INTRODUCTION TO MEDIEVAL THEOLOGY

Second Edition

This classic book, now in a second, expanded edition, is an invitation to think along with major theologians and spiritual authors, men and women from the time of St. Augustine to the end of the 14th century, who profoundly challenge our (post)modern assumptions. Medieval theology was radically theocentric, Trinitarian, scriptural and sacramental, yet it also operated with a rich notion of human understanding. In a postmodern setting, when modern views on "autonomous reason" are increasingly questioned, it is fruitful to reengage with premodern thinkers who did not share our modern and postmodern presuppositions. Their different perspective does not antiquate their thought, as some of the "cultured despisers" of medieval thought might imagine. On the contrary, rather than rendering their views obsolete, it makes them profoundly challenging and enriching for theology today.

RIK VAN NIEUWENHOVE is an associate professor of medieval theology at Durham University. He has authored many articles and books on medieval theology and spirituality, including *Thomas Aquinas and Contemplation* (Oxford University Press, 2021) and *Jan van Ruusbroec: Mystical Theologian of the Trinity* (University of Notre Dame Press, 2003), and he has coedited *The Theology of Thomas Aquinas* (University of Notre Dame Press, 2005) and *Late Medieval Mysticism of the Low Countries* (Paulist Press, 2008).

INTRODUCTION TO MEDIEVAL THEOLOGY

Second Edition

RIK VAN NIEUWENHOVE

University of Durham

CAMBRIDGE
UNIVERSITY PRESS

University Printing House, Cambridge CB2 8BS, United Kingdom

One Liberty Plaza, 20th Floor, New York, NY 10006, USA

477 Williamstown Road, Port Melbourne, VIC 3207, Australia

314–321, 3rd Floor, Plot 3, Splendor Forum, Jasola District Centre,
New Delhi – 110025, India

103 Penang Road, #05–06/07, Visioncrest Commercial, Singapore 238467

Cambridge University Press is part of the University of Cambridge.

It furthers the University's mission by disseminating knowledge in the pursuit of
education, learning, and research at the highest international levels of excellence.

www.cambridge.org
Information on this title: www.cambridge.org/highereducation/9781108839556
DOI: 10.1017/9781108884426

First edition © Rik Van Nieuwenhove 2012
Second edition © Cambridge University Press 2022

First published 2012
Reprinted 2014
Second edition 2022

A catalogue record for this publication is available from the British Library.

Library of Congress Cataloging-in-Publication Data
NAMES: Van Nieuwenhove, Rik, 1967– author.
TITLE: Introduction to medieval theology / Rik Van Nieuwenhove.
DESCRIPTION: Second edition. | Cambridge, United Kingdom : New York, NY, USA :
Cambridge University Press, [2022] | Series: Introduction to religion | Includes bibliographical
references and index.
IDENTIFIERS: LCCN 2021034466 (print) | LCCN 2021034467 (ebook) | ISBN 9781108839556
(hardback) | ISBN 9781108884426 (ebook)
SUBJECTS: LCSH: Theology, Doctrinal – History – Middle Ages, 600–1500. | BISAC:
RELIGION / Theology.
CLASSIFICATION: LCC BT26 .V36 2021 (print) | LCC BT26 (ebook) | DDC 230.09–dc23
LC record available at https://lccn.loc.gov/2021034466
LC ebook record available at https://lccn.loc.gov/2021034467

ISBN 978-1-108-83955-6 Hardback
ISBN 978-1-108-81334-1 Paperback

To my daughters, Anna and Muireann

Intelligere enim est simpliciter veritatem intelligibilem apprehendere. Ratiocinari autem est procedere de uno intellecto ad aliud, ad veritatem intelligibilem cognoscendam ... ratiocinari comparatur ad intelligere sicut moveri ad quiescere, vel acquirere ad habere, quorum unum est perfecti, aliud autem imperfecti.

Thomas Aquinas, *Summa Theologiae,* 1a q. 79, a. 8

Contents

Preface to the Second Edition   *page* ix
List of Abbreviations   xi

1   Introduction   1

PART I   THE LEGACY OF THE FATHERS

2   Augustine of Hippo   7

3   Monks and Scholars in the 5th and 6th Centuries: John Cassian, Boethius and Pseudo-Dionysius   27

PART II   EARLY MEDIEVAL THEOLOGIANS

4   Gregory the Great   39

5   John Scottus Eriugena and the Carolingian Renaissance   56

PART III   THE 11TH AND 12TH CENTURIES

6   Introduction: Renewal in the 11th and 12th Centuries   77

7   Anselm of Canterbury   83

8   Monks and Scholars in the 12th Century: Peter Abelard, Bernard of Clairvaux and William of St. Thierry   99

9   Hugh of St. Victor   121

10   Richard of St. Victor   138

11   Hildegard of Bingen   148

12   Peter Lombard and the Systematization of Theology   158

viii   *Contents*

PART IV THE 13TH CENTURY

13 Introduction: Mendicant Orders, Universities and Islamic
    Scholarship   181

14 Two Beguines: Mechthild of Magdeburg and Hadewijch   187

15 Early Franciscan Theology: Robert Grosseteste, Roger Bacon
    and the *Summa Halensis*   199

16 Bonaventure   232

17 Albert the Great   247

18 Thomas Aquinas   264

19 The Condemnations of 1277   306

20 John Duns Scotus   310

PART V THE 14TH CENTURY AND BEYOND

21 Introduction: Upheavals and Pluralism in the 14th Century   331

22 William of Ockham   335

23 Meister Eckhart   347

24 Jan van Ruusbroec and the Modern Devotion   359

25 Epilogue   367

Bibliography   368
Index   377

Preface to the Second Edition

The first edition of this book was published ten years ago. It filled an obvious gap in the market, and it is fair to say that it was well received by both scholars and general readers interested in medieval thought. I was especially delighted to see it appear on reading lists in a variety of subjects that cover not just medieval theology but also medieval literature (English, French, . . .), philosophy and art.

This second edition has been expanded by more than one quarter, and the text of the first edition has been slightly revised in a number of places. Errors and infelicities throughout the text have been rectified and bibliographies updated.

The first edition operated with the assumption that today's scholarly categories are often less than helpful when outlining medieval thought. Hence, besides mainstream theologians I included authors whom some would characterize today as mystical or spiritual writers. Similarly, while I included mostly authors writing in Latin, some writing in the vernacular also found a home in the book. Given this approach, it had been an oversight on my part not to include any women authors. In this revised edition, two chapters are therefore dedicated to female theologians: one features Hildegard of Bingen, who wrote in Latin, while the other considers the contribution of two beguines, Mechthild of Magdeburg and Hadewijch of Antwerp, who wrote in the vernacular (originally in Middle Low German and Middle Dutch, respectively). Few in the medieval period spoke so movingly as Hadewijch about the desire for God (a key theme in this book). Of course, many other female authors could have been selected for discussion. For reasons of constraints of space, I reluctantly decided not to deal with Julian of Norwich's attractive theology, as it is well covered in scholarship, especially in the English-speaking world. Likewise, I had to leave out Catherine of Siena's *Dialogues*, which offer a splendid example of how academic theology (such as Thomas Aquinas's) found an expression in an existentially relevant key in vernacular writings. Medieval theology was undoubtedly mainly an affair for men, but here too, as in other walks of life, women made a significant contribution, and the new chapters alert the reader to this.

Medieval thought was more plural than it is generally given credit for in another sense also. Latin theology was not only a Europe-wide enterprise, but it was itself in turn deeply indebted to Islamic and (to a lesser extent) Jewish scholarship. This influence occurred especially when the entire corpus of Aristotelian works was being received at the end of the 12th century and the beginning of the 13th. Given the nature of Aristotle's writings, it made itself most acutely felt in the world of philosophy. Even so, it was of major theological significance, impacting discussions on the nature of the intellect, immortality, the nature of happiness, the eternity of the world and so forth. Although it was not possible to dedicate a chapter to Avicenna and Averroes, Islamic influence now receives some attention in the context of the discussion of the elements that shaped scholastic theology in the 13th century (Chapter 13).

There were other lacunae. Thomas Aquinas and Bonaventure – understandably so – received considerable attention in the first edition. What was lacking, however, was an extensive discussion of some of the authors who exerted a major influence upon these two key thinkers. Hence, in this second edition, the reader benefits from a chapter on "Early Franciscan Theology" (Chapter 15) (drafted by my colleague Dr. William Crozier), which contains discussions of Robert Grosseteste, Roger Bacon and the influential _Summa Halensis_. A chapter on Albert the Great (Chapter 17) has also been included. He was the teacher of Thomas Aquinas and exerted a profound influence that lasted until the end of the medieval period (both in the school of "Albertism" and on Rhineland spirituality) and beyond.

I remain indebted in a variety of ways to the following colleagues: Lewis Ayres, John Betz, Patrick Connolly, Eamonn Conway, Boyd Taylor Coolman, William Crozier, Jos Decorte (†), Eugene Duffy, Rob Faesen, Russell Friedman, Karen Kilby, Katja Krause, Bernard McGinn, Simon Oliver, Philip L. Reynolds and Joseph Wawrykow.

I would also like to express my sincere gratitude to Beatrice Rehl, senior editor at Cambridge University Press, for enthusiastically and expertly guiding this second edition toward publication.

This edition, as was the first, is an exercise, not in theological nostalgia, but in retrieval for the sake of renewal. In this spirit, I dedicate it to my two beautiful daughters, Anna and Muireann.

Abbreviations

BDW	*Book of Divine Works* (Hildegard)
Brevil.	*Breviloquium* (Bonaventure)
CDH	*Cur Deus Homo* (Anselm of Canterbury)
Comm. Jn	*Commentary on John*
Comm. on Rom	*Commentary on Romans*
Confer.	*Conferences* (John Cassian)
Confess.	*Confessions* (Augustine)
Consol.	*The Consolation of Philosophy* (Boethius)
CT	*Compendium of Theology* (Thomas Aquinas)
De Civ. Dei	*De Civitate Dei* (Augustine)
De Doctr. Christ.	*De Doctrina Christiana* (Augustine)
De Lib. Arb.	*De Libertate Arbitrii* (Anselm of Canterbury)
De Pot.	*De Potentia* (Thomas Aquinas)
De Prim. Princ.	*De Primo Principio* (Duns Scotus)
De Sacr.	*De Sacramentis Christiane Fidei* (Hugh of St. Victor)
De Trin.	*De Trinitate*
De Ver.	*De Veritate* (Thomas Aquinas)
Dial.	*The Dialogues* (Gregory the Great)
Didasc.	*Didascalicon* (Hugh of St. Victor)
DTD	*De Tribus Diebus* (Hugh of St. Victor)
Enarr. in Ps.	*Enarrationes in Psalmos* (Augustine)
Enchir.	*Enchiridion* (Augustine)
Hex.	*[Collationes in] Hexaemeron*
Hom. Ev.	*Forty Homilies on the Gospels* (Gregory the Great)
Hom. Ez.	*Homilies on Ezekiel* (Gregory the Great)
Lect.	*Lectura* (Duns Scotus)
Mor.	*Moralia in Iob* (Gregory the Great)
MW	*The Major Works – Anselm of Canterbury*

Myst. Trin.	*Disputed Questions on the Mystery of the Trinity* (Bonaventure)
Op. Ox.	*Opus Oxoniense* (Duns Scotus)
Ordin.	*Ordinatio*
Past. Reg.	*Pastoral Rule* (Gregory the Great)
Quodlib.	*Quodlibetal Questions* (William of Ockham)
Rep. Par.	*Reportatio Parisiensis* (Duns Scotus)
ScG	*Summa contra Gentiles* (Thomas Aquinas)
Sent.	*Commentary on Peter Lombard's Sentences*
ST	*Summa Theologiae* (Thomas Aquinas)
TSB	*Theologia Summi Boni* (Peter Abelard)

CHAPTER I

Introduction

This book is written for anybody who wants to find out more about the ideas of the major theologians of the medieval period from the time of St. Augustine to the end of the 14th century. Rather than offering a survey of a myriad of theologians I focus on a limited number of key thinkers and expound their ideas in some depth. I opt for a text-focused approach – often quoting from primary texts – thus allowing the authors to speak for themselves as much as possible. I also incorporate brief comments on the historical and cultural background of each period, which will assist the reader in contextualizing the authors I discuss.

Although I would like to think this book is written in a clear style and explains complex issues in a lucid manner, this is not a textbook that offers a "standard" survey of key medieval thinkers, and this is for two reasons. First, one of the joys of writing this book was the opportunity it offered me to debunk "popular" accounts of medieval thought readers still come across in systematic textbooks, to which especially Augustine, Anselm and even Thomas Aquinas have fallen victim. Second, rather than offering disparate chapters on key figures I try throughout this book to make a sustained argument that contrasts (post)modern understandings of the nature of theology and human rationality with medieval ones. My overall aim, therefore, is to extend an invitation to *think along* with medieval authors. In a postmodern climate in which modern views on "autonomous reason" are increasingly questioned, it may prove fruitful to reengage with premodern thinkers who obviously did not share our modern and postmodern presuppositions. Their different perspective does not antiquate their thought, as some of the "cultured despisers" of medieval thought might imagine. On the contrary, rather than rendering their views obsolete it makes them profoundly challenging and enriching, perhaps more so than any postmodern critique of modernity could possibly be. For the postmodern, as a mirror image of the modern, is still determined by key assumptions of the modern.

Indeed, it could be plausibly argued that the postmodern critique is part and parcel of the history of modernity itself.

Medieval theology is radically theocentric, and God, for medieval theologians, is of course the Trinitarian God. This may not sound particularly surprising, but it is fundamentally different from those theologians who operate in the shadow of Schleiermacher (and his "anthropological turn" in theology), as well as from those who react against this anthropological turn by espousing a radical bibliocentric approach. This radical theocentric focus is both strengthened and exemplified by how medieval theologians conceived of human rationality. For them, human intelligence encompassed much more than reason. It also involved intellect. If reason is to be rational it has to have an openness toward that which transcends reason, and reason transcends itself by becoming intellect. This is a key theme to which I allude throughout this book.

Medieval theologians were desirous for God. Their whole thinking reached out toward the divine. There is a profound thrust toward the transcendent in medieval theology. In order to illustrate this I pay particular attention to how they conceived of the Christian life, especially their understanding of faith and love, two of the theological virtues. I also hope to show that the theocentric focus at the heart of medieval theology introduces an element of gratuity in the medieval mindset that is rather at odds with modern notions of instrumentalization and functionalization. From Augustine's invitation to "enjoy God solely" (*frui Deo*) to Meister Eckhart's notion of detachment, the medieval period contains rich resources to critique modern utilitarian and instrumentalizing perspectives on the world.

Thomas Aquinas wrote that there are two central mysteries in the Christian faith: the mystery of the Trinity and the Incarnation. The doctrine of the Trinity is at the heart of medieval theology, and broad-sweeping and often repeated claims about the alleged emphasis upon the divine unity in Latin theology at the expense of a true Trinitarian understanding of God are to be discarded as scholarly untenable. Indeed, the mystery of the Trinity shapes every aspect of the theology and spirituality of most of the figures I discuss.

While the patristic period witnessed major debates on the nature of the Person of Christ, medieval theology was drawn more toward soteriological questions. Here Anselm's analysis, often caricatured in modern scholarship, looms large. It is another aspect that retains my attention.

Discussions of the nature of the relation between faith and reason, the mystery of the Trinity, soteriology, Christian love and the transcendent thrust of medieval thought run like a thread throughout my examination of the authors I have selected. I hope focusing on these themes will provide this book with a measure of cohesion and unity.

Any selection of authors to be included is somewhat arbitrary. The first major author is St. Augustine. It is hardly an exaggeration to describe medieval theology as a footnote to Augustine. In line with the overall aims of this book, other patristic authors such as Boethius, John Cassian and Pseudo-Dionysius receive a more cursory treatment.

It is probably true to say that Gregory the Great's ideas were not all that original. Of course, and revealing, medieval authors did not consider originality a virtue in its own right. They were rather concerned with discovering truth. Gregory merits inclusion for the specific way he appropriates Augustinian views and adapts them for a more monastic setting. With Augustine, he shaped monastic theology well until the 11th century and beyond.

The Carolingian renaissance witnessed renewed theological activity in the West, and it is mostly remembered for the so-called Eucharistic controversy between Radbertus and Ratramnus. One theologian stood out amongst his peers, if only because he devised a daring synthesis of Augustinian and Greek theology. An engagement with the thought of John Scotus Eriugena is therefore well justified even if his influence on later medieval thought was admittedly somewhat limited.

Undoubtedly one of the towering figures of medieval theology is St. Anselm. His *Proslogion* (and its famous "ontological argument"), as well as his soteriology, are addressed at some length.

The 12th century is one of the most creative eras in the cultural history of the West. This is the time of Abelard and Heloise, the Cistercian revolution (Bernard of Clairvaux) and the School of St. Victor in Paris. The theology of Peter Abelard, Hugh and Richard of St. Victor is discussed, as well one of the most influential works of the medieval period: the *Sentences* by Peter Lombard. On one hand Peter Lombard's synthesis looked back by incorporating the Augustinian legacy into his *Sentences*. Its more systematic approach was, however, forward-looking and explains why it became the key text in the theology faculties of the universities founded throughout the 13th century. In contrast, Hildegard of Bingen's oeuvre is squarely set in the monastic culture of the 12th century. Defying categorization, it echoes Old Testament prophecy and vision.

Peter Lombard paved the way for scholastic theology, which flowered in the 13th century. This is the time of the rise of the universities, mendicant orders and, of course, the reception of the entire Aristotelian corpus, facilitated by Islamic scholarship. The inclusion of Bonaventure, Thomas Aquinas and John Duns Scotus does not need justification. Their achievements, however, are incomprehensible without some knowledge of their immediate predecessors such as Robert Grosseteste, Roger Bacon, Albert the Great and the highly influential *Summa Halensis*. Vernacular theology also came to its own, especially (initially) in the writings of women authors. In the 13th century their theology often took its lead from the Cistercian sources with which it was often closely associated. I discuss two examples – namely, Mechthild of Magdeburg and Hadewijch.

The Condemnations of 1277 are often seen as a caesura (perhaps more symptomatic than a causal factor) in the history of scholastic theology. While the impact of Duns Scotus's contribution to early modern developments is a matter for debate, most scholars agree that William of Ockham's thought originated in an intellectual climate very different from that of the 13th century. As I hope to explain, the most remarkable change is the more analytical and less intellective notion of theological reason.

It is inaccurate to claim that scholasticism came to an end with the arrival of nominalism. It is, however, fair to say that the theological scene in the 14th and 15th centuries is more pluralist and divided and less systematic or encompassing than before. The nature of reason (*ratio*) changes, and hence also its relation with faith. Metaphysics and theology and even theology and spirituality are increasingly considered separate and not just distinct from one another. Two important authors of this period (Meister Eckhart and Ruusbroec) are discussed so as to illustrate the ongoing vibrancy of medieval spirituality.

PART I

The Legacy of the Fathers

CHAPTER 2

Augustine of Hippo

LIFE AND SOURCES

Augustine was born in AD 354 in Thagasta (in what is now Algeria), North Africa, the son of a Christian mother and a pagan father. He studied rhetoric in Carthage, acquiring a profound knowledge of classical Latin literature, especially Cicero and Virgil. He became a gifted teacher of literature in Carthage, Rome and Milan. From 373 onward, Augustine, "living outside of himself," alienated from God – who was "more inward than his most inward part," as he recalled later in his *Confessions* (*Confess.* III.6 [II]) – was drawn into the circles of Manichaeism. The term *Manichaeism* is derived from Mani (AD 216–76), the Persian who founded this Gnostic religion. It was an extremely dualistic worldview with a very negative evaluation of matter, body and sexuality. The followers of the Manichean religion were divided into two classes: the elect, who had to remain celibate, and the auditors (or hearers), who were allowed sexual intercourse as long as it did not lead to offspring (for procreation contributed to the imprisonment of souls in the physical world). Augustine became an auditor in the Manichean religion, much to the heartbreak of his mother. After nine years, Augustine grew disillusioned with Manichaeism. In 383, he traveled to Rome, and it was there, at the age of thirty, that he gradually abandoned Manichean views, lapsing into a period of skepticism (*Confess.* V.10 [19]).

While in Milan, Augustine was to encounter a person who left an indelible mark on him: St. Ambrose, the local bishop. It was Ambrose who was to draw Augustine closer to the Catholic faith. Of particular significance, Augustine informs us, was the ways in which Ambrose interpreted the Scriptures. Once Ambrose demonstrated that difficult passages from the Old Testament could be legitimately interpreted figuratively, one of the main objections Augustine had long harbored against the Catholic faith vanished. He then decided to become a catechumen in the Catholic Church. It was at this time that Augustine, still searching for truth,

discovered Neoplatonic philosophy. This too was to have a major forma-
tive impact on Augustine's intellectual outlook.

Neoplatonism is a philosophy that revived Platonist tendencies in philosophy from the 3rd to 6th centuries AD. The major figures are the school's
founder, Plotinus (ca. 205–70), Porphyry (ca. 232–301) and Proclus (410–85).
Augustine must have read (in translation) some extracts from Plotinus's
main work, *The Enneads*, and a number of works from Porphyry. In
Neoplatonism we discern the following characteristics. First, there is
a strong emphasis on the One – the Absolute or the Good from which all
things emanate through a hierarchy. This Absolute principle is beyond being
and thought. Within the divine realm is a hierarchy: the One is absolute and
transcendent; it is supreme goodness. Somewhat lower is Mind or *Nous*.
Finally, there is Soul, which has the power to produce matter. The emphasis
upon hierarchy within the Godhead distinguishes the Neoplatonic understanding of the divinity from the Christian view of God as three equal
Persons in one Godhead. From the divine realm the material world flows
or emanates. In the process of emanation there is gradual loss, for every effect
is slightly inferior to its cause (the higher level is the cause of whatever is
immediately lower). Again, this is different from a Christian understanding,
in which God directly creates all things out of nothing rather than through
an elaborate hierarchy. Human beings have to transcend the multiplicity of
the material world in order to achieve union with the One. This entails
a practice of purification and introversion. This union with the One is being
achieved in transient ecstasy (e.g., *Enneads* 6.9.9).

Plotinus's mysticism is private and individual. It is also fairly intellectual. Christians will correct this view by emphasizing the role of grace and
community. Despite the important differences between Neoplatonic philosophy and Christianity (above all Christianity's emphasis upon the reality
of the Incarnation), Neoplatonism was to exert a lasting influence upon
Augustine. A number of aspects need to be mentioned.

First, the emphasis upon the utter transcendence of the One was to
strengthen further apophatic approaches to the Christian understanding of
God (itself heir to the Hebrew emphasis upon the unknowability of God).
Second, it contributed to an exemplarist metaphysics. This warrants some
clarification. Plato, the father of Western philosophy, had struggled with
the problem of how we can attain certain knowledge in a changeable and
material world. As is well known, the Greeks had made significant progress
in the area of mathematics and geometry. Taking his cue from the certainty
we can attain in the immaterial, theoretical world of mathematics, Plato
had argued that all things (a tree, a dog, a woman, the legal system)

participate in a transcendent, ideal world of spiritual forms. Our material world is therefore a mere reflection of this perfect world of forms. (Incidentally, Aristotle accepted the notion of forms, but he claimed that these forms only exist in material things, rather than in a transcendent realm – a view Thomas Aquinas would later adopt.) The spiritual forms or Ideas (the perfect, spiritual archetypes, models or exemplars of things) *in-form* the world: a dog is a dog, and not a tree, because its matter is "in-formed" by the Idea of "caninehood." These forms shape all things in the world and are the foundation of our certain knowledge of them.

Plotinus claimed that these divine ideas are found in the *Nous*, or the divine Mind, the second hypostasis within the Divinity. For Augustine, the divine ideas, models or exemplars (*aeternae rationes*) of all created things are contained in the Word, the second person of the Trinity. "There is but one Word of God, through which all things were made (John 1:1–6), which is unchanging truth, in which all things are primordially and unchangingly together, not only things that are in the whole of this creation, but things that have been and will be" (*De Trin.* IV. 3).

This doctrine of exemplarism allowed later theologians to connect the theology of the Trinity (especially the generation of the Word from the Father) with the theology of creation. It assisted them in seeing the whole of creation as a marvelous reflection of the beauty of the divine Word.

Another important view Augustine inherited from the "Platonists" (*Neoplatonism* is, of course, a modern scholarly term) is the notion that evil is absence of goodness. Evil is a defect of being and goodness in the same way that natural evil (e.g., blindness) is an absence of goodness (e.g., sight) (cf. *Confess.* VII.12.18 and *De Civ. Dei* XI.9 and 22: "'evil' is merely a name for the privation of good"). Given the fact that everything God created is something (good), God is not directly responsible for the evil in this world. Augustine was to use this doctrine to explain how evil that occurs in this world is not caused by God. This proved important for his departure from Manichaeism. Finally, there is a strong sense of longing for the immaterial, transcendent realm and for fulfillment beyond the material world – a longing that strongly appealed to Augustine.

During this time, Augustine also submerged himself in the Scriptures. One day, while sitting in the garden of his house in Milan, he heard a child singing *Tolle et lege*, "Pick up and read." Augustine opened St. Paul's letters and his eyes fell on Rom. 13:13–14, in which St. Paul admonishes his readers to abandon their orgies and drunkenness, requesting them to put on the Lord Jesus Christ. At that very moment all the shadows of doubts were dispelled (*Confess.* VII.12 [29]). He gave up his worldly career and started writing his first works, including the *Soliloquies*. Sometime later, during the Easter Vigil of 387, Augustine was baptized by Ambrose. He returned to North Africa, where he was ordained in 391. Five years later, he became the bishop of Hippo, a position he held until his death in 430. Apart from the *Confessions* his most important works are *The City of God* (*De Civitate Dei*), *The Trinity* (*De Trinitate*), *On Christian Doctrine* (*De Doctrina Christiana*), *Faith, Hope and Charity* (*Enchiridion*), sermons, a range of anti-Pelagian, anti-Manichaeist and anti-Donatist writings, and commentaries on the Scriptures, including on St. John, Genesis and the Psalms – that is, *Expositions of the Psalms* (*Enarrationes in Psalmos*).

THE RELATION BETWEEN PHILOSOPHY AND THEOLOGY, REASON AND FAITH

In his search for truth, Augustine engaged deeply with the philosophy of antiquity. This was to shape the way he viewed the relation between faith and reason and between theology and philosophy. Philosophy, which to him is a way of life rather than a discipline, is important as a *praeparatio evangelica*, a preparation for the Christian religion. Christianity is, however, the *vera philosophia*, the true philosophy. Again, although reason has its part to play in helping us understand our faith, it is the total relation to the soul that interests Augustine. Thus, it is not possible to separate Augustine's theology from philosophical considerations and vice versa. The attempt to attain fulfillment by merely relying on an independent philosophy would have struck him as undesirable.

His views on faith and reason have acquired a new relevance in our postmodern times, now that the modern Cartesian understanding of reason in terms of utter autonomy has been questioned. In a short treatise, *Faith in the Unseen*, he criticizes those people "who maintain that the Christian religion should be despised rather than embraced, because what it presents is not something tangible but something that demands faith in matters which lie beyond human vision." In the treatise, Augustine refutes this positivistic view by pointing out the fiduciary nature of human rationality and the significance of beliefs for human interactions. In *The Advantage of Believing* 12.26, he states that absolutely nothing in society would be safe if we decided not to believe anything that we cannot hold as evident. How can we procure convincing evidence of genuine love or friendship between people? The consequence of a radical positivistic stance would be "that human relationships are thrown into chaos" (*Faith in the Unseen*, 2.4). Radical skepticism is equally untenable: it is, after all, impossible to doubt everything, for when we doubt we always presuppose something as given. In a passage that may have inspired Descartes's *Meditations*, who, however, used it for radically different purposes, Augustine argues:

If you are not sure what I am saying and have doubts about whether it is true, at least be sure that you have no doubts about having doubts about this; and, if it is certain that you do have doubts, ask where this certainty comes from . . . Everyone who understands that he has doubts is understanding something true, and he is certain about this thing that he understands. He is certain therefore about something true. So then, everyone who has doubts whether there is such a thing as truth has something true in himself about which he cannot have any doubts, and there cannot be anything true except with truth. And so, one who has been able to have doubts about anything has no business to have doubts about truth.[1]

Augustine developed the same theme in *De Civitate Dei* xi.26, in language that clearly influenced Descartes ("'If I am mistaken, I exist.' A non-existent being cannot be mistaken; therefore I must exist, if I am mistaken.") For Augustine, radical skepticism and universal doubt are impossible. Every doubt is predicated on accepting something as true. It is intellectually incoherent to claim that we can doubt everything. Similarly, radical positivism, which only accepts those elements to be true that can be empirically shown to be true, is not a viable intellectual or existential option. The two extremes of radical skepticism and positivism have in common that they both deny important fiduciary aspects of the human search for meaning and truth.

In this context it may prove useful to draw attention to a distinction Augustine makes between reason and understanding or intellect (*intellectus*). It is characteristic of the human being to reason; however, the knowledge acquired by reason, and the glimpse of truth thus gained, is understanding. This distinction between reason and understanding or intellect will prove highly influential in later thinkers.

GRACE AND OUR SEARCH FOR GOD

Augustine was deeply aware of his powerlessness in turning toward God. He felt that only God could (and eventually did) pull him out of the abyss of sin. Sinful human beings, subject to selfishness from the earliest moments of infancy, are the prisoners of habits that become second nature. Only grace can restore authentic freedom. According to Augustine, Adam and Eve

---

[1] *True Religion (De Vera Religione)*, 39 [73], trans. Edmund Hill as *Saint Augustine: On Christian Belief* (New York: New City Press, 2005), 78–79.

initially enjoyed the divine assistance of grace and justice. However, when they sinned and turned away from God, they lost this divine assistance. Henceforward, human nature becomes "fallen." It is not utterly corrupt, but it has lost its original focus and justice. Because every member of the human family shares in Adam's human nature, all of humanity shares in the consequences of this Fall. We are all in need of the aid of divine grace to restore us to our pristine condition, and without this free gift of grace (which has become available in Christ's saving work), we cannot be redeemed.

Given the fact that some people die as unreconciled sinners, Augustine takes for granted that not all will be saved; only some belong to the elect. Initially, such as in his *Propositions on Romans*, §60, he taught that God freely bestows his grace upon those who would put it to good use. Given God's foreknowledge, he elects those whom he foreknew would believe in him. But then Augustine realized that this view effectively made God's grace dependent on the response of human beings – and this he felt to be unacceptable. So he later revised his teaching and argued that God freely bestows his grace upon some (and thereby will save them) and not upon others, and no reason can be given for this choice. This is the teaching of predestination.

Augustine's views hardened through his dispute with Pelagius, a British lay theologian who had a more positive understanding of human nature. *Pelagianism* refers to the doctrine that human beings can achieve their salvation by their own powers. Original sin is no more than Adam's bad example, which can be nullified if we follow the example of Christ. Original sin refers to the universality of sin, which results in a social habit after Adam had set a bad example. Death, for Pelagius, was a biological necessity, not a punishment from God. Against these views Augustine argued that grace is needed, even just to turn our will away from evil toward God. Original sin refers to an inherited defect that impairs the freedom of the will. Death is a punishment for sin. No pain or loss is undeserved. All of us are guilty of sin, and all of us therefore stand under judgment. In Augustine's analysis, the issue is not why God fails to save all. Rather, the issue is, why does God bother saving some? The practice of infant baptism, so Augustine contended, illustrates that people are in need of grace even before they commit actual and deliberate sins.

Some readers might perhaps be forgiven for thinking that Pelagius's views appear at first more attractive, perhaps even more "modern." They seem to safeguard human freedom more than Augustine's. Moreover, can it not be argued that Augustine's God is somewhat arbitrary, electing some and not others?

A number of points need to be made so as to avoid a simplistic interpret-ation. To appreciate Augustine's views, it may be useful to remember that Christianity sees the relationship between God and humanity in terms of love. Nobody, however, has, strictly speaking, an entitlement to the love of anybody else. You cannot force the other to love you. Love has to be freely given, and the same applies to God's grace: it is, quite literally, given gratuitously. As he puts it in *De Trin.* IV.2, grace is "not paid out as something earned but is given gratis; that is why it is called grace." Similarly, faith is a gift from God. It is not something we can attain by our own efforts. Moreover, as Luther realized, the notion that we cannot merit God's favor by our own initiative is not an infringement of human freedom; it is actually liberating. Pelagianism puts a terrible burden on the human person that is impossible to meet. Finally, we need to be careful about what exactly we mean when talking of human freedom. Augustine distinguishes between the freedom of choice (*liberum arbitrium*) and genuine freedom (*libertas*). Freedom of choice is not freedom in the full sense of the word. The latter freedom (*libertas*) refers to our orientation toward God through the enabling operation of divine grace upon our will. This *libertas*, or God-given freedom, is not a diminishment of our human freedom but a restoration and fulfillment. It was this kind of freedom, not the freedom of choice, that Adam lost in the Garden of Eden and that Christ restored.[2] It can be argued that the problem of a tension between grace and freedom does not exist for Augustine. As he sees it, grace does not diminish human freedom but actually enables it. True freedom for humans is God-given freedom. In comparison, freedom of choice is but a pale privil-ege. In short, Augustine's pessimism – or realism? – in relation to the impotence of fallen humanity to effect its own salvation is counterbalanced by a profound sense of God's powerful grace.

Even when we take into consideration Augustine's analysis of the gratuity of God's operation in us as existentially valid, I suspect most readers may still harbor a number of reservations. The key issue is predes-tination of some and not others:

God almighty, the supreme and supremely good creator of all beings, who assists and rewards good wills, while he abandons and condemns the bad . . . surely did not fail to have a plan whereby he might complete the fixed number of citizens predestined in his wisdom, even out of the condemned human race. He does not now choose them for their merits, seeing that the whole mass of humankind has been condemned as it were in its infected root; . . . each person can recognize that

---

[2] See Mary T. Clark, *Augustine of Hippo* (New York: Continuum, 2000), 50, with a reference to *Contra duas epistolas Pelagianorum ad Bonifacium Papam*, 1.25.

his deliverance from evils is due to an act of kindness freely granted, not owed to him by right, when he is exempted from sharing the final destiny of those whose just punishment he had shared. (*De Civ. Dei* xiv.26)

All of humankind shares in original sin through Adam, the "infected root." Therefore, all deserve to remain separated from God. However, God bestows his grace upon some and not others. When we seek to fathom why mercy is given to some, we cannot say. For the gratuitous nature of grace precludes the view that this bestowal is based on any prevenient merit. As Augustine argued in *Letter* 194, when we seek to know how mercy is deserved, we find no merit because there is none: grace would be made void if it were not freely given but awarded to merit. Of course, only God knows who the chosen few are. In my view, the key problem is not the abolishment of human freedom, as is often alleged, but rather Augustine's view that God's predestination is not universal. Undoubtedly Augustine did consider this kind of reservation unconvincing: "Who but a fool could think that God is unfair, whether he passes adverse judgment on one who deserves it or shows mercy to one who is unworthy?" (*Enchir.* 25 [98]).

In scriptural terms, Augustine can appeal to the favoritism Yahweh shows toward some and not others (e.g., Jacob over Esau, cf. Mal. 1:2–3 and Rom. 9:13). In the New Testament too are a number of texts that also seem to support Augustine's views on predestination, such as Rom. 8:28–30 and Eph. 1:4. On the other hand, at times Augustine has to do violence to the natural meaning of the text in order to maintain his teaching. He interprets 1 Tim. 2:4 ("God wants everyone to be saved") to mean that "nobody is saved except those whom he wills to be saved" (*Enchir.* 27 [103]). As we will see, in the 9th century a major controversy broke out over the issue of predestination, with Gottschalk claiming that Augustine had taught a double predestination, one toward heaven and the other toward hell. Calvin too was to radicalize ideas in his theory of double predestination. Augustine's view also entails that unbaptized babies are condemned because they share in the collective alienation that originated with Adam. This view, considered problematic, forced the Church in the Middle Ages to develop the doctrine of limbo.

AUGUSTINE AND THE BIBLE

We have already touched on the topic of Augustine's interpretation of the Scriptures. Some aspects of Augustine's approach to the Scriptures may strike us as quite modern. For instance, he expresses his annoyance at Christians who mistake what the Scriptures may say about a certain topic for solid, scientific knowledge. It is "quite disgraceful and disastrous," he writes, when non-Christians hear Christians talk nonsense about scientific topics, unjustifiably claiming the authority of the Scriptures for their erroneous views. "What is so vexing is not that misguided people should be laughed at, as that our authors should be assumed by outsiders to have held such views, and, to the great detriment of those about whose salvation we are so concerned, should be written off and consigned to the waste paper basket as so many ignoramuses" (*The Literal Meaning of Genesis* 1.19 [39]).[3] The Scriptures are not manuals on cosmology or science. But there are also ways in which Augustine's views on the Scriptures are rather different from ours, and this is where they can begin to challenge ours.

For Augustine, the Scriptures are the word of God. They form a coherent whole, and he is not shy about using one passage to throw light on an entirely different passage. He also resists an exclusively literal reading of the Scriptures, happily espousing allegory and typology. In *Enarr. in Ps.* 103 (Expos. 1.13), he defines allegory as follows: "Something is said to be an allegory when one meaning seems to be conveyed by the words, and a different meaning is symbolised for our minds."[4] A number of examples clarify this. In his book *The Literal Meaning of Genesis* 1.6 [12], Augustine comments on the opening verse of Genesis ("In the beginning [*In principio*] God made heaven and earth . . . And the Spirit of God was being borne over the waters."). Augustine takes *principium* ("the beginning" but also "the principle") to refer to the Word, in whom God the Father creates all things, while the Spirit is, of course, taken as a reference to the third Person of the Trinity. As long as interpretations are in accordance with the Rule of Faith they are legitimate (*De Civ. Dei* XI.32) and not arbitrary. For Augustine, the Bible is not primarily a historical book, although it does contain a lot of historically accurate accounts. The Scriptures are designed to nourish devout hearts. Just as the created world reveals and points to its Creator, so too the words of the Scripture are deeply symbolic, referring to a more profound reality. As Augustine knew from his own journey, a literalist interpretation of the Scriptures often stands in the way of faith.

In his disputes with the Manicheans, Augustine explains that many of the Old Testament events prefigure Christ and his Church. This is typology. An obvious example is how Adam prefigures Christ and Eve the Church:

---

[3] All translations by Edmund Hill from *Saint Augustine on Genesis* (New York: New City Press, 2002).
[4] All translations by Maria Boulding from *Saint Augustine: Exposition of the Psalms*, 6 vols. (New York: New City Press, 2000–04).

Adam was a type of the one who was to come, and when Adam slept, Eve was formed from his side. Adam prefigured Christ, and Eve prefigured the Church, which is why she was called the mother of the living (cf. Gen. 3:20). When was Eve fashioned? While Adam slept. And when did the Church's sacraments flow forth from Christ's side? While he slept on the Cross. (*Enarr. in Ps.* 40:9 [10])

As Eve was formed from the side of sleeping Adam (Gen. 2:21), so too the Church was formed from the side of Christ (cf. John 19:34). In a commentary on one of the verses from the Psalms, Augustine draws on Genesis and John's Gospel to weave an intricate and suggestive tapestry of theological interpretation. Again, this is not an arbitrary move: it is a Christocentric hermeneutic that remains faithful to the Rule of Faith.

CHRIST, SALVATION AND CHURCH

Augustine develops a number of soteriological themes. One of these is the release from Satan's bondage, explored in *De Trin.* XIII.16–18 and elsewhere. Augustine explains that by divine justice the human race was handed over to the power of the devil. Christ's humility neutralized the pride of sin, and as Christ had not committed any sin and yet was killed, the devil had to release humanity from his captivity. Anselm of Canterbury was to take issue with this account. It is, however, not all that important in Augustine's understanding of how Christ effected our salvation. Of much greater significance is the way we become incorporated into Christ and emulate his humility.

The theme of the humility of God (*humilitas Dei*, in *De Trin.* IV.4) runs throughout Augustine's oeuvre. Probably reflecting his own journey, Augustine is very much aware that there is something deeply humbling about having to accept that the transcendent God became human and died for us on the Cross. In this context, Augustine adopts the patristic theme of exchange: "becoming a partaker of our mortality he made us partakers of his divinity" (*De Trin.* IV.4).[5] Another theme he develops, and one that resonated with the early Edward Schillebeeckx, is the notion that Christ is the sacrament of our salvation (*De Trin.* IV.6). Christ's death and resurrection draw us toward a transformation that shares in and is made possible by his saving activity. The death of Christ can refer in a symbolic way to our death to sin – that is, repentance over our sins. Christ's death can also assist us in approaching our own sufferings and death as a participation in Christ. Similarly, Christ's resurrection can refer to our inner resurrection –

[5] All translations by Edmund Hill from *Saint Augustine: The Trinity* (New York: New City Press, 1991).

that is, our inner spiritual renewal – but it also prefigures and pledges our own bodily resurrection. In *Enchir.* 52, we read: "just as he suffered a true death, in us there is true forgiveness of sins, and just as his resurrection was true, so also is our justification true."[6] Thus, the life and death of Christ is existentially relevant for us here and now: Christians are called to "live within these mysteries" (*Enchir.* 53).

A particularly fruitful theme – and a very biblical one – in Augustine's soteriology is that of sacrifice (*De Trin.* IV.15–19 and *De Civ. Dei* x). It is worthwhile to elaborate on this as it also has profound implications for Christian spirituality.

In *De Civ. Dei* x.5, Augustine argues that God does not require sacrifices for his own gratification ("it is man, not God who is benefited by all the worship which is rightly offered to God").[7] Quoting Ps. 16:2, he contends that it would be foolish to assume that God needs our sacrifices: it is we, not God, who benefit from the worship offered to God. The purpose of past and present offerings is that "we may cleave to God and seek the good of our neighbour for the same end. Thus the visible sacrifice is the sacrament, the sacred sign, of the invisible sacrifice" (*Sacrificium ergo uisibile inuisibilis sacrificii sacramentum id est sacrum signum est*). God does not want the sacrifice of a slaughtered animal but he does desire "the sacrifice of a broken heart" (cf. Ps. 51:17), and this is the invisible, inner sacrifice Augustine has in mind. "Thus," Augustine writes, "the true sacrifice is offered in every act which is designed to unite us to God in a holy fellowship, every act, that is, which is directed to that final Good which makes possible our true felicity" (*De Civ. Dei* x.6). True sacrifices are "acts of compassion, whether towards ourselves or towards our neighbours, when they are directed towards God."[8] In offering our sacrifices "we shall be aware that visible sacrifice must be offered only to him, to whom we ourselves ought to be an invisible sacrifice in our hearts."[9] So what matters is the intention with which we make our offerings. Clearly Augustine has a very broad understanding of the notion of sacrifice: in that sense, our body can be a sacrifice when we discipline it for the sake of God. Even more so, the soul can be an instrument of sacrifice when it offers itself up to God, abandoning worldly desires and becoming transformed in submission to God (*De Civ. Dei* x.6).

---

[6] Translation by Bruce Harbert from *Saint Augustine: On Christian Belief* (New York: New City Press, 2005).

[7] *De Civ. Dei* x.5, trans. H. Bettenson as *St Augustine: The City of God* (Harmondsworth: Penguin, 1984).

[8] Ibid., x.6.   [9] Ibid., x.19.

The true nature of sacrifice can only be properly grasped from the perspective of the Cross and its reenactment in the Eucharist:

The whole redeemed community, that is to say, the congregation and fellowship of the saints, is offered to God as a universal sacrifice through the great Priest who offered himself in his suffering for us – so that we might be the body of so great a head – under the form of a servant. For it was this form he offered, and in this form he was offered, because it is under this form that he is the Mediator, in this form he is the Priest, in this form he is the Sacrifice ... This is the sacrifice which the Church continually celebrates in the sacrament of the altar, a sacrament well-known to the faithful where it is shown to the Church that she herself is offered in the offering which she presents to God. (*De Civ. Dei* x.6)

This is a dense quotation, as it weaves together Christological, Eucharistic, and ecclesiological themes. A key aspect of the argument is the living link between Christ and his Church. For Augustine, *Church* refers to the community of the believers. This community is the body of Christ (cf. Rom. 12:3ff.). This intimate union between Christ and his Church is established in and through the Eucharist, which reenacts the sacrifice of Christ on the Cross. Thus, on the Cross, Christ is both the priest who makes the offering and the offering itself (*oblatio*). The daily sacrifice of the Church – the Eucharist – is the sacramental symbol of this (*cuius rei sacramentum*), and the Church, being the body of Christ, learns to offer itself through him (*De Civ. Dei* x.20).

It has become clear that Augustine establishes a close link between the sacrifice of Christ on the Cross, the Eucharistic sacrifice and the community of the Church. These three themes are connected by the notion of the Body of Christ. This notion can refer to the body of the Incarnate Word, the historical Jesus. It can also refer to the Eucharistic body of Christ. Finally, it can refer to the community of the believers who are vivified by the Holy Spirit. In *Sermon* 272, preached to newly baptized Christians about to receive the Eucharistic bread for the first time, Augustine put it memorably: "Be then what you see and receive what you are." Through partaking in the body and blood of Christ we ourselves become the one body of Christ. As Christ addresses Augustine in the *Confessions*: "you will not change me into you like the food your flesh eats, but you will be changed into me" (*Confess.* VII.x [16]).

The spiritual implications of this theology are significant, for it allows us to consider our own afflictions as a participation in the redemptive suffering of Christ. Moreover, given the intimate link between Christ and his Church, Augustine makes the radical claim that the risen Christ continues to suffer in his members:

If he is the head, we are the limbs. The whole Church, spread abroad everywhere, is his body, and of that body he is the head ... Accordingly, when we hear his voice, we must hearken to it as coming from both head and body; for whatever he suffered, we too suffered in him, and whatever we suffer, he too suffers in us. Think of an analogy: if your head suffers some injury, can your hand be unaffected? Or if your hand is hurt, can your head be free from pain? ... When any one of your members suffers, all the other members hasten to help the one that is in pain. This solidarity meant that when Christ suffered, we suffered in him; and it follows that now that he has ascended into heaven, and is seated at the Father's right hand, he still undergoes in the person of his Church whatever it may suffer amid the troubles of this world, whether temptations, or hardship, or oppression. (*Enarr. in Ps.* 62:2)

In *Enarr. in Ps.* 61:4, drawing on Col. 1:24, Augustine makes the same point: our own sufferings can be interpreted as contributing to the universal passion of Christ: "He suffered as our head, and he suffers in his members, which means in us." This theology does not legitimize our sufferings, but it allows us to see them in a different light: as somehow sharing in Christ's saving activity. These soteriological ideas were to influence many key authors after Augustine such as Anselm, Bonaventure and Thomas Aquinas.

TRINITARIAN THEOLOGY

Augustine's work *De Trinitate*, consisting of fifteen books, is his most original and searching contribution to the understanding of the Christian God: "Nowhere else is a mistake more dangerous, or the search more laborious, or discovery more advantageous" (1.5). The work, one of the most genial theological books in history, can be roughly divided into two halves: Books I–VII, and Books IX–XV, with Book VIII as an important transitional chapter.[10]

In *De Trin.*, Augustine propounds many original theses that left a deep imprint on later theological thinking in the West. Indeed, it is fair to say that Trinitarian theology in the West is but a footnote to Augustine's seminal work. Key questions addressed in the book include: How can we claim that the three Persons are distinct when the Trinity works inseparably in everything God does?[11] How can there be distinction between the

---

[10] See Lewis Ayres, *Augustine and the Trinity* (Cambridge: Cambridge University Press, 2010) for a classic study of Augustine's Trinitarian theology.

[11] Augustine clearly states that "just as Father and Son and Holy Spirit are inseparable, so do they work inseparably" (*De Trin.* 1.7). This view safeguards monotheism. It does not, however, exclude the three Persons from acting inseparably in *distinct* ways (as, for instance, in the Incarnation).

three Persons given the oneness of God? How are Son and Holy Spirit distinct from one another? How can there be equality between the three Persons given the fact that the Father is the origin of the other Persons? How can we square texts from the New Testament that seem to suggest the inferiority of Christ with his supposed equality with God the Father – an issue of particular importance given the Arian challenge?

The last question can be relatively easily answered. Appealing to Phil. 2:6, on the self-emptying of the Son, Augustine argues that "in the form of a servant which he took, he [= the Son] is the Father's inferior; in the form of God in which he existed even before he took this other [form] he is the Father's equal" (*De Trin.* 1.14). In short, distinguishing between the human and divine natures of Christ (as the Council of Chalcedon was to do in AD 451), Augustine argues that texts that seem to attribute inferiority to the Son should be understood as referring to the human nature of Christ, not to his divine nature. This takes the sting out of the Arian critique. This allows Augustine to speak, for instance, of "a crucified God" (*deus crucifixus*), "owing to the weakness of flesh, though, not to the strength of [the] godhead" (*De Trin.* 1.28).

Books II–IV are mainly concerned with the divine missions, the sendings of Son (Incarnation) and Holy Spirit (such as at Pentecost). This brings us to Augustine's first, major contribution to later theology of the Trinity. For Augustine, everything we say about the inner nature of the Trinity has to be based on how the triune God reveals himself in the history of salvation – namely, in the sendings of the Son and the Holy Spirit. In Rahner's terms, the economic Trinity reveals the immanent Trinity. This is why Book IV contains an extended soteriological discussion, which illustrates how the mission of the Son reveals the eternal generation of the Son within the Trinity.

Books V–VII deal with the linguistic difficulties we encounter when speaking of the Trinity. Here we find, for instance, elaborate discussions of the notion of "Personhood." Augustine puts a distinct emphasis upon divine simplicity. In Aristotelian language, there is no distinction in God between his essence (what he is) and his "accidents." When we call something "simple," we are effectively saying that there is no difference between what it *is* and what it *has* (cf. *De Civ. Dei* XI.10). Whereas goodness, wisdom, justice and other attributes do not belong to our essence as human beings – we may have them as attributes – in God they do.

But then a question arises. How can we square divine simplicity with a distinction between the three Persons? Augustine's answer is to distinguish the Persons from one another in terms of their relationships.

"Although being Father is different from being Son, there is no difference of substance, because they are not called these things substance-wise but relationship-wise" (*non secundum substantiam dicuntur sed secundum rela-tiuum*) (*De Trin.* v.6). Although the Cappadocians had developed similar ideas, Augustine was the first in the West to introduce this notion. In this view, God is utterly "simple"; his being is identical with his attributes. Only the relations in which each of the Persons stands to the others are distinct. Father, Son and Holy Spirit are one God, but the Father is not the Son, and neither of them is the Holy Spirit (*De Civ. Dei* XI.10; *De Trin.* v.9).

The Arian critics had argued that the distinctions within the Godhead were either of substance (which would mean there are three gods) or accidental or nonessential (which would imply that there is no real distinc-tion between Father, Son and Holy Spirit). Against this, Augustine argued that the divine Persons were subsistent relations – that is, Father, Son and Spirit are relations in the sense that whatever each of them is, he is in relation to one or both of the others. "Father" and "Son" are co-relative terms, "opposites" in relational language. Only the mutual relations allow us to distinguish between the Persons within the Godhead: the Father is distinguished as Father because he begets the Son, and the Son is distin-guished as Son because he is begotten. The Holy Spirit similarly is distin-guished as he is "bestowed" by them; he is their common gift, a kind of communion of Father and Son.

It is clear that neither the Son nor the Holy Spirit is the Father, as there is a distinction between being an originator and being originated from. But how do we distinguish the Son from the Holy Spirit, seeing that the Holy Spirit too comes forth from the Father, as it says in the Gospel (John 15:26) (cf. *De Trin.* v.15)? Augustine's answer, which was to shape the whole of Latin theology – and cause a rift with the Eastern Orthodox Church – was that the Holy Spirit proceeds from the Father *and from the Son* (*Filioque*). Augustine can undoubtedly appeal to the biblical witness to make this case. His espousal of the *Filioque* follows from his key presupposition that whatever we say about the inner Trinity has to be based on the revelation of the Persons in the history of salvation. Given the fact that scriptural texts indicate that the Son too sends the Holy Spirit, it stands to reason that, within the inner nature of the Trinity, the Son too is involved in the spiration of the Holy Spirit.

In talking about the Persons of the Trinity we need to make an import-ant distinction between those words that are relationship words – and hence can only be said about one of the divine Persons – and words that can refer to the divine being, the whole Trinity. For instance, only the Second Person of the Trinity can be called "Son" or "Word." These are what we would call "personal names," as they are used relationship-wise (*relative intelligitur*) while other words such as "wisdom" or "goodness," are said about the divine being (*essentialiter*) (*De Trin.* VII.3), although they are associated with one Person in particular. In later terminology we would say that calling the Son "Wisdom" is a case of appropriation. Word and Wisdom are closely related in meaning. Only "Word" is a relationship term – that is, it contains an intrinsic reference to one of the other Persons (the Son is the Word of the Father), while the whole Trinity is "wise" (*De Trin.* VII.3). As Augustine explains, Father and Son are together one wisdom and one being because of divine simplicity (in which "to be" is the same as "to be wise"); they are not, however, both Word or Son. Only the Second Person is Son, which is a term of relationship (*relative dici*).

What about the word "Person" itself? It is a special case. "Person" is clearly used for all three within the Trinity. It is therefore not a relationship word. When we call the Father a "Person," he is so called "with reference to himself, not with reference to the Son or the Holy Spirit" (*De Trin.* VII.11). In that sense the word "Person" is like the word "God" – another non-relationship word. And yet the word "Person" is used for Father, Son and Holy Spirit each as the only term to denote what the three are in their distinctiveness. Hence we speak of three Persons, not three Gods. Augustine concludes that we retain the word "Person" for each of the divine three, so "as not to be reduced to silence when we are asked three what" (*De Trin.* VII.11).

The second part (Books IX–XV) treats of the image of the Trinity in the human soul. This too is a major innovation, although it was often misunderstood in the later tradition, such as by Peter Lombard (1 *Sent.* d.3.2), whose interpretation was in turn rectified by Thomas Aquinas (*ST* 1.93.7 *ad* 2). Augustine tries in *De Trin.* "to see him by whom we were made by means of this image which we ourselves are, as through a mirror" (*De Trin.* XV.14). Thus, he tries to find traces of the Trinity in the human person to assist him in penetrating deeper into the mystery of the triune God. In his search he reviews a number of different analogies. In Book VIII he mentions the Trinitarian character of charity: "You do see a trinity if you see charity" (*Immo uero uides trinitatem si caritatem uides*) (*De Trin.* VIII.12). After all, when we love somebody, we also love the love with which we love. And of course, God is love (1 John 4:8). Hence our love in its threefold dimension (the lover, what is loved and love) discloses something of the mystery of the Trinitarian God (*De Trin.* VIII.12–14). Augustine did not develop this analogy of love in any greater detail, but his hints proved fruitful inspiration for the Trinitarian theology of Richard of St. Victor.

Another analogy he develops (*De Trin.* x. 17–19) is that of memory (*memoria*), understanding (*intellegentia*) and will (*voluntas*). These three form one mind (*mens*), are equal to one another and therefore suggest a promising avenue to explore the mystery of the Three in One, especially if we construe it in dynamic terms (i.e., as acts rather than as static faculties), thus mirroring the divine processions. For whenever we use our intellectual powers (e.g., when I think about the city walls of Rome), a mental word (*verbum mentis*) is issued from the storehouse of *memoria*. The *verbum mentis*, or inner word, is a "word" before it is spoken aloud. It is even prelinguistic. (The linguistic expression of the inner word of Augustine compares to the Incarnation of the Word [*De Trin.* xv.20].) As Edmund Hill explains in his outstanding translation of *De Trinitate*, this mental word is "a mentally visible replica or image of the object of understanding latent in the memory. It can thus be regarded as an off-spring (*proles*) conceived from the parent memory" (p. 266; cf. *De Trin.* IX.12). But it requires an act of will to continue to think about something. Augustine concludes: "And so you have a certain image of the Trinity, the mind itself and its knowledge, which is its offspring and its word about itself, and love as the third element, and *these three are one* (1 John 5:8) and are one substance" (*De Trin.* IX.18).

Thus, Augustine draws a comparison between the inner workings of the mind and the Trinity. As an inner word is generated from memory, and the will rejoices in this knowledge (rather than eliciting it), so too the Word is generated from the Father, and the Holy Spirit is the bond between the Word and the Father.

Now, this may be a useful analogy, but Augustine's main aim is to disclose how we can participate in the life of the Trinity, become transformed and thus become a real image of the Trinity ourselves (*De Trin.* XIV.11). The mind is God's image "insofar as it is capable of him and can participate in him; indeed it cannot achieve so great a good except by being his image" (*De Trin.* XIV.11). In short, at the heart of *De Trinitate* is an existential call for renewal, to become more Godlike through faith and love, and in pursuing this call we will develop a better understanding of the Trinitarian God – insofar as this is possible in this life. This is why the second half of this book contains large excursions on sin, faith, salvation and other key theological themes.

Finally, this explains why, for Augustine, the real image of the Trinity in us is not found in the mind remembering, understanding and loving itself (cf. *De Trin.* XIV.9), but rather in it remembering, understanding and loving God: "This trinity of the mind is not really the image of God because the mind remembers and understands and loves itself, but because it is also able to remember and understand and love him by whom it was made ... Let it then remember its God to whose image it was made, and understand and love him" (*De Trin.* XIV.15). Actualizing the image-character within us is a lifelong process that will come to full fruition only when we meet God face to face (*De Trin.* XIV.23–25).

Augustine's achievement in *De Trinitate* is outstanding: he clearly argued that the historical missions of the Son and Holy Spirit reveal something of their inner processions within the Trinity; he explained the dogma of the Trinity in terms of subsistent relations; he developed the psychological analogy to the Trinity; he was responsible for the *Filioque*; and, finally, he developed a beautiful spirituality of the image: the soul reflects and reveals the Trinity best when it knows and loves God. Thomas Aquinas was to develop these ideas in greater detail.

AUGUSTINE'S SPIRITUALITY: THE FRUITION OF GOD

"It is our great misfortune not to be with him without whom we cannot be" (*Magna itaque hominis miseria est cum illo non esse sine quo non potest esse*) (*De Trin.* XIV.16). Our discussion of Augustine's soteriological and Trinitarian views has revealed that his theology is inextricably interwoven with a profound and multifaceted spirituality. One of the ways in which Augustine tried to express his view that God should be our ultimate concern in all our activities (intellectual or practical) is by his often-misunderstood distinction between enjoyment of God (*frui*) and use of things (*uti*). Augustine illustrates this distinction between enjoyment (*frui*) and use (*uti*) by referring to somebody who, while traveling to her homeland, has to make use of different means of transport. She should not abandon her final goal, which is the sole source of her fruition and fulfillment; if she does abandon her goal by treating the means as an end, she will never reach her true destination. Augustine attempts to make clear that only God should be our ultimate concern; no created being should be considered as the ultimate. Having distinguished between things that are to be enjoyed and things that are to be used, Augustine goes on to identify those things that do both the enjoying and using, saying (in *De Doctr. Christ.* 1.3): "We ourselves, however, both enjoy and use things, and find ourselves in the middle, in a position to choose which to do. So if we wish to enjoy things that are meant to be used, we are impeding our progress, and sometimes are deflected from our course, because we are thereby delayed in obtaining what we should be enjoying, or turned back from it altogether."[12] He then goes on to define "enjoyment." It consists "in clinging to something lovingly for its own sake." "Use" consists in "referring what has come your way to what your love aims at obtaining, provided, that is, it deserves to be loved" (*De Doctr. Christ.* 1.4). Everything we "use" needs to be referred back to our ultimate concern: God as the object of our fruition. Other human beings are not really to be enjoyed (as in *De Doctr. Christ.*) or, if we are willing to concede that they can be enjoyed, they should only be enjoyed "in God" (*De Trin.* IX.13).

It may seem to modern commentators that the notion that only God is to be enjoyed necessarily implies an instrumentalization of creation, including human persons. I would argue with Augustine and the medieval tradition after him that the opposite is the case: Augustine's radical theocentric focus – only God is to be enjoyed – is exactly what keeps us from either idolizing creation or contemptuously disregarding it. For only when our desire is immediately focused on God, and only indirectly on created beings, can we attribute intrinsic meaning to created beings. An analogy with friendship may clarify this: you can only reap the benefits of friendship (such as mutual support or consolation) if you do not directly aim for these benefits. If you target them immediately, you cease to be a friend (you may perhaps become a "social networker"). Similarly, when our desire is first focused on God, we can then, indirectly, treat created beings with the reverence that is due to them without subjecting them to a calculative or instrumentalizing approach.[13] In other words, "enjoying God only" does not imply, for Augustine, that we cannot consider created beings as having intrinsic value.[14] In short, the distinction between *frui* and *uti* allows Augustine to make clear how everything we do should be focused on God or have God as its ultimate reference. This is a key theme that runs throughout medieval theology, as we will see.

BIBLIOGRAPHICAL NOTE

The critical edition of key works by St. Augustine has been published in the Corpus Christianorum series (Turnhout: Brepols).

---

[12] All translations from *De Doctr. Christ.* are taken from Edmund Hill (trans.), *St. Augustine: Teaching Christianity* (New York: New City Press, 1996).

[13] For a fuller statement of this argument, see Rik van Nieuwenhove, "The Religious Disposition As a Critical Resource to Resist Instrumentalisation," *Heythrop Journal* 50 (2009): 689–96.

[14] This is why he can invite us in *Enarr. in Ps.* 0(4) no. 11: "Learn not to love, so you may learn to love; draw back, so that you may turn [to the Lord]; empty yourself, so you may be filled" – a passage Meister Eckhart was later to quote with approval in his *Book of Divine Consolation*.

The Augustinian Heritage Institute is producing excellent translations (some of which I have used in this chapter), such as *The Works of St. Augustine: A Translation for the 21st Century*, edited by John Rotelle and published in New York by New City Press. I have used *Saint Augustine, vol. 1/5 The Trinity*, translated by Edmund Hill (New York: New City Press, 1991); *Saint Augustine, vol. 1/11 Teaching Christianity (De Doctrina Christiana)*, translated by Edmund Hill (New York: New City Press, 1996); *Saint Augustine, vols. 111/15–20: Exposition of the Psalms* in 6 vols., translated by Maria Boulding (New York: New City Press, 2000–04); *Saint Augustine, vol. 1/8: On Christian Belief (including: True Religion [De Vera Religione])*, translated by Edmund Hill (New York: New City Press, 2005); *Saint Augustine, vol. 1/13: On Genesis*, translated by Edmund Hill (New York: New City Press, 2002). For the translation of the *Confessions*, I have used *Saint Augustine, Confessions*, translated by Henry Chadwick (Oxford: Oxford University Press, 1992). For *De Civitate Dei*, see the translation by Henry Bettenson, *St Augustine, Concerning the City of God against the Pagans* (Harmondsworth: Penguin, 1984).

The best introductions to Augustine's thought and life are: Matthew Levering, *The Theology of Augustine: An Introductory Guide to His Most Important Works* (Grand Rapids, MI: Baker, 2013); Henry Chadwick, *Augustine of Hippo: A Life* (Oxford: Oxford University Press, 2010); Carol Harrison, *Augustine: Christian Truth and Fractured Humanity* (Oxford: Oxford University Press, 2000) and Mary T. Clark, *Augustine of Hippo* (London: Continuum, 1994). For his theology of the Trinity, see Lewis Ayres, *Augustine and the Trinity* (Cambridge: Cambridge University Press, 2010).

CHAPTER 3

Monks and Scholars in the 5th and 6th Centuries
John Cassian, Boethius and Pseudo-Dionysius

JOHN CASSIAN AND LATIN MONASTICISM

Christian monasticism finds its origins in the Egyptian desert. Following the example of St. Anthony (d. 356), who, inspired by Matthew 19:21, sold everything and espoused the life of a hermit, men and women set up monastic cells in the Nile region. Monasticism took different forms. Some monks favored the anchorite or eremitic life; others adopted a more communal monastic life called cenobitic (Pachomius). The monastic movement spread to Palestine and Syria. After he left Rome, Jerome (d. 420) led the life of a hermit near Bethlehem, and spent years translating the Bible from Hebrew and Greek into Latin (the Vulgate).

John Cassian (d. 430) founded monasteries in Gaul (near Marseilles). His writings form one of the most important links between Egyptian monasticism and the Latin West. He visited the Desert Fathers in Egypt and adapted their way of life for his own monasteries. From here, these ideals spread through the rest of Gaul and abroad as far as Ireland, from which, in time, missionaries would be sent out to Scotland and northern England (Columba d. 597), and mainland Europe (Columbanus [d. 615], with monastic settlements in Luxeuil in Burgundy and Bobbio in northern Italy) to assist in the re-Christianization of Western Europe. John Cassian wrote two influential works for his communities: *The Institutes* and *The Conferences* (*Collationes*).[1] *The Institutes* deals with a wide range of ascetical issues from the garb of monks to ways of praying, but its main topic is the eight principal vices (gluttony, fornication, avarice, anger, sadness, acedia, vainglory and pride). *The Conferences* is the more voluminous work. As the title suggests, it consists of gatherings of Egyptian monks or "Abbas" (Fathers), who discuss topics such as prayer, renunciation, vices, repentance, the role of discretion (a virtue

---

[1] Boniface Ramsey has translated both works: John Cassian, *The Institutes* (New York: Newman Press, 2000) and John Cassian, *The Conferences* (New York: Newman Press, 1997).

that assists in distinguishing between good and bad), submission to elders, friendship and contemplation. The goal of the entire ascetical practice is purity of heart so as to reach the kingdom of heaven.

From a doctrinal perspective, John Cassian's views on justification and the cooperation between the human will and grace are most interesting. They are considered closer to the Eastern view of *synergeia* (harmonious cooperation between grace and free will) than to the Augustinian one. As Columba Stewart explains, "in a monastic context where the interplay of ascetical discipline, prayer, and the support of other human beings created the context for growth toward Christian perfection," Augustine's apparent downplaying of human initiative made little sense.[2] Cassian discusses the relation between divine grace and free will in *Conference* XIII, expanding views he had already touched on in Book XII of *The Institutes*. While not denying the necessity of grace in our conversion, he argues that "the grace of God always works together with our will on behalf of the good."[3] While for some, grace and free will may appear mutually opposed, we should acknowledge that "both are in accord, and we understand that we must accept both in like manner."[4] While Augustine had taught that our turning toward God is itself already the result of divine grace operating in us, Cassian allows for more scope for human initiative in our salvation: "For when God sees us turning in order to will what is good, he comes to us, directs us, and strengthens us."[5]

Prosper of Aquitaine, a follower of Augustine, harshly attacked Cassian's teaching.[6] Despite the Council of Orange's condemnation (in AD 529) of views that assert the role of human initiative in our salvation, John Cassian's approach represents an important minority view in the Latin West, distinct from the mainstream Augustinian tradition. As indicated, it exerted its appeal in a monastic context rather than in doctrinal theology. It is little coincidence that St. Benedict of Nursia (480–540), the father of Western monasticism, recommended the works of John Cassian in his *Rule*.

After leaving Rome in disgust over its decadence, Benedict lived in a cave as an anchorite. His holiness attracted followers and he eventually went to Monte Cassino, where he founded a famous monastery. Benedict's *Rule* was to shape monastic life in Western Europe profoundly until the middle of the 11th century and beyond, especially after Charlemagne imposed it on

---

[2] Columba Stewart, *Cassian the Monk* (Oxford: Oxford University Press, 1998), 19.
[3] John Cassian, *The Conferences* XIII.13.1 (trans. 481).   [4] Ibid., XIII.11.1 (trans. 477).
[5] Ibid., XIII.11.5 (trans. 478).   [6] See Stewart, *Cassian the Monk*, 19–22 and 79–81.

all monasteries. The *Rule* is very short – not more than about twelve thousand words – yet it covers all aspects of religious life (such as how to deal with visitors, sick people and disobedient people, how the days should be organized, how to deal with conflicts etc.) without being rigid. The main emphasis is upon obedience. The *Rule* was written so that those who follow it may "by the labor of obedience" return to God "whom they have abandoned by the sloth of disobedience." There is obedience of heart and body to the Gospel, to the *Rule* itself and to the abbot, the vicar of Christ within the community. Obedience has to be full-hearted and without "murmuring for any cause whatsoever, by any word whatsoever, or any gesture." As Richard Southern rightly points out, this emphasis on obedience should not be misconstrued in authoritarian terms.[7] Obedience is not an end in itself but must be seen in relation to a transformation of the self (within the community) and a restoration of a relationship with God. To attain these goals, self-abnegation (the fruit of obedience) is necessary: the monks are to have nothing of their own; they are expected to put up with poverty, illness and harshness because through these things we return to God.

BOETHIUS

Manlius Severinus Boethius was born around AD 480 into a noble Roman family. He absorbed the philosophies of Aristotle, Plato and Neoplatonism. He had the intention to translate the complete works of Plato and Aristotle from Greek into Latin. If he had succeeded in doing this, Western thought and culture in the medieval period would arguably have been very different. As it turned out, he managed to translate Aristotle's *Categories* and *On Interpretation*, as well as Porphyry's *Isagoge* (*Introduction*) to the last-mentioned work. Together with a number of textbooks on logic written by Boethius himself, they formed the so-called Old Logic (*Logica vetus*).[8] It was in Boethius's works and translations that medieval thinkers would encounter the problem of universals, which would lead to heated discussions in the 12th century and beyond. Boethius composed textbooks on the *quadrivium*, not all of which have survived. He himself coined the phrase *quadrivium*, denoting "the fourfold path," to refer to arithmetic, geometry,

---

[7] Richard Southern, *Western Society and the Church in the Middle Ages* (Harmondsworth: Penguin, 1990), 218–23.

[8] In the 12th century, Boethius's translations of Aristotle's *Prior Analytics*, *Posterior Analytics*, *Sophistic Arguments* and *Topics* were discovered. They were to be known as the New Logic (*Logica nova*).

astronomy and music. As John Marenbon explains, these disciplines, all mathematical in nature, assist the student in making the transition from the world of the senses to the more certain things of intelligence.[9] Boethius is also remembered for writing short theological treatises on topics such as the Trinity and the Person of Christ, as well as a work commonly known as *De Hebdomadibus*, dealing with the goodness of being.

Above all else, however, Boethius is remembered for his book *The Consolation of Philosophy*, written under rather dramatic circumstances. Boethius had entered into service with Theodoric, the ruler of the Ostrogoths, but fell out of favor with him and was convicted of high treason. Boethius wrote *The Consolation* in prison in Pavia, while he was awaiting execution.

The *Consolation* is divided into five books. In the first book, we find Boethius in prison, lamenting his fate: "I have been parted from my possessions, stripped of my offices, blackened in my reputation, and punished for the services I have rendered."[10] A Lady then enters the room. She has fiery eyes and is vibrant, but it is impossible to put an age on her, although she clearly is not young. She wears a dress in which two Greek letters are visible in the embroidery – θ (Th) and Π (P) – standing for theoretical and practical philosophy. The Lady, who symbolizes Philosophy or Wisdom, rebukes Boethius for his melancholy and grief. He has forgotten his own identity and appears "unaware of the goal to which creation proceeds."[11] Boethius mistakenly assumes that Fortune has changed toward him, but that is not the case: it simply belongs to the nature of Fortune to be fickle and inconstant (*Consol.* II.1). Instead of seeking happiness outside of himself, Boethius should be looking for fulfillment within (*Consol.* II.4).

Lady Philosophy surveys Fortune's gifts – riches, honor, power, bodily pleasures – and none of them are a secure source of happiness. In *Consol.* III.10, she then goes on to explain the nature of true happiness. She argues that the ultimate good can only be God. In this context she states in passing that "nothing better than God can be imagined" – an insight Augustine had already expressed (*De Doctr. Christ.* 1.7.7) and Anselm of Canterbury was to develop half a millennium later in his *Proslogion*. Now, since we become happy by achieving happiness, and happiness itself is divinity, we can only become happy by attaining divinity, or at least by participating in it (*Consol.* III.10). Thus, our search for happiness is ultimately a search for

[9] John Marenbon, *Boethius* (Oxford: Oxford University Press, 2003), 14.

[10] *Consol.* 1.4. All translations by P. G. Walsh from *Boethius: The Consolation of Philosophy* (Oxford: Oxford University Press, 1999), 13.

[11] *Consol.* 1.6, trans. 17.

the highest good. This goodness is God, which all things desire (*Consol.* III.II). While Boethius exclaims that Lady Philosophy has revealed the very center of truth to him, he still harbors difficulties. "The consuming cause of my depression is this, that in spite of the existence of a good ruler over the world, it is at all possible for evils to exist, or to go unpunished." Given the goodness, omniscience and omnipotence of God, how can we make sense of evil (*Consol.* IV.I)?

Evidently drawing on Plato's thought, Lady Philosophy explains that goodness is its own reward, just as wickedness is punishment in its own right for bad people (*Consol.* IV.3). Indeed, people disfigured by vices are actually subhuman. Their wretchedness lies precisely in this disfigurement of their character. According to Lady Philosophy, we either participate in the divinity through a virtuous life, or we degenerate into some kind of animal-like status (*Consol.* IV.3).[12]

The discussion then moves on to the topic of Providence. Lady Philosophy identifies Providence with divine reason itself (*Consol.* IV.6). Hers is a deeply rational world where each gets his just rewards. Every fortune, pleasant or harsh, is bestowed to either reward or exercise the good and to punish or correct the wicked. "They are either just or useful" (*Consol.* IV.7, trans. 94). In the fifth and final book, we find an influential discussion on the relation between divine foreknowledge and contingency and human freedom. Lady Philosophy's interlocutor, Boethius, summarizes the problem well: "If God foresees all things and cannot be in any way mistaken, then what Providence has foreseen will happen, must inevitably come to pass" (*Consol.* V.3, trans. 100). If there were any validity in this objection, it would follow that there cannot be any genuine freedom of will (*Consol.* V.3). And this in turn would compromise everything Lady Philosophy has been saying, especially her call to embrace a virtuous life.

In order to deal with this problem, Lady Philosophy points out, as a preliminary observation, that the nature of knowledge and its acquisition depends as much on the capacity of the knower as on the object known (*Consol.* V.4). This is what scholars call "the modes of cognition principle."[13]

Before I examine in more detail how Lady Philosophy applies this principle to the case at hand, I want to pause and consider the example she gives to clarify her meaning because it touches upon the self-transcending

---

[12] From this it follows, perhaps surprisingly, that the wicked are happier if they suffer punishment than if no deserved punishment constrains them (*Consol.* IV.4). Dostoevsky's Raskolnikov (from his novel *Crime and Punishment*) would agree.

[13] John Marenbon, *Boethius* (Oxford: Oxford University Press, 2003), 130ff.

nature of human knowledge, which is a key theme I hope to develop in this book.

Let's say, for instance, we observe a person. The senses (*sensus*) will perceive her shape in matter; the imagination (*imaginatio*) will visualize her shape (*figura*) independently of matter; reason (*ratio*) rises higher still and abstracts the (Platonic) universal form of humanity; and the eye of understanding (*intellegentia*), finally, transcending the boundaries of the created world, contemplates (*contuetur*) the simple Form, which is divine, with the pure sight of the mind (*Consol.* v.4). Each aspect of our perceptional and cognitive apparatus has a different object. The senses perceive a particular, material thing. The imagination grasps a sensible, particular image. Reason distils an abstracted, universal form, and intelligence or understanding gazes upon the divine Form. Now, sensation and imagination can never quite perceive the universal form, abstracted from matter, as this is within the remit of reason. This illustrates that cognition is dependent on the capacity of the knower as much as on the object of knowledge.

I have dwelt on this for two reasons. First, as suggested already, the distinction between reason and intellect, found in Augustine, illustrates the self-transcending nature of human rationality. While reason is typically human, it is subject to a higher kind of intelligence – namely, intellect – which is divine. I allude to this topic throughout this book.

Second, having made the case that cognition depends at least partly on the capacity of the knower, Lady Philosophy then goes on to apply this principle to God's knowledge of future contingent events. She explains that God knows future events in ways different from how we do – simply because his mode of cognition (and being) differ from ours. "Just as we have decreed that the imagination and the senses ought to yield to the reason, so we would regard it as most just that the human reason should defer to the divine mind" (*Consol.* v.5, trans. 109). More specifically, God in his eternity knows things in ways different from how we know them. His knowledge transcends all movement and time, abiding in the simplicity of the present. God's eternity "possesses simultaneously the entire fullness of life without end; no part of the future is lacking to it, and no part of the past has escaped it" (*Consol.* v.6, trans. 111). For God, all things (past, present and future) are known in an eternal present moment. Boethius uses the metaphor of a man gazing out on the world from the top of a mountain, which proved very popular.[14] Let's develop this image in more detail.

---

[14] Thomas, for instance, adopts it in *ST* 1.14.13 *ad* 3.

Consider three people walking: one is walking toward a bridge across a river (for him, the bridge is in the future), another person has crossed the bridge already (for her, the bridge lies in the past), and a third person is at present walking over the bridge. If somebody sitting on top of a mountain were to look down on these three people, he would in one single, present moment see what is past, present and future for them. This is how we should imagine God's eternity. Events that take place in time can be known in God's eternal now. God's knowledge of future events does not compromise their contingent nature (i.e., it does not necessitate them). "A future happening which is necessary when viewed by divine knowledge seems to be wholly free and unqualified when considered in its own nature" (*Consol.* v.6, trans., 112–13).

In short, God's knowledge of future and contingent events does not necessitate them. Boethius's espousal of a virtuous life has not proved futile. God's eternal knowledge does not compromise the true freedom and contingency of our world.

Since this is the case, man's freedom of will remains intact ... God continually observes with foreknowledge all things from on high, and his eternal vision, which is ever in the present, accords with the future nature of our actions, and dispenses rewards to the good and punishments to the wicked. The hopes which we rest in God, and the prayers addressed to him, are not in vain. (*Consol.* v.6, trans., 114)

God's world is both rational and just. Boethius can die in peace.

PSEUDO-DIONYSIUS

I conclude this survey of patristic authors with a brief discussion of an author who wrote in Greek. He called himself Dionysius, pretending to be St. Paul's convert mentioned in the Acts of the Apostles (Acts 17:34). In reality, we are probably dealing with a Syrian monk from the end of the 5th or the beginning of the 6th century. Dionysius's deception worked well until the beginning of the Reformation, when Erasmus was one of the first to express his doubts. Until that time his works enjoyed immense prestige and authority. As we will see, John Scottus Eriugena translated some of his works into Latin, but they only began to make a massive impact with new translations and commentaries from the end of the 12th and the beginning of the 13th century onward. The works of Pseudo-Dionysius injected a strong mystical, apophatic and symbolic element into Latin theology. The Dionysian corpus proved a major source of influence on scholastic theologians (e.g., Bonaventure, Albert the Great and Thomas Aquinas), the Rhineland Mystics (such as Meister Eckhart and his school) and, in the English-speaking world, on the anonymous author of *The Cloud of Unknowing* (14th century), while in Spain John of the Cross too underwent his influence.

The main writings that have been preserved are *The Divine Names, The Mystical Theology, The Celestial Hierarchy, The Ecclesiastical Hierarchy* and a number of *Letters*. In *The Divine Names*, Pseudo-Dionysius examines a number of names (such as "Good," "Being," "Life," "Wisdom," "Power" and so forth) and wonders whether they are applicable to God, starting from the loftier and more abstract ones and then descending to more particular ones (such as "Peace"). In *The Mystical Theology*, Pseudo-Dionysius ascends through denial of names to ultimately enter the realm of speechlessness: when talking about God, our language utterly fails. This is the way of "unknowing" – a way that makes the reader aware of the utter transcendence of God.

The often somewhat obscure remarks of Pseudo-Dionysius were later systematized as consisting of three distinct but closely intertwined ways. First, there is the *affirmative* way, where we affirm something of God. We say, for instance, "God is good." This is a positive or "cataphatic" statement. Second, we *deny* this affirmation: this is the negative way: "God is not good." Why? Because we use the word "good" in a creaturely manner. We are, in fact, attributing a creaturely notion ("goodness" as we know it) to God, and God is not good the way we are. Finally, there is what later scholastic theologians called the *super-eminent* way, or the way of excellence: here we say that "God is supra-goodness." Now, the third way is not some kind of affirmative way, albeit in a more sophisticated guise. In the third way, we attribute words to God (such as "supra-being," "supra-wisdom"), *but we do not actually fully understand what they mean.* In order to highlight the inadequacy of our language about God, mystical theologians often play games with language so as to instill in the reader a sense of the mystery of God. A classic example is: "God is light" (affirmative statement); "God is darkness" (denial of affirmative statement); "God is a luminous darkness" (super-eminent way). Here, language breaks down. We can never quite grasp God's mystery.[15] It is the goal of mystical theology to make the reader aware of this divine mystery; this awareness will lead to a different way of relating to God, ourselves and the world, and is not merely intellectual in nature. Pseudo-Dionysius

---

[15] On this, see Denys Turner, *The Darkness of God: A Study in the Negativity of Christian Mysticism* (Cambridge: Cambridge University Press, 1995).

developed this aspect in a highly symbolic manner in his work *The Ecclesiastical Hierarchy*. He describes how we attain union with God or deification (to become Godlike) through our participation in the rites of the Church.

BIBLIOGRAPHICAL NOTE

John Cassian

Boniface Ramsey has translated the two main works as John Cassian, *The Institutes* (New York: Newman Press, 2000) and John Cassian, *The Conferences* (New York: Newman Press, 1997). The best introduction to his thought is Columba Stewart, *Cassian the Monk* (Oxford: Oxford University Press, 1998).

Boethius

I have used the translation by P. G. Walsh, *Boethius: The Consolation of Philosophy* (Oxford: Oxford University Press, 1999). John Marenbon has written an excellent introduction, *Boethius* (Oxford: Oxford University Press, 2003), with many references to primary and secondary literature. Also very helpful is Noel Harold Kayler and Philip Edward Phillips (eds.), *A Companion to Boethius in the Middle Ages* (Leiden: Brill, 2012).

Pseudo-Dionysius

For a translation, see Colm Luibheid (trans.), *Pseudo-Dionysius: The Complete Works*. Classics of Western Spirituality (New York: Paulist Press, 1987). For a good introduction, see Andrew Louth, *Denys the Areopagite* (London: Continuum, 2002).

PART II

Early Medieval Theologians

CHAPTER 4

Gregory the Great

HISTORICAL BACKGROUND

Between the death of Augustine and the papacy of Gregory the Great (590–604), the Western world changed beyond recognition. Already during Augustine's lifetime a number of major events had taken place that were to lead to a radically new political, socioeconomic and cultural state of affairs. Due to pressure from the Huns, who had arrived in Eastern Europe around AD 376, Germanic tribes were forced to move into the Roman Empire. The Visigoths were eventually to settle in the Iberian Peninsula (where the Suevi, another Germanic tribe, occupied the northwest). The Franks had occupied most of Gaul (with the exception of Burgundy) and the Low Countries. The Vandals made their way through Spain and settled in northern Africa. Angles and Saxons moved into the east of Britain, where the Christian Britons unsuccessfully attempted to defend themselves against the pagan invaders. (These historic events later found literary expression in the legend of King Arthur and the knights of the Round Table.) The map of Europe had been radically redrawn, with Franks in Gaul, Visigoths in Spain and Ostrogoths in Italy.

Italy had proved particularly vulnerable. In 476, Odoacer, a Germanic general, sent the imperial regalia to the emperor of Constantinople, thereby effectively staking a claim for his own authority in Italy. The gesture had mainly symbolic significance. At the request of Emperor Zeno (in AD 489), Theodoric, an Arian, attempted to introduce a measure of stability in Italy, reigning from AD 493 until his death in AD 526. He held court at Ravenna, encouraging a revival of classical learning and culture. Less than a decade after Theodoric's death, Emperor Justinian attempted to reconquer the West. In Italy, this led to wars, destruction, starvation and plagues for almost two decades. In AD 568, three years after the death of Justinian, the Ostrogoth era ended, when a new Germanic tribe invaded Italy: the Lombards. Their main centers were around Milan, Spoleto and Benevento.

Gregory originated from a rich family with strong Church connections. He converted some of his properties into monasteries and became a monk himself – the happiest time of his life, as he was to recall later. Around AD 579, the pope sent him to Constantinople as papal ambassador (*apocrisiarius*). After he had returned to Italy and served another spell in the monastery, Gregory was elected pope in AD 590. Gregory was an able administrator, pastoral leader, monk, bishop, diplomat and theologian. In the English-speaking world, he is remembered for sending forty Benedictine monks as missionaries to the Anglo-Saxons under the leadership of Augustine of Canterbury.

WORKS AND ESCHATOLOGICAL OUTLOOK

One of Gregory's most popular books was *The Dialogues*, consisting of four parts. It contains miracle stories about Italian saints, which may strike the modern reader as mildly bizarre and naive. For instance, in the first part, Gregory recalls a story about Boniface, bishop of Ferentis, who one day walked into his garden, only to discover that all his vegetables were covered in caterpillars. Boniface prayed to Christ and the caterpillars duly left (*Dial.* 1.9 [15]). The story is more sophisticated than we might give it credit for. It is inspired by a similar story from *The Life of Saint Anthony* (50.9) by Athanasius, which reveals how the Christian saint recaptured the harmony between prelapsarian man and the rest of creation. Moreover, these stories strike us as incredulous because we are imbued with a positivistic worldview. Gregory would dispute our presuppositions, pointing out that things we consider scientifically explicable are equally remarkable and revealing of God's power. In his most important work, *Moralia in Iob*, Gregory challenges those who have become dull to the consideration of the wondrous nature of creation. We are astonished that five thousand people were fed with five loaves, and yet every day the grains of seed that are sown are multiplied in rich harvest, and no one wonders. Similarly, all are astonished to see water turned into wine, and yet each day the earth's moisture is drawn into the root of the vine and turned by the grape into wine, and no one wonders. Gregory concludes: "Full of wonder then are all things, which we never think to wonder at because ... we have, by habit, become dull to the consideration of them" (*Mor.* VI.18).[1]

---

[1] I use the translation by Members of the English Church as *Gregory the Great: Morals on the Book of Job*. 4 vols. (Oxford: John Henry Parker, 1844).

Gregory himself comments in one of his sermons: "You see the great wars ravaging the world, the great blows daily destroying the people ... Cities have been laid waste, fortified places overthrown, churches and monasteries destroyed, fields reduced to wasteland" (*Hom. Ev.* 17). He was not exaggerating when he remarked that he lived "in a barbaric age" (*tempus barbarici*) (*Hom. Ev.* 17) in which Italy was being "handed over to be struck by the pagans' sword" (*Hom. Ev.* 1).[2] In Gregory's apocalyptic times, the present and the future worlds converge. "As the present world approaches its end, the future world is now so near at hand that it almost touches us, and therefore its nature is more clearly revealed. We stand, as it were, in the twilight of the dawn, and the light [of the end times] is already breaking in" (*Dial.* IV.43 [1]). Thus, the supernatural is deeply woven into the way people experience and interpret the world of ordinary experience. In Gregory's world, invisible reality exists alongside the visible reality it sustains and determines.[3]

Unlike Augustine (who had generally shown greater reticence on eschatological speculation), Gregory's world is one in which the eschaton impacts the here and now, and he is therefore happy to speculate more freely about eschatological issues. For instance, in relation to the fate of souls after death, he claims that the souls of the just will enter heaven and dwell in the presence of Christ before they are reunited with their bodies in the resurrection (cf. *Dial.* IV.26; *Mor.* IV.56; *Mor.* XIII.48). This view was to determine some of the discussions at the beginning of the 14th century on the nature (and time) of the beatific vision. Again, Gregory considers in much greater detail the nature of the fires of purgatory – which will cleanse minor misdemeanors (*Dial.* IV.41) – hell (*Dial.* IV.44) and the benefits of offering Mass for the dead (*Dial.* IV. 57).[4] Of particular interest are his views on the devil. As F. H. Dudden observed many years ago, Gregory's devil is "already the cunning impostor, full of tricks and devices, with whom the Middle Ages were familiar."[5] The devil is portrayed with flaming mouth and flashing eyes (*Dial.* 11.8), or under the form of a little black boy (*Dial.* 11.4); the devil holds court in a ruined temple, receiving reports of

---

[2] I use the translation by David Hurst, *Gregory the Great: Forty Gospel Homilies* (Kalamazoo, MI: Cistercian Publications, 1990).

[3] Carole Straw, *Gregory the Great: Perfection in Imperfection* (Berkeley: University of California Press, 1988), 10.

[4] In *Dial.* IV.48, Gregory suggests that fear of damnation may suffice to cleanse people of the stain of small misdeeds. Peter Abelard was to adopt this idea.

[5] F. H. Dudden, *Gregory the Great: His Place in History and Thought, vol. 2* (London: Longmans, Green and Company, 1905), 368.

the mischief his demons have accomplished during the day (*Dial.* III.7, inspired by John Cassian's *Confer.* VIII.16.1–4).

While eschatological issues concern part IV of *The Dialogues*, part II is rightly famous for the portrayal of the Life of St. Benedict, whose rule Gregory celebrates (*Dial.* II.36) as being unsurpassed in wise moderation or discernment (*discretione praecipuam*).[6] It is in this part of *The Dialogues* that we find a description of the famous vision St. Benedict enjoyed, standing near a window, contemplating the world reduced to a single ray of light (*Dial.* II.35).

Another popular work was Gregory's *Regula Pastoralis* (*Book of Pastoral Rule*), traditionally translated into English (in the 9th century) as *Pastoral Care*. In this book, Gregory outlines the qualities bishops and pastoral leaders should possess such as compassion, humility, unselfishness and God-centeredness, maintaining a right balance between interiority and active involvement with their fellow humans. It contains valuable advice how a pastor should admonish his faithful, with particular sensitivity to the state of life of each. Just as Benedict's *Rule* was to shape profoundly monastic life in the West for centuries to come, so Gregory's *Regula Pastoralis* proved equally influential in the formation of priests.

Some of Gregory's major works find their origin in sermons he gave to his own monastic community or to a wider congregation. A famous example of sermons he preached to his wider community is the *Forty Gospel Homilies* (*XL Homeliarum in Evangelica*), already referred to. His most important works, however, are his *Homiliae in Hiezechihelem* (*Homilies on Ezekiel*) and, above all, his *Moralia in Iob* (*Morals on the Book of Job*). There is also a brief *Expositio in Canticum Canticorum* (*Commentary on the Song of Songs*), as well as more than eight hundred letters. These letters are of immense value, providing us with a unique insight into his times. They also proved a major source in the formation of canon law.

GREGORY AND THE BIBLE

Gregory's major work is *Moralia in Iob*, extending over almost two thousand pages. No major theologian had written a commentary on the Book of Job before Gregory's time. It is not particularly surprising, however, that Gregory felt attracted to this particular book. As is well

---

[6] The notion of *discretio* is an important one, both for Gregory and for St. Benedict. It appears its meaning gradually shifted from wise discernment ("the discernment of the spirits") to moderation.

known, the problem of innocent suffering is the key issue addressed in the Book of Job. God allows the devil to inflict enormous suffering on Job in order to test Job's faithfulness. Job loses everything (his family, his riches, his health), with the exception of his wife, who admonishes him "to curse God, and die!" (Job 2:9).[7] Given the times in which Gregory lived and his own ill health, the Book of Job was bound to appeal to him.

It is impossible to appreciate Gregory's contribution to spirituality and theology without a proper understanding of the hermeneutical presuppositions that govern his reading of the Scriptures. For Gregory, the Bible is a single book that deals with one major theme: Christ and the mysteries of faith. This implies that his approach is deeply intertextual – that is, Gregory can use one passage from the Bible to illuminate another one, even if they were written during a totally different era. This kind of approach may strike us as unhistorical or uncontextualized. It is true that more often than not Gregory is not concerned with a text's historical context. As a matter of fact, this kind of concern would, in his view, be rather misplaced. To borrow one of his metaphors: when you receive a letter from a great person, it is rather absurd to ask what kind of pen he used to write it. Similarly, it is superfluous to inquire who the human writer of a biblical text is, since "at any rate the Holy Spirit is confidently believed to have been the Author" (*Mor. Pref.* 2). Rather than looking behind the text, we should be concerned with pondering its true meaning and how it may transform us.

As divinely inspired writings, the Scriptures can appeal to readers at different levels, from theological novices to seasoned readers. Gregory uses a memorable simile to illustrate this point. The Scriptures are, as it were, a kind of river, which is both shallow and deep, wherein the lamb may walk and the elephant may float at large (*Mor. Ad Leand.* iv). Thus, the Scriptures have different levels of meaning. There is, in the first place, the prima facie meaning of the text, which Gregory calls the historical sense. At least in principle, the historical or literal sense is the root or foundation of more profound spiritual senses (the typological-allegorical and tropological senses), although he acknowledges that a literal interpretation may not be possible in every instance. This is how Gregory distinguishes between the three senses:

I shall run quickly through some passages with a historical exposition; some I shall examine by means of allegory for their typological sense [*per allegoriam quaedam typica investigatione*]; others again I shall discuss by means of allegory only for their moral bearing [*per sola allegoricae moralitatis instrumenta*]; some, finally, I shall

---

[7] The Vulgate has (euphemistically perhaps): *Benedic Deo et morere*: "Bless God, and die."

investigate thoroughly in all three ways . . . First I shall establish the historical sense as fundamental; then I shall erect [on this foundation], by means of the typological sense, a mental edifice as a stronghold of faith; finally, by means of the moral sense I shall as it were complete the building by a coat of paint. (*Mor. Ad Leand.* iii)[8]

I explain these different senses (literal or historical, allegorical in the strict sense or typological and moral) through examples of Gregory's exegesis from the first part of his *Moralia*. In doing so, I also have the opportunity to uncover his theological concerns.

Gregory explains in the preface to his *Moralia* that Job can stand for the historical man Job. This is the literal sense. In a typological-allegorical sense, Job stands for Christ. Job's sufferings announce and point toward the salvific sufferings of Christ and can only be properly understood from that angle. This typological meaning (in which Job is a type or prefiguration of Christ) is closely associated with the moral or tropological meaning, in which Job represents us, the Church. The theological reason the typological-allegorical (or Christ-centered) meaning and the tropological meaning (what the text means for how we should live) are so closely linked is that Christ (the Head) and the Church (his Body) enjoy an intimate union (*Pref. Mor.* 14). Following a lead from Augustine, Gregory claims that the glorified, risen Christ still suffers in his Body. If the torments we suffer did not reach the Head, He would never have cried out to his persecutors on behalf of his afflicted members: "Saul, Saul, why do you persecute me?" (Acts 9:4). Similarly: "If our agony were not his pain, Paul, when afflicted after his conversion, would never have said: 'I fill up those things that are wanting of the sufferings of Christ in my flesh' (Col. 1:24)" (*Mor.* III.25). This intimate link between Christ and his Church is foundational for the allegorical (Job should be interpreted as Christ) and moral interpretations Gregory goes on to offer. Therefore, because Job is a sign of Christ, foretelling in his afflictions the mysteries of Christ's passion (*sacramenta passionis*, cf. *Mor. Pref.* 14), and because of the union between Christ and his Body, the Church, Job can be a type of both Christ and the Church (*Mor.* 1.33). As Gregory suggests in *Mor.* xx.1, the text of the Book of Job, by telling the past (the historical or literal sense), announces the future (the saving activity of Christ, i.e., the typological-allegorical sense) and points out how we should live (the moral-allegorical, or tropological sense). Let me now examine specific examples of Gregory's exegesis.

---

[8] I have used (and partially modified) R. A. Markus's translation of this passage in his book *Gregory the Great and His World* (Cambridge: Cambridge University Press, 1997), 46.

In the beginning of the Book of Job, we find that "seven sons and three daughters were born to him" (Job 1:2). In a tropological vein, Gregory interprets the seven sons as the seven virtues of the Holy Spirit – namely, wisdom (*sapientia*), understanding (*intellectus*), counsel (*consilium*), strength (*fortitudo*), knowledge (*scientia*), piety (*pietas*) and fear of the Lord (*timor Domini*).[9] The three daughters may symbolize laypeople ("the weaker multitude of the faithful"), but they can also refer to the three states of Christian life in the Church – namely, clergy, monks and married people (*Mor.* 1.18–20). Continuing his exegesis on the sons who called for their three sisters to eat and drink with them (Job 1:4b), Gregory interprets the three sisters now as referring to the three theological virtues of faith, hope and love (*Mor.* 1.46). These rejoice in the good works and are strengthened by them, "and after the meal they long to be refreshed by the dew of contemplation" (*Mor.* 1.46). Here Gregory alludes to a major theme in his theology: how the active life of charitable activity interfaces with a life of contemplation. I return to this topic later.

In his comments on Job 2:8 ("he took him a potsherd to scrape the humor withal, and he sat down upon a dunghill"), we find another example of Gregory's creative allegorical interpretation. A potsherd is made of clay baked in fire. The potsherd symbolizes our human nature, made of clay (cf. Gen. 2:7) and assumed by the Son ("He took himself a potsherd"). This flesh was rendered strong by the fire of his Passion, bestowing it with immortality (the Resurrection). The humor refers to our sinfulness, which is purified by Christ (*Mor.* III.33). The same verse can also be interpreted in a moral sense. In that case, the potsherd refers to the frailness of our mortality and the humor refers to sinful thoughts. In this moral reading, "to scrape the humor with a potsherd" is to ponder on the course and frailty of our mortal state and thereby purge our sinful thoughts (*Mor.* III.58).

Allegorically, the "dunghill" on which Job sits symbolizes the humility of the Word who assumes flesh. Thus, Job's isolation, sitting outside on a dunghill, prefigures that of Christ, rejected by his own people (John 1:11) and crucified outside the city walls in Calvary (*Mor.* III.34). In a moral sense, "to sit on a dunghill" refers to repentance over "the dung of our sins" (*Mor.* III.60). It expresses how we despise our own sinfulness in true repentance and humility.

---

[9] This list of seven gifts of grace (*dona septiformis gratiae*), or the seven gifts of the Holy Spirit, as they were to be called in the later tradition, is inspired by Isa. 11:2, and through Gregory they proved highly influential in medieval spirituality.

Some of these interpretations may strike the modern reader as fanciful or strained. The problem is that modern readers approach texts (and how to interpret them) in ways radically different from premodern authors. Modern readers assume that the meaning of a text can be *uncovered* by attending to its historical and literary *contexts*. These presuppositions are not self-evident. First, texts can yield meaning outside historical and literary contexts. An example is the liturgical context. When Matt. 8:8 is transferred into a liturgical context (when receiving the Body of Christ), its meaning is transformed. Second, in a modern understanding, words hide a true meaning that can be uncovered, or exposed: reading is understood here as a kind of archaeological activity in which meaning is excavated. As Robert Wilken has pointed out in an illuminating contribution, Gregory's strategy is different: it is more akin to composition than modern interpretation.[10] It moves from the true meaning (Christ) to the words, rather than the other way around. The whole of the Old Testament is about Christ and the mysteries of the Christian faith and needs to be understood in light of these.

This explains why Gregory interprets the Old Testament through the lens of the New Testament and reads the Bible as a single, coherent book. In *Hom. Ez.* 1.6.15, Gregory famously wrote that "what the Old Testament promised, the New showed forth, and what the one covertly announced, the other openly proclaimed manifest" (*Et quod Testamentum Vetus promisit, hoc Novum exhibuit; et quod illud occulte annuntiat, hoc istud exhibitum aperte clamat*).[11] In short, Gregory reads the Old Testament as a Christian book, and pondering its words and metaphors illustrates and further enriches his (and our) understanding of these Christian mysteries.

In Gregory's exegesis, the Scriptures are therefore like a piece of art. As John Moorhead has helpfully pointed out, great pieces of art and music are open to ever-new readings; they always open up new avenues. So too the Scriptures are open to multilayered readings, partly depending on the spiritual discernment of the reader.[12] In a famous passage from *Hom. Ez.* 1.7.8, Gregory writes that divine words grow with the reader (*cum legente crescunt*), for the deeper one understands the Scriptures the deeper they penetrate into the reader. Thus, our disposition as readers (*sensus legentium*) will determine how much meaning we can uncover in the Scriptures

---

[10] See R. W. Wilken, "Interpreting Job Allegorically: The Moralia of Gregory the Great," *Pro Ecclesia* 10 (2001): 213–26.

[11] *Gregory the Great: Homilies in the Book of the Prophet Ezekiel*, trans Theodosia Tomkinson (Etna, CA: Center for Traditionalist Orthodox Studies, 2008), 105.

[12] John Moorhead, *Gregory the Great* (London: Routledge, 2005), 20–21.

(*Hom. Ez.* 1.7.9). As Gregory puts it: "God is the more gloriously revealed to the mind who seeks him the more he is sought with insight and interiority" (*subtilius atque interius*).[13] If a spiritual transformation is both the result and the precondition of ever more profound interpretations of the Scriptures, it follows that God's revelation is not closed. For Gregory, interpretation is a dynamic, ongoing process that attempts to find ever-new horizons of divine meaning, and this is only possible after we have become receptive to "the hidden words" spoken (cf. *Mor.* v.50).

Gregory's spiritual readings in his *Moralia* and other works proved a major source of inspiration for future Christian exegetes. As Robert Wilken observed, "No exegetical work from the early church was more admired, studied, excerpted, and cited than Gregory the Great's large commentary on the Book of Job, the *Moralia*."[14]

In the later Middle Ages, four senses were identified – the literal, allegorical, moral and anagogical senses. Tracing the exact historical path of this development is beyond the scope of this work.[15] John Cassian was one of the first Latin authors to list all four senses of Scripture together in *Confer.* xiv.viii.1. Apart from the historical sense he mentions the spiritual sense, which in turn is subdivided into three senses – allegory, tropology (moral sense) and anagogy (eschatological sense, referring to "heavenly secrets"). In *Confer.* xiv.viii.4, Cassian uses the example of "Jerusalem" from Ps. 147:12 to illustrate this fourfold sense. "According to history it is the city of the Jews. According to allegory it is the Church of Christ. According to anagogy it is that heavenly city of God 'which is the mother of us all' (Gal. 4:26). According to tropology it is the soul of the human being, which under this name is frequently either reproached or praised by the Lord."[16] This fourfold sense was to become classic doctrine in later centuries. Bonaventure[17] and Thomas Aquinas,[18] for instance, adopted it. Augustine of Dacia (in turn quoted by Nicholas of Lyra ca. AD 1330) phrased it as follows in the 13th century: *Littera gesta docet, quid credas allegoria, moralis quid agas, quo tendas anagogia* ("The Letter teaches events; Allegory what you should believe; Morality teaches what you should do; Anagogy what you should aim for").

---

[13] *Expositio In Canticum Canticorum* 4, trans. Denys Turner in *Eros & Allegory: Medieval Exegesis on the Song of Songs* (Kalamazoo, MI: Cistercian Publications, 1995), 219. See also *Mor.* xx. 1.

[14] Wilken, "Interpreting Job Allegorically," 213.

[15] See the massive overview by Henri de Lubac, *Medieval Exegesis*, 4 vols. (Grand Rapids, MI: Eerdmans, 1998ff.).

[16] John Cassian, *The Conferences*, trans. Boniface Ramsey (New York: Newman Press, 1997), 510.

[17] St. Bonaventure, *Brevil.*, Prol. 4; *Hex.* xiii.11.   [18] Thomas Aquinas discusses it in *ST* 1.1.10.

CHRISTOLOGY AND SACRIFICE

We saw in Chapter 2 that Augustine developed a rich theology of sacrifice in his *De Civitate Dei*. Gregory adopts this theology wholeheartedly and develops it. According to him, the Son perpetually intercedes for us with the Father. Indeed, the Incarnation itself is "an offering for our purification" (*oblatio nostrae emundationis*). Through the mystery of his humanity Christ offers a perpetual sacrifice (*perenne sacrificium immolat*; cf. *Mor.* 1.32), which restores our relationship with the Father (cf. *Mor.* xxiv.4). Other soteriological themes are: our deliverance from the rule of the devil (*Mor.* xvii.46; xxxiii.14), including the famous metaphor of the fishhook that catches the devil (*Hom. Ev.* 25; *Mor.* xxxiii.14); the notion of exchange and union between the Head and its members (cf. the beautiful passage from *Mor.* iii. 25, referred to earlier, on how Christ still suffers in his Body on earth and how we, the Church, glory in Christ, the Lord in heaven); Christ as example (*Mor.* xxi.11); and the significance of his descent into hell (*Mor.* iv. 56; xii.13; xiii.49; xx.26).

Central in his soteriology, as well as in his eschatology, is the Eucharist. In a beautiful passage from *Dial.* iv, Gregory first makes the point that the Victim of the holy sacrifice (*uictima sacrae oblationis*) can be of benefit to the dead. He then continues in a lyrical vein:

Let us remember what this sacrifice, which for our forgiveness always re-enacts (*imitatur*) the passion of the Only-begotten Son, means for us. Who among the faithful would doubt that at the exact moment of immolation heaven is opened to the voice of the priest; that the choirs of angels are present at the mystery of Jesus Christ; that the highest is united to the lowest; that heaven and earth are joined; that the visible and the invisible become one? (*Dial.* iv.60 [30])

Like Augustine before him, Gregory emphasizes that we must offer ourselves up to God with a contrite heart, for "when we celebrate the mystery of the Passion of our Lord, we must imitate what we do." In short, the Eucharist only becomes for us a real offering to God when we ourselves have become an offering to God through the Eucharist (*Dial.* iv.61 [1]). Gregory's emphasis on the Eucharist as an offering ties in with his monastic views. As Carole Straw has argued, sacrifice, which is at the heart of the monk's life, is transferred to the Church at large.[19] What makes Gregory's approach unique is the emphasis upon the ways in which the Christian needs to appropriate these mysteries. Much of what we today would call "Christian spirituality" is included in Gregory's moral sense. It is this aspect of Gregory's thought that explains his appeal throughout the centuries.

[19] Straw, *Gregory the Great*, 181.

LOVE AND DESIRE

Gregory's theological spirituality is permeated by a deep nostalgia for our prelapsarian state, or (and this amounts to the same) a burning desire for fulfillment in the afterlife. Indeed, in a beautiful book Jean Leclercq calls Gregory "the doctor of desire."[20] Interestingly, Gregory claims that in our very desire for God in this life we already draw closer to God: "A person who desires God with his whole heart already possesses the one he loves; no one could love God unless he possessed the one he loves" (*Hom. Ev.* 30). Similarly, in *Hom. Ev.* 14 he reminds his congregation that to love with a desire for heavenly things is already making a start toward reaching fulfillment in God. Drawing on Augustine, Gregory claims that desire is the form love assumes when the beloved is absent.[21] Given God's transcendence and our ineptitude in drawing close to him, God will always remain somewhat elusive to us. Given God's absence, our desire for God is a true sign of our love for him. The following text from *Mor.* 1.34 beautifully expresses Gregory's sense of nostalgia and exile and his desire to rest in the contemplation of God:

There are some people that live their lives in a neglectful manner. While they crave transient things, they fail to pay heed to things eternal; or they consider them contemptible insofar as they know them at all . . . While they are ignoring the things from above which they have lost, they are of the opinion, unhappy wretches, that they are on the right track. They never raise the eyes of their mind towards the light of truth for which they have been created. They never bend the keenness of their desire (*acies desiderii*) to the contemplation of their eternal country. Forsaking themselves amidst those things in which they are cast away, they love the exile (*exilium*) which is their lot, as if it was their home country. They rejoice in the darkness they undergo as if in the brightness of light. In contrast, when the minds of the elect perceive that all transient things are as nothingness, they seek out for which things they have been created. Nothing brings them satisfaction, but God. Their mind, wearied by the laborious search, finds rest in the hope and contemplation of its Creator, and longs to have a place among the citizens above. Each one of them, while yet in the body an inhabitant of the world, in mind already soars beyond the world; they bewail the weariness of exile they endure, and with the incessant incitements of love urge themselves on to the country on high.

Gregory, thirsty for things eternal, considers this world, which we are merely passing through, as a source of sorrow. Quoting Eccles. 1:18 ("He that increases

---

[20] Jean Leclercq, *The Love of Learning and the Desire for God* (New York: Fordham University Press, 1982).

[21] See Augustine, *Enarr. in Ps.* 118 (8).4. The notion that in seeking God we find him is inspired by Augustine's *Confessions* 1.1.

knowledge increases sorrow") he concludes: "He that already knows the heights he does not as yet enjoy, is the more grieved for the low condition, in which he continues to be held." And yet, in our very desire for God, who will always elude us, a measure of satisfaction is found. This is Gregory's version of the notion of *epektasis*. It means that our longing for God will never be fulfilled and yet, in our very longing, we attain some degree of fulfillment, which only increases our desire even further. "Merely to love things above is already to mount on high (*sursum ire*); and whilst with longing desire (*magno desiderio*) the soul thirsts for heavenly things, in a marvellous way it tastes the very thing it longs to get" (*Mor.* xv.53).[22] It is especially in contemplation that we can find some degree of satisfaction, as we will see shortly.

Desire, which is partly fulfilled in the dynamic of desiring itself, is, of course, also a source of sadness, a kind of holy sadness, which grieves over the fact that we cannot behold him whom we love (cf. *Mor.* ix.45). It also leads to a kind of restless seeking (*Mor.* x.13; v.11). In a captivating sermon (*Hom. Ev.* 27), Gregory illustrates this restless longing and seeking by referring to Mary Magdalene who searched for the Lord at the tomb (John 20:11–18). This text, in turn, is illuminated with a reference to the Bride of the Song of Songs (Sg. 3:1–2), who goes about the city, searching through its squares and streets for the one she loves. In appealing language, Gregory describes the anxious longing of the Bride/Mary Magdalene, her burning desire and persevering search. Again we find an eloquent expression of *epektasis* and the dialectic of fulfillment in unfulfillment. "She persevered in seeking, and so it happened that she found him. It came about that her unfulfilled desires increased, and as they increased they took possession of what they found."

Gregory's views on desire have implications for the way he sees the relation between love and knowledge. Indeed, "by desire the understanding may be augmented" (*intellectus augeatur*) (*Mor.* xx.61). To this topic I now turn.

KNOWLEDGE AND LOVE

If we did not know God, however opaquely, we would not love him either (*Mor.* xvi.33). Faith, which is the only kind of knowledge we have of God in this life (*Hom. Ez.* ii.4.13), is a dynamic process, implying growth (*Mor.* xxii.49). The very limitations inherent in faith generate desire. As God veils his glory, our desire and love increase (*Mor.* xvi.33). Given the

---

[22] Incidentally, our desire for God reflects God's desire for us. In Gregory's view, God's love is erotic and not just agapeic. Our Lord desires to be loved by us (*Mor.* xv.53).

inexhaustibility of God's mysterious nature, our love will even continue to grow in the afterlife, when we meet God face to face (*Mor.* xxv.16). In short, Gregory insists that knowledge is a necessary foundation for love.

But the inverse is also the case – that is, in order to know God, you need to love and desire him. This is the reason why some people who have a deep love of God can have a more intimate grasp of the truths of the Christian faith than more learned theologians (cf. *Mor.* vi.12). Gregory relates the story of Sanctulus, an illiterate priest who volunteered to sacrifice his life for that of a deacon who was about to be executed by a group of Lombards (*Dial.* iii.37 [20]). In charity Sanctulus embodied that which he lacked in knowledge. Sanctulus's "learned ignorance" (*docta ignorantia*) is far superior to our "inept knowledge" (*indocta scientia*). But even those who are theologically literate cannot progress in understanding God without love: it is through desire and understanding that we come to God (*Hom. Ez.* ii.2.13). The power of love (*uis amoris*) is "an engine of the soul (*machina mentis*) which draws the soul out of the world, and lifts it on high . . . For in contemplation, if love does not stimulate the mind, the dullness of its tepidity stupefies it" (*Mor.* vi. 58). Or again, in a passage (from *Hom. Ev.* 27.4), which was to be quoted time and again: "When we love the supercelestial things we have heard about, we already know the things we love, because love itself is knowledge (*amor ipse notitia est*)."[23]

"The supercelestial things we have heard" refers to faith. This precedes love. But in loving God we also come to know him, for faith is a living knowledge of God's dwelling in the soul. Faced with the immeasurable mystery of God the intellect needs to be permeated by love in order for us to approach God. Therefore, we should not interpret Gregory's phrase "love as knowledge" in anti-intellectualist terms. What he means is that we cannot know the living reality of God unless we love him. He is not suggesting that we should relate to God only or even primarily in a purely affective manner.

CONPUNCTIO, CONTEMPLATION AND ACTION

We have already mentioned that for Gregory, contemplation constitutes a foretaste of heavenly rest. In Gregory's reading, the life of contemplation and the longing for God that is inextricably linked with it find an eloquent expression in the Song of Songs. Commenting on the verse "May he kiss me with the kisses of his mouth," he writes:

---

[23] William of St. Thierry quotes it, as does Thomas Aquinas (*ST* ii–ii.172.4 *ad* 2).

Consider the soul of any one of the elect, who with constant desire burns with love to see her Bridegroom; for though in this life it is not possible to enjoy a perfect vision, she is able to contemplate his excellence and she is touched by this self-same love (*ex ipso amore conpungitur*). And this "being touched" (*conpunctio*) which is the work of love, which is the burning of desire, is a kind of kiss; whenever the soul kisses God, then it is touched by God. (*Expositio in Canticum Canticorum* 18)

We recognize a number of themes: the link between love, desire and contemplation. The key term in the quotation is *conpunctio* and its derivative *conpungitur*. As Denys Turner (whose translation I have used) helpfully explains, *conpunctio* refers to "a new beginning, a conversion . . . a new awareness of love, of sorrow and so a conversion of the *heart* to God."[24] Bernard McGinn summarizes: because of his deeply felt sense of the radical insufficiency of all terrestrial goods, Gregory's notion of compunction is not restricted to sorrow for sin; it also involves "the whole of the Christian's attitude towards present existence in relation to the underlying desire for the stability and joy of heaven."[25] As a radically new disposition, implying conversion, *conpunctio*, with humility and purity of heart, prepares the way for contemplation.

    Contemplatio, Dom David Hurst suggests, should be translated as "attentive regard" for God in all things. For Gregory, the contemplative life involves a kind of disposition. Commenting on Job 5:26 ("You shall enter into the grave in abundance"), he claims that the grave denotes the life of contemplation (see also *Mor.* v.9), "which as it were buries us dead to this world, in that it hides us in the interior world away from all earthly desires" (*Mor.* vi.56). The reference to desire is significant, for the contemplative disposition is intimately linked with refocusing our desire: it is "to hold fast with the whole mind to the charity of God, our neighbor, but to abstain from external action; to cleave (*inhaerere*) to the sole desire for the Creator" (*Hom. Ez.* ii.2.8). In a powerful metaphor, he describes the mental struggle of the contemplative life, "when it stretches the spirit in spiritual things, when it strives to transcend everything which is bodily seen, when it narrows to extend (*angustat ut dilatet*)" (*Hom. Ez.* ii.2.12). The contemplative life entails a radical theocentric focus of our mind and desire: in that way it both narrows and extends. Out of the tension between the contemplative disposition and the responsibilities of the active life, true holiness is born.

---

[24] Turner, *Eros & Allegory*, 251n38.
[25] Bernard McGinn, *The Presence of God: A History of Western Mysticism. Vol.* ii: *The Growth of Mysticism: From Gregory the Great to the Twelfth Century* (London: SCM, 1995), 48–49.

Augustine had already commented on the life of leisure (*otiosus*), the life of action (*actuosus*) and the combination of the two (*ex utroque composito*) (in *De Civ. Dei* XIX.19). The latter is therefore not a third kind of life, but rather the integration of the other two. This is also Gregory's teaching. Although Gregory clearly prefers the joys of contemplation, he is effectively radically transforming the pagan ideal of *theoria* (and its disdain for an active life) by treating the two aspects (activity and contemplation) as constituting each in its own right an integral part of the Christian life. So it is that in *Mor.* VI.57 he compares the two lives to the two eyes in the face – a metaphor that suggests their equal importance. Christ himself lived these two aspects in full harmony (*Mor.* XXVIII.33). In doing so, he embodied the two precepts of love – that is, love of God (which Gregory associates with the contemplative aspect) and love of neighbor (which he associates with the active life) (cf. *Past. Reg.* 1.7). The Incarnation itself is sufficient proof of God's radical solidarity with humanity, and the Christian should therefore never decline a life of active service (*Past. Reg.* 1.5). This ideal of the *vita mixta*, as it was later called, was to have a long and fruitful history in Christian spirituality.

In a memorable passage (in *Mor.* V.3), Gregory describes how the Christian feels himself in exile in this world, caught between this world and the bliss of the eternal country. Having ceased to retain the world in his affections, "the world still ties down that person by its business, and he indeed is already dead to the world, but the world is not yet dead to him" (*Mor.* V.4). While inwardly contemplative and focused on God, we must outwardly discharge our worldly functions. In the very tension that this *vita mixta* (the mixed life, combining charitable activity and contemplation) implies, Christian salvation is found: "For by a marvellous pitifulness of the divine Nature it comes to pass, that, when he, who aims at contemplation with a perfect heart, is busied with human affairs, his perfect mind at once profits many that are weaker, and in whatever degree he sees himself to be imperfect, he rises therefrom more perfect to the crowning point of humility" (*Mor.* V.5). As Carole Straw has made clear, commenting on this passage: for Gregory, "sacrifice is the obedient return to bear the imperfection of the carnality one has abnegated; a reluctant return to the world and all its temptations in obedience to God's commands of charity. Paradoxically, perfection lies in the recognition of one's imperfection."[26]

Gregory has explained his ideal of the mixed life by commenting on a number of biblical texts. One is the story of Jacob and his two wives (cf.

---

[26] Straw, *Gregory the Great*, 188.

Gen. 29:15ff.). Gregory compares the soul to Jacob, who desires the fair but barren Rachel (symbolizing the contemplative life), but who is given the bleary-eyed but fruitful Leah (symbolizing the active life):

Blessed Jacob had indeed desired Rachel but in the night accepted Leah because all who are turned to the Lord have desired the contemplative life and seek the quiet of the Eternal Kingdom, but must first in the night of this present life perform the works which they can, sweat with effort, i.e., accept Leah in order that they afterward rest in the arms of Rachel ... Rachel was a seer, and sterile, Leah truly purblind, but fertile, Rachel beautiful and barren, because the contemplative life is splendid in spirit but, whereas it seeks to rest in silence, it does not produce sons from preaching ... Leah truly is purblind and fertile because the active life, while it is engaged in labor, sees less but when, now by word now by example, it kindles its neighbors to follow suit, it produces many sons in good work.[27]

Gregory explicitly reminds us "that just as a good order of life is to strive from the active to the contemplative, so the spirit frequently reverts from the contemplative to the active, so that the active life may be lived more perfectly because the contemplative has kindled the mind" (*Hom. Ez.* II.2.II).

Another classic biblical pericope (already used in a similar way by John Cassian in *Confer.* I.viii.I) that lends itself well to a similar interpretation is the story of Mary and Martha (Luke 10:38ff.). Martha represents the active life, while Mary symbolizes the contemplative life. One of the reasons the contemplative life is "the best part" (Luke 10:42) is that the active life will pass away: in the afterlife, there will be no need to engage in charitable activity. The contemplative life, in contrast, which is begun here, will be perfected in heaven (*Hom. Ez.* II.2.9).

Although Gregory argues that the mixed life is superior to either the active or the contemplative as such, it is clear that the active life finds its ultimate meaning and fulfillment in contemplation. This too is an important insight, rather alien to the modern outlook.[28]

Although Gregory is clearly deeply indebted to Augustine, he appropriates the Augustinian material in his own way, with his own distinct

---

[27] *Hom. Ez.* II.2.8, trans. Tomkinson, 287. See also *Mor.* VI.61: "When the mind seeks the ease of contemplation, it sees more, but it is less productive in children to God."

[28] See the insightful book by Josef Pieper, *Happiness and Contemplation* (South Bend, IN: St. Augustine Press, 1998), 92–93: "We must recognize that the whole of morality points to something beyond itself ... All practical activity, from practice of the ethical virtues to gaining the means of livelihood, serves something other than itself. And this other thing is not practical activity. It is having what is sought after, while we rest content in the results of our active efforts. Precisely that is the meaning of the old adage that the vita activa is fulfilled in the vita contemplativa." As Thomas Aquinas puts it: "The active life is a disposition to the contemplative life" (*ST* II–II.181.1 *ad* 3).

emphases, and much of the Augustinian legacy was channeled through Gregory's writings. The vividness of his writings, their existential relevance, his colorful metaphors and his keen observation of human nature guaranteed him a place as one of the four doctors of the Church and the first important theologian of the medieval period.

BIBLIOGRAPHICAL NOTE

The critical edition of *Moralia in Iob* is available in *Corpus Christianorum* (Turnhout: Brepols), vols. clxiii, clxiiiA, clxiiiB. For the *Moralia*, I used the translation by Members of the English Church as *Gregory the Great: Morals on the Book of Job*, 4 vols. (Oxford: John Henry Parker, 1844). It is available online at www.lectionarycentral.com/GregoryMoraliaIndex.html. For *Hom. Ev.* I used the translation by David Hurst, *Gregory the Great: Forty Gospel Homilies* (Kalamazoo, MI: Cistercian Publications, 1990); for *Hom. Ez.* see *Gregory the Great: Homilies on the Book of the Prophet Ezekiel*, trans. Theodosia Tomkinson (Etna, CA: Center for Traditionalist Orthodox Studies, 2003). An excellent aid is Bronwen Neil and Mathew J. Dal Santo (eds.), *A Companion to Gregory the Great* (Leiden: Brill, 2013).

CHAPTER 5

John Scottus Eriugena and the Carolingian Renaissance

INTRODUCTION: THE CAROLINGIAN RENAISSANCE

John Scot(t)us Eriugena was an Irish scholar residing at the court of Charles the Bald, grandson of Charlemagne, king of the Franks. Charlemagne stood at the beginning of a cultural renaissance (*renovatio*), a blossoming of the arts and intellectual life. Eriugena is mainly remembered for his voluminous work *Periphyseon* (*On Nature*) or, in its Latin title, *De Divisione Naturae* (*The Division of Nature*), a dialogue between a Master (*Nutritor*) and his disciple (*Alumnus*). Other important works are his *De Divina Praedestinatione* (*Treatise on Divine Predestination*), the *Homily on the Prologue of John* and an incomplete *Commentary on the Gospel of John* (part of which is lost: all we have is the commentary on John 1:11–29; 3:1–4, 28; 6:5–14).

We do not know when Eriugena was born – he seems to have died some time around AD 870 or not too many years afterward. He arrived at the court of Charles the Bald in the 840s. He knew Greek and translated the complete works of Pseudo-Dionysius, *Ambigua* and *Quaestiones ad Thallassicum* by Maximus Confessor and Gregory of Nyssa's *De hominis opificio* (*On the Making of Man*). These authors had a major impact on Eriugena's own thought, and he quotes extensively from their works in his own *Periphyseon*. Some of the main themes he adopts from Pseudo-Dionysius are the emphasis on the unknowable nature of God, the roles of negative and positive theology and the themes of procession and return.

After the turbulences of previous centuries (discussed earlier), Charlemagne (AD 742–814), sometimes called *Pater Europae* (Father of Europe) was crowned emperor by Pope Leo III on Christmas Day of the year 800. This event had more than a symbolic significance: it illustrates how the papacy turned its attention away from Byzantium toward the West – thereby reinforcing the political and cultural separation between the Latin West and the Greek East. For the first time after the collapse of the Roman Empire, Western Europe was united under one head: from Frisia and Saxony in the north to the Pyrenees and northern Italy (with the exception of the papal regions) in the south, and Bohemia and Dalmatia in the east. Charlemagne had three sons and initially divided his realm into three parts, but in AD 813, he crowned his only surviving son, Louis the Pious, emperor in the magnificent Palatine Chapel at Aachen. After the death of Charlemagne, Pope Stephanus performed the ceremony in Reims, creating an important historical precedent: emperors are crowned by popes, preferably in Rome. Charlemagne himself moved around (*Vagobundus Carolus*) throughout his empire, thus failing to establish one major center of power and administration, which partly explains the later fragmentation of the Carolingian empire. Under Louis the Pious, monasteries were reorganized and the Benedictine Rule was enforced throughout the empire.

After Louis's death and a series of dynastic disputes, the empire was divided amongst Charlemagne's grandsons into three parts in AD 843 (Treaty of Verdun): the western part (later France) was given to Charles the Bald, at whose court Eriugena Scottus would reside; the eastern part (later Germany) was given to Louis the German, while the Middle Kingdom (including the Low Countries, Burgundy and Italy) was given to Lothair. The Middle Kingdom did not prove politically viable.

Partly due to the lack of a proper political center, family rivalry and external pressure (from Muslims in the south, Magyars in the east and Vikings who presented a constant threat throughout the 9th century in the North Sea regions), the Carolingian empire proved politically unsuccessful; however, as suggested earlier, a genuine cultural rebirth (renaissance) took place under the Carolingians that was to have a lasting legacy in many areas. Charlemagne tried to create a culture for his new Christian empire, attracting scholars from all over Europe (Lombards, Visigoths, Anglo-Saxons, Franks and Irish), promoting the arts, the foundation of schools, the copying of Scripture, the study of classic literature and the Fathers and so forth. Because Charlemagne wished to have a reliable text of the Latin Bible (Jerome's Vulgate), he cultivated the study of Latin and its most important authors. Study of the seven liberal arts (*grammatica, rhetorica, dialectica, arithmetica, geometria, astronomia, musica*) was encouraged in cathedral schools. It was Martianus Capella (4th century) who, in his *De Nuptiis Philologiae et Mercurii* (*The Marriage of Philology and Mercury*), had bequeathed the tradition of the seven liberal arts to the Middle Ages. Eriugena knew this work and wrote a commentary on it.

Like his grandfather, Charles the Bald (AD 822–77) ruled from a peripatetic court, which mainly traveled across the Isle-de-France region. However, a prominent place of learning was in the Laon region and it is here that Eriugena wrote and taught, according to the testimony of the local bishop, Pardulus.[1] Eriugena seems to have enjoyed the personal protection of the king, which was to prove significant in light of the opposition the theological views of the Irishman elicited at the time.

THEOLOGICAL DEBATES IN THE 9TH CENTURY

Lively theological debates, in which Charles the Bald took a personal interest, illustrate the newly found intellectual confidence and sophistication. Important topics discussed in the 9th century include iconoclasm (the Byzantine emperor Leo III issued an edict forbidding images, evoking opposition from iconophiles), the *Filioque* question, the nature of the presence of Christ in the Eucharist and predestination.[2]

The Eucharistic controversy was ignited by Paschasius Radbertus, the abbot of Corbie (d. 860), who wrote *De Corpore et Sanguine Christi* (*The Body and Blood of Christ*), one of the first medieval treatises on the Eucharist. In it, he argued that, after the consecration, the bread and wine are identical with the historical flesh and blood of Christ, as it was "born of Mary, suffered on the cross, and rose again from the tomb."[3] Thus, although the historical body and blood have the mere appearance of bread and wine in the Eucharist, for Radbertus, the relation between the Eucharistic body and the historical body was one of identity.[4] Paschasius Radbertus (like his opponent Ratramnus) struggled to address the issue properly. How can something be a reality if it is only an image?[5] For Radbertus, the bread and wine, perceived by the senses, are *figura*, while the Eucharistic Body of Christ, perceived with the eyes of faith, is the truth

---

[1] See John O'Meara, *Eriugena* (Oxford: Clarendon, 1988), 14.

[2] For an overview of some of these issues and the intellectual context from which they arose, I have benefited from Dermot Moran, *The Philosophy of John Scottus Eriugena: A Study of Idealism in the Middle Ages* (Cambridge: Cambridge University Press, 1989), 7–26.

[3] Paschasius Radbertus, *De Corpore et Sanguine Domini*, 1.2 *CCCM* 15. For a partial English translation, see George E. McCracken, *Early Medieval Theology* (Louisville, KY: Westminster John Knox Press, 2006), 94–108.

[4] See Jaroslav Pelikan, *The Christian Tradition: A History of the Development of Doctrine, vol. III: The Growth of Medieval Theology (600–1300)* (Chicago: Chicago University Press, 1978), 75.

[5] See Edward Kilmartin, *The Eucharist in the West* (Collegeville, MN: Liturgical Press, 1998), 83.

(*veritas*). This Eucharistic body is identical to the body of the historical Jesus. Radbertus therefore argues for the real presence of Christ by adopting an extreme, almost physicalist view of the Eucharist. Because of the adoption of this physicalist view, he has to introduce the distinction between *veritas* (the reality of the Body and Blood, identical with that of the historical Jesus) and *figura* (the outward appearance of bread and wine, which does not look anything like Body and Blood).[6]

Ratramnus used some of these key terms in a rather different manner. For him, *veritas* refers to what is perceptible to the senses (which comes close to what Radbertus meant by *figura*). Thus, for Ratramnus, truth or reality refers to the empirical reality. By figure, he means "a kind of overshadowing that reveals its intent under some sort of veil."[7] Ratramnus denies the identification of the historical and Eucharistic body: "Nothing is more absurd than to take bread as flesh and to say that wine is blood."[8] There is only a "resemblance" between the two. The Eucharistic bread and wine are called the body and blood in a manner similar to the way we still call any annual Easter the day of resurrection (although there was only one day of resurrection, centuries ago).[9]

While Ratramnus is often credited with a more symbolic understanding of the Eucharist, the presuppositions that govern his account are actually more positivistic than those of Radbertus. For Ratramnus, what is real is, in the first instance, that which is obvious and factual.[10] Both Radbertus and Ratramnus struggle to make sense of the relation between reality and symbolism. Radbertus, concerned to emphasize the real presence of Christ, stresses the identity of the body of the historical Jesus and the Eucharistic body. His is a radical physicalist-realist position. Ratramnus, on the other hand, adopts an almost empiricist understanding of reality, and therefore he cannot make this identification: the bread and wine simply do not look like flesh and blood. Hence, he argues that the bread and wine veil the Body and Blood. Neither Paschasius Radbertus nor Ratramnus see the

---

[6] Paschasius Radbertus, *De Corpore et Sanguine Domini* IV: "If we truthfully examine the matter, it is rightly called both the truth (*ueritas*) and a figure (*figura*), so that it is a figure or character of truth because it is outwardly sensed. Truth, however, is anything rightly understood or believed inwardly concerning this mystery." McCracken, *Early Medieval Theology*, 102.

[7] Ratramnus, *De Corpore et Sanguine Domini* § 7; McCracken, *Early Medieval Theology*, 119.

[8] Ratramnus, *De Corpore et Sanguine Domini* § 11; McCracken, *Early Medieval Theology*, 121.

[9] Ratramnus, *De Corpore et Sanguine Domini* § 37: "And although the Lord's body, in which he once suffered is one thing, and the blood, which was shed for the salvation of the world, is one thing, yet the sacraments of these two things have assumed their names, being called Christ's body and blood, since they are so called on account of a resemblance with the things they represent." McCracken, *Early Medieval Theology*, 128–29.

[10] Ratramnus, *De Corpore et Sanguine Domini* § 8.

corporeal as something that *reveals* the spiritual. Radbertus's physicalist position as well as Ratramnus's notion that the corporeal veils the spiritual are in marked contrast to the truly symbolic outlook of Eriugena Scottus.

Because the Mass was increasingly seen as a sacrifice, Radbertus's position, which emphasized the identity of the historical and the Eucharistic, was favored in the later tradition.[11] The controversy about the nature of the Eucharistic presence would resurface in the 11th century (not to mention during the Reformation). During a synod held in Vercelli in 1050, the views of Berengar of Tours, who appealed to the views of Ratramnus (although he erroneously attributed the work to Eriugena), were condemned. It is no coincidence that during the 11th-century controversy the works of Ratramnus on the Eucharist were attributed to Eriugena. For in his *Commentary on John*, Eriugena argues that we offer up Christ in a spiritual manner, consuming the Eucharistic bread and wine with our mind and not with our teeth (*mente non dente comedimus*).[12] Still, as an author deeply imbued with the legacy of Greek Neoplatonism, Eriugena has a much stronger sacramental understanding of the world than Ratramnus. All material things point to a truer, spiritual reality, and this applies equally, if not more, to the Eucharistic bread and wine.

Eriugena shows the influence of Greek thought on a number of issues. One of these is the *Filioque*. *Filioque* refers to the belief, inspired by the work of Augustine (see Chapter 2), that the Holy Spirit proceeds from the Father *and from the Son* (in Latin: *Filioque*). The Spanish Church interpolated the *Filioque* in the Creed during the third Council of Toledo (AD 589), and from Spain this innovation made its way north to France and Germany. Rome would continue to recite the Creed without the *Filioque* until the beginning of the 11th century. Eriugena is well aware that the *Filioque* is a later, Latin addition to the Nicene-Constantinopolitan Creed from AD 381,[13] and in *Periphyseon*, we find the *Alumnus* (the student) saying that he is "not too preoccupied with this question" – as long as the co-equality of the Persons and the role of the Person of the Father as the sole source of the Trinity are safeguarded.[14] Drawing a comparison between the sun, its ray and the brightness it causes, on one hand, and the processions within the Trinity, on the other, Eriugena in his role of *Nutritor* (the teacher) had shown himself fairly sympathetic to the moderate Greek view, which allows for the notion that the Holy Spirit proceeds from the Father

---

[11] For a short and useful summary, see Pelikan, *The Growth of Medieval Theology*, 74–80.

[12] *Commentary on John* 1.xxxi.311B.   [13] *Periphyseon* 601C; 612B.

[14] *Periphyseon* 612D. I use the translation by I. P. Sheldon, revised by John O'Meara (Washington, DC: Dumburton Oaks, 1987).

through the Son. The brightness does not proceed from the sun and the ray as from two causes; rather it proceeds from the sun through the ray. Similarly, with moderate Greeks we can say that the Holy Spirit (= the brightness) proceeds from the Father (= the sun) through the Son (= the ray) rather than from the Father and the Son, which is the Latin view.[15]

It is certainly remarkable to encounter a Latin author in the 9th century so well versed in Greek language and theology. By the beginning of the 6th century, few Westerners spoke Greek, and due to the impact of the barbarian invasions the western half of the Roman Empire had drifted further and further away in political, cultural and linguistic terms from the eastern half. The 9th century witnessed an unfortunate dispute between Pope Nicholas and Photius, Patriarch of Constantinople, with mutual excommunications (in AD 863 and 867). Relations were restored in AD 867, but they remained tense and would significantly worsen in 1054 (the Great Schism), reaching their low mark in AD 1204 (the taking of Constantinople during the fourth crusade).

Perhaps the debate on predestination – another Augustinian legacy – also illustrates Eriugena's Greek theological sympathies. A monk called Gottschalk argued for a double predestination: good people are destined to salvation, the others to damnation. This resulted in a major debate. His opponents argued that God predestines only his elect. Hincmar, the bishop of Reims, called on Eriugena to settle the issue – but the outcome was rather different from what Hincmar expected or desired. In AD 851, Eriugena wrote a relatively short work, *De Divina Praedestinatione* (*Treatise on Divine Predestination*) in which he argued that, in order to solve the difficulty, one had to have recourse to reason. Eriugena contended that we cannot properly speak of predestination in God: since God is simple and beyond time, foreknowledge and other temporal notions do not apply to him. Moreover, seeing that sin and evil are nothing but absence of goodness (the Neoplatonic notion of *privatio boni*), they cannot be caused by God. Human beings are free, and if they choose evil, this is due to their own free will, not to God. Thus salvation is open to all and God does not predestine anybody. Hincmar was not pleased. First, Eriugena denied predestination altogether – or rather, he identified it with God's being, goodness and simplicity and therefore nothing is foreknown or predestined in the strict sense.[16] Second, he applied

---

[15] Ibid., 609A–C.

[16] As Eriugena puts it in the epilogue to the *Treatise on Divine Predestination*, 130: "The one eternal predestination of God is God, and exists only in those things that are, but has no bearing at all on those that are not."

philosophical reasoning to a theological problem. As Eriugena puts it in another work, nobody enters heaven except by means of philosophy (*nemo intrat in coelum nisi per philosophiam*).[17]

ERIUGENA'S VIEWS ON FAITH AND REASON

Eriugena evoked criticism for this strong emphasis upon reason. Nevertheless, it would be a mistake to see him as a champion of a kind of rationalism *avant la lettre*. Eriugena draws explicitly on Augustine's early work *On True Religion* (*De Vera Religione*), 5, 8, when stating that "true philosophy is true religion and conversely that true religion is true philosophy," or that the exercise of philosophy is nothing but "the exposition of the rules of true religion by which the supreme and principal cause of all things, God, is worshipped with humility and rationally searched for."[18]

For Eriugena, there can be no doubt that "our salvation takes its beginning from faith."[19] In his *Homily on the Prologue to the Gospel of John*, Eriugena argues that Peter (who symbolizes faith and virtuous action) enters the tomb of Christ (interpreted here allegorically as the Holy Scriptures) first, while John (who symbolizes contemplation and knowledge) waits for him: "For if Peter symbolizes faith, then John signifies the intellect. Therefore, since it is written: 'Unless you believe you will not understand,' faith necessarily enters first into the tomb of Holy Scripture, followed by intellect, for which faith has prepared the entry."[20] Just as Peter preceded John, so faith must precede reason, which, nevertheless, has an important role to play in explaining its implications and hidden treasures. The main reason it would be a gross misunderstanding to label Eriugena a rationalistic author or even a philosopher in the modern sense of the word is the fact that for him reason merely assists us in instilling in us an ever more profound sense of the divine mystery and hiddenness.

Philosophy and faith flow from the same source of divine Wisdom, and true faith and true reason do not conflict with one another.[21] Given his strong negative theological stance, reason does not abolish faith but deepens it – it makes it more profoundly aware of the incomprehensibility and otherness of God. For Eriugena, this growing illumination or awareness of

---

[17] See *Annotationes in Marcianum*, ed. Cora E. Lutz (Cambridge, MA: Harvard University Press), 64, 23–24, quoted by E. Jeauneau, *Homelie*, 263n1.
[18] *Treatise on Divine Predestination* I.1, p. 7.   [19] *Treatise on Divine Predestination* I.4, p. 9.
[20] *Homily* III.284D–285A; all translations by Christopher Bamford, *The Voice of the Eagle: The Heart of Celtic Christianity* (New York: Lindisfarne Press, 1990), 23.
[21] *Periphyseon* 511B.

the divine otherness and darkness will come to full fruition in the afterlife only.[22] In our mortal state, there are only the delights of an arduous and never-ending search for truth. This kind of search is held only among the wise, "to whom nothing is more pleasing to the ear than true reason, nothing more delightful to investigate when it is being sought after, nothing more beautiful to contemplate when it is found."[23] Undaunted by the seeming impossibility of the path, aided by the grace of God, the wise will return time and again to the contemplation of Truth, and reaching it they will love it, abide in it and find rest in it.[24]

In order to appreciate Eriugena's views on the relation between theology and philosophy, we need to remember that the medieval view of intellectual understanding is much richer than the modern understanding of reason (*Vernunft, raison*). Medieval authors distinguish between reason (*ratio*) and intellect or understanding (*intellectus*). Commenting on Jesus' reply to the Samaritan woman (John 4:16: "Go and call your husband"), Eriugena not only illustrates that he is well versed in allegorical readings of the Scriptures by claiming that the Samaritan woman represents the rational aspect (*anima rationalis*) of the soul while the husband represents the mind or intellect (*animus, intellectus, mens*); more importantly he then goes on, having referred to 1 Cor. 11:3, to indicate a hierarchy within human understanding:

The head of the rational soul (*anima rationalis*) is her husband, that is, her intellect (*intellectus*), and the head of the intellect is Christ. For the natural order of the human creature is as follows: the soul should be subject to the governance of the mind (*mens*), and the mind should be subject to Christ. In this way, the whole human being is united, through Christ, to God and the Father.[25]

Eriugena offers us a rich portrayal of human understanding and intellect, one that is much deeper than what reason can offer us and one that may challenge our modern positivistic (and therefore reductionist) mindset, which merely "sticks to the facts." For Eriugena, as for us, reason is a discursive faculty (*ratiocinatur*) geared toward this physical world.[26] But reason is only one facet of human understanding: there is also intellect

---

[22] Commenting in *Homily* xii, on "And the light shone in the darkness," Eriugena states: "The Light shines in the darkness of faithful souls and shines there more and more, beginning in faith and leading to knowledge" (*a fide choans, ad speciem tendens*), p. 39. This knowledge refers to the beatific vision.

[23] *Periphyseon* 512B, p. 109.   [24] Ibid., 744B, p. 383.   [25] *Commentary on John* iv.v.336A, p. 305.

[26] *Periphyseon* 755B and 754D: When the soul is preoccupied with the divine, it acts as mind (*mens*), spirit (*animus*) and intellect (*intellectus*); when it is occupied with this physical world and its causes, it is called discursive reason (*ratio*).

(*intellectus*), which can, in this life, intuit more profound mysteries in the heights of contemplation, and it can pass on these insights, however opaquely, to reason.[27] The scholastics will develop these ideas in more detail, and I return to them in due course.

ERIUGENA ON THE RELATION BETWEEN
GOD AND CREATION

Let me now look in some more detail at Eriugena's major work, *Periphyseon*, which itself consists of five books. In Book I, Eriugena introduces the reader to the four divisions of nature, God as the uncreated creator and the main tenets of negative theology. Book II examines the second division of nature: procession through the primordial causes is the cause of diversity in the visible world. It also reduces the four divisions to two and then to one. Book III deals with the created effects and the five days of creation. Book IV deals with the sixth day of creation and contains a treatise on human nature. Book V sketches the *reditus*, the return of things to their Source. Let me unpack all of this. (Incidentally, this is exactly how Eriugena tackles the question of God and creation too: when you are confronted with a problem (i.e., a mathematical puzzle or a broken-down engine), you take it apart first, and then you put it back together.) This is precisely what Eriugena will do: first he will divide (unpack) "Nature," and then he will put it back together (the so-called *reductio*).

According to Eriugena, creation is a manifestation of God. Everything finds its origin in God, proceeds from him (*exitus*) and returns to him (*reditus*). Eriugena emphasizes that you cannot think of creation without reference to God and vice versa. God and creation ought to be thought of together, and Eriugena calls this "Nature" (*Natura*). "Nature" is then divided into four:
(1) That which creates and is not created: God as the cause of this world.
(2) That which is created and creates: the causes of all things in the Word.
(3) That which is created and does not create: the world.
(4) That which is not created and does not create: God as the end of all things.
"Nature" therefore refers to both God and the world (although Eriugena sometimes uses *Natura* to denote created reality only). If you examine these

---

[27] *Commentary on John* IV.V.336B.

divisions, you will notice that the distinctions between (1) and (4) obviously do not exist in God – they exist only in the human mind because of its finitude. The distinction between (2) and (3) exists both in mind and in reality.

Eriugena pursues this in Book II.[28] Here, Eriugena gives a summary of the divisions of *Natura* and "reduces" them as follows. Seeing that in God there can be no duality (beginning and end have no temporal reality in God), (1) and (4) are identical in reality. Similarly, (2) and (3) both refer to created reality. The four divisions can therefore be reduced to two: God and creation. Then Eriugena makes a surprising move: he further reduces these two divisions to one: Creator and creation are one.[29] How does Eriugena make this point plausible? He argues that all things participate in God and cannot exist apart from him. Despite this reduction into unity, Eriugena does retain a basic distinction between the self-manifestation of God (theophany) and God. Deirdre Carabine makes the point well: "The final resolution of the four divisions of *natura* to one can indeed be said to 'unite' the finite and the infinite but only insofar as that which is infinite refers to God's self-manifestation in theophany. The final dialectic operative in Eriugena's thought is that while God can be understood as part of universal *natura*, the infinite nature of the divine essence can only be hinted at, never grasped. God remains transcendentally above all things."[30] Or Eriugena himself affirms that "that the creative Cause of the whole universe is beyond nature and beyond being and beyond life and wisdom and power and beyond all things which are said and understood and perceived by any sense."[31] Thus, God is manifest in creation, and creation totally participates in God, yet God remains transcendently unmanifest:

For everything that is understood and sensed is nothing else but the apparition of what is not apparent, the manifestation of the hidden, the affirmation of the negated, the comprehension of the incomprehensible, the understanding of the unintelligible, the body of the bodiless, the essence of the superessential, the form of the formless, the measure of the measureless, the number of the unnumbered, the weight of the weightless, the materialization of the spiritual, the visibility of the invisible.[32]

In creating the world, God expresses himself, reveals himself, creates himself (*a se ipso creatur*), as Eriugena puts it.[33] In creating, God who is no-thing becomes some-thing; he moves from non-being or nothingness into

[28] *Periphyseon* 527Bff.   [29] Ibid., 528B.

[30] Deirdre Carabine, *John Eriugena Scottus* (Oxford: Oxford University Press, 2000), 33.

[31] *Periphyseon* 621D–622A.   [32] Ibid., 633A–B.   [33] Ibid., 454A.

being, yet all the while he remains transcendent: "And while it is eternal, it does not cease to be made, and made it does not cease to be eternal, and out of itself it makes itself, for it does not require some other matter, which is not itself in which to make itself."[34] Obviously, Eriugena holds divine transcendence and immanence in a delicate balance: while the whole of creation is theophany – the manifestation of God in the world – God remains different from his creation. Given the fact that Eriugena shares Gregory of Nyssa's view that God's being is infinite and incomprehensible (because inexhaustible), he can argue that God, in manifesting himself in the world, can also begin to comprehend himself:

The divine nature . . . allows itself to appear in its theophanies, willing to emerge from the most hidden recesses of its nature in which it is unknown even to itself, that is, knows itself in nothing because it is infinite and supernatural and super-essential and beyond everything that can and cannot be understood, but by descending into the principles of things and, as it were, creating itself, it begins to know itself in something.[35]

Perhaps a modern analogy can clarify the point Eriugena is trying to make. Imagine that you are in a strange, indefinable mood, impossible to capture, even to yourself. However, when you improvise on the piano, listening to the music you produce, it suddenly dawns on you how you feel. So too with God and his creation: it is only when God externalizes himself that he can begin to perceive his own mystery, as in a mirror. Nevertheless, although God can be known as Creator, he remains unknowable as uncreated, even to God's self, and all the more so to us: if anyone who saw God understood what he saw, it would not be God he saw but one of these creatures that derive their existence and unknowability from him.[36]

THE FOUR DIVISIONS AND *EXITUS* AND *REDITUS*

Let us now return to the division of nature. (1) As indicated, the uncreated creator is, of course, God as the source of all. As we have seen, the divine essence is no-thing, the ineffable and incomprehensible and inaccessible brilliance of divine goodness, surpassing all beings.[37] (2) The things that have been created and create are the primordial causes – that is, the Platonic "forms" or "ideas" existing in the Word of God. They remain in the Word, yet they move outward into created effects. They participate in God's eternity but they are not coessential.[38] They are created in the

---

[34] Ibid., 678D.   [35] Ibid., 689B.   [36] Ibid., 920C.   [37] Ibid., 643B.   [38] Ibid., 561D–562A.

beginning in the Word and share in the unknowability of God (Eriugena identifies them with "the waste and the void hanging over the abyss" in Genesis; similarly, the "*Fiat lux!*" of Gen. 1:3 refers to their procession into created effects – from invisibility to visibility, from unknowability to knowability). Eriugena's view on creation implies that all visible and corporeal things are the symbol of something incorporeal and intelligible[39] – which obviously implies a positive evaluation of the whole of creation. For Eriugena, the whole world has a sacramental value.

(3) From the primordial causes created things flow forth, such as material things, trees and plants (life), animals (they have senses), human beings (they have reason and share in intellect) and angels (they have intellect): they are created but do not create.

Before I deal with the return of all things, I need to discuss the role of humanity in the created world. As a Christian Neoplatonist, Eriugena argues that the true essence of the human person resides in the Word, and is therefore spiritual. The fact that we share with animals a bodily, material nature is the result of the Fall. In its *spiritual* (or "ideal"/"formal") way of being, human nature is eternal, causal and created as intelligible. In its *corporeal* aspect, it became temporal, caused and material. Exploiting the fact that there are two creation stories in Genesis (Gen. 1–2:4 and Gen. 2:5ff.), Eriugena distinguishes between two creations of human nature: in the "first" creation, a spiritual body and soul were created in the image of God; in the "second" creation, human beings acquired materiality (made from the clay of the earth, cf. Gen. 2:7), temporality and division between the sexes.[40] However, these two creations took place simultaneously, which implies that human nature, as soon as it was created, fell into sin.[41] When God created humanity, he therefore simultaneously created the consequences of our sin even before we had sinned! Our mind and reason are creations of the goodness of God; other parts, such as our body – "the tunics of skin," as Gen. 3:21 has it – and the sexual differentiation it involves, were created on account of the transgression which was foreknown.[42]

The notion that sexual differentiation is a result of the Fall is bound to strike us as somewhat strange. It is a view that probably finds its remote origins in the discourse by Aristophanes in Plato's *Symposium* 189e–193e, and that Gregory of Nyssa had adopted in his *De Imagine*, chapters 16 and 17 – a text Eriugena was familiar with. Maximus Confessor too adopts this view in his *Ambigua* 41 (1308C–1309B), a text Eriugena cites in Book 11 of

---

[39] Ibid., 865D–866A.   [40] Ibid., 797C and 817A–D.   [41] Ibid., 807B–C.   [42] Ibid., 818D.

Periphyseon.[43] Some modest biblical sources support his view: first, there is the creation story in which the human being (in a generic sense) is created in God's image, and only later the text says, "male and female he created them" (Gen. 1:27). According to Eriugena, by the use of the singular, the unity of the human nature before the Fall is indicated ("In the image of God he created him"), but then the plural is used in reference to the division of that nature after the Fall: "Male and female he created them." More important are the eschatological texts, especially Paul's assertion in Gal. 3:28 that "in Christ Jesus there is neither male nor female."[44] Given the fact that our origin mirrors our end, these texts about the resurrection of Christ reveal something about our initial stage. Eriugena actually admits that the resurrected Christ *appeared* as male but he claims – rather unconvincingly – that this was merely to make sure his disciples would recognize him.[45] This is an instance in which Eriugena's Neoplatonism (and its typical reservations about the goodness of our sexual being) gets the better of his Christian views.

One of the more interesting aspects of Eriugena's views is that his negative theology is reflected in an equally negative anthropology. The human mind knows that it is, but it does not know what it is, and it is this characteristic "which reveals most clearly the Image of God to be in man":

For just as God is comprehensible in the sense that it can be deduced from his creation that he is, and incomprehensible because it cannot be comprehended by any intellect whether human or angelic nor even by himself what he is, seeing that he is not a thing but is superessential: so to the human mind it is given to know one thing only, that it is – but as to what it is, no sort of notion is permitted to it; and, a fact which is stranger still and, to those who study God and man, more fair to contemplate, the human mind is more honoured in its ignorance than in its knowledge ... just as the negation of God accords better with the praise of his nature than the affirmation and it shows greater wisdom not to know than to know that Nature of which ignorance is true wisdom and which is known all the better for not being known.[46]

The human being, like God himself, cannot be defined or comprehended. Neither God nor the human being can be grasped; they are not a "what."

The human being shares with the angel intelligence and reason, and he shares with animals the possession of a material body and the five senses: therefore humanity occupies a central role in the created world, containing every creature in himself. "In man is contained the universal creature" (*in*

---

[43] Ibid., 532Cff. and 536D–537C.   [44] Ibid., 894B.   [45] Ibid., 894B and 594A–D.
[46] Ibid., 771B–C.

homine universam creaturam contineri). "The whole of creation is divided into five parts; the creature may be a body, or a living being, or a sensible being, or a rational being, or an intellectual being. All these five parts are in every way found in man."[47] Like angels, we enjoy the use of mind and reason; like animals, we enjoy the use of physical sense and the capacity to administer our body.[48]

The notion that the human being is the universal creature is very important: it allows Eriugena to say that the whole created universe was brought forth in humanity after the Fall, and it also explains the pivotal role of resurrected man in the return of all things. The creation of the body and the material world, the propagation via sexual means, the loss of intellect (we now have to rely on the senses to acquire knowledge) are all the result of our first sin – defined as turning away from God, abandoning the image of God, to become like irrational, mortal animals.[49] Paradise therefore refers to the "ideal" human nature in the image of God; seeing that human beings sinned as soon as they were created, for Eriugena, paradise refers to the future rather than to the past. This brings us to the theme of *reditus*, the return of all things to God.

(4) The Return of all things into their Source – that which is not created and does not create – is described in Book v. We have seen that humanity occupies a central role in the created world; similarly, in the return of all things into God humanity plays a key role. When we have reached the bottom of the pit – when we die and our body dissolves – the return starts.[50] Eriugena distinguishes the following stages: (a) the body dissolves and returns into the four elements of the sensible world from which it was composed; (b) in the resurrection, each shall take his own body out of the common fund of the four elements; (c) the body is changed into spirit; (d) the spirit (and the whole human nature) shall revert to its primordial causes; (e) the spirit with the primordial causes is absorbed into God as air is absorbed into light.[51] Thus, human nature (and all things in human nature) does not perish but is transformed into something better.

Given the fact that "the Return and the resurrection are one and the same thing," there is a strong Christological dimension to this cosmic process.[52] The goal of the world lies in the causes out of which it originated, and to these it must return.[53] But as the Word is the Cause of all causes, the

---

[47] Ibid., 755B, pp. 396–97. Eriugena applies the word *cosmos* (in *Commentary on John* III.vi.321A) to the human being, but he refrains from using the word *microcosm* in the light of Gregory of Nyssa's critique of this concept, which he quotes in *Periphyseon* 793C.

[48] Ibid., 755B.   [49] Ibid., 761A; 817D; 846A.   [50] Ibid., 875C.   [51] Ibid., 876A.

[52] Ibid., 979D.   [53] Ibid., 892D.

final End of the world is the Word: the common end of the whole creation is the Word of God.[54] From the unification of the division of the human being into the two sexes, the return and unification through all the other divisions start.[55] In the resurrection, sexual differentiation will be done away with, human nature will be made one, and there will be only human beings as it would have been if the human being had not sinned. Through the resurrection of the human being, the "universal creature" in whom the whole of creation is contained, the inhabited globe will be transformed into paradise. Earthly bodies will be changed into heavenly bodies. Next there will be a unification of the whole sensible creature, followed by a transformation into the intelligible, so that the universal creature becomes intelligible. Finally, the universal creature will be unified with its Creator and will be in him and one with him.[56] This unification does not involve the confusion of individual essences and substances: despite the strong Neoplatonic thrust of his cosmic vision, Eriugena nevertheless tries to harmonize it – perhaps unsuccessfully in this instance – with the Christian belief in individual immortality of humans.

It probably has become clear by now that Eriugena rejects a literal understanding of the Genesis story: human nature was never in paradise (understood as a place). As suggested earlier, Eriugena takes the references to "paradise" to refer to the primordial, ideal human nature that exists in the mind of God, and to which creation is drawn back. As Eriugena puts it, commenting on the resurrected Christ:

From this we learn that the Paradise which he entered when he rose from the dead is nothing else but that very integrity of human nature which he restored in himself, and in which the First Man, had he not sinned, would have continued in glory. This is the Paradise promised to the Saints. Partly, in their souls, they have entered it already; partly, in their bodies, they are still outside. So did he in himself achieve the unification of Paradise and the inhabited globe. He was the Paradise of the inhabited globe himself.[57]

This is by any standards an extraordinary understanding of paradise. Clearly, Eriugena refuses to understand paradise in a crude material sense. At the time of the general resurrection, Christ will convert into spirit all things humanity acquired from this material world after its transgression, and will bring it into an equal share of the heavenly glory of the angels.[58] Finally, Eriugena while quoting Maximus Confessor, states that Christ will "effect the unification of the created nature with the nature

---

[54] Ibid., 893A.   [55] Ibid., 893C.   [56] Ibid., 893C–D.   [57] Ibid., 895A.   [58] Ibid., 895B–C.

that is not created" – that is, God.[59] An interesting implication of Eriugena's views is that nothing created will be lost. His doctrine implies that my dogs will have a share in the afterlife: with and in the human nature, my canine friends will return into their causes and principles. "All things visible and invisible are created in man, and are therefore destined to rise again with him on the last day."[60]

The last judgment too will not take place in any physical place, but each person, good or evil, will behold Christ's coming in herself, in her own conscience, and each person will be judge of her own deeds and thoughts.[61]

Hell will be nothing else than a kind of "psychological" torment: the disappointment and hunger and deprivation of the covetous will of the wicked for the things they used to desire so inordinately.[62] The wicked will be tormented with grief and sorrow – and that is their hell.[63] Similarly, reward refers to imaginations of good things. The saints, however, will enjoy the theophanies of divine energies and become deified, becoming one with God.[64]

ERIUGENA'S LEGACY

Eriugena's impact on the thought of the Middle Ages after the 9th century is difficult to ascertain.[65] It certainly was not pervasive. A number of important authors such as Anselm of Canterbury (d. 1109), Hugh of St. Victor (d. 1141) and Alain of Lille (d. 1202) may have been familiar with some of Eriugena's ideas. In the first half of the 12th century, a summary of *Periphyseon*, entitled *Clavis physicae* (usually attributed to Honorius Augustodunensis), became an important vehicle for the dissemination of Eriugena's ideas, despite the fact that it only existed in a very limited number of manuscripts. Meister Eckhart may have been familiar with *Clavis*. One of the manuscripts of *Clavis* was later owned by Nicolas of Cusa, who was deeply influenced by Eriugena.

Periphyseon was fairly well known in the 12th and 13th centuries – sufficiently well known for the followers of Amaury of Bene (d. 1207) to appeal to it in their defense of their own alleged pantheistic views. This led to an official condemnation of the book in 1225 by Pope Honorius III. After this condemnation, few people openly aligned themselves with

---

[59] Ibid., 896A. [60] Ibid., 907A; 912Cff. [61] Ibid., 996C. [62] Ibid., 936A–B.
[63] Ibid., 955B; 961Bff. [64] Ibid., 905A.
[65] For a short but helpful survey of Eriugena's influence, see Moran, *The Philosophy*, 269–81.

Eriugena's works.[66] Nevertheless, Eriugena's influence continued. Eriugena's translations of the Dionysian corpus proved influential. His translation of *The Mystical Theology* was sent to the papal librarian Anastasius, who added *scholia* (explanatory notes translated from Greek manuscripts present in Roman libraries). Around the middle of the 13th century, an anonymous scholar added relevant excerpts from *Periphyseon* to this manuscript, and in this format the book (now containing Eriugena's translation, the *scholia* translated by Anastasius and the excerpts from *Periphyseon*) came to be used as a textbook for Dionysian studies at the University of Paris.[67]

Eriugena's *Homily* exerted some influence and was widely read and copied in the 12th century because it was attributed to Origen. Thomas Aquinas, for instance, quotes it eight times in his *Catena Aurea* (*The Golden Chain*), a selection of texts from the Church Fathers on the four Gospels he compiled. Similarly, in his own *Commentary on the Gospel of St. John*, Thomas Aquinas refers to the *Homily* half a dozen times.[68]

The *Commentary on the Gospel of John* has been preserved in one manuscript – probably the autograph – from Laon. Given the fact that there was only one manuscript, we may be inclined to think that this work did not exert any influence. However, this was not the case. At least from the 12th century onward it began to make an impact as several passages were incorporated into the *Glossa Ordinaria* (a standard commentary on the Scriptures in the Middle Ages containing explanations and comments from Jerome, Augustine, Gregory the Great, Bede, John Chrysostom, Origen and so forth). According to some scholars, Anselm of Laon (d. 1117) was responsible for the gloss on Paul, and perhaps, St. John's Gospel. Given the fact that the manuscript was in the possession of the School at Laon, it becomes clear why the *Glossa Ordinaria* contained several passages from Eriugena's *Commentary*. In this manner, Eriugena's ideas found an outlet. It is probably through this medium that Thomas Aquinas will use a number of extracts in his own *Commentary on John*, the *Catena Aurea* and even the *Summa Theologiae*, although he is unaware that they actually go back to Eriugena.[69]

---

[66] In 1684, three years after *Periphyseon* was printed, it was duly put on the index of prohibited books.

[67] See L. Michael Harrington (ed.), *A Thirteenth-Century Textbook of Mystical Theology at the University of Paris: The Mystical Theology of Dionysius the Areopagite in Eriugena's Latin Translation with the Scholia translated by Anastasius the Librarian and Excerpts from Eriugena's Periphyseon.* Dallas Medieval Texts and Translations 4 (Leuven: Peeters, 2004).

[68] For the impact of the *Homily*, see Jeauneau, *Jean Scot, Homélie*, 130–67.

[69] See Jeauneau, "Introduction," in *Jean Scot, Commentaire sur l'Évangile de Jean*, 61–62. The passage Jeauneau identifies from the *Summa* is *ST* III.38.1.

Today, Eriugena's oeuvre enjoys a renewed interest for a number of reasons. In Eriugena, we encounter an author who bridges the gap between the Latin West and the Greek East. Even when Eriugena draws on Latin sources (such as Augustine), he develops, at times, theological views that are reminiscent of Greek views, which illustrates that scholarly distinctions between the theologies of the "Latin West" and the "Greek East" should not be applied too rigorously. His views on the relation between God and creation are quite remarkable. Eriugena is also an interesting exponent of negative theology, and some scholars have linked his ideas with those of Meister Eckhart and even with those of German idealism. While Eriugena develops a number of approaches and themes we encountered in earlier authors (such as the sacramental understanding of the world and allegorical readings of Scripture), he also occupies a relatively original position in the Latin West by adopting a moderate Greek stance on the procession of the Spirit, and he is a fine representative of the profound medieval views on human understanding and intellect. The best reason, however, to engage with Eriugena's works is the sheer splendor of his majestic vision, which is unrivaled in Western theology. Eriugena's world is full of symbolism, pregnant with pointers toward the divine, caught up as it is between its origin (*exitus*) and its final goal (*reditus*): God, the Alpha and the Omega.

BIBLIOGRAPHICAL NOTE

The following editions are still available: for *Periphyseon*, see the complete translation into English by I. P. Sheldon, revised by John O'Meara (Washington, DC: Dumburton Oaks, 1987). There is also a multivolume bilingual edition (Latin-English translation) *Iohannis Scotti Eriugenae Periphyseon (De Divisone Naturae)*, ed. I. P. Sheldon-Williams, L. Bieler and E. Jeauneau, published by the Dublin Institute for Advanced Studies, 1968ff. The *Homily on the Prologue to the Gospel of St. John* has been translated into English (with annotations) by Christopher Bamford as *The Voice of the Eagle: The Heart of Celtic Christianity* (New York: Lindisfarne Press, 1990). E. Jeauneau produced an excellent bilingual edition (Latin-French) of the *Homily* in Sources Chrétiennes series no. 151 (Paris: Cerf, 1969) as *Jean Scot. Homélie sur le Prologue de Jean*. In the same series, we also find the bilingual edition of Eriugena's *Commentary on John* as *Jean Scot, Commentaire sur l'Évangile de Jean*, introduced and translated by E. Jeauneau. Sources Chrétiennes no. 180 (Paris: Cerf, 1999). Mary Brennan translated *De Divina Praedestinatione* as *John Scottus Eriugena: Treatise on Divine Predestination*, with an introduction by A. Wohlman (South Bend, IN: University of Notre Dame Press, 1998).

The best introduction remains Deirdre Carabine, *John Eriugena Scottus* (Oxford: Oxford University Press, 2000). More comprehensive is Adrian Guiu (ed.), *A Companion to John Scottus Eriugena* (Leiden: Brill, 2019).

PART III

The 11th and 12th Centuries

CHAPTER 6

Introduction
Renewal in the 11th and 12th Centuries

In the second half of the 9th century, the Carolingian world gradually disintegrated. After the creation of three independent kingdoms (Treaty of Verdun), further divisions occurred and central authority all but disappeared. Economic contraction and military impotence accompanied political disintegration. Europe became increasingly vulnerable to military attacks. Viking raids at the beginning of the 9th century turned into more permanent invasions in the second half of the century, with Vikings settling in Ireland, Frisia, England, Normandy and elsewhere. In the East, the Magyars went on plundering sprees until Otto the Great (936–73) called a halt to it in 955. In Southern Europe, Islamic incursions into the Mediterranean islands (Sicily, the Balearic Islands), the south of France and Italy further disclosed the weakness of Europe.

The Church too suffered decline during the 10th and 11th centuries. In a climate of economic downturn, simony was epidemic while local potentates seized Church property. During the 10th and early 11th centuries, the papacy became an economic commodity bought and sold by rivaling Roman families. The colorful, infamous career of Pope John XII (955–63) represents the low point of the papacy at that time.

A number of significant changes during the 11th century would culminate in a radically transformed society in the 12th. I can only briefly mention some of the main contributing factors that led to the renaissance of the 12th century. Incursions from raiders had led to a clustering of population around local strongholds. The local baron offered his peasants protection in return for a share of the proceeds. A concentration of resources and manpower resulted in more efficient agricultural practices and technological innovations (more efficient ploughs and mills), as well as the expansion of arable land through the growth of "new towns" from the late 11th century. The local lord encouraged these developments, thereby gaining income from previously unproductive lands.

In political terms, the end of the 10th century and the beginning of the 11th century are important, with the gradual centralization of power in three feudalized states in Europe – namely, Germany, France and England. Otto the Great (936–73) engaged in military campaigns in the East, reduced the power of his ducal vassals and installed bishops and abbots in his fiefs, thereby securing a close alliance between state and Church in Germanic lands. Otto was crowned emperor in AD 962 by Pope John XII: it is here that we find the origins of the "Holy Roman Empire," as it was called in the 12th century. In France, Hugh Capet assumed power in AD 987 in the royal domain, which had effectively shrunk to the area around Paris. The Capetians initially exerted little power but it grew steadily, and Hugh's descendants were to occupy the royal throne until AD 1328. In 1066, under the leadership of William the Conqueror, England was invaded by the Normans – the descendants of the Vikings who had settled in Normandy. William introduced centralized power in England, and this was also to affect the Church: the king attempted to control all ecclesiastical appointments. This policy was to lead to a clash between the king and Anselm of Canterbury, whose work I consider shortly.

In the south, the new vitality of Europe found expression in the *Reconquista*, the reconquest of Spain, with the recapture of Toledo in AD 1085 by Alfonso VI of Leon and Castile. The epic of *El Cid* (inspired by Rodrigo Diaz de Vivar) reveals some of the complex relations between Muslims, Christians and Jews in the Iberian Peninsula at that time. Valencia was captured in 1238; Seville was taken ten years later. Only in 1492, with the fall of Granada, was Spain fully united under Christian rule. As we will see in Chapter 13, the encounter with flourishing Islamic culture in Spain proved of major significance for Western thought because it provided Western scholars access to the works of Aristotle, which was to shape scholastic theology.

Finally, the most obvious illustration of Western expansion is the crusades. The first crusade (1095–99), called by Pope Urban II at the request of the Byzantine emperor, was the only one that succeeded in military terms. After the short reign of Godfrey of Bouillon, his brother Baldwin was crowned king of Jerusalem in AD 1100, ruling over the Latin kingdom of Jerusalem, a vulnerable kingdom caught between Muslims and Byzantines. After the fall of Edessa, a second crusade was organized (1147–49), with the active support of Bernard of Clairvaux. The crusade proved a total failure: the army went to Palestine (which was not under threat), and then attacked Damascus, an ally of the crusader states. A third crusade followed (1189–93), involving Richard the Lionheart of England,

Philip Augustus of France and Frederick Barbarossa of Germany. The fourth crusade (1202–04) ended in the capture of Constantinople (Byzantium) – a new low in the history of the relations between Latin and Greek Christians. Other crusades followed, including a children's crusade (in 1212), and they all ended in debacle.

The end of the 10th and the first half of the 11th century is also an important period of Church reform. First I need to mention the Cluniac reform. The abbey of Cluny was founded around AD 910. It benefited from considerable privileges and freedom from secular powers, allowing it to enjoy tremendous growth. With papal sanction Cluny was allowed to welcome any monk who had left his monastery in search of a stricter rule. This reform movement spread gradually throughout Europe, and by the second half of the 11th century, Cluny counted around 2,000 affiliated houses. By AD 1100, Cluny had grown extremely wealthy and powerful. Two new monastic orders, both Benedictine in inspiration, were founded in order to challenge the increasing worldliness of Cluny at that time: the Carthusians (in AD 1084) and the Cistercians (in AD 1098). The first order (called after its motherhouse, La Chartreuse, near Grenoble) was founded by Bruno of Cologne. He established a community of hermits who were to lead austere lives devoted to solitary contemplation and prayer in individual cells.

The second order, the Cistercians, was founded in 1098 by St. Robert, Abbot of Molesme, in a deserted and uninhabited part of the Diocese of Chalons-sur Saône, today the Diocese of Dijon. In this region lay a marsh covered with rushes and coarse grass called in the language of the country *cistels*; hence the name Cistell or Cîteaux (Lat. *Cistercium*). Here St. Robert and his companions founded the Order of Cîteaux and commenced the literal observance of the Rule of St. Benedict. St. Robert built the first monastery of the Cistercian Order, which he named *Novum Monasterium* (New Monastery) to distinguish it from the monastery of Molesme from which he and his brethren had come. St. Robert was elected abbot of Cîteaux, but when he was recalled to Molesme a year afterward, he was succeeded by St. Alberic, who gave the monks the white habit and placed the monastery immediately under the protection of the Holy See. Under St. Alberic's successor, St. Stephen Harding, the number of subjects was significantly increased by the arrival of St. Bernard and his thirty companions, all young noblemen from Burgundy. From then on the order began to expand rapidly. In little more than fifty years the number of foundations grew to more than 300 – an unprecedented growth. The Cistercians had had their strongest expansion behind them by 1200 and were overcome by the new orders of the 13th century. (Between AD 1118 and 1200, the Cistercian abbeys grew in number from 7 to 525; by AD 1500, there were 742 abbeys.) The Cistercians fled from society and were rigorous and disciplined, leading a life of following Christ in poverty and austerity.[1] They developed a beautiful spirituality, the main exponent of which is St. Bernard of Clairvaux (1090–1153).

Whereas the Cistercians were an offshoot from the Benedictines, the Augustinian canons were a new order altogether. St. Augustine had never written a Rule; he had, however, written a letter of spiritual advice to religious women about life in community. It was a general letter exhorting them to have all things in common, to pray together at certain times, to dress without distinction and so forth. During the period AD 1075–1125, a large number of communities following the Rule of St. Augustine appeared all over Western Europe. Their emphasis was different from the Benedictine movement. They served society and led a practical life focused on apostolic activity in the world (preaching, hospitals, administration). They attracted endowments of minor aristocracy and townspeople who regarded an Augustinian house as a type of foundation within their means and a religious ideal within their understanding. Their unpretentious houses attracted many small gifts and benefactions. As Richard Southern puts it: "Living under a modest Rule the canons performed modest services for men of moderate means and moderate needs."[2] They provided burial places for townsfolk and masses for the dead, schools and hospitals, and administrative services as clerks. In an increasingly busy and complex age, they offered more than the Benedictine monks could.[3] Near Paris, William of Champeaux, a Master in Theology, and a number of his students, including Gilduin, withdrew to a chapel dedicated to St. Victor and founded a religious community as canons regular. It met with the support of King Louis VI, as it further consolidated Paris as a center of national importance – something that was of major significance in political terms to the new dynasty. They also received papal approval in AD 1114. Gilduin became abbot, leading the community for forty years (1114–55). It was during this time that Hugh of St. Victor (discussed shortly) joined the community and effectively founded the theological school known as the Victorines. The foundation of St. Victor on the outskirts of Paris by William of Champeaux is thus part of the

[1] See Richard Southern, *Western Society and the Church in the Middle Ages: The Penguin History of the Church*, vol. II (Harmondsworth: Penguin, 1990), 250–72.
[2] Ibid., 247.   [3] Ibid., 241–50.

reform movement that attempted to harmonize priestly orientation with new learning. The Victorines were scholars who lived in an enclosed community, thereby overcoming the growing rift between monks and scholars.

Another order took its inspiration from this so-called Rule of St. Augustine – namely, the canons of Prémontré, also called the Norbertines after their founder, St. Norbert of Xanten. He was born around AD 1080 and led an uneventful life as a secular canon attached to the church in Xanten until he underwent a conversion experience (in AD 1115). He chose Prémontré (near Reims) as the site for his first foundation – although Norbert himself did not mean to found a new order but rather hoped to renew the movement of the canons through the original Rule of St. Augustine.

After a period of decline, the papacy too was reformed. Pope Leo IX (1049–54), cousin of Emperor Henry III of Germany, was one of the early exponents of the reform movement. Leo traveled around Europe, opposed simony and clerical marriage and created the College of Cardinals. In 1059, a momentous step was taken in the history of the papacy: it was promulgated by a synod that the pope had to be elected by the College of Cardinals, thereby reducing interference in papal elections by secular powers (both Roman and imperial). Another practice that was condemned was lay investiture – that is, the practice by which secular rulers appoint clergy. This led to the so-called investiture contest, which initially came to a head in the conflict between Pope Gregory VII (1073–85) and Henry IV. The issue, however, was not limited to the regions under imperial control, as the stand-off between Anselm of Canterbury and King William II illustrates.[4]

The 12th century was a time of major intellectual and artistic flowering. The intellectual and artistic developments in different areas were impressive: canon law was developed, chivalric literature (*Roman de la Rose*) blossomed and churches were built in the new Gothic style characterized by soaring heights and flooded with light.[5] An early exponent of this new architectural style was the Abbey Church of St. Denis (AD 1144), built under the auspices of Abbot Suger. From here the style, with its pointed arches and flying buttresses, spread throughout Europe.

No less impressive were changes in the theological scene. An important contributory factor to the intellectual revival was the growth of cathedral

---

[4] In Germany and Italy, some kind of compromise was reached in AD 1122 in the Concordat of Worms.

[5] The (derogatory) label "Gothic" dates from the postmedieval period. It was initially called the French Style (*Opus Francigenum*).

schools. Gregory VII decreed that every episcopal church should have its own school. This amounted to an official recognition of the importance of cathedral schools and contributed to the shift of the focal point of intellectual creativity away from Benedictine monasteries to these new centers of learning, out of which universities would grow in the early 13th century. This new setting allowed for greater mobility of students and teachers and also secured greater intellectual autonomy. It is in this context that we must understand the debates between Roscelin of Champagne, William of Champeaux, Peter Abelard and his opponent, St. Bernard of Clairvaux. In the latter's view, Abelard basically applied the strict criteria of dialectic and logic to the tenets of Christian faith, assuming that they can be rationally explained without reference to revelation or the authority of the Church Fathers. Hugh and his school attempted to harmonize Abelard's alleged rationalist tendencies with the traditional monastic approach.

CHAPTER 7

Anselm of Canterbury

Anselm was born in Aosta (northern Italy) in 1033, which at that time was part of Burgundy. He moved to France and studied at the Benedictine monastery of Bec, in Normandy, where the illustrious Lanfranc was teaching. In 1060 Anselm took his vows as monk. When Lanfranc left Bec, Anselm succeeded him as principal teacher. In 1078 Anselm was elected abbot. It was around this time that he wrote the *Proslogion*, which I discuss shortly. In 1093 Anselm was asked to become Archbishop of Canterbury, a responsibility he reluctantly assumed. Given the investiture struggle between the Church and the rulers of England, Anselm's initial misgivings about his episcopal duties proved well founded. His years as archbishop were "a time of grief and affliction."[1] Anselm died on April 22, 1109.

ANSELM AND THE 11TH CENTURY

Anselm lived in a period in which reason and dialectic acquired a renewed significance in the intellectual history of the West. When dialectic was applied to theological mysteries, the outcomes were at times theologically unacceptable. Berengar of Tours (d. 1088) is an example of this more controversial approach. Augustine had made a distinction between *sacramentum* and *res*, between the sacramental sign and the reality to which it refers. Appealing to this distinction and arguing that something is either a sign or the reality it refers to, Berengar concluded that the consecrated bread and wine (the sacramental sign) cannot possibly be the reality (*res*) that is the real body and blood of Christ. Although Berengar may only have wanted to deny a physicalist interpretation of the presence of Christ in the Eucharist, and not the real presence as such, his contemporaries

[1] For an in-depth study of Anselm's life and context, see Richard Southern, *Saint Anselm: A Portrait in a Landscape* (Cambridge: Cambridge University Press, 1990). For this quotation, see page 231.

83

(including Lanfranc) took exception to his views. Later theology would solve the issue by introducing a threefold distinction between sacramental sign (*sacramentum tantum*), the reality of grace it refers to (*res tantum*) and that which can be both (*sacramentum et res*).

The controversy that broke out over the status of *universalia* should also be seen in this context. Anselm became embroiled in it through Roscelin, a secular master from northern France who was to teach Peter Abelard. Roscelin was an early defender of radical nominalism. The nominalist view holds that our universal categories exist only in the mind, and they do not have a foundation in reality. Thus, the nominalist claims that universal categories are mere words or names (*nomines* in Latin). There are, for instance, individual human beings but there is no such thing as "humanity," which is just a name and does not have any ontological reality. Realism, on the other hand, teaches that *universalia* do have an existence outside the mind: our universal concept of humanity does have an ontological foundation. This is the view of both Plato and Aristotle. They differed, however, in that the former claimed that these universals exist in a transcendent realm (the realm of the forms), whereas the latter argued that universals only exist *within* individual things. The discussion was to flare up again in the next generation, with Peter Abelard refuting the naive, ultrarealist position of William of Champeaux (d. 1120), who defended the view that the one and the same nature is essentially (*essentialiter*) and wholly present in individual members of species. Abelard ridiculed this position, arguing that it implied that the same thing ("humanity") could be present in different places at the same time.[2]

These issues are theologically relevant. A nominalist position, for instance, will find it difficult to accommodate the view that we all share in the corruption of Adam's nature after the Fall. Similarly, in relation to Trinitarian theology: if the nature shared by the three divine Persons has no ontological foundation but is a mere word or name, then it becomes difficult to avoid the accusation of tritheism – a charge Roscelin was to face at the Council of Soissons in 1092.

While Anselm is best known for his works *Monologion, Proslogion* and *Cur Deus Homo* (*Why God became Human*), he also wrote a number of

---

[2] If the one and the same identical substance ("humanity" as William understood it) is present in Plato and Socrates, and Plato and Socrates are in different towns, it follows that the same substance is simultaneously present in different places. Or if the universal "animality" really exists in two species, such as man and horse, the same animality that is rational in man is irrational in horse. One and the same thing (animality) is both itself and its contrary, which is impossible. See also Armand Maurer, *Medieval Philosophy* (Toronto: Pontifical Institute of Medieval Studies, 1982), 61–63.

influential smaller treatises, such as *On Truth* (*De Veritate*), *On Free Will* (*De Libertate Arbitrii*) and *On the Fall of the Devil* (*De Casu Diaboli*).[3] Initially written by Anselm at the request of Pope Urban (for the Council of Bari), but only finished in 1102, *On the Procession of the Holy Spirit* defends the Latin view on the legitimacy of the *Filioque*.

REASON AND FAITH IN ANSELM'S WORKS

I have already had occasion to allude to the new rationalism that characterized the 11th century. The status of Anselm's works, and the key argument in the *Proslogion* in particular, has caused considerable debate amongst scholars. For some, Anselm is a philosopher who explicitly rejects any appeals to the Scriptures. In the prologue to the *Monologion* he states, for instance, that he wrote this book at the request of his brethren who specified "that nothing whatsoever [was] to be argued on the basis of the authority of the Scriptures; but the constraints of reason (*rationis necessitas*) concisely to prove, and the clarity of truth clearly to show, in the plain style, with everyday arguments, and down-to-earth dialectic, the conclusions of distinct investigations" (*MW* 5). Again, in *Monologion* 1, he writes that he hopes to convince his readers by reason alone (*sola ratione*). In his most famous work, the *Proslogion*, he writes about the proof of the existence of God in the following terms:

I began to ask myself if it would be possible to find one single argument (*unum argumentum*), needing no other proof (*probandum*) than itself, to prove (*ad astruendum*) that God really exists, that he is the highest good, needing nothing, that it is he whom all things need for their being and well-being, and to prove whatever else we believe about the nature of God.[4]

While this may sound as a purely philosophical approach, in his preface to the *Proslogion* Anselm tells us that he considered the *Monologion* "An Example of Meditation on the Meaning of Faith," while he characterizes the *Proslogion* as "Faith Seeking Understanding" (*Fides quaerens intellectum*). This suggests that Anselm is not attempting to dislodge the claims of faith in favor of a philosophical discourse. Thus, when he writes that he does not want to argue on the basis of the Scriptures, he merely rejects appealing to scriptural proof texts. In short, for Anselm, the contrast is not

---

[3] I use the translation by Brian Davies and Gillian Evans (eds.), *Anselm of Canterbury: The Major Works* (Oxford: Oxford University Press, 1998). This work is abbreviated as *MW*.

[4] Translation by Benedicta Ward in *The Prayers and Meditations of Saint Anselm [With the* Proslogion*]* (Harmondsworth: Penguin, 1986), 238.

between faith and reason, or between theology and philosophy (as it came to the fore from the end of the 13th century), but rather between theological reason and an uncritical appeal to scriptural proof texts. Anselm is not working in a context in which theology and philosophy had already become disengaged from one another. On the contrary, Berengar's and Roscelin's approaches illustrate this very engagement. Anselm was to do the same, but in a more balanced manner.

For Anselm, theological activity presupposes faith, informed by the Scriptures and ongoing reflection on them in the tradition. By pondering and reasoning about the mysteries of faith, he hopes to penetrate deeper into their riches, without aiming to abolish the fideistic nature of these claims. Reason does not prove faith, nor does it provide a foundation for it, but reason assists us in disclosing to some degree the beauty and coherence of faith.

In any case, it must be remembered that the proofs for God's existence are only part of a broader theological project. For instance, in his first major work, the *Monologion*, Anselm argued for the existence of a supreme Good in which all things participate in a finite manner (*Monol.* 1–4) – an argument that is Platonic in inspiration as it presupposes a hierarchy of perfection. Anselm then goes on to argue for creation out of nothing and for the distinct attributes of the divinity (simplicity, eternity, omnipresence, immutability) as well as its Trinitarian nature. He makes the case for Trinitarian differentiation (the generation of the Word from the Father) by appealing to the creative act of God: if God creates everything through himself – that is, through the Word (*Monol.* 9–12) – then God and Word are consubstantial (*Monol.* 29). However, by using the teaching of exemplarism (*exemplum* in *Monol.* 9), itself an Augustinian legacy based on the fusion of Platonic thought and biblical teaching (John 1:1–3), Anselm makes plausible the claim that there is inner differentiation within the Godhead. I cannot unpack Anselm's reasoning in the *Monologion* in any detail in this context. Rather, I focus my attention on the *Proslogion*.

THE *PROSLOGION*: THINKING AND DESIRING GOD

The *Proslogion* was written in AD 1077, around one year after Anselm had finished the *Monologion*. The work is rightly famous for its so-called ontological proof for the existence of God (Kant) which, however, is only discussed in chapters 2–3, while the treatise comprises twenty-six chapters in total. Anyone who reads the whole work (which is only about twenty-five pages) will be struck by the fact that it is both intellectual and prayerful. The title itself suggests that Anselm is addressing God.[5] The work can be legitimately characterized as mystagogical, but it is mystagogy in which intellect has a key role to play. Intellect and desire cannot be separated in the *Proslogion.* Anselm's is a desirous intellect. By pondering the mysteries of faith he draws closer to God; theological thinking is a foretaste, however inadequate, and inchoative participation in the vision of God. For Anselm, the understanding we acquire in this life stands midway between faith and the vision of God we all desire.[6]

After having acknowledged in chapter 1 his inability to draw near to God, given his fallen nature, and having reiterated that he does not seek to understand so as to believe, but he believes so as to understand (Is. 7:9), Anselm (perhaps inspired by Augustine's *De Doctr. Christ.* 1.7.7) introduces the famous argument for the true existence of God in chapter 2:

> Now we believe that You are something than which nothing greater can be thought (*aliquid quo nihil maius cogitari possit*). . . . And surely that-than-which -a-greater-cannot-be-thought cannot exist in the mind alone. For if it exists solely in the mind, it can be thought to exist in reality also, which is greater.[7]

A thorough discussion of the validity and the reception of Anselm's argument is beyond the scope of this book.[8] The most obvious objection is that the fact that we can think of something perfect does not necessarily imply its existence. This line of attack was taken by Thomas Aquinas (who may have known the argument from the *Proslogion* only secondhand) in *ST* 1.2.1 and *ScG* 1.11.[9] It was, however, also formulated in Anselm's time by

---

[5] *Proslogion* means address – that is, speaking to somebody. *Monologion* means soliloquy or inner dialogue.

[6] See Anselm's remarks in the "Commendation" of *Cur Deus Homo*, addressed to Pope Urban II: "I consider that the understanding which we gain in this life stands midway between faith and vision (*speciem*). It follows, in my view, that the nearer someone comes to attainment of this understanding, the nearer that person approaches to vision, for which we all pant in anticipation." *MW* 260 (trans. partly modified).

[7] *MW* 87.

[8] See Brian Davies's contribution, "Anselm and the Ontological Argument," in Brian Davies and Brian Leftow (eds.), *The Cambridge Companion to Anselm* (Cambridge: Cambridge University Press, 2004), 157–78 for a penetrating analysis. Jos Decorte, whose discussion has influenced my reading of the *Proslogion*, hardly exaggerates when he states that the history of the reception of the ontological argument reflects the history of Western philosophy. See Jos Decorte, *Waarheid als Weg. Beknopte Geschiedenis van de Middeleeuwse Wijsbegeerte* (Kapellen: Pelckmans, 1992), 108–21.

[9] *ScG* 1.11.3: "From the fact that that which is indicated by the name *God* is conceived by the mind, it does not follow that God exists save only in the intellect. Hence, that than which nothing greater cannot be thought will likewise not have to exist save only in the intellect" (trans. by Anton Pegis as *Saint Thomas Aquinas, Summa contra Gentiles. Book 1: God* (Notre Dame, IN: University of Notre Dame Press, 1975), 82).

a monk called Gaunilo from the abbey of Marmoutiers, who wrote a reply to the *Proslogion* entitled *Pro Insipiente* (*On Behalf of the Fool*). The reference to "the fool" is inspired by Psalms 14:1 ("The Fool has said in his heart: there is no God"). Quoting this verse in *Prosl.* 2, Anselm had duly considered the counterargument that "it is one thing for an object to exist in the mind, and another thing to understand that an object actually exists." In Anselm's view, however, if one really ponders the full meaning of the notion "something-than-which-nothing-greater-can-be-thought," this counterargument does not hold water.

Gaunilo gives the example of a most perfect, paradisiacal island, which, if Anselm's reasoning was valid, would of necessity exist: "Since it is more excellent to exist not only in the mind alone but also in reality, therefore it must needs be that it exists. For if it did not exist, any other land existing in reality would be more excellent than it, and so this island, already conceived by you to be more excellent than others, will not be more excellent."[10] He adds, somewhat harshly: "If, I say, someone wishes thus to persuade me that this island really exists beyond all doubt, I should either think that he was joking, or I should find it hard to decide which of us I ought to judge the bigger fool." It is an indication of Anselm's magnanimous nature that he insisted that Gaunilo's criticism – as well as his own reply to it – was to be added to the publication of the *Proslogion*.

In that reply, Anselm points out that Gaunilo mistakenly identifies "that which is greater than everything" (Gaunilo's interpretation of Anselm's text) with "that-than-which-nothing-greater-can-be-thought" (Anselm's phrase).[11] The former concept is formed in an empirical way; the latter is not. Again, the former may very well prove very imperfect indeed; the latter cannot.[12] Most important of all, whereas "that-than-which-nothing-greater-can-be-thought" leads the mind to reach out toward that which will always elude it, "that which is greater than everything" can be grasped by the mind. Thus, the latter does not result in a dynamic of cognitive transcendence that the "that-than-which-nothing-greater-can-be-thought" evokes. Indeed, pondering God as

---

[10] *MW* 109.

[11] "You often reiterate that I say that that which is greater than everything exists in the mind, and that if it is in the mind, it exists also in reality, for otherwise that which is greater than everything would not be that which is greater than everything. However, nowhere in all that I have said will you find such an argument" (*MW* 116).

[12] See *MW* 116 and B. Davies, "Anselm and the Ontological Argument," 165.

"that-than-which-nothing-greater-can-be-thought" compels our mind to make a qualitative jump and induces a kind of intellectual disclosure.[13]

In other words, Anselm is not saying that God is the most perfect thing and that he therefore must exist. His approach is both more sophisticated and apophatic. Some commentators have actually argued that Anselm's phrase "that-than-which-nothing-greater-can-be-thought" does not immediately describe God's nature but suggests, rather, how we should think about God. In this interpretation Anselm's argument does not explicitly reveal what God is but indicates how we should think about God.[14] Even when we do not go as far as this, the prescriptive rule (how to think about God) does lead us to a number of important conclusions: if God is genuinely that-than-which-nothing-greater-can-be-thought, then he cannot simply exist in the mind, but he also has to exist in reality (*Prosl.* 2) and his nonexistence is unthinkable (*Prosl.* 3). It follows that he is the supreme being who made everything else from nothing (*Prosl.* 5). God is whatever it is better to be than not to be (ibid.), such as perceptive (*Prosl.* 6), omnipotent (*Prosl.* 7), merciful and impassible (*Prosl.* 8), just (*Prosl.* 9), limitless and eternal (*Prosl.* 13).

Before we proceed, let us have one more look at the argument Anselm develops. For no matter how Anselm may have considered his argument, it is undeniable that in the history of Western thought it was treated as a proper proof for the existence of God. Thomas Aquinas attacks Anselm on two counts: first, as we mentioned earlier, he denies, as Gaunilo had, that we can deduce the existence of something from the mere concept we have of it. From Anselm's reply to Gaunilo (§ 4) we conclude that Anselm was perfectly aware of this objection and that he agrees that it generally holds, but, in his view, it does not apply in this case (i.e., the concept of God).[15]

Kant (who may have known the argument only through the *Meditations* of Descartes) argued that the central flaw of the argument is that it treats "existence" as "a real predicate" while effectively existence is "not anything

---

[13] Jos Decorte, drawing on the work of I. T. Ramsey, offers an illuminating analogy. I request students to imagine a square; then I ask them to change this square into an octagon, then a dodecagon and so forth. Finally, I ask them to add an infinite number of angles: they smile, for their minds have made a qualitative jump (they have, rather unproverbially, circled a square). See Jos Decorte, *Raak me niet aan. Over middeleeuws en postmiddeleeuws transcendentiedenken* (Kapellen: Pelckmans, 2001), 202.

[14] Decorte, *Waarheid als Weg*, 116.

[15] Anselm, *Reply to Gaunilo*: "It is the distinguishing characteristic of God that he cannot be thought of as not existing." *MW* 116.

that could be added to the concept of a thing."[16] Although I cannot discuss Kant's critique here, it is not clear that it holds water.[17]

Gaunilo had also argued that we do not actually have a proper understanding of that-than-which-nothing-greater-can-be-thought. Again, Thomas Aquinas was to make a similar point: because we do not know the essence of God, Anselm's proposition is not self-evident *to us* (*ST* 1.2.1). If we were God and had a proper understanding of God's nature, then the proposition "God exists" would indeed be self-evident, for God is his own existence.

This is a much more interesting critique than the first one. It is not clear, however, that Anselm holds the view that that-than-which-nothing-greater -can-be-thought is necessarily a clear and distinct idea (as it was for Descartes), or that its clarity and distinctness are necessary for the validity of his argument. This is confirmed by *Prosl.* 14, a key turning point in the treatise. Here Anselm almost despairingly questions the value of his theological speculations thus far:

> Have you found, O my soul, what you were seeking? You were seeking God, and you found him to be something which surpasses all things, and that than which nothing greater can be thought, and to be life itself, light, wisdom, goodness, eternal blessedness and blessed eternity, and to exist everywhere and always. If you have not found your God, how is he this which you have found, and understood so truly and certainly? If you have found [him], why is it that you do not experience what you have found? Why, O Lord God, does my soul not experience (*sentit*) You if it has found (*invenit*) You? (*Prosl.* 14; my trans.)

Anselm's soul desires to see more of God, but it sees nothing beyond what it has seen, except darkness, due to his intellectual and moral limitations (sin), as well as the dazzling light of God's glory (*Prosl.* 14). This is

---

[16] Immanuel Kant, *Critique of Pure Reason*, trans. Norman Kemp Smith (New York: St. Martin's, 1965), A 599/B 626.

[17] First, it is not clear that Anselm is committed to the view that existence is a characteristic of things. He is committed to the premise that something that only exists in the mind cannot be thought of as that-than-which-nothing-greater-can-be-thought. This does not necessarily mean that he treats existence as a property of things. As Brian Davies observes, Anselm seems to be "contrasting objects of thought and saying that one of them cannot be sensibly described as that-than-which-nothing-greater-can-be thought – the one in question being, of course, something which exists only in the mind" ("Anselm and the Ontological Argument," 171). Moreover, critics of Kant have pointed out that the truth of Kant's dictum ("Existence is not a real predicate") is anything but self-evident. See Allen Wood, *Kant's Rational Theology* (Ithaca, NY: Cornell University Press, 1978), 100–23 for a more in-depth discussion. It may very well be that a modern understanding of being (which is much poorer than the medieval one) lurks behind Kant's critique. For Kant, when we say "God is," we attach no new predicate to the concept of God, but only *posit* the subject with all its predicates. For Anselm and medieval thinkers in general, saying that "God is" allows us to derive a whole series of predicates (omnipresence, eternity, goodness, justice). What are "real predicates" for Kant are, for Anselm, effectively predicates derived from understanding God as *true being*.

a moment of crisis in the *Proslogion*. Theological constructions, no matter how brilliant, do not fulfill Anselm's desire for union with God.[18]

Prosl. 15 appears to be a new start, in which Anselm remains more sensitive to the utter transcendence of God. He now describes God as "greater-than-can-be-thought" (*quiddam maius quam cogitari possit*). This new way of characterizing God cannot be derived from the first phrase (that-than-which -nothing-greater-can-be-thought): that-than-which-nothing-greater-can-be -thought is not necessarily identical with that-which-is-greater-than-can-be-thought. However, Anselm does refer to his first phrase to argue for its necessity: "Since it is possible to think that this could exist, if you are not this, then a greater than you can be thought; and that will not do" (*Prosl.* 15).

Anselm acknowledges that he cannot comprehend God, but now he has a better understanding why he cannot grasp God: no matter how hard our intellect searches for God, it cannot grasp him because God is greater-than-can-be-thought.[19] He has, in other words, acquired a measure of insight into the limitations of reason when "raiding the inarticulate" (T. S. Eliot):

In truth, Lord, this is that light inaccessible in which you dwell. Nothing can pierce through it to see you there. I cannot look directly into it, it is too great for me. But whatever I see, I see through it, like a weak eye that sees what it does by the light of the sun, though it cannot look at the sun itself. (*Prosl.* 16)[20]

In the remainder of the treatise Anselm continues, in a prayerful and searching manner, to reconsider some of the attributes he had ascribed to God in the first half of the treatise. Central in this discussion is the notion of God's simplicity (cf. *Prosl.* 19: *simpliciter es*: You simply *are*.). The attributes that the mind perceives in a multiple and scattered way (i.e., truth, life wisdom, goodness, blessedness, eternity cf. *Monol.* 18), due to its intellectual narrowness, are all simply one in God: that kind of division into different attributes is foreign to that-than-which-nothing-greater-can-be-thought (*Prosl.* 18). Because of divine simplicity, God has these attributes in his own ineffable way (*Prosl.* 17: *in tuo ineffabili modo*).

The importance of the notion of simplicity (which had already been discussed in *Monol.* 17) in Anselm's apophatic strategy is further highlighted in *Prosl.* 22: "You alone, Lord, are what You are and You are who You are." After this clear allusion to God's name in Ex. 3:14, Anselm continues to argue that God, as the one who exists truly and simply (*Et tu es qui proprie et simpliciter es*), is immutable, eternal and the highest good.

[18] Decorte, *Waarheid als Weg*, 117ff.   [19] Ibid., 118.
[20] Translation by Benedicta Ward from *The Prayers and Meditations of Saint Anselm. With the Proslogion* (Harmondsworth: Penguin, 1973), 257.

Toward the end of the *Proslogion* its mystagogical dimension becomes increasingly evident:

Now arouse yourself, my soul, attend with all your mind, and think as much as you can about the nature and extent of so great a good. For if each good thing is delightful, think carefully how delightful must be that good which holds within it the joy of every good, and not such a good as we experience in created things, but as different as Creator is from creature. For if life that is created is good, how good must the life of the Creator be? ... If the wisdom that knows everything that is made is loveable, how loveable must that wisdom be that made all things out of nothing? (*Prosl.* 24, trans. Ward, 263)

The insight, however inadequate, into God's supereminent, ineffable goodness is not futile. For it awakens in us the desire for a full enjoyment of that goodness. Through knowing and loving God, and, in doing so in this life, enjoying him, our lives are inscribed into a path that will come to full fruition when we are one with God in the afterlife. Our whole life derives its focus and meaning from this orientation. As Anselm prays in the final chapter of *Proslogion*:

> My God,
> I pray that I may so know you and love you that I may rejoice in you.
> And if I may not do so fully in this life,
> let me steadily go on
> To the day when I come to that fullness.
> Let the knowledge of you increase in me here,
> And let it there come to its fullness.
> Let your love grow in me here,
> And let it there be fulfilled,
> So that here my joy may be in a great hope,
> And there in full reality.   (*Prosl.* 26)[21]

ANSELM ON FREEDOM

After the *Monologion* and *Proslogion* Anselm wrote three short treatises called *De Veritate* (*On Truth*), *De Libertate Arbitrii* (*On Freedom of Will*)

---

[21] Ibid., 266–67. In the *Monol.* 74–76, Anselm has beautifully described this orientation in terms of the theological virtues. Here he notes that we have to exert ourselves to attain this good, which is God, by love and desire. In order to even attempt this, we need hope. But love and hope are impossible without faith: "Belief paves the human soul's way to the supreme essence; by believing we progress toward the supreme essence" (*MW* 78).

and *De Casu Diaboli* (*On the Fall of the Devil*). I now briefly discuss his understanding of free will and truth.

It is probably fair to say that the modern understanding of freedom can be characterized in terms of freedom of choice: if you are not compelled to do something, you are free. For Anselm, this is a deficient understanding of freedom. He refuses, for instance, to equate freedom with the ability to either choose the good or to reject it. If freedom was understood in those terms, it would follow that neither God nor the good angels (who are unable to sin) would have free will (*De Lib. Arb.* 1). For Anselm, the will is therefore not some kind of neutral, indifferent capacity. We are only free when we actively will goodness. Perfect freedom will actually imply the *inability* to sin: when we cannot help but be attracted to goodness and avoid sin, we are close to holiness.

A different way of putting this is that true freedom is the capacity for preserving rectitude of will for the sake of rectitude itself (*De Lib. Arb.* 3: *libertas arbitrii est potestas servandi rectitudinem voluntatis propter ipsam rectitudinem*). The key term here is *rectitudo*, or rightness, which is closely associated with "truth." Anselm had already discussed the concept of *rectitudo* in more general terms in his dialogue *On Truth*. There (*De Ver.* 10) Anselm had made the point that things are "right" ("rectitudinous") when they are or do what they ought. In Anselm's understanding, what things are in their essence (i.e., what they ought to be) ultimately refers to their conformity with their spiritual existence or essence in the divine mind. Things are true when they are rectitudinous – that is, when they conform with their true, ideal essence. In short, they are "rectitudinous" when "they are that which they are in the highest truth" (*De Ver.* 7; *MW* 160). Rectitude – the conformity of things with their true essence or being – is the cause of all truth (*De Ver.* 10). Truth in turn is defined (*De Ver.* 11) as "rectitude perceptible by the mind alone." Moral truth or justice is also defined in terms of rectitude: justice is "rectitude of the will preserved for its own sake" (*De Ver.* 12). Ultimately, things as diverse as actions or propositions are true because they are in accordance with truth. If anything, Anselm's adoption of the Platonic worldview fuels the theocentric focus of his theology. Everything we do, desire or think has to have a reference to God (its rectitude) in order to be truthful. The theme of rectitude also plays an important part in his soteriology. For sin has resulted in a distortion of the creaturely order and this lack of rectitude needs to be addressed.

ANSELM'S SOTERIOLOGY

Anselm developed an influential theory of salvation in his work *Cur Deus Homo* (finished in AD 1098). The title of the work can be translated in two ways: first as "Why Did God Become Human?" but also as "Why a God-Man?" The treatise has left a deep imprint on Catholic theology throughout the centuries. His theory has also been sharply criticized. Theologians of a liberal mindset, for instance, will want to question the notion that saving significance is attributed (allegedly) to the suffering of an innocent man, Jesus of Nazareth. It has been argued that the Anselmic theory of satisfaction comes dangerously close to turning God into a vindictive, punitive God who needs a bloody sacrifice before he becomes reconciled with this sinful world. The theory of satisfaction, so it is further alleged, is legalistic, transactional, more indebted to feudal categories than to the Scriptures and effectively glorifies innocent suffering instead of providing us with resources to challenge it.[22] In agreement with this critique, Edward Schillebeeckx has famously argued that we have been saved "despite the Cross."[23] He writes: "Many existing theories of our redemption through Jesus Christ deprive Jesus, his message and career of their subversive power, and even worse, sacralize violence to be a reality within God. God is said to call for a bloody sacrifice which stills or calms his sense of justice."[24]

Let us serenely examine the issues in some more detail. In *Cur Deus Homo*, written as a dialogue between Anselm and his pupil Boso, Anselm first dispenses with the theory of the devil's rights. The view that the devil had any legitimate claims over God in relation to humanity simply does not hold water for Anselm (*CDH* 1.7). He then outlines his own views in the remainder of the book, arguing for the "necessity" of the incarnation as follows. Given the fact (1) that all of humanity was subject to human sin; (2) that sin distorts the right order (*rectitudo* or *rectus ordo*) that God had established in his creation and creates "a debt" we owe to God (to the will of whom all creatures ought to be subject);[25] (3) that it is necessary in light

---

[22] For the notion that Anselm's theory of satisfaction is profoundly shaped by feudal categories (especially honor), see, for instance, Southern, *Saint Anselm*, 221–27.

[23] Edward Schillebeeckx, *Christ: The Christian Experience in the Modern World* (London: SCM, 1980), 729.

[24] Edward Schillebeeckx, *The Church: The Human Story of God* (London: SCM, 1990), 125.

[25] *Cur Deus Homo* 1.11 The translation used is by Brian Davies and Gillian Evans from *Anselm of Canterbury: The Major Works* (Oxford: Oxford University Press, 1998), 260–356. The language of "debt" is inspired by the Our Father ("Forgive us our debts") (*debita nostra* in Matt. 6:12), referred to in *CDH* 1.19.

of God's justice and honor that this debt does not remain outstanding;[26] (4) that humanity, because of the Fall, was not in a position to make satisfaction to God, although the onus is actually on humanity to do so (as *we* have incurred the debt); and (5) that only God, being sinless, could repay the debt we had incurred, it follows that it was "necessary" that somebody who was both God (who could make restitution) and Man (who ought to make restitution) did it (*CDH* II.6).

Stating the theory in such a brief manner is bound to give fuel to the popular criticism that has been raised against it. Let me now deal with some of this critique. First, the idea that God's anger was somehow appeased by the sacrifice of his Son need not detain us, as the idea of a changeable God was unacceptable to medieval theology.[27] Salvation is *pro nobis*; it affects us and our relation with God rather than God himself. It is not as if God is in need of redemption. Anselm's God does not feel offended by sin. "Nothing can be added to, or subtracted from, the honor of God, in so far as it relates to God himself" (*CDH* I.15). Earlier Anselm had clarified what "repaying God's honor" entails: it is "our righteousness or uprightness of will." This righteousness, Anselm states, is "the sole honor, the complete honor which we owe to God and which God demands from us" (*CDH* I.11). For Anselm, honoring God means nothing else than living a life of virtue in obedience to God's will: "When such a being [a rational being] desires what is right, he is honoring God, not because he is bestowing anything upon God, but because he is voluntarily subordinating himself to his will and governance, maintaining his own proper station in life within the natural universe, and, to the best of his ability, maintaining the beauty of the universe itself" (*CDH* I.15).

Second, those who argue that Anselm's views are indebted to feudal categories rather than to the Christian faith should remember that the notion of "satisfaction" has patristic roots.[28] If anything, as Jaroslav Pelikan observed many years ago, Anselm's notion of satisfaction bears more resemblance to the developing penitential system of the Church of the 11th century than to feudal categories.[29] For instance, when Anselm asks Boso how he hopes to make restitution to God for his sin, Boso replies:

---

[26] *CDH* I.11: "Everyone who sins is under an obligation to repay to God the honor which he has violently taken from him, and this is the satisfaction which every sinner is obliged to give to God."

[27] *CDH* I.8 (in which it is being argued that the divine nature is immutable and impassible) and I.15.

[28] See, for instance, Tertullian, *De Poenitentia*, chapter 5, *CCSL* 1.328.

[29] Jaroslav Pelikan, *The Christian Tradition: A History of the Development of Doctrine, vol. III: The Growth of Medieval Theology (600–1300)* (Chicago: Chicago University Press, 1978), 143–45: "'Satisfaction,' then was another term for 'sacrifice' and Christ's sacrificial act of penance made even human acts of satisfaction worthy, since of themselves they were not."

"Penitence, a contrite and humbled heart, fasting and many kinds of bodily labor, the showing of pity through giving and forgiveness, and obedience" (CDH 1.20). Anselm will go on to argue that this may not be sufficient, as creatures owe everything to God anyhow. Only Christ can readdress the imbalance caused by sin. But Anselm does not question the nature of the satisfaction Boso proposes. He merely argues that, in his view, it will prove insufficient.

Third, the popular critique that the justice of Anselm's God overrides his mercy shows a disturbing lack of firsthand knowledge of the text. Anselm explicitly states that one of the main purposes of his work is to show how divine justice and mercy are harmonized in the Cross of Christ. Indeed, at the end of the *Cur Deus Homo*, after it has been explained how Christ, the God-man, "satisfies" on behalf of humanity and thereby restores the right order within the universe, we find Anselm concluding:

Now the mercy of God which, when we were considering the justice of God and the sin of humankind, seemed to be dead, we have found to be so great, and so consonant with justice, that a greater and juster mercy cannot be imagined. What, indeed, can be conceived of more merciful than that God the Father should say to a sinner condemned to eternal torments and lacking any means of redeeming himself, "Take my only-begotten Son and give him on your behalf," and that the Son should say, "Take me and redeem yourself." For it is something of this sort that they say when they call us and draw us towards the Christian faith. (*CDH* II.20)

Finally, Anselm's understanding of sacrifice is influenced by the Augustinian notion of sacrifice. Augustine had argued that God does not need any sacrifices for his own gratification but he only desires what sacrifices signify: "a heart that is broken and humbled" (Ps. 51:18) – which is exactly the language Boso adopts to talk of repaying the debt (*CDH* 1.20). As we saw in Chapter 2, for Augustine, sacrifice has to be seen as a form of (self-)gift that mirrors the sacrifice of Christ. Understood against this larger context it becomes clear how Anselm's terminology can vary from "paying our debts," "making satisfaction" (*satisfacere*) and "offering," to the language of "(self-)giving" (*dare, datio, tradere se*) without any noticeable differences. Examples of the latter can be found throughout St. Anselm's text. One example will suffice: "Is it not fitting that man, who, by sinning, removed himself as far as he possibly could away from God, should, as recompense to God (*satisfaciendo*), make a gift of himself in an act of the greatest possible self-giving (*dare*)?" (*CDH* II.11). This quotation (and the treatise in general) suggests that "making satisfaction" centers around restoring a relationship with God through the self-gift of Christ.

Indeed, the sacrifice of the God-man is both a divine self-gift and a gift of humanity to God in Christ: "because Christ himself is God, the Son of God, the offering he made of himself was to his own honour as well as to the Father and the Holy Spirit; that is, he offered up his humanity to his divinity" (*CDH* II.18).

In short, we need to understand "satisfaction" not as something directed toward God but rather toward the relationship between God and humanity: satisfaction is a cleansing of the sinner (and creation) in relation to God. Anselm gives the example of a beautiful, precious pearl (humanity) that falls in mud and gets dirtied (sin). Would it make sense to put the pearl back into the treasure chest without cleaning it first? Boso agrees: "Surely it would be an appreciably better course to keep and store his pearl clean, rather than dirtied, would it not?" (*CDH* I.19). This illustrates that making satisfaction must be understood in terms of purification of the sinner. This being so, it follows that if God were to forgive sins without this purification having taken place, the relationship between God and humanity would not really be restored. Even if God were to forgive sins without asking for penance, we would not arrive at happiness (*CDH* I.24). In Christ God allows *humanity* to restore the relationship with its Creator.[30] Justice requires that evil does not prevail and is being penalized; however, the "satisfaction" Christ effects through his obedience and love, as displayed in his passion, renders "punishment" unnecessary: whereas "satisfaction" is popularly misunderstood in terms of meeting the demands of vindictive justice (Christ is being punished on our behalf), for Anselm satisfaction (which should be understood in terms of penance) rules out punishment: *aut poena aut satisfactio*. This is of major importance: Anselm's view on the relation between satisfaction and punishment actually implies a *critique* of the popular misinterpretations of his theory in terms of penal substitution.

This is not to say that Anselm's theory is immune to criticism. For instance, Anselm fails to clarify the connection between Christ's satisfactory activity and our participation in it. This is the main weakness of his theory and has contributed to its misunderstanding in transactional terms. Again, his understanding of "forgiveness of sins" seems at times rather limited (namely in terms of non-punishment).

Undoubtedly, the Cross should not be the sole focus of soteriological reflection. Modern theologians are right in emphasizing other themes as

---

[30] Of course there are other reasons why to forgive sin out of mercy alone without asking for restitution would be unfitting. For instance, God would be dealing with sinner and non-sinner in the same way. "This incongruity extends even further: it makes sinfulness resemble God. For, just as God is subject to no law, the same is the case with sinfulness" (*CDH* I.12).

well, such as the inauguration of the Kingdom or the redeeming value of the life of Christ. But to ignore the centrality of the Cross in our salvation or to argue that we have been saved "despite the Cross" is both unscriptural and untraditional.[31] Anselm has made clear that it is theologically plausible to argue for the centrality of the Cross without having to espouse a problematic, vindictive concept of God. On the other hand, it must be admitted that Anselm pays little attention to the life of Christ and that he does not sufficiently link soteriology with Trinitarian theology.

Anselm's overall achievement was considerable. His theory of salvation proved extremely influential, while his so-called ontological argument for the existence of God has continued to intrigue theologians and philosophers since. In an age of increasing rationalism he managed to strike a right balance between respecting the mysteries of faith and our attempts to understand them through reasoning in light of the key teaching of the faith. While he does not use proof texts from the Fathers or the Scriptures to develop his theology, it is clear that the whole of his theology is permeated and shaped by the Christian faith. Anselm, as a Benedictine monk, represents the old, monastic world, and yet he also displays a new kind of confidence in human reason. His work combines the best of both worlds.

BIBLIOGRAPHICAL NOTE

For primary texts, see F. S. Schmitt (ed.), *S. Anselmi Cantuarensis Archiepiscopi Opera Omnia*, 6 vols. (Edinburgh: T&T Nelson, 1946–61).

For a translation (which I have used), see Brian Davies and Gillian Evans (eds.), *Anselm of Canterbury: The Major Works* (Oxford: Oxford University Press, 1998). An older translation by Jasper Hopkins, *Anselm of Canterbury*, 4 vols. (New York: Mellen Press, 1974–76) has retained its value.

For good introductions to Anselm's thought, see Brian Davies and Brian Leftow (eds.), *The Cambridge Companion to Anselm* (Cambridge: Cambridge University Press, 2004) or Sandra Visser and Thomas Williams (eds.), *Anselm of Canterbury* (Oxford: Oxford University Press, 2008).

---

[31] Schillebeeckx, *Christ*, 729.

CHAPTER 8

Monks and Scholars in the 12th Century
Peter Abelard, Bernard of Clairvaux and William of St. Thierry

PETER ABELARD

Peter Abelard was born in Brittany around 1079. Before he founded his own school in 1102 he attended lectures with Roscelin and William of Champeaux. After an illness we find him in Paris (ca. 1108). Abelard appears to have had a propensity for antagonizing some of his teachers (such as William of Champeaux on the issue of universals, and Anselm of Laon, the most famous biblical exegete of his time). The bright and flamboyant Abelard attracted many students, often to the chagrin of other Masters (if Abelard's own account is to be believed). In 1115 or 1116 he began an affair with a young and attractive student, Heloise, the niece of his host Fulbert, a canon of Notre Dame in Paris. Abelard later recalled: "With our lessons as a pretext we abandoned ourselves entirely to love . . . with our books open before us, more words of love than of our reading passed between us, and more kissing than teaching."[1] Heloise fell pregnant but was reluctant to marry Abelard lest it hinder his scholarly career, and when the marriage took place it was conducted in secrecy. Heloise joined a monastery without taking the veil, and Fulbert, presumably assuming that Abelard had abnegated his promise to marry Heloise, sent a band of men to inflict the ultimate humiliation on Abelard's manhood. As he later recalled it: "They cut off the parts of my body whereby I had committed the wrong of which they complained."[2] Abelard then joined the Abbey of St. Denis and from one of their houses he continued teaching, not just on logic and dialectic, as he had done before, but also on theology. His major contribution of this period is the *Theologia Summi Boni*, which, unfortunately, landed him in more troubled waters. It was condemned at the

---

[1] *Historia Calamitatum*, trans. Betty Radice, in *The Letters of Abelard and Heloise* (Harmondsworth: Penguin, 1974), 67.
[2] Ibid., 75.

Synod of Soissons in 1121, and Abelard was forced to burn his own work. In 1122 (after difficulties with his fellow monks at St. Denis) he founded his own oratory. If Abelard had hoped to live as a hermit, the great number of students who flocked to him made this impossible. Abelard stayed at this hermitage (dedicated to the Paraclete or the Comforter) for about five years. Here he rewrote and expanded his previous work on theology, now called *Theologia Christiana*. Around 1126 Abelard was elected the abbot of St. Gildas in Brittany, where the unruly monks clashed with their new abbot who, zealous for reform, unsuccessfully tried to impose adherence to their monastic rule. In 1133 he returned to Paris where he taught for a number of years until he was silenced by St. Bernard and a number of other influential Cistercian monks. Bernard had seen to it that a number of theses drawn from Abelard's works were condemned at the Council of Sens in 1140 or 1141 before Abelard had the opportunity to defend himself. Through the intervention of his friend Peter the Venerable, abbot of Cluny, the excommunication was revoked and it was agreed that Abelard was to remain at Cluny without setting up another school. It is perhaps here that Peter Abelard finally enjoyed some peace. He died on April 21, 1142. He was buried at the Paraclete, where Heloise was later (d. 1164) laid to rest with him. Their remains were transferred in 1817 to the cemetery Père-Lachaise.[3]

It is probably fair to say that Peter Abelard epitomizes the changing dynamics of Western society in the 12th century. It would, however, be a mistake to cast the conflict between Abelard and St. Bernard of Clairvaux in terms of innovators versus conservatives. Both Abelard and Bernard were innovators; they differed, however, in the ways they conceived of innovation.

Today, Peter Abelard is mainly discussed in philosophical monographs for his views on universals and his critique of ultrarealist positions. He himself appears to have espoused a moderate realist conceptualism.[4] Universality only applies to words, not to things. But for him, words carry meaning – they are not sounds. We can meaningfully use universal concepts because there are similarities between the way things are. The intellect, with the aid of the imagination (which can form images of what is

---

[3] There are a number of excellent overviews of Peter Abelard's thought. See John Marenbon, *The Philosophy of Peter Abelard* (Cambridge: Cambridge University Press, 1997), Constant Mews, *Abelard and Heloise* (Oxford: Oxford University Press, 2005) and concisely Jean Jolivet, *La Theologie d'Abelard* (Paris: Cerf, 1997).

[4] See Jos Decorte, *Waarheid als Weg. Beknopte Geschiedenis van de Middeleeuwse Wijsbegeerte* (Kapellen: Pelckmans, 1992), 105.

common to a species), considers what universal words and statements denote, and considers their truth value.[5] In what follows I focus on those works that deal with more immediate theological issues.

Most of our knowledge of Abelard's colorful life stems from his highly readable autobiographical piece entitled *Historia Calamitatum* (*The Story of My Disasters*), written around the time he was about to leave St. Gildas. Heloise appears to have come across the *Historia* accidentally, and an exchange of letters between Abelard and Heloise ensued. Together with the *Historia* these attractive letters are the best known of Abelard's (and Heloise's) literary output. Abelard also revised his *Theologia* – effectively a third version – which became known as *Theologia Scholarium* (ca. 1135). Before this work Abelard had already produced an interesting work in dialogue form called *Collationes* or *Dialogue between a Philosopher, a Jew, and a Christian*. The work, written some time in 1125–35, is quite original. It differs from traditional Christian works in which Jewish views are criticized from a Christian perspective. In Abelard's *Dialogue* both the Jew and the Christian have to defend their views before the Philosopher who only accepts rational arguments. The Philosopher, for instance, questions why anyone should be asked to adhere to the Old Law given the fact that, in his view, the natural law suffices.[6] Through the natural law we already have an innate sense of basic moral precepts; God's revelation of the Old Law is therefore superfluous. The Jew retorts that the Old Law is more universal than the natural law: "You will realise that your law too, which you call 'natural,' is included within ours."[7] The revealed law commands perfect love of God and one's neighbor, and it is precisely in this that the natural law consists as well (by the Philosopher's own admission).[8] The precepts and commands that are added in the revealed law are concerned, "not so much with what constitutes a holy way of life as with safeguarding it."[9] The Philosopher remains unconvinced. The second book treats of the encounter between the Philosopher and the Christian. A whole range of issues are explored, such as the relation between faith and reason, the nature of the highest good and the greatest evil with excursions on virtues and vices, and heaven and hell. In relation to eschatological

---

[5] John Marenbon, *Early Medieval Philosophy* (London: Routledge, 1988), 138. For an in-depth discussion, see Marenbon, *The Philosophy of Peter Abelard*, chapter 8.

[6] Natural law, "that is the knowledge of morals, which we call 'ethics' is made up just of moral precepts, whereas the teaching of your [the Jew's] laws adds to them various commands to do with external signs, which seem superfluous to us." Translation from John Marenbon and Giovanni Orlandi (eds.), *Peter Abelard: Collationes* (Oxford: Clarendon, 2001), 10. In what follows I refer to the paragraphs and page numbers of this edition.

[7] *Dialogue* I. 45 (p. 55). [8] Ibid., I. 43 (p. 53). [9] Ibid., I. 45 (p. 55).

issues, Abelard, like Eriugena before him, appears particularly reluctant to interpret heaven and hell in literalist or material fashion.[10] Indeed, following a hint from Gregory the Great, Abelard's Christian suggests that the very pain of death may suffice "for the purgation of any sin which is not deserving of eternal damnation."[11] The Christian and the Philosopher agree on a definition of "good" and "evil," after which the *Dialogue* concludes. Abelard, who had put himself in the seat of arbitrator who was to sit in judgment over the outcome of the dialogue between the three spokespersons, never gives his verdict: it is left to the reader to decide whose arguments are most convincing.

Around the same period Abelard produced another important work, entitled *Sic et Non* (*Yes and No*). The book has often been considered a precursor to some of the more systematizing works of a later era (such as Peter Lombard's *Sentences*). It is a *collectio sententiarum*, a collection of views from the Fathers that often outline seemingly opposing views on important theological issues. The first chapter, for instance, is entitled "That Faith Must Be Strengthened by Rational Arguments, and the Opposing View." Abelard suggests a number of strategies to deal with apparent contradictory views, such as: Is the text authentic? Was it corrupted by a copyist? Does the wider context within which the sentence is found dissolve the contradiction (for many medieval books consisted merely of excerpts or florilegia)? Was the view expressed later retracted (as with Augustine)? Or perhaps the same words hold different meanings for different authors. Abelard's approach in *Sic et Non* is therefore not skeptical but entirely respectful of the tradition he inherited: he tries to harmonize dissenting voices from the tradition.

We also have a work called *Ethica* or *Scito te ipsum* (*Know Thyself*), written sometime in 1138–39. The *Ethica* remained unfinished: the second book consists of less than two pages.[12] The first book deals with sin and acting badly; the second was to have dealt with virtues and acting well. In this work Abelard argues that sin is not to be identified with vice (which merely inclines us to sin); nor is sin to be identified with any deed. The latter view may be surprising. Abelard's point is that our activities and bodily movements are morally "neutral." What matters is the intention with which we perform these activities. Killing somebody, for instance, can

---

[10] *Dialogue* II, 183–98 (pp. 191–203).

[11] *Dialogue* II, 195 (p. 201, with helpful notes by the editors).

[12] For an English translation of *Scito te ipsum* as well as the *Dialogue*, see Paul Vincent Spade (trans.) *Peter Abelard: Ethical Writings: His Ethics or "Know Yourself" and His Dialogue between a Philosopher, a Jew, and a Christian* (Indianapolis, IN: Hackett, 1995). I use this translation in what follows.

be legitimate (in war) or unjustified (murder). The act of killing as such is neutral; what matters is the intention with which we kill. Sin should therefore be identified with consent to what is inappropriate. This consent to what is inappropriate is but "scorn for God and an affront against him."[13]

In this context Abelard draws an interesting distinction between what we want or desire and our consent to it, which appears to be of a second order or meta-order. We can, for instance, desire to sleep with a married woman but refrain from consenting to this desire.[14] Given the moral neutrality of acts, it follows that whoever consents to commit an inappropriate act is already fully guilty, even though he may not have the opportunity to commit the act.[15] Nor is the bodily pleasure which we may find in an illicit act (gluttony, sexual gratification) necessarily sinful, as a colorful example of Abelard's illustrates.[16] Abelard's view – that neither the act nor the bad will as such are sinful – was singled out for criticism (and condemnation) by his opponents. Clearly, Abelard advocates a strongly interiorized notion of morality. The objection that society hands out punishments on account of acts rather than intentions does not hold for Abelard. First of all, intentions are known only to God, not to the others; moreover, often bad deeds are punished (even when the person is not guilty of a sinful act but may have been merely negligent) to set proper examples.[17] Abelard's radical emphasis upon interior consent is not morally disruptive of ethical traditions and values. On the contrary, these are presupposed. Still, in Abelard's theological ethics there is a shift toward interiority which, according to M. D. Chenu, should be situated in the discovery of self in the first half of the 12th century.[18]

If some of Abelard's views on ethics proved troublesome, his views on faith and reason, soteriology and theology of the Trinity evoked even more

---

[13] *Ethics*, chapter 2, pp. 2–3.   [14] Ibid., chapter 2, p. 6.

[15] "We consent to what isn't allowed when we don't draw back from committing it and are wholly ready to carry it out should the opportunity arise. So whosoever is found in this condition has incurred complete guilt. Adding on the performance of the deed doesn't add anything to increase the sin." *Ethics*, chapter 2, p. 7.

[16] "For example, if someone forces a monk, bound by chains, to lie amongst women, and he is led into pleasure – but *not* into consent – by the bed's softness and the touch of women around him, who can venture to call this pleasure nature has made necessary a 'sin'?" *Ethics*, chapter 2, p. 9 (trans. partly modified).

[17] Ibid., chapter 5, pp. 17–18.

[18] See Jolivet, *La Théologie d'Abélard* (pp. 100–01), who refers to Marie-Dominique Chenu, *L'Éveil de la Conscience dans la Civilisation Médiévale* (Paris: Librairie J. Vrin, 1969), 17–32. Chenu calls Peter Abelard "the first modern person." The emphasis on the role of interior consent is not new as such. The downright denial of the moral relevance of acts is.

consternation. Although it is not clear whether he knew Anselm's *Cur Deus Homo*, Abelard too, in his important *Commentary on Romans*, rejects the view that humanity was held in legitimate bondage by the devil.[19] The devil did not enjoy any legitimate claims over us. In what, then, does the saving efficacy of Christ's life and death consist? On this issue Abelard was to be subjected to severe criticism by St. Bernard of Clairvaux. Abelard had written:

How gruesome and unjust it seems, that somebody would have demanded the innocent blood as some kind of ransom, or that it would have pleased him in some manner or other that an innocent person be killed; not to mention the notion that the death of his Son would have pleased God so much that through it the whole world would have become reconciled with him.[20]

Abelard, referring to John 15:13, continues to give his own view on the efficacy of Christ's saving activity:

It seems to me that our justification in the blood of Christ and reconciliation with God consists in this, namely, that through this unique grace that he displayed to us – namely that the Son assumed our nature and taught us through his words and his example, unto death – he has bound us closer to him in love (*nos sibi amplius per amorem adstrinxit*); therefore, the true love of anybody who is the recipient of such a favor of divine grace will not recoil from suffering (*tolerare*) for his sake.[21]

As St. Bernard saw it, Abelard had reduced the significance of Christ's saving activity to a mere example he had set. To put it in modern scholarly terms, in Bernard's view, Abelard's understanding of salvation is utterly subjectivist (it is something that happens to us) while a balanced soteriology should be objectivist as well: Christ's saving work has effected a real change in the world (such as the remission of sin and punishment, the end of our alienation from God and the reconciliation of God and world). In *Letter* 190 Bernard maintains that for Abelard, Christ's saving work consists, not in "the power of the Cross or the price of Christ's blood, but in the improvement of our own way of life."

It is correct to say that Abelard puts a particular emphasis upon the love of Christ, exemplified in his death, which entices us to abandon our sinful ways and to espouse a life of Christian love. The subjective transformation, effected

---

[19] See *Comm. on Rom.* 3.26. There is a bilingual (Latin-German) edition in the Fontes Christiani series by Rolf Peppermüller: *Abaelard. Expositio in Epistolam ad Romanos – Römerbrief-Kommentar*, 3 vols. (Freiburg: Herder, 2000), and an English translation by Steven R. Cartwright as *Peter Abelard: Commentary on the Epistle to the Romans* (Washington, DC: Catholic University of America Press, 2011).

[20] *Comm. on Rom.* 3.26 (117).   [21] Ibid.

by Christ's life and death, refers to our change of heart, which frees us from disordered concupiscence. However, as Thomas Williams has argued, an exclusively subjectivist view of salvation is incoherent: "Only if there is an objective transaction can there be the subjective transformation."[22] Abelard was aware of this and identifies the objective aspect with the remission of punishment. For Abelard, original sin refers to our liability to punishment for sin rather than some kind of inherited guilt of the soul. It is this liability to punishment on account of Adam's sin that Christ's Passion dissolves.[23]

Abelard's doctrine of the Trinity was considered highly controversial, not in the least because it was intrinsically bound up with another highly sensitive issue: the relation between faith and reason. Indeed, in his *Historia Calamitatum* Abelard claims that his treatise on Trinitarian doctrine was written

for the use of my students who were asking for human and logical reasons on this subject, and demanded something intelligible rather than mere words. In fact they said that words were useless if the intelligence could not follow them, that nothing could be believed unless it was first understood, and that it was absurd for anyone to preach to others what neither he nor those he taught could grasp with the understanding: the Lord himself had criticised such "blind guides of blind men" [Matt. 15:14].[24]

This quotation reflects Abelard's own approach. Faith must be rationally examined. It also indicates the limits of his rationalism, for Abelard's rational examination of faith implies, obviously, that faith precedes reason.

The treatise he refers to in the quotation from his *Historia* is a work generally known under its title *Theologia Summi Boni*, a book that deals with the divine unity and Trinity. As we indicated earlier, it met with opposition at the Synod of Soissons in 1121, and Abelard subsequently redrafted the book. Later versions are known as *Theologia Christiana* (*A Christian Theology*) and *Theologia Scholarium* (*A Theology for Students*). In these later versions Abelard expanded the views he had outlined in his *Theologia Summi*

---

[22] Thomas Williams, "Sin, Grace, and Redemption," in Jeffrey Brower and Kevin Guilfoy (eds.), *The Cambridge Companion to Abelard* (Cambridge: Cambridge University Press, 2004), 258–78, especially page 262. Williams explains in his typically lucid fashion: "For unless the Passion actually accomplishes something, unless there is an 'objective transaction' made in and through the death of Christ, there is nothing about the Passion to inspire our love: pity perhaps, or sympathy, but not love or gratitude."

[23] *Comm. on Rom.* 5.19 (164): "The forgiveness of sin is nothing other than the remittal of punishment, and God bearing our sins means nothing else that he takes the punishment of our sins on himself." One wonders whether this understanding of forgiveness implicitly introduces a penal dimension into Abelard's soteriology.

[24] *Historia Calamitatum* 78.

Boni without fundamentally changing them. As the *Theologia Summi Boni* (*A Theology of the Supreme Good*) contains the gist of his Trinitarian thought I focus mainly on this work.[25]

The *Theologia Summi Boni* is divided into three books. The first book discusses the distinction between the three Persons in God and the scriptural and philosophical sources for the doctrine of the Trinity. The second book treats of objections that can be raised against the belief in the oneness and Trinitarian nature of God. The third book, then, provides answers to the objections raised.

One of the most striking aspects of Abelard's theology of the Trinity is his treatment of Power (*potentia*), Wisdom (*sapientia*) and Goodness or Benevolence (*benignitas*) as personal names of Father, Son and Holy Spirit respectively. Most scholars today (following D. Poirel) accept that Abelard may have drawn his inspiration from Hugh of St. Victor's *De Tribus Diebus* (*On the Three Days*), which I discuss in the next chapter. But Hugh had not treated these perfections as personal names. Abelard does, and in this he proves himself at odds with some of the key insights of Augustine.

The reader will recall that in *De Trin.* VII Augustine had argued that "Father," "Son" and "Holy Spirit" are personal names denoting the relations between the divine Persons. Augustine treats "Power," "Wisdom" and "Goodness" as appropriations. For instance, the three Persons are "wise," and therefore "Wisdom" is not a personal name. It is, however, especially associated with the Word (a personal name), who reveals the Father and calls us to follow him by living wisely.[26]

Abelard, on the other hand, tries to show that "Power," "Wisdom" and "Goodness" are personal names.[27] He does this by attempting to establish a connection between these names and the divine processions. More specifically, he argues that Wisdom is generated by Power by claiming

---

[25] I refer to this work as *TSB*, followed by the number of the book and the chapter. For an edition (Latin text and German translation), see *Peter Abaelard. Theologia Summi Boni. Tractatus de Unitate et Trinitate Divina*, introduced and translated by Ursula Niggli (Hamburg: Felix Meiner, 1997). Jean Jolivet produced a French translation as *Abélard. De L'Unité et de la Trinité Divines* (Paris: Librairie J. Vrin, 2001). All translations are my own.

[26] Cf. *De Trin.* VII.5 and *De Trin.* VII.3, trans., 221: "Therefore the Son is not Word in the same way as he is wisdom, because he is not called Word with reference to himself, but only in relationship to him whose Word he is, just as he is Son in relationship to the Father; but he is wisdom in the same way as he is being. And therefore one wisdom because one being. . . . Word is to be understood relationship-wise, wisdom being-wise."

[27] *TSB* I.2: "The name 'Father' refers to Power; the name 'Son' refers to Wisdom; and the name 'Holy Spirit' refers to the positive disposition (*bonus affectus*) towards creatures." See also *Comm. on Rom.* 1.20.

that Wisdom itself is a kind of power – namely, the power of discernment (*potentia discernendi*).[28] This power of discernment (i.e., the Son, or Wisdom) issues from the Power who is the Father. From Power and Wisdom Goodness proceeds. For anybody who is all-powerful and wise will be good. Therefore, Goodness (i.e., the Holy Spirit) proceeds from the Father and the Son.

In a theological climate in which Augustine's teachings set the standard of orthodoxy, these views were bound to elicit censure – and they did. Before I discuss the criticism raised against Abelard's views I must alert the reader to one obvious advantage – or drawback (depending on your theological stance).

The implication of Abelard's views is that it allows him to claim that philosophers of antiquity already witnessed to the doctrine of the Trinity. This, in turn, provides him with a powerful justification for his own engagement with philosophy as a legitimate intellectual pursuit as a Christian. Indeed, the final chapter of *TSB* III. 5 drives home the universality of the knowledge of the Trinitarian God in an explicit manner: "Saying that God is Father, Son, and Holy Spirit means the same as saying that God is powerful, wise, and good. Because no sound person, be it Jew or Gentile, disputes this, it seems that this faith [in the Trinity] is shared by all."[29] Abelard discusses the scriptural witness as well as those philosophical writings (mainly Plato's *Timaeus*) that support the belief in a powerful, wise and good God.[30] Indeed, Abelard goes to great lengths to interpret Plato's discussion of the soul of the world in line with the Christian views on the Holy Spirit – despite some obvious difficulties.[31] This strategy allows Abelard to claim that "the differentiation within the divine Trinity has not been first disclosed by Christ, although he taught it with clarity and openness. For divine inspiration has revealed it through the Jewish prophets and Gentile philosophers . . . so as to entice them to the worship of the one God."[32]

In the second book Abelard draws on philosophical arguments – more specifically arguments from dialectics, one of the disciplines of the *trivium* – to

---

[28] See *TSB* III.2.

[29] *TSB* III.5. See *Comm. on Rom.* 1.19–20. Knowledge of the Holy Trinity is accessible "without recourse to the Scriptures through natural reason" (*etiam sine scripto per naturalem rationem manifestum*). Roger Bacon was to entertain similar ideas in the 13th century.

[30] *TSB* I.5.

[31] In *Timaeus* 37a Plato suggested that the soul of the world (*anima mundi*) was created in time. Abelard solves this difficulty by arguing that while the Holy Spirit is eternal and uncreated, the effects of the Holy Spirit are created (*TSB* III.4). In other words, by interpreting Plato's views on the creation of the soul of the world in terms of the created effects of the Holy Spirit Abelard can continue to identify Holy Spirit and the Platonic soul of the world.

[32] *TSB* I.2 (p. 8).

refute those "false dialecticians" who attack faith in the Trinity, thus combating them with their own weapons.[33] More particularly, he addresses the central issue in Trinitarian theology: how can we square the belief in the oneness of God with the belief in three Persons?

TSB II.2 lists a range of objections against the Trinitarian understanding of God. A detailed discussion of these objections would be both tedious and repetitive. Most can be summarized as follows. "If God is one in his substance, is he not also one in his Persons? Or, if he is triune (*trinus*) in his Persons, is he then not also triune in his substance?"[34] In short: how can sameness (in the divine substance) be reconciled with difference (amongst the Persons)?

Abelard describes the difference of Persons in terms of a difference in definition or property. The following quotation encapsulates some of Abelard's key insights. Discussing the divine substance, which is the *same* in the three divine Persons, he explains the meaning of sameness in the Trinity:

> The same, I mean, in relation to the essence (*essentialiter*), in the manner the substance of a heavy dagger and a short sword is the same, or the substance of this human being and this animal. Nonetheless, the Persons (i.e., the Father, Son, and Holy Spirit) are different (*diversa*) from one another in the same way that things differ according to their definition. Indeed, although the essence which the Father is, is the same as that which the Son and the Holy Spirit are, nonetheless the property (*proprium*) of the Father, insofar as he is Father, differs from that of the Son, or from that of the Holy Spirit. For the Father is named "Father" because he is powerful; the Son is named "Son" because he has the power to discern (*potens discernere*); and the Holy Spirit is thus called because he is good. The property of the Father consists in being powerful; that of the Son in being wise; and that of the Holy Spirit in being good.[35]

Let me unpack this quotation. The last sentence illustrates the point made earlier – namely, that Abelard treats power, wisdom and goodness as relative or personal names. Instead of saying that powerfulness is being attributed to the First Person because he is Father (and origin of the Trinity), Abelard turns it around: the First Person is called "Father" because he is powerful (*pater ex eo tantum dicatur quod potens est*). The quotation also makes clear that the Persons differ from one another in their definition or property but are otherwise the same. In order to clarify this, Abelard provides us with two analogies. In both cases (short sword and

---

[33] *TSB* II, prol. Abelard may be using a standard rhetorical device to make a case for his own use of dialectics. Or perhaps he has in mind the Trinitarian views of Roscelin.

[34] *TSB* II.2 (p. 98).   [35] *TSB* II.4 (p. 142).

dagger; an individual human being and that animal) we are dealing with things that are the same but differ nonetheless in their definition. In Henry the human being and the animal nature coincide in reality. Nonetheless, the definitions of Henry as a human being and as animal differ. The difference between human beings and animals is their *differentia* – that is, the property (such as "rationality") that together with a genus ("animal") constitutes a species ("humans").[36]

Bernard of Clairvaux was to take grave exception at this analogy, which Augustine before him had considered inadequate.[37] In his view the comparison between the divine substance and the Persons on one hand and genus and species on the other is totally inappropriate. He argues that genus has precedence over species, while there is no hierarchy in God. It is clear that St. Bernard took Abelard's comparison at face value. Now, first of all, Abelard is very much aware that these are mere analogies (*aliqua similitudine*), and that words, when applied to God, change in meaning.[38] Moreover, Abelard tried to make clear how we can coherently speak of the difference between Persons while upholding the claim that the three Persons are one and the same divinity. He was not trying to imply some kind of hierarchy between the divine unity and the Persons, as between genus and species.

Abelard tried to make clear that the definitions of the three Persons differ because they have different properties – namely, power, wisdom and goodness.[39] They are therefore distinct, but this distinctness does not rule out divine oneness. Another analogy Abelard develops is that between a wax statue and the wax out of which this statue is made. They are numerically the same thing, but the wax and the waxen statue have different properties.[40] Just as a wax image is wax, yet one cannot identify the image with the wax, so the Son is distinct from the Father. Again, this

---

[36] Humans (= species) are rational (= differentiating property) animals (= genus). In Abelard's view the animal nature of the human individual never exists in separation from its instantiation in individual animals, such as a particular human being (e.g., Henry). See *TSB* III.2 (p. 204).

[37] See St. Augustine, *De Trin.* VII.II.

[38] *TSB* II.3 (p. 120). See also *Comm. on Rom.* I.20: *per similitudinem corporalium rerum* (through an analogy or comparison with corporeal things).

[39] *TSB* II.4 (p. 146).

[40] As Jeffrey E. Brower explains, the property of the waxen image is "being made from wax." The property of wax is different. It is "being the wax from which something is made." In this way Abelard can show that "the subject of the first property is distinct from the subject of the second property, even if their subjects are the same in essence." See Jeffrey E. Brower, "Trinity," in *The Cambridge Companion to Abelard*, edited by Jeffrey E. Brower and Kevin Guilfoy (Cambridge: Cambridge University Press, 2004), 246. In *Comm. on Rom.* I.20 he develops the analogy of the bronze statue.

analogy should not be taken to imply any kind of modalism – although it must be admitted that Abelard occasionally pushes the analogy too far.[41]

William of St. Thierry (d. 1148), to be discussed soon, alerted Bernard of Clairvaux to some of the more problematic aspects of Abelard's theology. Both wrote a number of texts in which they singled out some of the more controversial passages from Abelard's writings (or those attributed to him), often without paying due attention to the context. The most famous piece is Bernard's *Letter* 190 to Pope Innocent II, also known as *The Treatise on the Errors of Abelard*. The outcome of Bernard's actions was condemnation of Abelard at the Councils of Soissons (1121), more censure during the Council of Sens and, finally, condemnation by Pope Innocent II shortly before Abelard's death.

I have already alluded to some of Bernard's criticism. In general he takes exception to the rationalistic approach of Peter Abelard, who wants to grasp the most profound mysteries through reason. Bernard considers Abelard's appeal to gentile sources utterly unconvincing: "While he is exerting himself to turn Plato into a Christian, he only proves that he himself is a pagan."[42] Bernard also makes a number of more specific points. The main one centers on treating "Power," "Wisdom" and "Goodness" as personal names – an issue William of St. Thierry had also raised in his own *Disputation against Abelard*.[43] Bernard argues that Abelard's view, which teaches "that omnipotence in the proper sense belongs to the Father exclusively, and Wisdom to the Son ... is false. For the Father, too, is truly Wisdom, and the Son, too, is truly Power ... What is common to both cannot be the distinct property of one of them" (*quod est commune amborum, non erit proprium singulorum*).[44] If the Father is Power in a personal way, does this imply that the Son only has some power (as Wisdom, or the power to discern) and the Holy Spirit none at all? In

[41] Abelard suggests that as an individual man (e.g., Jack Sparrow) is derived from animality, or a waxen statue from wax, and not conversely, so too Wisdom is derived from Power, but not the other way around. Wisdom implies Power (i.e., the Power to discern) but not the other way around (*sed non e converse*; cf. *TSB* iii.2, 208). This makes perfect sense if you accept with Abelard that Power and Wisdom are personal names. It does raise the question, however, whether he can still hold that the Father is wise in his own right, or whether the Son is omnipotent. The last point was taken up by St. Bernard, who sarcastically wrote that for Abelard, the Father is omnipotent, the Son is semi-potent and the Holy Spirit is impotent. See Bernard of Clairvaux's criticism of Peter Abelard in *Tractatus de Erroribus Abaelardi*, chapter 3 (effectively *Letter* 190 addressed to Pope Innocent II).
[42] *Tractatus de Erroribus Abaelardi*, chapter 4, no. 9.
[43] See William of St. Thierry, *Disputation against Abelard* 2, *PL* 180:250A–B. William will return to this topic in his insightful (and very Augustinian) book *The Enigma of Faith*, nos. 49–50. John Anderson translated the work as *William of St. Thierry: The Enigma of Faith* (Kalamazoo, MI: Cistercian Publications, 1973).
[44] *Tractatus de Erroribus Abaelardi*, ch. 3 no. 5 (1058D).

Bernard's estimation, this smacks of Arianism. We have already seen that Bernard, quoting Abelard out of context, takes issue with the analogy of genus and species to describe the relation between God's unity and the three Persons.

Bernard also criticizes Abelard's definition of faith. Abelard had defined faith as "a judgement (*existimatio*) of things not seen."[45] St. Bernard had misinterpreted Abelard, supposing that, for Abelard, faith is a mere matter of opinion with no solid basis in reality to support its truth claims, "as if everyone is at liberty to think and say [on the truths of Christian faith] whatever they please, and as if the edifying truths of our religion would somehow float around between different vague opinions, instead of being firmly based on the certainty of truth."[46] The key text for Bernard is the Letter to Hebrews 11:1, which he considers a definition of faith: "the substance of things hoped for, the evidence (*argumentum*) of things not seen." In Bernard's view, Abelard was undermining the certainty of faith, reducing it to mere speculation. Thus, Bernard did not simply take issue with the rationalism of Abelard; he also questioned the erosive and relativizing effect of Abelard's stance. Abelard's views represent those of the academics, "who doubt everything but do not know anything" (*Academicorum sint istae aestimationes, quorum est dubitare de omnibus, scire nihil*).[47] On this score too Bernard's criticism is unfair. As Marcia Colish has argued, the word *existimare* is used in Romans to denote firmly held convictions (such as in Rom. 8:18), and to interpret it (as Bernard does) in terms of wavering opinions is incorrect.[48] Thus, Abelard's *existimatio* can be translated in English as "conviction" rather than "opinion."[49]

Again, Bernard takes issue with Abelard's soteriology, arguing that he reduces the salvation Our Lord effected to nothing but a good example we are called to imitate.[50] Here Bernard accuses Abelard of Pelagian tendencies: if Christ only set a good example, but did not really effect our salvation, the onus remains on ourselves to procure our salvation. While some scholars celebrate Abelard as a supposedly attractive alternative to the alleged transactionalism of Anselm, we have already indicated that Abelard too accepts an objective aspect in our salvation. Once more, Bernard's critique of this issue is therefore to be treated with caution.

---

[45] *Theologia Scholarium* 1.2.
[46] Bernard of Clairvaux, *Letter* 190, known as *Disp. Adversus Abaelardum* (my trans.).
[47] *Disp. Adversus Abaelardum*, cap. 4.
[48] Marcia Colish, *Peter Lombard* (Leiden: Brill, 1994), 494.   [49] Ibid.
[50] *Tractatus de Erroribus Abaelardi*, chapters 5–9.

I have mentioned Bernard of Clairvaux and William of St. Thierry as critics of Abelard. It is now time to examine their contribution in its own right. Bernard's skepticism toward "academics" suggests that when engaging with their writings we will encounter a different climate, one in which theology is more monastic and spiritual than dialectical.

BERNARD OF CLAIRVAUX

Perhaps every Christian theologian is a theologian of love – but none more so than Bernard of Clairvaux. Bernard entered the Cistercian monastery of Cîteaux (near Dijon) at the age of twenty-three, together with some thirty relatives (Bernard did not like half measures). Cîteaux had been founded by Robert of Molesme in 1098, his aim being to renew the Benedictine rule and inspiration. After the entrance of Bernard in Cîteaux the monastery began to flourish. Within three years Bernard was sent to found a new monastery at Clairvaux. From it many dependent monasteries originated – some 360 by the time of the death of Bernard in 1153. There were foundations from Ireland (e.g., Mellifont) to Poland, from Scandinavia to Spain. But under the inspiration of Bernard, the Cistercian movement was also the source of a school of spirituality that gained an immense popularity in its own time and has had a continuing influence on Christian spirituality down through the centuries. Through his prestige and the power of his order, Bernard grew extremely influential, which can be illustrated by the fact that he effectively determined the election of one of his pupils to the papacy as Eugene III in 1145. Bernard almost single-handedly brought about the condemnation of Peter Abelard. He was also a major influence in the organization and propagation of the second crusade.

Bernard's most important work is *86 Sermons on the Song of Songs*. In these *Sermons* Bernard developed in an original manner the three traditional stages of spiritual progress. He describes, first, a purification or penitential preparation, symbolized by the kiss of the feet of our Lord. Second, there is illumination and the practice of virtue, symbolized by the kiss of the hands. Finally, we reach contemplation and union with the divine lover: the kiss of the mouth. Other important works are *On Consideration*, written for Eugene III, and an early treatise *On Grace and Free Choice*. I would like to focus, however, on a short work – namely, *On Loving God (De Diligendo Deo)*.[51]

---

[51] I have used the following translations: *Bernard of Clairvaux: Selected Works*, trans. Gillian R. Evans, intro. by Jean Leclercq. Classics of Western Spirituality (New York: Paulist Press, 1987); Bernard of

In *On Loving God* VII.18–22, Bernard writes that nothing finite can satisfy human desire. In colorful and existentially appealing language Bernard describes how human desire wanders in vain from one momentary satisfaction to another, exhausting itself without finding fulfillment. We remain constantly more dissatisfied because of what eludes us than satisfied with what we possess. Even that which we have acquired with lots of toil we will lose one day; even if our insatiable desire could possess the whole world but God, boredom will eventually overwhelm us. We walk in circles, wanting whatever will satisfy our desires, yet foolishly rejecting that which would lead us to our true end, "which is not in consumption but in consummation."[52] In order to escape this vicious circle we need to refocus our desire on God. Only this will secure our true fulfillment or consummation. Bernard raises the question of "why and how God should be loved."[53] He answers that God himself is the reason why he is to be loved. And he should be loved "without measure" (*sine modo*).[54] To explain this in more detail Bernard distinguishes between four kinds or degrees of love, based on the object and the fundamental orientation or motivation of our love. First, we love ourselves for our sakes. This is natural self-love. Bernard calls this love "carnal." It is exactly its carnal character that allows the Incarnate Word to draw it out of its self-centered orientation. This, as we will see, is one of Bernard's key insights: the Incarnation appeals to our carnal nature and forms the foundation of our transformation.[55] With "carnal" love we are preoccupied with the satisfaction of our immediate needs and the needs of those around us: "carnal" love can be extended to others and thus become social.[56]

When we learn to love that we receive many good things from God, we learn to love God for our own benefit. This is the second degree of love. Here we love God for our own advantage, but not yet for God's own sake.[57]

In the third degree we love God for God's sake. Our love becomes gratuitous and free, seeking nothing in return. We simply love God, not because God is good to us, but because God is good. This, however, is not the climax of our transformation. In the final degree, which Bernard

---

Clairvaux, *On Loving God* (Kalamazoo, MI: Cistercian Publications, 1995); Bernard of Clairvaux, *On the Song of Songs*, vols. I–IV (Kalamazoo, MI: Cistercian Publications, 1971–80). A good commentary with secondary literature can be found in Bernard McGinn, *The Presence of God: A History of Western Christian Mysticism, vol.* II: *The Growth of Mysticism* (London: SCM, 1994), 162–224.

[52] *On Loving God* VII.19, p. 22.   [53] Ibid., VIII.23, p. 25.   [54] Ibid., VIII.23.

[55] See, for instance, *Sermon on the Song of Songs* 6.3. The same theme can be found in *Sermon* 20.6–9. For commentary and literature, see McGinn, *The Growth of Mysticism*, 167–68, 175–77.

[56] *On Loving God* VIII, 23–25.   [57] Ibid., IX, 26.

suggests would normally only be achieved in the afterlife, we love ourselves for the sake of God.[58] Here we have attained a disposition of utter selflessness and radical theocentricity. Even the way we relate to ourselves is now determined by the way we relate to God.

Bernard attached a letter, originally addressed to Carthusian monks, to the treatise. In it he describes the transformation of our love for God by drawing on ancient metaphors (inspired by John Cassian) of slave, hireling and son. The slave does God's works out of fear; the hireling fulfills God's will out of self-interest and lust for reward. Bernard perceptively characterizes them: "The slave and the mercenary have a law of their own which is not from the Lord. The former does not love God and the latter loves something more than God."[59] The sons, in contrast, have genuine charity, loving God for his own sake. Theirs is true freedom of spirit and gratuitous love. In the *Sermons on the Song of Songs* 83.4 Bernard captures the nature of gratuitous love best: "[It] is its own merit, its own reward. Love has no cause or fruit beyond itself: its fruit is its use. I love because I love. I love that I may love." Few medieval authors have described the gratuitousness of love of God as beautifully as St. Bernard.

We have already alluded to the theme – so influential in the theology and piety after him – of Christ's carnal nature in our conversion. Bernard develops this idea in a number of his *Sermons on the Song of Songs*. As a fallen race, we are engrossed in the bodily, material world. Therefore, salvation is impossible unless God takes on a body: "He offered his flesh to those who knew flesh so that through it they might come to know the spirit too."[60] God, in the Person of the Word or the Son, takes on our fallen fleshly condition in order to free us from imprisonment and restore the original human possibility of attaining the spiritual through what is bodily. In a sense we are being seduced: because of the Fall, we are now inclined toward material, bodily things rather than spiritual things. This explains why it was necessary for God to assume a bodily nature in Christ. This is perhaps Bernard's most original innovation: he puts a strong emphasis on the necessity of the carnal starting place for our appropriation of saving grace. Therefore, in his sermons Bernard links our transformation and deification to the various mysteries of Christ's life.

This "carnal" starting point should help us rise from a carnal to a mature spiritual love. This mature spiritual love is linked with Christ's spirit – as in his resurrection and ascension. By attending, by being focused on the life, death and resurrection of Christ, the believer

---

[58] Ibid., x, 29.   [59] Ibid., xiii, 36, p. 37.   [60] *Sermon on the Song of Songs* 6.3.

will be gradually transformed. Thus, there is a link between Christ's life, death and resurrection and our own spiritual progress. (a) The Incarnation is a "carnal" or fleshly starting point: here we are attracted with carnal love to the flesh of the God-man (this is the most basic level of human attraction). (b) Passion: we begin to love his spirit (in a carnal way) when we are struck with sorrow at the remembrance of his death for our sake. (c) Resurrection and Ascension: we love the spirit of Christ spiritually when we become one with him in his resurrection and ascension (the events through which his flesh becomes spiritual). Thus, we too have to "ascend" to heaven (in a figurative manner) through our incorporation in Christ. This means a turning away from sin and a radical love for God. This is more than following a moral example; it is becoming incorporated in the Body of Christ, his life and death. This is the heart of St. Bernard's Christology: "No one ascends to heaven save he who descended from heaven (John 3:13) – the one and the same Lord is both Bridegroom as Head and Bride as Body."[61] Because we become part of the Body of Christ through participation in the Christian life and community, we share in Christ's rewards.

I would like to conclude my discussion of St. Bernard with some brief comments. First, Bernard's mysticism is not individualistic but communal. When Bernard talks of the relation between the Bridegroom and the Bride, the Bride is not in the first place the individual soul but rather the believer as member of the wider Church. Similarly, when Bernard refers to "experience," he does not have in mind a psychological, privatized experience (inner states of feeling, or a person's interiority); he has in mind a personal appropriation and existential embodiment of the communal faith, deeply connected with Christian faith and liturgy.

Second, union with God does not mean that we have a direct, immediate, unmediated contact with God. Although Bernard is often understood in this way we should understand "union with God" and "divine presence" in terms of intention, in particular a loving intention or focus: "A person is present to God to the extent that the person loves him."[62] The more we are able to love God, the more he is present to us. Union with God means a perfect union of wills and never involves any form of identity with God. Bernard states clearly that union with God is always mediated.

Third, this "mediated" character by its very nature implies a dialectic of yearning and lack of final fulfillment. We will always long for God in this life

---

[61] Ibid., 27.7.

[62] *Liber de Praecepto et Dispensatione* 19.60; quoted by McGinn, *The Growth of Mysticism*, 190.

because we never fully attain union with God. The partial loving union we attain only inflames our desire even further. Our desire for God will never find compete fulfillment in this life. It is this desire for God that permeates Bernard's writings; and this is perhaps one of the reasons why Dante considered him the greatest contemplative, the one who was to lead Dante to the vision of the Holy Trinity in his *Divine Comedy* (*Paradiso, canto.* 31ff.).

WILLIAM OF ST. THIERRY

William was born in Liége sometime in the final quarter of the 11th century. The details of his life are sketchy. We know he became abbot of the Benedictine monastery of St. Thierry near Reims. He was, however, attracted by Bernard of Clairvaux's reform movement, and he joined the Cistercian abbey of Signy (in the Ardennes). He was a close friend of Bernard, and perhaps the greater theologian of the two. Some of his works were handed down throughout the centuries under Bernard's name – despite the distinctive nature and originality of some of William's insights.

Apart from a *Disputation against Abelard,* he wrote a number of relatively short but attractive mystical theological treatises, such as *Meditations, The Nature and Dignity of Love, The Mirror of Faith* and *The Enigma of Faith,* as well as the somewhat longer *Expositions on the Song of Songs* and *On Romans.* His most influential work was the so-called *Golden Epistle,* a letter or treatise written for the Brothers of Mont Dieu, a Carthusian house near Reims. William died in 1148.

An in-depth overview of William's mystical theology is beyond the confines of this chapter. In what follows I mainly focus on those aspects of his doctrine that stand in sharp contrast with those of Peter Abelard (as interpreted by William) but that nonetheless bring out William's own contribution. I largely concentrate on *The Enigma of Faith* and *The Mirror of Faith* to outline his views on the relation between faith, reason and desire, and the Trinitarian foundation of these views.

The Enigma of Faith is deeply indebted to Augustine's *De Trinitate* and summarizes some of its key teachings on Trinitarian theology. In his *Disputation against Abelard* 2 (*PL* 180:250A–B), William had criticized Abelard for treating power, wisdom and goodness (or love) as personal names for the Father, Son and Holy Spirit, respectively. He reiterates the point in *The Enigma of Faith.*[63] William also raises some interesting issues on

---

[63] The appropriation or attribution of Power, Wisdom and Goodness to the Father, Son and Holy Spirit respectively is "done for distinction of person that they may be distinguished not that they

the relation between faith and reason. Clearly this is one of the areas in which he considered his position radically different from Abelard's.

In William's opinion, reason should be subordinated to faith. For him too theology is faith seeking understanding. Quoting Isaiah 7:9 (in Vulgate) — "Unless you believe you will not understand" — he writes that the person who believes by loving may deserve to understand what he believes.[64] Reason can only come to proper fruition when it is enriched by faith and desire for God. In a scarcely veiled reference to Abelard, William castigates "the proud and puffed-up person" who comes to the door of faith and instead of entering, begins to dispute with the doorkeeper about the rules of admission — only to find the door slammed in his face.[65] This does not mean, however, that William endorses an anti-intellectualist stance. He acknowledges that very few people will submit to the teachings of the Christian faith with an utterly simple and unquestioning mind. Most people will want to grow in understanding the faith.[66] Far from downplaying reason, William exalts it, as long as it does not attempt to acquire an unsustainable autonomy. "Let man consider that there is nothing in his nature which is better than his own intellect by which he desires to understand God."[67] For William, intellect (*intellectus*) is closely linked with desire and love, as this quotation makes clear — and this kind of desiring intellect is the highest aspect of human nature (*nil in natura sua esse melius*). For William (somewhat misquoting Gregory the Great), love itself is a kind of understanding.[68] As he writes in the *Exposition on the Song of Songs*: "Love of God itself is knowledge of him; unless he is loved, he is not known, and unless he is known, he is not loved."[69] Again, reason and love, the two eyes of the contemplative mind, should become one:

Contemplation has two eyes, reason and love . . . And when they are illumined by grace, they are of mutual assistance, because love gives life to reason and reason gives light to love. . . . Often when these two eyes faithfully cooperate, they become

---

may be separated. Except for relative names by which the Father, Son and Holy Spirit are spoken of in relation to one another and which are individual and proper to a single person, by whatever name one of the persons is designated, they are all likewise designated, because they are all one in that by which they are named" (*Enigma* no. 49, p. 82). If Wisdom were a personal name of the Son (as Abelard has it), then the Father could only be wise through the Son, but then "the Son would not be so much the Son of the Father as his essence" (*Enigma* no. 50, pp. 82–83) — and this is the Sabellian heresy.

[64] William of St. Thierry, *The Mirror of Faith*, translation by Thomas Davis (Kalamazoo, MI: Cistercian Publications, 1979), no. 9.

[65] *Mirror* no. 6. [66] *Mirror* no. 16. [67] *Enigma* no.18, p. 50.

[68] In *Adv. Abl.* II (PL 252C) William writes: *amor ipse intellectus est*. In *Hom. Ev.* 27.4 Gregory had written: *amor ipse notitia est*.

[69] *Exposition on Song of Songs* (Kalamazoo, MI: Cistercian Publications, 1968) no. 76, p. 64.

one; in the contemplation of God, where love is chiefly operative, reason passes into love and is transformed into a certain spiritual and divine understanding which transcends and absorbs all reason.[70]

The intellect that desires God and freely subjects itself to faith culminates in a loving contemplation: "the understanding of one thinking (*intellectus cogitantis*) becomes the contemplation of one loving" (*contemplatio amantis*).[71] Few authors have written so eloquently about the interpenetration of love, faith and knowledge. However, William gives his teachings on the necessity of faith and the relation between faith and reason a Trinitarian basis. It is here that he makes his most interesting contribution.

William's key point against the perceived rationalism of Abelard is this: unless we have faith and love, which themselves are a participation of the Holy Spirit in us, we cannot relate to the mysteries of the Triune God. For William, vision implies participation. Unless we share in the Holy Spirit, the common bond between Father and Son, we cannot know and love the triune God:

The Father and the Son reveal this to certain persons then, to those to whom they will, to those to whom they make it known, that is, to whom they impart the Holy Spirit who is common knowing or the common will of both. Those therefore to whom the Father and the Son reveal [themselves] recognise them as the Father and the Son recognise themselves, because they have within themselves their mutual knowing, because they have within themselves the unity of both, and their will and love: all that the Holy Spirit is.[72]

Unless we participate in the Holy Spirit (the bond of knowledge and love between Father and Son), we will not be able to know and love the Triune God. We can only know and love God with a love and knowledge bestowed to us through the indwelling of the Holy Spirit. This is why Abelard's alleged rationalism (and his claim that pagan philosophers had knowledge of the Triune God) is so mistaken. The fact that the Holy Spirit is the bond of both knowledge and love also explains why William insists that both intellect and love are necessary in our union with God. The intimate union or perichoresis of intellect and love reflects the mutual indwelling of the divine Persons within the Trinity.

---

[70] Ibid., no. 92, trans. Mother Columba Hart, 74. See also *The Nature and Dignity of Love* no. 21.

[71] *The Golden Epistle* no. 249, trans. Theodore Berkeley (Kalamazoo, MI: Cistercian Publications, 1971), 92.

[72] *Mirror* no. 31, pp. 75–76.

BIBLIOGRAPHICAL NOTE

Peter Abelard

The Latin text of *Theologia Christiana* is available in *CCCM*, vol. xii (Turnhout: Brepols, 1969); for *Theologia Scholarium* and *Theologia Summi Boni*, see *CCCM*, vol. xiii (Turnhout: Brepols, 1987).

For an English translation of *Scito te ipsum*, as well as the *Dialogue*, see Paul Vincent Spade (trans.), *Peter Abelard: Ethical Writings. His Ethics or "Know Yourself" and His Dialogue between a Philosopher, a Jew, and a Christian* (Indianapolis, IN: Hackett, 1995). Steven R. Cartwright translated the *Commentary on the Epistle to the Romans* in The Fathers of the Church. Mediaeval Continuation Series. Vol. 12 (Washington, DC: Catholic University of America Press, 2011).

There are a number of excellent overviews of Peter Abelard's thought. See John Marenbon, *The Philosophy of Peter Abelard* (Cambridge: Cambridge University Press, 1997); Constant Mews, *Abelard and Heloise* (Oxford: Oxford University Press, 2005).

William of St. Thierry

The reader will find the most important spiritual treatises of William in the Sources Chrétiennes Series (Latin-French translation). All the works by William I have mentioned have been translated in the Cistercian Fathers Series: *The Golden Epistle* (Kalamazoo, MI: Cistercian Publications, 1971); *The Mirror of Faith* (Kalamazoo, MI: Cistercian Publications, 1979); *The Enigma of Faith* (Kalamazoo, MI: Cistercian Publications, 1973); *The Nature and Dignity of Love* (Kalamazoo, MI: Cistercian Publications, 1981); *Exposition on The Song of Songs* (Kalamazoo, MI: Cistercian Publications, 1968). The Latin text of several of his treatises has been published in the Sources Chrétiennes series. In English, a concise but very useful overview of his thought (especially his mystical theology), with many references to secondary literature, is Bernard McGinn, *The Presence of God: A History of Western Christian Mysticism, vol. II: The Growth of Mysticism: From Gregory the Great to the Twelfth Century* (London: SCM Press, 1995), 225–74. Also useful is the short chapter in Anne Hunt, *The Trinity: Insights from the Mystics* (Collegeville, MN: Liturgical Press, 2010), 1–22. For a more comprehensive overview, see F. Tyler Sergent (ed.), *A Companion to William of Saint Thierry* (Leiden: Brill, 2019).

Bernard of Clairvaux

The complete works are available in *Sancti Bernardi Opera*, 8 vols., ed. Jean Leclercq, C. H. Talbot and Henri Rochais (Rome: Editiones Cistercienses, 1957). Online: Bernard of Clairvaux's works are available at: www.binetti.ru/bernardus. See also the relevant volumes from the Sources Chrétiennes series (Latin-French translation).

Bernard's main works have been translated in the Cistercian Fathers series, including his *Sermons on the Song of Songs*, 4 vols. (Kalamazoo, MI: Cistercian Publications, 1971–80) and *On Loving God*, trans. Emero Stiegman (Kalamazoo, MI: Cistercian Publications, 1995).

For secondary literature, see Bernard McGinn, *The Growth of Mysticism*, 158–224 and Brian Patrick McGuire (ed.), *A Companion to Bernard of Clairvaux* (Leiden: Brill, 2011).

CHAPTER 9

Hugh of St. Victor

BIOGRAPHICAL BACKGROUND AND CONTEXT

Our knowledge of Hugh's life is fairly limited. We do not know where Hugh was born – he may have been of Saxon descent or (less likely) of Flemish origin. He was born at the end of the 11th century and died on February 11, 1141. Hugh was the main theologian of the Augustinian school of St. Victor near Paris, founded by William of Champeaux, the teacher and adversary of Peter Abelard. While Peter Abelard claimed in his *Historia* that William withdrew into St. Victor after his views on universals had been exposed as untenable, a more charitable reading would suggest that William's withdrawal was not so much in response to Abelard's challenge as perhaps an expression of the desire to recapture the ideals of monasticism in the world of new learning. The canons regularly attempted to combine the new world of scholarship with a traditional communal life of prayer. This ideal also found expression in their spirituality. Hugh, too will attempt to harmonize the rationalism of Abelard with the monastic devotion of Bernard. Thanks to Hugh, the abbey of St. Victor became an important center of learning. A letter of recommendation, written in 1136 by St. Bernard on behalf of Peter Lombard, suggests that the future author of *The Sentences* visited St. Victor; he probably studied with Hugh. Other students include Petrus Comestor (who proved an immediate source for Ruusbroec's *The Spiritual Tabernacle*) and, of course, Richard of St. Victor, whose original theology of the Trinity I discuss later.

Hugh is credited with having produced the first major summary of medieval theology, his so-called *De Sacramentis Christiane Fidei* (*The Sacraments of the Christian Faith*), and an influential "pedagogical" work, *Didascalicon de Studio Legendi*. Hugh also wrote a number of texts associated with spirituality, such as the so-called Ark-treatises (*De Archa Noe*, *Libellus de Formatione Arche* and *De Vanitate Mundi*), as well as an extended *Commentary on the Celestial Hierarchy* by Pseudo-Dionysius, thereby contributing to the renewed interest in the Pseudo-Dionysian corpus during the second half of the 12th century and beyond. A final work, a brief *Soliloquy*, a dialogue between a person and his soul, brings the mystical bent of Hugh's oeuvre into prominence.

In what follows I deal with his views on pedagogy, the sacraments and the theological virtues of faith and love. I, however, begin with a discussion of an early work, *De Tribus Diebus Invisibilis Lucis* (*The Three Days of the Invisible Light*).

DE TRIBUS DIEBUS AND THE SACRAMENTAL UNDERSTANDING OF CREATION

De Tribus Diebus offers a highly attractive introduction to Hugh's theological and spiritual thought, especially to his views on the role of beauty in theology. The "Three Days" mentioned in the title of the treatise refer to fear of the Lord (in response to God's Power), truth (in response to God's Wisdom) and love (in response to God's Goodness) (*DTD* 26).[1] God's Power, Wisdom and Goodness (*benignitas*) must of course be understood in a Trinitarian way, and are appropriated to Father, Son and Holy Spirit respectively. In *De Tribus Diebus* Hugh does not explicitly state that this is a case of appropriation. In *De Sacramentis*, written after the condemnation of Peter Abelard at Soissons, he was to make the point explicitly.[2]

The immensity of things reveals the divine Power, while the beauty (*decor*) of creatures manifests divine Wisdom, and their usefulness (*utilitas*) reflects the divine Goodness (*DTD* 16). Hugh pays particular attention to the beauty of the created world, which reveals the divine Wisdom. Few medieval theologians, with the exception of Eriugena and Bonaventure, have spoken so eloquently of the sacramental nature of the created world:

This entire sensible world is like a book written by the finger of God, that is, created by divine might. Individual creatures are like shapes that are not the product of human design, but they are invested by God to manifest and, in a way, to signify his invisible Wisdom. Imagine an illiterate person who looks at an open book: he will see shapes but will not understand the written letters. Similarly, the foolish and sensual person does not perceive the things that are of God (1 Cor. 2:14); he will look at visible creatures as merely external appearances

---

[1] All references are to the chapters in the critical edition by Dominique Poirel (ed.), *De Tribus Diebus, CCCM 177* (Turnhout: Brepols, 2002), 3–70.

[2] In *De Sacr.* 1.3.26, Hugh is careful to stress that the three Persons are powerful, wise and good on account of their shared divine nature. It is a case of appropriation (the word he uses in *De Sacr.* 1.3.25 is *attribuitur*).

but he will not be able to understand their meaning. The spiritual person, on the other hand, who can judge all things (1 Cor. 2:15), knows, when contemplating the external beauty (*pulcritudo*) of things, how to admire in this the inner Wisdom of the Creator. (*DTD* 4)

In a number of highly lyrical passages Hugh speaks of "the artwork of the universe" (*machina uniuersitatis*), praising the astonishing beauty, harmony and diversity of our created universe (*DTD* 4–13). It is especially beauty that draws the mind to God. While the immensity of creation relates first and foremost to the sheer existence or being of things, beauty is related to the form of created things.[3] He explains why:

Existence (*essentia*) as such, without form (*absque forma*), can be characterized as a kind of formlessness. That which exists without form, resembles God insofar as it exists, but it differs from God insofar as it lacks form. That which has form bears a greater resemblance to God than that which is lacking in form. From this it follows that the beauty of created things, which is closely related to their forms, better discloses God than the immensity of created beings, which only relates to their existence. (*DTD* 16)

Similarly, beauty surpasses usefulness in its revelatory character. Usefulness, Hugh writes, has to do with fulfilling a function (*utilitas uero ad actum*). Beauty, on the other hand, relates to the nature (*habitus*) or character of something, which is more essential and abiding than mere function: after all, "the character of a thing is a natural given, while it receives its function only by appointment" (*DTD* 16). In short, the nature or form of a thing is of greater importance than the function it is asked to fulfill. Hugh obviously adopts an anti-instrumentalizing stance, considering the function of something (what it can do) as far less important than what it is (its true nature or form). He summarizes: "This is why, in the acquisition of knowledge, the image (*simulacrum*) of beauty takes precedence over both immensity and usefulness, for it is more radiant in its revelation (*quia est in manifestatione euidentius*)." More than the sheer existence or the usefulness of things, it is their beauty that draws us near to God. The reason why the beauty of the forms of things has the power to draw us near to God is ultimately Christocentric and even Trinitarian: "It is beautifully fitting (*pulcre*) that we begin our quest for wisdom with the image (*simulacrum*) of this Wisdom. For it is through Wisdom that the Father has revealed himself, both when he bestowed fleshly being on his Wisdom, but also when he created the world through his Wisdom" (*DTD*

---

[3] This insight is probably partly inspired by the fact that the classic Latin word *forma* can mean both form and beauty. The words Hugh uses for beauty are *decor* and *pulcritudo*.

16). Thus, the beauty of creation reflects and manifests the Word of God, through whom all things have been made and who himself became Wisdom incarnate, drawing all things to God. Hugh's is a theological perspective that Bonaventure was to adopt enthusiastically.

Amongst all created beings the rational creature discloses the divinity most properly. By following the path of introversion, examining her own spiritual nature, the human person becomes aware that her own immaterial, invisible essence cannot have been created out of matter, "for everything which originates from matter, is necessarily corporeal" (*DTD* 17). Only God, as his own Cause, had the ability to create things out of nothing. Hugh then goes on to argue for God's unity and immutability. He argues that divine perfection implies immutability. Finally, Hugh engages in Trinitarian speculation. Following the Augustinian path of interiority as a way toward God, Hugh, having discerned traces of the Trinity in the human mind, intellect and love, discusses the Father, Son and Holy Spirit.

The arguments he develops in this context are not particularly original. More original are the final pages of the treatise. After the height of contemplation of the Holy Trinity, having moved from creation to the divine Persons, Hugh makes a surprising move: "Let us now return, and through a fitting contemplation of God's Wisdom, go to the rational creature, and then, from the rational creature to the material creation" (*DTD* 25). In returning this way, we follow the order of creation, in which the human person, as God's image, has priority over the rest of creation. The spiritual implications are significant: the Christian who has attained union with Father, Son and Holy Spirit is called to share the delights of this union with others: "If we there have contemplated Power, let us bring down the light of the fear of God; if we there have contemplated Wisdom, let us bring down the light of truth; if we there have contemplated Goodness, let us bring down the light of love" (*DTD* 26). This theme is in turn developed in a Christological manner by drawing an intricate connection between the three days of the invisible light (i.e., fear of the Lord, truth and love) and the *triduum*. As Christ is our example and sacrament (*exemplum et sacramentum*), his death, burial and resurrection become the pattern of our own spiritual death, burial and resurrection. In a stirring conclusion to his treatise Hugh weaves these different strands together:

Power evokes fear, Wisdom enlightens, and Goodness fills us with joy. On the day of Power we die through fear; on the day of Wisdom we are buried far from the noise of this world through contemplation of the Truth; and on the day of Goodness we are being resurrected through love and desire for things eternal. For Christ died on the sixth day; was laid in the tomb on the seventh; and rose on the eighth day. As a consequence, in a similar manner, Power, in its day, will kill worldly desires; Wisdom will bury us in its day in the hidden depth of contemplation; and Goodness, in its day, will resurrect us and raise us to life through desire for divine love. For the sixth day is the day of suffering; the seventh the day of rest; and the eighth day is the day of resurrection. (*DTD* 27)

Didascalicon

The arts had enjoyed a revival under Carolingian rule, as noted in Chapter 5. Medieval authors were familiar with the theoretical reflection on the arts during antiquity, such as the book *On the Arts and Disciplines of the Liberal Letters* by Cassidorius, a pupil of Boethius. In this work Cassidorius deals with grammar, rhetoric and logic (the so-called *trivium*) and arithmetic, astronomy, geometry and music (*quadrivium*). Together these constitute the seven liberal arts. The intellectual climate of the 12th century, with its new preoccupation with nature and cosmology, the discovery of self and human rationality, further constitute the context in which Hugh's early work on pedagogy and the role of the Arts, entitled *Didascalicon*, should be understood.[4]

Hugh's *Didascalicon* is often called a "pedagogical work," which is correct as long as we remember that its philosophical scope is much broader than the modern understanding of this word, in terms of methodology of teaching. In my view it is exactly this more profound understanding of what proper education is about – effectively its transcendental thrust – that makes Hugh's work so alien and yet so revolutionary to us. Thus, in the *Didascalicon* Hugh lists all major scientific areas and how one should embark on their study, as one would expect from a pedagogical work. But it also outlines the focal point of all study: through study of the arts fallen humanity can begin to be restored, share in the Wisdom of God and reestablish union with Him. As Hugh himself puts it:

This, then, is what the Arts are concerned with, this is what they intend, namely, to restore within us the divine likeness, a likeness which to us is a form but to God is

---

[4] Cosmological speculation flowered in the School of Chartres. The main representatives of this school were Bernard of Chartres, William of Conches, Bernardus Silvestris and Gilbert of Poitiers. Especially through an engagement with Plato's *Timaeus* they tried to disclose the inner rationality of the created order.

his nature. The more we are conformed to the divine nature, the more do we possess Wisdom, for then there begins to shine forth again in us what has forever existed in the divine Idea or Pattern (*in ratione*) coming and going in us but standing changeless in God. (*Didasc.* II.I)[5]

The goal of the *Didascalicon* is the restoration in us of the image of the divine Wisdom, the second Person of the Trinitarian Godhead. Through study we share in the Word, the primordial Idea or Pattern of all things, through whom the Father has created all things, and restored after the Fall. This view, which considers study a path toward reunion with God, allows Hugh to locate scientific pursuits in a broader theological framework. The opening sentence of Book I of the *Didascalicon*, inspired by Boethius's *The Consolation of Philosophy* III.10.1:37, reminds the reader of how all our pursuits have a religious thrust: "Of all things to be sought, the first (*prima*) is that Wisdom in which the Form of the Perfect Good stands fixed (*Omnium expetendorum prima est sapientia, in qua perfecti boni forma consistit*)." *Prima* ("the first") does not mean the first in a sequence but it refers, rather, to "the ultimate reason" that motivates all existence.[6]

Hugh would be highly uncomfortable with scientific pursuits that are subjected to the demands of the economy, without any reference to Wisdom and human salvation; and he would also reject the ideal of knowledge for the sake of knowledge. Consider the following passage:

Of all human acts or pursuits, then, governed as these are by Wisdom, the end and the intention ought to regard either the restoring of our nature's integrity, or the relieving of those weaknesses to which our present life lies subject . . . This is our entire task – the restoration of our nature and the removal of our deficiency. (*Didasc.* 1.5)

Pursuing knowledge for the sake of knowledge falls short of his demand that study should be aimed at "the relieving of those weaknesses to which our present life lies subject." A mercenary pursuit of knowledge made subservient to economic demands, without reference to the religious dimension of "the restoration of our integrity," is equally undesirable in Hugh's way of thinking.

Let's now consider in some greater detail Hugh's division of the sciences or arts in the *Didascalicon* and how they are embedded in a theological frame-work. As indicated, given the fallenness of human nature, we need a program of cognitive and moral restoration, assisting us to become re-conformed to

---

[5] I use the translation by Jerome Taylor, *The Didascalicon of Hugh of Saint Victor: A Medieval Guide to the Arts* (New York: Columbia University Press, 1991).

[6] See Ivan Illich, *In the Vineyard of the Text: A Commentary on Hugh's "Didascalicon"* (Chicago: Chicago University Press, 1993), 14.

God's Wisdom. This explains Hugh's broad perspective: it does not merely involve theoretical sciences (*theoretica*); it extends to practical sciences – that is, morality (*practica*) – as well as mechanical arts (*mechanica*) such as hunting, agriculture, even theater and others. Logic (*logica*) serves as an auxiliary science. Thus, Hugh has identified four fields of knowledge: the theoretical, the practical, the mechanical and the logical (*Didasc.* 1.4–5, 8,11). Hugh's incorporation of the mechanical sciences reveals the spirit of a new age, in which non-monastic pursuits such as commerce and theater are positively evaluated.

The mechanical sciences include fabric-making, armament, commerce, agriculture, hunting, medicine and theatrics (*Didasc.* 11.20). How do these pursuits fit in the orientation toward God, which Hugh puts at the heart of his pedagogy? In his view, they contribute to "the relief of the weaknesses to which our present life lies subject," which is one of the two goals identified by Hugh, of human pursuits when governed by Wisdom (the other being the restoration of the integrity of our nature). In that sense rather "mundane" activities such as commerce or theatrics retain an orientation toward the transcendent. Commerce, for example, "reconciles nations, calms wars, strengthens peace, and commutes the private good of individuals into the common benefit of all" (*Didasc.* 11.23). Similarly, Hugh considers theatrics, often scorned by medieval authors, favorably: it offers an entertaining diversion, "refreshing the mind," and assists in keeping us from pursuing morally problematic distractions (*Didasc.* 11.27).

The restoration of the integrity of our nature occurs also through the pursuit of knowledge on one hand, and the attainment of virtue on the other. Hugh therefore distinguishes between theoretical (or speculative) and practical or ethical sciences (*Didasc.* 1.8). Logic, finally, is a foundational discipline as it provides ways of distinguishing between correct and erroneous arguments.

Hugh then goes on to subdivide the theoretical (*theoretica*) in theology, mathematics and physics. Mathematics, in turn, is subdivided into arithmetic, music, geometry and astronomy (*Didasc.* 11.6), which make up the traditional *quadrivium*. The practical is divided into ethical, economics and political. I have already mentioned the subdivisions of the mechanical. Logic, the fourth part, contains grammar and theory of argument, which in turn is further subdivided into dialectic and rhetoric (*Didasc.* 111.1).

Although all the arts tend toward the single end of philosophy (i.e., attainment of and growth in conformity to Wisdom), they each have their own integrity and distinctive approach (*Didasc.* 11.17).

Hugh's vision of the arts as pathways to the divine implies a proper mental discipline or disposition of learning. This discipline is the topic of

Book III of *Didascalicon*. Key to it is humility – that is, the willingness to learn from all sources and, once one has become learned, to avoid the traps of arrogance (*Didasc.* III.13). Other important factors are quiet (both interior and exterior), as well as insistent application to our work.

Books IV to VI mainly deal with how to read the Bible, and a threefold sense of the Scriptures, where Hugh underscores the significance of the historical sense, besides the allegorical and tropological. Some commentators consider the division between the two parts of the *Didascalicon* deeply problematic. It is alleged that the first part of the book – namely, *Didasc.* I to III – is more philosophical, thus reflecting the new, more secular preoccupation with the liberal arts. The second part (Books IV–VI), which treats of the Scriptures and how to read them, would supposedly reflect a more traditional, monastic perspective.

Although there may be a number of tensions, we should refrain from overemphasizing these. First, in the *Prologue* to *De Sacr.*, Hugh points out the usefulness of the *trivium* for a proper understanding of the historical sense (*historia*), and the *quadrivium* for allegory and tropology. This clearly implies that, for Hugh, there is no tension between the pursuit of the arts and engagement with Scripture. Second, we have to be cautious in reading too much into a perceived contrast between Hugh's positive evaluation of philosophy (whereby he relies heavily on authors from antiquity, including some Church Fathers) in the first half, and his negative remarks about the philosophers of his own day. For Augustine, for instance, true philosophy and Christianity are intrinsically linked; indeed, Christianity is the true philosophy. But in his own day, Hugh is confronted with more secular understandings of philosophy (especially dialectics) such as Abelard's, which may sit somewhat more uneasily with the traditional, Augustinian understanding, or indeed Hugh's own. Hugh's *Didascalicon* attempts (in my view successfully) to retrieve the older understanding of philosophy and learning and to apply it in the new context of the 12th century, while at the same time criticizing perceived excesses such as Abelard's. It is in this light that we need to understand his critique of the writings of philosophers in the second part of the *Didascalicon*, or his scathing remarks about those Masters who make a living out of their fees and who attract snobbish students who brag more about the amount of fees they pay than about knowledge acquired (cf. *Didasc.* III.18). Similarly, in *Didasc.* V.8, Hugh admonishes his students to "Study, but do not be preoccupied with it (*Lege, et occupari noli*). Study can be a practice for you; it is not your objective (*sed non propositum*)." This reinforces Hugh's point that the pursuit of knowledge, without reference to the goal of the restoration of fallen humankind, is not desirable. It is mere curiosity (in Augustine's or Bernard's sense of the word).[7] The pursuit of knowledge must lead to a gradual transformation of the human person. It involves not just study or instruction, but also meditation (in Hugh's sense, not in the modern sense), prayer, (moral) action and, finally, contemplation (*Didasc.* v.9). Indeed, the goal of all learning – that is, the restoration of the human person, provides us with a glimpse of eternal bliss, even in this life:

The start of learning, thus, lies in reading, but its consummation lies in meditation; which, if any man will learn to love it very intimately and will desire to be engaged very frequently upon it, renders his life pleasant indeed, and provides the greatest consolation to him in his trials. This especially it is which takes the soul away from the noise of earthly business and makes it have even in this life a kind of foretaste of the sweetness of the eternal quiet. (*Didasc.* III.10)

For Hugh, "Wisdom is a kind of moderator (*moderatrix*) of all human activities" (*Didasc.* 1.4). All human activities should have an orientation toward God. This means that every discipline of learning can be critically questioned: What is this discipline (*quid sit*)? Why should it exist (*quare sit*)? And how (*quomodo*) does it contribute to Hugh's ideals of restoration of the integrity of human nature, or the relieving of those weaknesses to which we are subject?[8]

De Sacramentis

Hugh's most important work is called *De Sacramentis Christianae Fidei* (*The Sacraments of the Christian Faith*).[9] As indicated earlier, it is often hailed as the first theological *summa*. Unlike later *summae*, which present

[7] Augustine had condemned the pursuit of knowledge that does not contribute to a more profound understanding and participation in Christian salvation. He had distinguished between wisdom ("the intellectual cognizance of eternal things") and knowledge ("the rational cognizance of temporal things" cf. *De Trin.* XII.25). Wisdom relates to our transformation through participation in the Trinity: when we remember, understand and love God, we become wise (cf. *De Trin.* XIV.15). Knowledge includes the knowledge of faith regarding the salvific events of Christ's life and death (*De Trin.* XIII.24). Thus, according to Augustine, there is knowledge that is useful – namely, insofar as it "strengthens the saving faith which leads to true happiness" (*De Trin.* XIV.3). However, the pursuit of knowledge for its own sake, without reference to our salvation, is sternly rejected by Augustine, as it includes "a great deal of superfluous frivolity and pernicious curiosity" (ibid.). Hugh shares this concern: the pursuit of knowledge should always be embedded in a salvific context; *curiositas* is therefore considered sinful, for it is not rooted in a dynamic that draws us closer to God.

[8] The threefold question (*quid, quare, quomodo*) is adopted from Hugh's text *On Meditation* (*De Med.* 1). It is clear that an implementation of Hugh's vision in today's third-level institutions that claim a Christian heritage would have a transformative power.

[9] When quoting I use the translation by Roy Deferrari, *Hugh of Saint Victor: On the Sacraments of the Christian Faith* (Cambridge, MA: Medieval Academy of America, 1951).

the Christian faith in a systematic way (following an order of exposition dictated by pedagogical or speculative concerns), Hugh attempts in *De Sacr.* to outline the Christian faith and its mysteries in a manner that reflects the salvific-historical sequence. That is, from creation (*opus conditionis*) and Fall to restoration (*opus restaurationis*) and redemption (including the sacramental economy), unto the renewal of the earth (eschatology).

Hugh has a broad understanding of the notion of sacrament. He defines it, briefly, as "the sign of a sacred thing" (*rei sacre signum*) or, more accurately, as "a corporeal or material element set before the senses without, representing by similitude and signifying by institution and containing by sanctification some invisible and spiritual grace" (*De Sacr.* 1.9.2). Three aspects are important in this definition: similitude to that of which it is the sacrament, institution and sanctification. In baptism, for instance, water is the sacrament or the sign. Its similitude is its cleansing character: just like water washes away the stains of the body, so too baptismal water cleanses the iniquities of the soul. Baptism was instituted by Christ; and in it a spiritual grace is conferred (sanctification). Hugh interprets these three aspects in a Trinitarian way: the first aspect was made by the Creator, institution was established by the Savior, and sanctification occurred through the Holy Spirit (*De Sacr.* 1.9.4).

The first aspect, the material similitude, is not necessarily a thing (such as water, or bread and wine). It can also take the form of a deed (when making the sign of the cross) or words (e.g., prayer) (*De Sacr.* 1.9.6). This illustrates Hugh's broad understanding of "sacrament." It includes, for instance, what were later called the sacramentals. Even faith itself is a kind of sacrament for Hugh because it points toward future contemplation (*De Sacr.* 1.10.9), as I show later.

For now, let me examine, by way of example, what Hugh has to say on the Eucharist. In a previous chapter I briefly touched on the Carolingian debate between Paschasius Radbertus and Ratramnus. I argued that both authors found it difficult to relate reality and image. In the 11th century, Berengar of Tours (d. 1088) raised a similar problem. Drawing on Ratramnus's *De Corpore et Sanguine Domini* (which he incorrectly attributed to Eriugena), he argued that the bread and wine are not the true Body and Blood, but merely a likeness (*similitudo*) or figure (*figura*). Berengar made a sharp distinction between the *sacramentum* (the bread and wine) and the *res sacramenti* (the Body and Blood). Recalling that Augustine had defined a sacrament as "a sign of a sacred reality" (*Letter* 138), Berengar reasoned that if something is a sign, it cannot be at the same time that which it refers to. Therefore, if the bread and wine are a sacrament – that is, a sign of the real Body and Blood of Christ – the bread and the wine cannot be the real Body and Blood. Berengar's views evoked major opposition, from Lanfranc of Bec amongst others, and were condemned at different synods, including the Lateran Synod of AD 1079.

Hugh alludes to these Eucharistic controversies in *De Sacr.* 11.8.6. He rejects the view that something has to be either an image (*figura*) or reality/ truth (*veritas*) and argues instead that the sacrament of the altar is both truth and figure. He then continues to distinguish between visible appearance of the sacrament (*species visiblis*), truth of body (*ueritas corporis*) and virtue of spiritual grace (*uirtus gratie spiritualis*). The appearance refers to bread and wine; the truth of body refers to what we believe to be present under that appearance – namely, "the true body which hung on the cross and the true blood of Jesus which flowed from his side."[10] Through participation, in faith and love, in the Eucharist, grace is infused in us: this is the third element – that is, the power or virtue of the sacrament:

[W]hen the body of Christ is eaten, not what is eaten but he who eats is incorporated with Him whom he eats. ... He who eats and is incorporated has the sacrament (*sacramentum*) and has the substance (*rem*) of the sacrament. He who eats and is not incorporated has the sacrament but not the substance of the sacrament. (*De Sacr.* 11.8.5)

The incorporation in Christ occurs through faith and love. Hugh thus adopts a middle view between a strong objectivist standpoint (which holds that grace operates without proper disposition of its recipients) and a subjectivist view (which considers the sacrament only a figure).[11] This quotation also suggests that Hugh distinguishes between *sacramentum* and *res* (understood here as the grace that comes with worthy participation in the sacrament) – apparently one of the first medieval theologians to do so.[12] This distinction was to acquire major significance in later scholastic sacramental theology.

Another issue that was to exert the minds of future theologians until the 13th century was how to account for the change (*mutatio*) of bread and wine into the Body and Blood of Christ. Hugh anticipates the later teaching of transubstantiation:

Through the words of sanctification the true substance of bread and the true substance of wine are changed (*conuertitur*) into the true body and blood of Christ,

---

[10] *De Sacr.* 11. 8.7.   [11] Paul Rorem, *Hugh of Saint Victor* (Oxford: Oxford University Press), 101.
[12] Edward Kilmartin, *The Eucharist in the West* (Collegeville, MN: Liturgical Press, 1998), 146.

the appearance of bread and wine alone remaining, substance passing over into substance (*et substantia in substantiam transeunte*). . . . We say that essence has been changed into the true body itself and that the substance of bread and wine has not been reduced to nothing because it ceased to be what it was, but rather that it has been changed because it began to be something else which it was not. (*De Sacr.* 11.8.9)

Hugh, rejecting theories of consubstantiation (conceiving of the change in terms of the addition of the body and blood to the bread and wine) and annihilation (in which the bread and wine were understood to be destroyed at the time of consecration), espouses a theory of conversion (in which the substances of bread and wine are converted into the body and blood of Christ).[13]

Amidst these theological speculations Hugh does not lose sight of the true meaning of the Eucharist: through a worthy reception of the Eucharist we partake in the divinity (*De Sacr.* 11.8.8); it is food for the soul, not the body, changing us into Christ (*De Sacr.* 11.8.13).

HUGH ON FAITH AND LOVE

We need to understand Hugh's characterization of faith in *De Sacr.* 1.10.2 in light of the controversy surrounding Abelard.[14] Hugh first examines the nature of faith, quoting Hebrews 11:1: "Faith is the substance of things to be hoped for, the evidence of things that appear not" (*Substantia rerum sperandum, argumentum non apparentium*). Following Augustine (*De Trin.* XIII.3), Hugh argues that through faith "the invisible good things which are not yet present" are present in our hearts. Faith in the mysteries of God (this is what is meant by "the invisible good things") already amounts to their subsistence in us (*ipsa fides eorum in nobis est subsistentia eorum*). God is utterly ineffable and beyond comprehension (*incogitabilis*). Faith itself is the only way in which God and his mysteries dwell in us. So Hugh does not consider the description of faith in Hebrews 11:1 as a definition in the strict sense (i.e., as spelling out the essence of faith), but he sees it rather as a description of what faith does: through it God begins to dwell or subsist in us.[15]

Hugh goes on to clarify the epistemological status of faith by recalling the consequences of the Fall for human knowledge. He does this by

[13] Ibid., 146.   [14] See Marcia Colish, *Peter Lombard*, 2 vols. (Leiden: Brill, 1994), 494.
[15] It is clear that Hugh treats *substantia* in Hebrews 11:1 as synonymous with *subsistentia* and its derivatives.

distinguishing between three "eyes": the eye of the flesh (*oculus carnis*), with which we perceive the world outside; the eye of reason (*oculus rationis*), with which the soul could see itself and the things which were in itself; and the eye of contemplation (*oculus contemplationis*), with which the soul could see "God within itself and those things which were in God." After the Fall, the eye of contemplation has become extinguished and the eye of reason has become bleared. Only the eye of the flesh – our empirical perception, in more modern language – remained fully intact, allowing for indubitable knowledge within a limited scope. As a result of our fallenness, reason only allows us to attain doubtful and disputable knowledge. Faith is therefore necessary, Hugh claims, as it recaptures something of the initial contemplation we enjoyed in paradise. As prelapsarian man was allowed the contemplation of God and his mysteries within himself, so too, albeit in a far less perfect manner, fallen humanity can to some degree enjoy the indwelling of God and his mysteries within itself through faith.

Hugh then offers a general definition of faith that proved rather influential. It is worth quoting the relevant passage: "Faith is a kind of certainty of the mind in things absent, established beyond opinion and short of knowledge (*supra opinionem et infra scientiam*)" (*De Sacr.* 1.10.2). An opinion is characterized by lingering doubt: we waver between different views. Faith, however, is characterized by a kind of certainty and is therefore different from mere opinion. But faith does not attain the status of full-blown knowledge, in which we grasp the thing itself as when present. So although there is certainty in faith, it is a certainty of conviction rather than certain knowledge. It is only in the afterlife that we will attain certain knowledge, when faith passes over into vision.

Hugh's analysis of faith implies that faith is not just an intellectual affair: it also has an affective dimension, which refers to the constancy or firmness in the act of believing (*De Sacr.* 1.10.3). He distinguishes between faith by which there is belief (*fides qua creditur*), and that which is believed by faith (*quod fide creditur*) – that is, the cognitive aspect. This distinction between the act of faith and the contents of faith, useful in its own right as it avoids an over-intellectualist understanding of faith, also has a number of interesting implications. First, it allows us to account for the faith of those who are not theologically well-versed ("the simple-minded in the Holy Church"): the affective aspect of their faith is stronger than the cognitive, although the latter aspect is not entirely absent. It also allows Hugh to explain how faith can both grow intellectually and deepen devotionally.

Another question Hugh tackles is whether faith changes over time. Does it evolve? Do the Old Testament patriarchs have the same faith as

Christians from the 12th century? Hugh argues that they had the same faith although its cognitive dimension has evolved. He makes this point by drawing an analogy between those who have an intellectually profound grasp of faith and the faith of "the simple." They share the same Christian faith although the cognitive dimension is not the same. Similarly, people living before the coming of Christ had the same faith as those after the Incarnation, yet the cognitive aspect was obviously not identical. In adopting this view, Hugh combines a strongly universalistic stance that does not, however, exclude the possibility for faith to evolve throughout the ages.

In summary, faith is a sacrament (in Hugh's broad sense of the word) that refers to future contemplation. Faith is a foretaste of contemplation of God, in which our ultimate bliss consists: "If, then, the highest good is rightly believed to be man's contemplation of his Creator, not unfittingly is faith, through which he begins in some manner to see the absent, said to be the beginning of good and the first step in his restoration" (*De Sacr.* 1.10.9). This restoration is strengthened through a more profound knowledge of faith and an increase in the ardency of our love for God (*De Sacr.* 1.10.9). This brings me to the next topic I want to discuss: love of God and neighbor.

Both in secular (chivalric) and religious (Cistercian) literature of the 12th century, the theme of love figured prominently. Hugh too dealt with the topic of love in a number of places, but his most extensive discussion can be found in *De Sacr.* 11.13.6ff.

Commenting on the great precept (Matt. 22:37–39), Hugh argues that God should be loved on account of himself, while we should love our neighbor on account of God. To love God means to wish to possess him; to love our neighbor on account of God means that we love our neighbor because he possesses God or may possess God. In Hugh's own words: "Just as when I love man on account of wisdom I love him on this account, because I love wisdom itself, and surely I would not love man, if I did not love wisdom, the very thing on account of which I love him; so when I love my neighbour on account of God, I love him, because I love God" (*De Sacr.* 11.13.6). After all, when we are drawn toward goodness, justice and truth as present in our neighbor, we love the neighbor in God, "because God is goodness, and justice, and truth" (ibid.). The passage resonates with Augustinian ideas and with Augustine's Neoplatonic metaphysics of participation. It reinforces the notion that love of our fellow men is essentially triangular in nature: while we love God directly, our love of our neighbor is on account of

God (*propter Deum*). Hugh therefore develops a triangular understanding of love, faithful to the Augustinian tradition. This view (a typical instance of the medieval thrust toward the transcendent) will be shared by Thomas Aquinas, as we will see.

Hugh argues that if we really love ourselves, we love that in which the good of our soul consists – that is, God. Hence, if we were to claim to love something more than our own soul, we would effectively love that something more than God. The same applies to our love of neighbor: it too has to become rerouted, so to say, via God:

[I]f you love something [other than God] more than your own soul, surely you are proven to love this same thing more than God, because you love your own soul only in this, that you love its good which is God. Therefore, first love your own soul by loving the good of your own soul. Then love also your neighbour as yourself by loving the good for him which you love for yourself. For to love him is to love good for him. (*De Sacr.* 11.13.10)

The key sentence here is: "First love your own soul by loving the good of your own soul." Hugh is suggesting that we can only properly love ourselves by loving the good of our soul. This good is God. Hence Hugh adopts the Augustinian notion that our love for ourselves and neighbor has to be for the sake of God. When loving our neighbor for God's sake, we do not fail to love our neighbor as intrinsically valuable. On the contrary, the very fact that our love for neighbor is embedded in our love for God implies that we can love the other in a truly non-possessive, gratuitous manner for what he or she is. We can love many good things belonging to our neighbor – but it is only when we love him for the sake of God (when we love and desire the Good that is God, for him) that our love becomes truly unselfish. When we love God, the good for ourselves and for our neighbor coincide. This is why loving God does not exclude love of neighbor but implies it: "true good is not possessed with envy" (*De Sacr.* 11.13.10). True love for God is, by its nature, non-exclusivist.

As suggested, the triangular dynamic of love also extends to ourselves. When we love God we also love ourselves, for God is the good of our soul. In loving God we therefore love ourselves. This is why it was not necessary to have a third precept (i.e., we are not commanded to love ourselves, but only God and our neighbor).

We should not love our neighbor (or anything else for that matter, with the exception of God) more than we love ourselves, for "if you love something more than your own soul, surely you are proved to love this same thing more than God, because you love your own soul only in this, that you love its good which is God" (*De Sacr.* 11.13.10). Similarly, we cannot truly want the salvation of others at the expense of the eternal damnation of our soul. For choosing the perdition of your soul (and the separation from God it involves) would effectively imply that you do not love yourself – and would thus be contrary to the command to love yourself. After all, "how does one love one's neighbor when one does not love oneself?" Hugh asks (*De Sacr.* 11.13.10). Consenting to your own damnation for the sake of the salvation of others would effectively imply that you love other people more than you love God.

In this context Hugh also criticizes one-sided, disinterested love. He criticizes foolish people (*stulti*) who "love with pure and gratuitous (*pura et gratuita*) and filial love," seeking or desiring "nothing" from God. This kind of disinterested love, Hugh argues, is effectively indifference: "I as man would not wish to be loved thus by you. If you should so love me that you did not care about me, I would not care about your love. You should see if it is worthy for you to offer to God what man would worthily reject" (*De Sacr.* 11.13.8).

This polemic is highly interesting, and I cannot think of any other passage in *De Sacr.* where Hugh displays such a strong sense of irritation. He takes issue with those who claim out of an inflated sense of piety (cf. *De Sacr.* 11.13.7) to love God in a radically selfless, disinterested way without even desiring God for themselves. They want to avoid, at all costs, to appear mercenary, and therefore they reject all desire and need in their love for God (*De Sacr.* 11.13.8). The discussion is of importance for at least two reasons. First, Hugh identifies (without putting it in those terms) two kinds of Christian love. The first kind is utterly disinterested, radically agapeic, without any reference to the human self and her desires.[16] The second kind of love is a more erotic kind of charity, acknowledging the desires and needs of the lover. Hugh vehemently rejects the first version of charity, effectively unmasking it as indifference ("If you should so love me that you did not care about me"). Paradoxically, when all references to the loving subject are suppressed, the object of our love disappears too: if we do not desire the other, we do not love her or him. Hugh's wholesome defense of desire in human love for God does not commit him to a mercenary account of love. Having defined love for God as wishing to possess him, Hugh adds, significantly: "Not anything from him but himself, that is, freely (*gratis*)." So if we love God for any other reason than himself, our love may become mercenary. But if we love God, and

[16] Agapeic love has found a modern defense in Anders Nygren's book *Agape and Eros*.

desire him and nothing else, we love truly, and do so in a gratuitous, non-mercenary manner.

Hugh's views on love capture the transcendent thrust of his theology quite well. We have seen that this theocentric focus is present in his early work (*De Tribus Diebus*), implying a powerful sacramental vision of the world. It also shapes his understanding of the Arts in his *Didascalicon*. Finally, it finds expression in his mature work, *De Sacramentis*, and nowhere more explicitly so than in his discussion of love. Having quoted Matthew 22:37, he concludes:

Extend and force yourself as much as you can. . . . Love with your whole heart and your whole soul and your whole mind, that is: with your whole intellect and your whole affection and your whole memory; as much as you understand, as much as you know, as much as you are equal to, so much do you love. (*De Sacr.* 11.13.9)

BIBLIOGRAPHICAL NOTE

For *DTD*, see Dominique Poirel (ed.), *De Tribus Diebus. CCCM 177* (Turnhout: Brepols, 2002). For a translation, see Boyd Taylor Coolman and Dale Coulter (eds.), *Trinity and Creation: A Selection of Works of Hugh, Richard and Adam of St. Victor* (Turnhout: Brepols, 2010), 49–102. For the *Didasc.*, I have used the translation by Jerome Taylor, *The Didascalicon of Hugh of Saint Victor: A Medieval Guide to the Arts* (New York: Columbia University Press, 1991). For *De Sacr.*, I have used Roy Deferrari (trans.), *Hugh of Saint Victor on the Sacraments of the Christian Faith* (Eugene, OF: Wipf and Stock, 2007). The Latin text is available as *Hugonis de Sancto Victore De Sacramentis Christiane Fidei*, ed. Rainer Berndt (Asschendorff: Monasterii Westfalorum, 2008).

There are two excellent overviews of Hugh's thought: Paul Rorem, *Hugh of Saint Victor* (Oxford: Oxford University Press, 2009) and Boyd Taylor Coolman, *The Theology of Hugh of St Victor: An Interpretation* (Cambridge: Cambridge University Press, 2010).

CHAPTER 10

Richard of St. Victor

Richard of St. Victor, originally from Scotland, joined the canons regular at St. Victor at an unknown date. It is unclear whether he arrived before the death of Hugh of St. Victor. Nevertheless, he was deeply influenced by Hugh's thought. He was elected prior in AD 1162 and fulfilled this function until his death on March 10, 1173. He wrote scriptural commentaries, including the *Book of Selections* (*Liber Exceptionum*), sermons and letters, as well as a number of theological (*The Trinity*) and mystical treatises. Amongst the latter, *The Twelve Patriarchs* (also called *Benjamin Minor*) and *The Mystical Ark* (or *Benjamin Major*) have received most scholarly attention.[1] In *The Twelve Patriarchs*, Richard interprets in a mainly tropological manner the story of Jacob and his wives, their handmaids and their offspring so as to illustrate the moral preparation of the soul necessary for contemplation. Although, like Hugh, Richard considers the historical sense important as a foundation, in his mystical treatises, he interprets the texts mainly in a spiritual manner. I examine two aspects of this thought: his views on contemplation and human understanding, and his original theology of the Trinity.

In *The Mystical Ark*, we find a fairly detailed discussion of contemplation. It is first defined rather generally as "the free, more penetrating gaze of the mind, suspended with wonder concerning manifestations of wisdom."[2] In a penetrating analysis, Richard then goes on to distinguish between six modes of contemplation, effectively covering all degrees of human knowledge. Following Boethius, he distinguishes between three levels of knowing: through the imagination (directed at what we can perceive with our senses), through reason (directed at intelligible things [*intelligibilia*]) and through understanding (directed at intellectible things [*intellectibilia*]).[3] By

---

[1] Translated by Grover A. Zinn in *Richard of St Victor: The Twelve Patriarchs. The Mystical Ark. Book Three of the Trinity* (New York: Paulist Press, 1979).
[2] *The Mystical Ark* 1.4. All translations from Zinn.
[3] These distinctions in the human hierarchy of knowledge (as well as the neologism *intellectibilia*) are inspired by Boethius, *The Consolation of Philosophy* v.4.

the "intelligible," Richard means invisible things that can nevertheless be understood by reason. The "intellectible" refers to invisible things that cannot be understood by human reason (*The Mystical Ark* 1.7). An example of the latter is the mystery of the Trinity, which I discuss in greater detail in what follows.

Before I do so, I want to briefly examine how Richard characterizes contemplation in *The Mystical Ark*. Contemplation differs from thinking and what Richard calls meditation in a number of ways. First, Richard explicitly states that all three forms can relate to the same object. "We regard one and the same object in one way by means of thinking, we examine it in another way by means of meditation and we marvel at it in another way by means of contemplation" (*The Mystical Ark* 1.3). It is therefore not the case that contemplation only relates to divine things. We can approach creaturely things with a contemplative mindset too. These three modes are therefore distinct ways of relating to the same things. They are, in Richard's words, "a kind of sight of the soul" (*The Mystical Ark* 1.4). We are dealing with different kinds of "attention." Whereas *thinking* is discursive, wandering "here and there in all directions without any regard for arriving" using mainly the imagination, *meditation* is a more focused investigation by the soul, drawing mainly on reason in its search for truth. *Contemplation* draws on understanding. Instead of being discursive, it grasps things in one vision and rests in the perception of wisdom it perceives (*The Mystical Ark* 1.3–4). Meditation has nothing to do with meditative practices in the modern meaning of the word. Rather, it is a kind of focused intellectual effort. Also, the boundaries between thinking, meditation and contemplation are not strict. Meditation, for instance, when it attains truth, may pass over into contemplation (*The Mystical Ark*. 1.4). Thus, each stage has an inner dynamic toward self-transcendence.

Given the fact that these boundaries are fluid, Richard can draw a broad picture of contemplation that incorporates elements of thinking and meditation. In *The Mystical Ark* 1.6, he introduces a hierarchy of six kinds of contemplation. The first two are in the imagination, the following two in reason and the last two in understanding. In each case, imagination, reason and understanding can both stoop down to a level underneath it, and pass over into a higher level. Let me unpack this.

Contemplation of sensible things (e.g., a beautiful rose) occurs in the imagination. In the first kind of contemplation (in the imagination and according to imagination only), we give our attention to the beauty and diversity of the visible things that we perceive with the senses, and we marvel at the manifestation of the beauty of it all. We marvel but do not think about it.

In the second kind of contemplation, discovery and knowledge enter the frame. While contemplating the things that are in the imagination, we begin to consider things from a more rational point of view. We may ask, for instance, what is the cause of this thing and its beauty? Richard calls this contemplation in the imagination according to reason (*in imaginatione et secundum rationem*). Although this is in the imagination, reason has come down to the level of imagination.

The third kind of contemplation is formed in reason according to imagination (*in ratione et secundum imaginationem*). Here we reason about invisible things but we do so by drawing on similitude of visible things, which is why Richard states that this third kind of contemplation occurs in reason (for we think) according to imagination (for we use a similitude drawn from an image of visible things). In this case, imagination transcends its own realm into the realm of reason.

The fourth kind of contemplation is formed in reason and according to reason (*in ratione et secundum rationem*). Here, we direct our attention toward things that the imagination does not know but that the mind knows by means of reason. At this level, pure understanding makes its entry, lowering itself, so to speak, from its own distinct level.

The fifth kind of contemplation is above reason yet not beyond reason (*supra sed non praeter rationem*). Here, we are dealing with things we cannot discover by relying on human reason only but, once shown to us by divine revelation, we can give our intellectual assent to them. Richard gives the example of an understanding of the divine nature as revealed in the Scriptures.

The sixth kind of contemplation is that which is engaged with those things that are above reason and seem to be beyond or even against reason. Richard mentions "almost all the things we are told to believe concerning the Trinity of persons" (*The Mystical Ark* 1.6).

In this brief scheme, Richard has captured the whole range of human contemplation, from contemplating modest creaturely things in the first and second kind of contemplation (sensible things), via intelligible things (three and four), to intellectible things (five and six). An attractive aspect of Richard's account is that contemplation, for him, is not some kind of meditative technique. It is, as I mentioned, a kind of focus or attentive regard with which we approach the world and God. Richard's description of the self-transcending nature of imagination, reason and intellect is another appealing feature. Reason (*ratio*) reaches out beyond itself and comes to fulfillment in understanding, which, in turn, transcends itself:

Although the three highest taken together [i.e., contemplation 4–6] cannot exist without pure understanding, in the first of these (that is: in the fourth) understanding inclines itself to reason; in the fifth, understanding raises reason to itself; in the sixth, understanding transcends reason and, as it were, abandons everything below itself. Again: Although in the middle there are four taken together that cannot exist without reasoning, in the second kind of contemplation, reason stoops down to imagination, as it were to the lowest things; in the third, it draws imagination with it, as it were, to higher things; in the fourth it receives and conducts understanding, which descends, as it were, below itself; in the fifth, reason rises above itself, as it were, to understanding and alludes to it in its sublime things. (*The Mystical Ark* 1.8)

Few authors in the medieval tradition rival Richard's description of the thrust toward the transcendent at the heart of human knowledge. I will now discuss his understanding of God as Trinity. Before I do this, however, I want to examine briefly the nature of his argument for the existence of God.

THE TRINITY

From the contingency and finitude of creation, Richard argues that there must be a being that is its own origin.[4] For if there were no being which is its own origin, there would be no principle capable of bringing into existence those beings that are not their own existence (1.8). The counterargument that perhaps the whole world has always existed simply clashes with our experience of contingency. Rather than examining the merits of Richard's argument in its own right I would like to pause and examine the way this argument reveals something of how Richard sees the relation between faith and reason. For Richard's argument is, of course, not a philosophical proof in the strict sense: when he states that our reasoning (*ratiocinando*) leads us "from the visible to the invisible," "from the transient to the eternal, from the worldly to the supra-worldly, from the human to the divine" (1.8), he stands squarely in the Anselmic tradition of faith seeking understanding:

To understand these truths of which it has been rightly said "If you do not believe, you will not understand," you must enter by faith. But we must not immediately halt here; rather we should constantly reach out towards a more intimate and profound understanding, and with a complete studiousness and highest diligence

---

[4] For the text of Richard's *De Trinitate*, I used Richard de Saint-Victoire, *La Trinité*, ed. Gaston Salet. Sources Chrétiennes 63 (Paris: Cerf, 1998).

penetrate deeper from day to day, through newly acquired insights into an understanding of our faith. (1.3)

Richard's theology of the Trinity both arises from and results in a contemplative disposition. He describes it as a ladder by which we climb from a reflection (*speculatio*) of the visible to contemplation (*contemplatio*) of the invisible mystery of God (1.10), who will always remain beyond our grasp (1.19). In short, Richard, writing long before the modern divide between faith and "autonomous" reason, requires from his readers an almost aesthetic receptivity toward the world in order to be able to see the world as a pointer to the mystery that grounds it. Bonaventure adopts and develops this stance.

Having discussed in the second book of *De Trinitate* divine attributes such as uncreatedness, immutability, eternity, infinity, incommunicability, indivisibility and simplicity, Richard goes on in book three to examine the divine plurality. How can we square the unity of the divine substance with a plurality of Persons?

PLURALITY OF PERSONS AND THE ORDER OF LOVE

Given that within God there is plenitude of goodness, and goodness implies true love (*caritas*), Richard states that love demands a plurality of Persons, for love by its nature entails an orientation toward an other. Perhaps the reader might object: Surely God could bestow his love on a created being? Divine love does not therefore necessarily imply a plurality of Persons within the divine nature. Against this, Richard argues that "the proper order of love" demands that God does not bestow the fullness of his love on someone who should not be supremely loved (III.2). This claim, crucial in his argument, may strike us as implausible at first, especially in light of the gift of God's Son to humanity. On the other hand, Richard may well appeal to our own experience to support his argument. There is, for instance, something inordinate, something "not quite right," about loving your pet with the same intensity as you would love a human being. Therefore, perfect love requires equality (III.7; v.16) – an observation that will also allow Richard to resist any suggestion of subordinationism within the Trinity (III.7).

Not only does it belong to the nature of love to be shared, but it is only when love is reciprocated that it is a source of supreme happiness. Richard then takes his analysis of love one step further. If love is to be genuinely perfect, it must have a triadic structure.

Certainly in mutual and very fervent love nothing is rarer or more magnificent than to wish that another be loved equally by the one whom you love supremely and by whom you are supremely loved. And so the proof of perfected charity is a willing sharing of the love that has been shown to you. So a person proves that he is not perfect in charity if he cannot yet take pleasure in sharing his excellent joy . . . Therefore it is necessary that each of those loved supremely and loving supremely should search with equal desire for someone who would be mutually loved (*condilectus*) and with equal concord and willingly possess them. Thus you see how the perfection of charity requires a Trinity of Persons. (III.II, trans. 384–85)

This analysis of love is at the heart of Richard's theology of the Trinity. Love between only two divine Persons would not be perfect; it would be somewhat self-enclosed and exclusivist, at odds with the harmonious (*concordialis*) and shared or communal (*consocialis*) nature of love (III.20). The key term is *condilectus*, a term coined by Richard himself. It can be translated as "co-beloved," the one who is loved by two lovers as the perfect expression and union of their love.[5] It is with the co-beloved (*condilectus*) that the others share the delights of the love they harbor for each other (VI.6; III.14 and 15).

DIVINE PLURALITY AND THE INTRICACIES
OF PERSONHOOD

In order to illuminate the mystery of the Three in One, Richard considers the meaning of the word "person" at length. He rejects the traditional Boethian definition of personhood (i.e., "an individual substance of a rational nature") and defines it instead as "an incommunicable existence (*incommunicabilis exsistentia*) of the divine nature" (IV.18, 22). Two aspects are striking: Richard prefers *exsistentia* over *substantia*, and he replaces "individual" with "incommunicable."

In relation to the first point, Richard points out that the word "exist-ence" (*exsistentia*) is derived from the word "exist" (*exsistere*). This word consists of two parts: "ex" (from, out of) and "ist" (*sistere*), which means "to be." While the word *sistere* seems to denote something that is, the word "exist" (*exsistere*) does not simply denote being, but it also seems to contain a reference to a kind of origin. Something "exists" when it has its being from elsewhere or from somebody else. "What does to exist (*exsistere*) mean

---

[5] As Richard puts it: "Shared love (*condilectio*) is properly said to exist when a third Person is loved by two Persons harmoniously (*concorditer*) and in community (*socialiter*), and the affection of the two Persons is fused into one affection by the flame of love for the third" (III.19).

but to be (*sistere*) from (*ex*) somebody, to receive one's substantial being from somebody?" (IV.12; also IV.23).

Thus, Richard's analysis of divine existence already points to his understanding of persons in terms of origin, which is the only way in which the Persons can be distinguished from one another without compromising the divine unity (IV.15). He is aware of the importance of this discovery: "Thus we have found what we had been looking for: how there can be distinction (*alteritas*) of Persons without any distinction (*alteritas*) of substances" (IV.15).

This brings us to the issue of incommunicability (or distinctiveness): although the three divine Persons share the divine nature (*exsistentia communis*), the Persons themselves are constituted by their own unique way of being: their *exsistentia incommunicabilis* (IV.16–17) – that is, those personal characteristics that cannot be shared. The personal characteristic or property (*proprietas personalis*) is that which bestows on each of the Persons that which makes him distinct. To claim that a personal property could be shared would amount to saying that an individual person could be two persons (IV.17). Thus, the divine Persons share the one divine substance in their own distinct manner (IV.19). In this way, there can be a plurality of existences or hypostases within the unity of the divine substance (IV.20). In short, for Richard, the divine being itself – understood as love – yields an inner plurality of Persons who differ in their origin. It is through the origin of the divine Persons that we can discern their distinguishing properties (V.1). Let me examine in more detail how the Persons differ through their origin.

In the first part of his book, Richard had argued for the existence of God as *causa sui* on the basis that to deny this would lead to an infinite regress. He now applies a similar reasoning to the Trinity: there must be a Person in the divinity who is his own Cause and does not derive his being from another. Otherwise there would be an infinity of Persons in the Godhead (V.3). Richard will identify this Person with the Father, who alone is his own origin (*innascibilis*), and it is this characteristic that constitutes him as a unique (*incommunicabilis*) existence (V.5).

Recalling his arguments from Book III about the nature of love and the need for a co-beloved (*condilectus*), Richard distinguishes in Book V between love that is freely bestowed (*gratuitus*), freely received or owed (*debitus*) or a combination of both (i.e., freely given and owed, *ex utroque permixtus*) (V.16):

Love is freely given (*amor gratuitus*) when one freely bestows one's love on somebody from whom one has not received anything. Love is owed (*amor debitus*) when one returns (*rependit*) to the one who freely bestowed his love nothing but love. Love is a combination of both (*ex utroque permixtus*) when one freely receives and freely bestows love. (v.16)

The Person who freely bestows (*communicare*) the plenitude of his love is, of course, the Father (v.17). The Son both receives and bestows love (*permixtus*): he receives love from the Father and bestows it on the Holy Spirit (*Filioque*) (v.19). Richard usually describes the Spirit as the one who merely receives love. At times Richard seems to suggest that the Holy Spirit, as the One who merely receives love, does not bestow his love on another (divine) Person: the property of the Holy Spirit is to possess love without giving it to another Person (*Proprium autem Spiritui sancto habere nec alicui dare*) (vi.11). Especially in those passages where Richard is at pains to distinguish the Holy Spirit from the Second Person (the Son, the Image of the Father), he emphasizes that the Holy Spirit, unlike the Son, does not share in the spirative plentitude of the Father: "No person whatsoever receives from the Holy Spirit the plenitude of the divinity. For this reason he does not express in himself the image of the Father" (vi.11). However, we should not take this to mean that the Holy Spirit does not love the other Persons (i.e., the Father and the Son). The quotation just cited (the Spirit "returns" [*rependit*] love) suggests that the Holy Spirit too loves the other Persons, but the nature of this love is different: whereas the Father loves with a love that is utterly gratuitous or freely given, the Holy Spirit loves with a love that is totally owed and the Son loves with a love that is a mixture of both.

DIVINE NAMES

For Richard, each of the divine Persons shares the divine love in his own distinctive manner (v.20). In Book vi, Richard discusses the distinctiveness of the divine Persons by way of origin in more detail by examining the personal names (Father, Son, Holy Spirit, Word, Image, Gift) and appropriations (power, wisdom, goodness). As we saw in a previous chapter, a personal name is a name that strictly applies to one of the Three Persons only. When a name can be applied to the Trinity as such but is especially associated with one of the three Persons, it can be appropriated. For instance, "Wisdom" is usually appropriated to the "Word" (a personal name), although, strictly speaking, the whole Trinity is "wise."

"Father" is the personal name of the First Person of the Trinity as he is the origin of the Trinity, while "Son" is the name of the Second as he is generated by the Father (vi.4). The Third Person is called "Holy Spirit" as he is the common love (*amor qui communis est ambobus*) of Father and Son, which is then breathed – *inspire* – into the hearts of the saints by the Father and the Son. As air is necessary for the life of the body, so too the divine Spirit is necessary for a saintly life (vi.10): here an interesting connection is made between Richard's theology of the Trinity and Christian spirituality.

The Son is also called "Word" as this name points to the fact that the Son reveals or expresses the glory and truth of the Father – in the same way as a word originates from the heart of a person (vi.13). Richard combines here an "intrapersonal" explanation, at least partly derived from Augustine (*De Trin.* xv.20,23,24), with an "interpersonal" analysis of love. This illustrates that, for him at least, the psychological and social model are not mutually exclusive.

The Holy Spirit, as the expression of the love between Father and Son, is also called "Gift" (vi.14). As creaturely beings we receive everything from God, and in our sanctification we become "configurated" to the Spirit – that is, we learn to love God with a love that is utterly owed or received. The Holy Spirit in which we share is the "outcome" of the Love between Father and Son. This too is traditional Augustinian teaching (*De Trin.* v.15,16). In this instance, Richard's approach allows him to argue convincingly how the mission of the Holy Spirit reveals the procession of the Spirit (whereas in the case of the mission of the Word the link with Love both received and given remains unclear).

For Richard, the Trinity is a mystery of interpersonal Love. Developing a sophisticated analysis of the "ecstatic" nature of Love, he develops an original model in which the Father is the Origin of the Trinity and the Son is the one who receives this Love from the Father and bestows it, with the Father, unto the Holy Spirit, who receives it. The immediate appeal of Richard's model is that it seems to do full justice to the New Testament understanding of God as love.

While Richard's exposition has often been hailed as an alternative to the Augustinian one, scholars have long noted that Richard draws his inspiration from Augustine's *De Trinitate* (see *De Trin.* viii.12,14; ix.2). Augustine's so-called psychological model implies a close link between our "psychology" and the intra-Trinitarian processions, and it therefore offers resources to link the theology of the Trinity with spirituality – that is, how to participate in the life of the Trinity. In Richard's interpersonal model, this link is not so easy to establish.

Richard's ideas were highly influential. St. Thomas Aquinas initially commented on them with some apparent approval (in *De Pot.* 9.9), but he later criticized the key presupposition (the necessity of love to be shared), which, he suggested, only holds "in the case of one not having perfect goodness" (*ST* 1.32.1 *ad* 2). It was mainly Franciscan theologians, including St. Bonaventure, who were to espouse and develop some of Richard's key insights.

BIBLIOGRAPHICAL NOTE

For the text of Richard's *De Trinitate*, I used Richard de Saint-Victoire, *La Trinité*, ed. Gaston Salet. Sources Chrétiennes 63 (Paris: Cerf, 1998). A translation of Richard's entire *De Trinitate* can be found in Boyd Taylor Coolman and Dale Coulter (eds.), *Trinity and Creation* (Turnhout: Brepols, 2010), 195–382. Grover A. Zinn translated some of Richard's works in *Richard of St. Victor: The Twelve Patriarchs. The Mystical Ark. Book Three of the Trinity* (New York: Paulist Press, 1979).

For context and theology, see Hugh Feiss and Juliet Mousseau (eds.), *A Companion to the Abbey of Saint Victor in Paris* (Leiden: Brill, 2017).

CHAPTER II

Hildegard of Bingen

St. Hildegard of Bingen, also known as the Sybil of the Rhine, was one of the most remarkable women of the 12th century. She was a visionary theologian, prophetic reformer, composer of remarkable music that soars up to the heavens, natural scientist and healer. She was declared a Doctor of the (Catholic) Church in 2012.

Born into a family of lower nobility in AD 1098 in Bemersheim (the Rhineland), Hildegard (1098–1179) was pledged as a tithe to the service of God at the age of eight. She was initially placed in the care of a recluse called Jutta of Sponheim with whom she was enclosed in 1112 in the abbey of Disibodenberg. In order to participate in the divine office and read the Bible, Hildegard, as a Benedictine nun, acquired a basic knowledge of Latin. When Jutta died in 1136 Hildegard was elected prioress.

From her biography we know that from her infancy Hildegard suffered with ill health and severe headaches. As a child, from the age of five, she received visions. As she informs us in a "Declaration" that precedes her first major work, the *Scivias*, when she was forty-two years of age she received a prophetic call to write down and interpret these visions. She describes how she was gazing at a heavenly vision in which she contemplated a great splendor, from which a voice from heaven resounded, commanding her, "a fragile human, ashes of ashes, and filth of filth" to write down what she sees and hears. Since she is "timid in speaking, and simple in expounding, and untaught in writing," she is told to "speak and write these things not by a human mouth, and not by the understanding of human invention, and not by the requirements of human composition," but as she sees and hears them "on high in the heavenly places in the wonders of God."[1] In colorful language she describes how heaven was opened. A fiery light of exceeding brilliance came and permeated her brain and inflamed her whole being,

---

[1] Hildegard of Bingen, *Scivias*, trans. Mother Columba Hart and Jane Bishop (New York: Paulist Press, 1990), 59.

"not like a burning but like a warming flame, as the sun warms anything its rays touch." Immediately, she adds, she knew the meaning of the exposition of the Scriptures.

These were of course bold claims. In a generally patriarchal society, such as the Latin medieval one, where only a limited number of women acquired real power and authority, Hildegard appeals to her own very frailty and powerlessness to justify the authoritative claims she makes. The voice from heaven asserts that Hildegard, timid and fearful, stricken by sickness and enduring great pains in the body, was a chosen medium of revelation. A critique of the dignitaries of her time and an affirmation of her own prophetic status is implied: anyone who disputes the veracity of Hildegard's claims is effectively questioning the authority of God who speaks through her.[2]

Her belittling of herself as a poorly educated, weak woman should alert us that we should be hesitant about naively hailing her oeuvre as somehow proto-feminist.[3] Her writings have been shaped by the context in which she found herself. The fact that she could not benefit from the formal education male religious of her social standing would have enjoyed (such as attending cathedral schools) undoubtedly had implications for her oeuvre. Having said this, Hildegard's writings at times also subvert traditional gender notions while appearing to subscribe to them. For instance, she makes the point that man signifies the divinity while woman signifies the humanity of the Son of God.[4] This view appears to reflect the medieval view of superiority of men. As Barbara Newman observes, however, Adam symbolizes but does not share the divine nature; in contrast, Eve, insofar as she prefigures Mary, shares and bestows the humanity of the God-man.[5]

Throughout her writings she conveys her insights through rich use of striking imagery and symbolism rather than by expounding her views in

---

[2] Hildegard stresses in the "Declaration" that she received the visions "while awake" and not in dreams, sleep or delirium, or by the ears. She saw the visions with "a pure mind and the eyes and ears of the inner self."

[3] In *Scivias* 11, 6 [76], assuming the divine voice, she writes about women (in the context of a discussion of women and priesthood) as follows: "Those of female sex ... are an infirm and weak habitation, appointed to bear children and diligently nurture them. A woman conceives a child not by herself but through a man, as the ground is plowed not by itself but by a farmer. Therefore, just as the earth cannot plow itself, a woman must not be a priest." More generally, in *BDW* 1, 4 [65] she informs us that "woman is weak and looks to man to be cared for by him, just as the moon receives its strength from the sun. So too should she be subject to man and ever ready to serve him." Translations from *The Book of Divine Works* are by Nathaniel M. Campbell (Washington, DC: Catholic University of America Press, 2018).

[4] *BDW* 1, 4 [100], tr. 238.

[5] Barbara Newman, *Sister of Wisdom: St Hildegard's Theology of the Feminine* (Berkeley: University of California Press, 1997), 93.

a systematic manner. The rich visual nature of her writings is reflected well in the surviving illuminated manuscripts. These illuminations mattered to Hildegard. The Rupertsberg manuscript, dating from 1165, contained some marvelous ones in vibrant color that vividly illustrated her visions and assisted her readers. Unfortunately, it was lost during the Second World War at Dresden.[6] Thankfully, black-and-white reproductions had been made. Another manuscript, known as the Riesencodex (Wiesbaden), may also have been produced under her supervision shortly before her death. It contains almost all her writings.

Hildegard enjoyed the assistance of another nun, Richardis von Stade, and the support of a monk called Volmar who until his death in 1173 helped her with the editorial work of her main theological works. Through the support of her local bishop Henry of Mainz and Bernard of Clairvaux, she secured the encouragement and blessing of Pope Eugenius III.

For all her protestations of frailty and weakness, Hildegard was a strong personality who tenaciously pursued her own goals in the face of opposition. In 1148, after yet another vision, she expressed a desire to move her community to a new foundation at Rupertsberg, despite trenchant opposition from the abbot of Disibodenberg. Hildegard's determination prevailed and the community moved two years later to St. Rupertsberg in Bingen am Rhein. When her assistant and friend Richardis decided to leave her to become abbess of Bassum, Hildegard did everything in her power (even appealing – unsuccessfully – to the pope) to prevent this. The premature death of Richardis "resolved" the issue. Similarly, at the end of her life, in 1178, Rupertsberg was placed under interdict when Hildegard refused to exhume a nobleman who had been excommunicated from the monastic churchyard. Hildegard claimed that he had died in a state of grace and therefore refused to yield to the request of exhumation. For six months Hildegard and her community were deprived of Mass and the divine Office. The interdict was only lifted a few months before her death.

As indicated, her oeuvre is rich and diverse. She wrote books on healing and herbal medicine (*The Book of Simple Medicine*, also called *Nine Books on the Subtleties of Different Kinds of Creatures*, and *Causae et Curae* or *The Book of Composite Medicine*); she wrote around four hundred letters, which included correspondents such as emperor Frederick Barbarossa, King Henry II of England and Queen Eleanor, and four popes; she preached sermons (from 1158 onward), which was a highly unusual thing for

---

[6] Barbara Newman, "Introduction," p. 25 from Hildegard of Bingen, *Scivias.* trans. Mother Columba Hart and Jane Bishop. Classics of Western Spirituality (New York: Paulist Press, 1990).

a woman to do; she wrote astonishing liturgical music and hymns (collected as *Symphonia*) and a musical morality play (*Ordo Virtutum*).[7]

Her main theological contributions can be found in three major works. The first one is the *Scivias*, already mentioned, on which Hildegard worked for ten years until its completion in 1152. The title is a contraction of *Scito vias Domini*, "Know the ways of the Lord." This may be a reference to Jeremiah 5:4, where the prophet laments those who do not know the ways of the Lord (*ignorantes viam Domini*). If so, this would confirm that Hildegard sees herself as an apocalyptic prophetess whose vocation it is to recall God's people to paths of righteousness and true devotion. As is the case with her other theological works, each book of the *Scivias* consists of a number of visions, the meaning of which is explained. Book One deals with the Creator and Creation, opening with an expansive vision that describes the Lord of the universe seated on an iron-colored mountain. Other visions – there are six altogether in Book One – deal with the Fall, the cosmos, the human soul and body, and the choirs of angels. Book Two contains explanations of seven visions broadly concerning Redemption, including a vision of the Son of God, the Trinity, the Church, confirmation and the three orders in the Church (religious, secular clergy and laypeople), Christ's sacrifice as the marriage of the Son with the Church, and the devil and his temptations. The third and final book consists of thirteen visions, and broadly covers the history of salvation from the Fall to a climactic vision of the last judgement and a symphony of praise.

In 1158–63 Hildegard wrote *The Book of the Rewards of Life* (*Liber Vitae Meritorum*). As the title suggests, the main theme is virtue and vice. The final installment in her trilogy of visionary theology, *The Book of Divine Works* (*Liber Divinorum Operum*), was finished in 1173. It consists of three parts and treats of the theophany of divine love and the macrocosm; a commentary on the creation in which she offers literal, allegorical and tropological readings of John's Prologue and Genesis's opening; and the city of God surrounded by the wheel of eternity with theophanic love as its central axis.

Given the nature of her oeuvre and the "opacity of its visionary style," it is very difficult to summarize Hildegard's theology.[8] The visual element is of fundamental importance to Hildegard: her visions find their most immediate expression in the paintings that illuminate her manuscripts,

---

[7] The recordings of her entire musical oeuvre by the justly celebrated *Sequentia Ensemble* are warmly recommended. See www.sequentia.org/projects/hildegard.html.

[8] Nathaniel M. Campbell, "Introduction," from *Hildegard of Bingen: The Book of Divine Works*, trans. Nathaniel M. Campbell (Washington, DC: Catholic University of America Press, 2018), 22.

which are then described and interpreted by Hildegard. Anyone who rapidly "scans" her writings for original theological insights will be disappointed. Her writings need to be read slowly and be ruminated upon, to allow its rich symbolism to permeate the imagination of the reader. Hildegard invites us to enter into a different outlook or vision upon the world, encouraging us to come to see what she "sees": a world that is deeply sacramental, permeated and vibrant with the power of divine goodness, in which all things are interconnected. As Patricia Zimmerman Beckman notes, Hildegard's visions seek not simply to describe but to induce revelatory experience in her readers. Hildegard, she comments, lives "in an integrated world where winds, herbs, celestial music all reveal an incarnational God." Her visions "serve as a handbook of God's illuminating power throughout all creation."[9] In what follows I sketch some of her central ideas and emphases.

MACROCOSM AND MICROCOSM

Hildegard inhabits a universe in which all things are intimately interconnected, which allows her to establish some striking associations. Hers is therefore a deeply symbolic worldview. Both horizontal interconnections and a vertical sacramentality operate in her writings. Consider the second *Vision* from Book 1 of *The Book of Divine Works*. Hildegard sees a cosmic wheel (perhaps inspired by Ez. 1:15ff) consisting of six intersecting circles joined seamlessly together. In the middle of this cosmic wheel is the image of a human being. The wheel symbolizes divine foreknowledge and operation, which has neither beginning nor end, and which both surrounds or supports all things created and yet transcends everything in spatial and temporal terms.[10] The first circle symbolizes bright fire, the first of the elements, which "pervades all of creation and supplies to it the joy of its light, signifying the power of God, who is above all things and who grants life to things."[11] Underneath this circle is one of black fire, which represents the hellish fire of judgment. This circle is only half as thick as the circle of

---

[9] Patricia Zimmerman Beckham, "Lives and Visions" from Edward Howells and Mark McIntosh (eds.), *The Oxford Handbook of Mystical Theology* (Oxford: Oxford University Press, 2020), 213. In this contribution Beckham also discusses the writings of North American author Annie Dollard. This is a felicitous choice: both authors draw the reader into a profoundly sacramental vision of the world.

[10] *BDW* 1, 2 [2]: "And as a circle surrounds and contains all that lies inside of it, so holy divinity contains and exceeds all things infinitely, for no one can divide or overcome it in its power, or bring it to an end" (pp. 54–55).

[11] *BDW* 1, 2 [4], tr. 55.

the bright fire: God's grace and mercy exceed his judgment.[12] The third circle contains ether, the second element. It proceeds from the bright and black fire like lightning. It symbolizes the penitence of sinners, which issues from an awareness of the grace of God (the bright fire) and the fear of God (black fire). Beneath this is a circle of watery air (water being the third element), representing holy works, "which cleanse unclean works like water washing away some filth."[13] In the fifth circle is bright, white air, which holds back the floods of the upper waters. It signifies discretion (a major Benedictine virtue) that strengthens holy works with moderation, preventing them from becoming excessive. Later in the book Hildegard will characterize discretion as the firmament, symbolizing the heavenly and contemplative life above the earthly or active life. But it is also the "ladder between them, on which human minds ascend to heaven through good works and also descend to earth because of the flesh's needs."[14] In other words, discretion is a virtue that assists us in keeping heavenly and earthly matters in an appropriate balance, as a perfect integration of the contemplative and active lives, symbolized by Mary and Martha, respectively. A sixth circle consists of thin air, which appears to pervade the entire wheel, "for all things are quickened and sustained by it." It resembles the right desires that permeate our entire life of virtue under the guidance of the Holy Spirit.

The image of a human being in the middle of the wheel signifies humankind, which occupies a central place in the universe. Hildegard describes God as a light and life force that permeate the entire universe, especially humankind: every work of God flourishes through humankind, whom he made in his image and likeness. Just as God made humankind as his handiwork, so too humankind may share in God's work by caring for the rest of creation.[15] The head and the feet of the figure that accompanies the second vision are placed above and below the circle of strong, bright air. This symbolizes humankind as a microcosm, an idea we have encountered earlier in the writings of Eriugena Scotus. Hildegard's symbolic imagination develops this notion in a rich variety of ways. Like her predecessors, she finds the different dimensions of reality (material, vital, sensitive, rational, . . .) reduplicated and concentrated in the human being. As our material universe consists of earth (the fourth element) and stones, we are made of flesh and bones to which our soul is joined. A person's length (in stature) and breadth (with arms and hands extended from the chest) are

---

[12] *BDW* I, 2 [4].   [13] *BDW* I, 2 [6], tr. 57.   [14] *BDW* II, 1 [27], tr. 301.
[15] *BDW* I, 1 [2], tr. 35.

equal, just as the firmament has equal length and breadth. Similarly, the roundedness of the human head resembles the roundedness of the firmament. Even the three upper elements are present in the human head: the bright fire, together with the black fire beneath, from the top of the skull to the forehead; the pure ether from the forehead to the end of the nose; and the watery air, together with the strong, bright white air placed beneath it, from the nose to the throat.[16] These three elements in turn are associated with three powers in the soul Hildegard identifies (albeit somewhat obscurely): comprehension (by which we know celestial and terrestrial things within God's power), intelligence (by which we can recognize some things as evil) and motion (by which the soul is moved in the performance of good deeds).[17]

"In man," Hildegard writes, "God signified his entire work in the human form." "Man" in this context refers to every human being but also the man Christ. In other words, in the Incarnation the Son of God assumes every aspect of the created world, and in doing so, perfects the work of creation. The human form, then, is the image of God in a strong sense: the human brain, which rules the body, symbolizes the lordship of God; the human eyes, through which we discern things, reveal the divine foreknowledge; the nostrils manifest divine wisdom, which is "the aromatic principle of order in skills," as the sense of smell identifies the qualities of each thing. The human mouth signifies the Word of God through which he created all things, as words pronounced by the mouth express the inner intelligibility of all things.[18]

FALL AND SALVATION

It will have become clear that Hildegard has a positive understanding of creation, in which God dwells as a life-giving force, both immanent and transcendent. God created all things because he generously desired to share his glory, so that the entirety of creation could rejoice with and in God, who protects created things "as a hen gathers her young under her wings."[19] This harmony was disturbed by the sin of Adam and Eve. Given the intimate union between humankind and the rest of creation, it is not surprising that Hildegard retains the biblical and patristic notion that the Fall had cosmic repercussions. The disobedience of Adam and Eve cast a shadow over the rest of creation, which continues to struggle and groan toward deliverance.[20] When Cain murdered his brother, for instance, "the

---

[16] *BDW* I, 4 [14–17].   [17] *BDW* I, 4 [17].   [18] *BDW* I, 4 [105].   [19] *BRL* I, 118.
[20] *BDW* II, 1 [15].

whole earth trembled" as his crime had deprived the earth of the wholeness of sanctity, "just as a woman is left without a husband's solace in widowhood."[21] As a consequence of this disobedience, creation, which had been subjected to Adam and Eve, turned against them, so that they, having lowered themselves, might be held in check by creation.[22] Thus, our mortality and struggles serve their purpose in our reorientation toward God. Similarly, when she raises the question as to why God made humans such that they could sin, Hildegard answers by arguing that sin is a test: "Gold must be tested in the fire, and precious stones, to smooth them, must be polished. . . . Hence, O foolish humans, how can that which was made in the image and likeness of God exist without testing?"[23]

Incidentally, Hildegard presents an interesting account of the traditional story of the Fall of Adam and Eve, extending the Augustinian notion of evil as absence of goodness by describing Adam's sin as one of omission. She hints at this in *Scivias* II, 1. The vision describes how after the creation of heaven and earth the blazing fire of the divinity offers a white flower to Adam. Its scent reaches Adam's nostrils, but he does not taste it with his mouth or touch it with his hands. Hildegard interprets this as follows: Adam "tried to know the wisdom of the Law with his intelligence, as if with his nose, but did not perfectly digest it by putting it in his mouth, or fulfil it in full blessedness by the work of his hands." As a consequence, by not seeking God "either by faith or by works" he failed to attain true know-ledge of God and "sank into the gaping mouth of death."[24] Thus, the disobedience of our first parents is not an instance of self-assertive pride but it is a failure to anchor their entire existence in God, with ongoing ramifications throughout the cosmos and history. The connection Hildegard identifies between human sin and the disturbance or even disfiguration of the entire natural world should not fail to resonate with readers in the twenty-first century.

Hildegard adopts a variety of soteriological models. One of these is the patristic theory of the devil's rights whose claim over humankind was broken by the redemptive work of the innocent Christ – a model of salvation Anselm had rejected in his *Cur Deus Homo*.[25] Elsewhere, she employs a more medicinal model: Christ is the physician who treats the sick person who longs to be cured.[26] In this vein she adopts the metaphor of sinful humankind as a precious pearl that fell into the mud (as Anselm had done) and which needs to be purified and restored.[27]

---

[21] *BDW* I, 2 [47].   [22] *Scivias* I, 2 [27].   [23] *Scivias* I, 2 [29].   [24] *Scivias* II, 1 [8].
[25] *BDW* III, 4 [5].   [26] *Scivias* I, 3 [30].   [27] *Scivias* I, 2 [33].

More fundamentally, Hildegard's sacramental vision extends to her soteriology. In *Scivias* 11, 6 Hildegard sees Christ on the Cross, the central beam of which is planted into an altar. The blood that flows from the side of the crucified Christ is retained in a chalice held by a woman who symbolizes the Church. This blood, having streamed into the Eucharistic chalice, brings salvation and spiritual regeneration to souls,[28] and appears into heaven,[29] pleading that salvation should be granted. Similarly, in a powerful metaphor she describes the Cross and the altar as a winepress where wine has to be pressed out so as to replenish and sanctify humankind.[30] Adopting more bridal imagery, Hildegard characterizes the Church as the Bride of Christ who has been offered a dowry (the body and blood of Christ), which she can offer to the Creator for the sanctification of the world.[31]

The divine glory and transcendence, described in language truly reminiscent of the Old Testament, blazes throughout Hildegard's theological writings. Her profoundly cosmic and sacramental worldview may both challenge and enrich ours. While her theological insights may not always be original or presented in a systematic manner, her writings, imaginative and replete with striking associations, continue to exert their distinctive appeal to this day.

BIBLIOGRAPHICAL NOTES

Hildegard's theological works are available in the following translations: Mother Columba Hart and Jane Bishop (trans.), *Scivias*. Classics of Western Spirituality (New York: Paulist Press, 1990).

Bruce Hozeski translated *The Book of the Rewards of Life* (Oxford: Oxford University Press, 1994) and Nathaniel M. Campbell translated *The Book of Divine Works* (Washington, DC: Catholic University of America Press, 2018).

Secondary

The following are helpful: Sabina Flanagan, *Hildegard of Bingen 1098–1179: A Visionary Life* (London: Routledge, 1998); Anne King-Lenzmeier, *Hildegard of Bingen: An Integrated Vision* (Collegeville, MN: Liturgical Press, Michael Glazier, 2001); Jane McAvoy, *The Satisfied Life: Medieval*

---

[28] *Scivias* 11, 6 [1].   [29] *Scivias* 11, 6 [3].   [30] *Scivias* 1, 3 [31]; II, 6 [29].   [31] *Scivias* 11, 6 [4].

Women Mystics on Atonement (Eugene, OR: Wipf and Stock, 2009), especially chapter 4; Barbara Newman, *Sister of Wisdom: St Hildegard's Theology of the Feminine* (Berkeley: University of California Press, 1997); Debra Stoudt, George Ferzoco and Beverly Kienzle (eds.), *A Companion to Hildegard of Bingen* (Leiden: Brill, 2013).

The website of the International Hildegard of Bingen Society offers some interesting resources: www.hildegard-society.org/p/home.html.

For her music, see www.sequentia.org/projects/hildegard.html.

CHAPTER 12

Peter Lombard and the Systematization
of Theology

Peter Lombard was born in northern Italy, perhaps in Novarra. We first encounter a reference to him in a brief letter by St. Bernard of Clairvaux (dating from around 1138), in which he commends Peter to Gilduin, abbot of St. Victor in Paris. Here Peter found a vibrant center of intellectual activity, and he was to stay in Paris for the remainder of his life. He embarked on a successful ecclesiastic career, even becoming bishop of Paris shortly before his death in July 1160.

Peter is best known for his work *The Sentences*, consisting of four parts (or "Books").[1] *The Sentences* is a work that is very much at the service of the Church and the defense of faith (*Prologue* 1–4). Peter states that his aim was to write a book that brings together the views of the Fathers in a collection of "sentences" so that "the one who seeks them shall find it unnecessary to rifle through numerous books" (*Prologue* 5). Giulio Silano makes the point that *The Sentences* may be compared to a legal casebook: jurisprudence is unapologetic (its relevance is not disputed), and it draws on authorities to settle legal difficulties. Similarly, Peter's *Sentences* is an invitation to students of theology to engage in theology and draw on important theological authorities to solve theological issues. The main goal of *The Sentences* is therefore to draw students into the theological discipline and to teach the skills necessary to pass sound theological judgments when confronted with theological difficulties.[2]

As with any casebook, the selection of the opinions is crucial. Peter explicitly states that he opts for a balanced approach, steering clear of excesses and self-indulgent choices (*Prologue* 4). This approach partly explains the success of the book. Alexander of Hales adopted it as a study manual and from then onward it established itself as the classic handbook

---

[1] Magistri Petri Lombardi, *Sententiae in IV libris distinctae*, ed. Ignatius Brady, 2 vols. Spicilegium Bonaventurianum 4 and 5 (Grottaferrata: Editiones Collegii S. Bonaventurae Ad Claras Aquas, 1971, 1981).

[2] See Giulio Silano's "Introduction" to his translation of *Peter Lombard: The Sentences Book 1: The Mystery of the Trinity* (Toronto: Pontifical Institute of Medieval Studies, 2008), xix–xxvi.

on which later theologians wrote commentaries (e.g., Bonaventure, Thomas Aquinas, Duns Scotus, all the way to Martin Luther and beyond).

FRUI AND UTI, AND THE STRUCTURE OF PETER LOMBARD'S SENTENCES

When discussing Augustine, I have alluded to the distinction between *frui* and *uti*. Augustine used this distinction to make clear that in all our dealings with created things we should retain a theocentric focus: only God is to be "enjoyed." This distinction structures the four books of *The Sentences*; moreover, Peter makes a number of most helpful clarifications that may assist us in capturing the full meaning of Augustine's terminology.

The title of the first chapter of the first distinction (d.1.1.1) of Book 1 reads "All teaching concerns things or signs." In the fourth book of *The Sentences* Peter will deal with signs or sacraments. The first three books treat of "things." In order to differentiate between these things, Peter introduces the Augustinian distinction between enjoyment (*frui*) and use (*uti*). Indeed, Peter opens the second chapter of his first distinction as follows:

As Augustine says in the same place [*De Doctr. Christ.* I, c.3], "in the case of things, we must consider that there are some things which are to be enjoyed, others which are to be used, and yet others which enjoy and use" (*Id ergo in rebus considerandum est, ut in eodem Augustinus ait, quod res aliae sunt quibus fruendum est, aliae quibus utendum est, aliae quae fruuntur et utuntur*).

Similarly, the crucial sentence in the *Epilogue* (d.1.3.11), which concludes the first distinction, reads:

"Of all that has been said since we began our discussion of things severally, this is the summation" [*De Doctr. Christ.* I, c.35]: that some things are to enjoyed, others to be used, and yet others enjoy and use (*quod aliae sunt quibus fruendum, aliae quibus utendum, aliae quae fruuntur et utuntur*); and among those which are to be used, there are even some through which we come to joy (*et inter eas quibus utendum est, quaedam sunt per quas fruimur*), such as the virtues and powers of spirit.

I quote this text at some length (including the Latin) as recent commentators have misinterpreted Peter's distinction, arguing that he introduces a third category of things – namely, "those that are to be enjoyed and used" (in the passive sense).[3]

---

[3] Marcia Colish, *Peter Lombard*, 2 vols. (Leiden: Brill, 1994), 79: "As for human beings, they are to be enjoyed as well as used. They deserve to be treated as moral ends; and indeed the created universe is

In reality, Peter only distinguishes between "things to be used," "things to be enjoyed" and "things that enjoy and use" in the active sense, not in the passive sense. So there is no talk of "things to be enjoyed and used." As a matter of fact, Peter makes clear that only God is to be enjoyed, and all other things are to be used. Of the things that are to be used, there are some through which we can enjoy God.

Following Augustine, Peter explicitly addresses the question of whether we should enjoy our fellow men (d.1.3.4). Peter answers negatively, drawing on a passage from *De Doctr. Christ.* 1.37: "When you enjoy a human being in God, you are really enjoying God rather than the human being." Although Peter does not always resolve tensions in his sources, he clearly does in this instance. We should only enjoy God.

When dealing with the question whether the virtues are to be used or enjoyed (d.1.1. 3.7–10), Peter again includes a number of quotations from Augustine. These citations suggest that virtues are not to be enjoyed (d.1.3.7). However, he then quotes Ambrose, who seems to suggest that the virtues are indeed to be loved for their own sake (d.1.3.8). Peter settles the issue as follows – and I quote him in full because in this citation Peter sets straight many modern (mis)interpretations of Augustine:

Wishing to remove the seeming contradiction of these authorities, we say that the virtues are to be sought and loved for their own sake (*propter se petendae et amandae sunt*), and yet only for the sake of beatitude (*et tamen propter solam beatitudinem*). They are to be loved for their own sake, because they delight those who possess them with a sincere and holy delight and give birth in them to a spiritual joy. However, we are not to stop here; we must climb higher. Do not let the course of love end here, nor let this be the limit of delight, but let this joy be related to that highest good, to which alone we must adhere wholly, because it alone is to be loved for its own sake and nothing is to be sought beyond it, since it is the highest end. – And so Augustine says that we love the virtues for the sake of beatitude alone, not because we do not love them for their own sake, but because we refer our very love of them to that highest good (*referimus ad illud summum bonum*), to which alone we are to adhere and in which we are to remain and place the summit of our joy. And so it follows that the virtues are not to be enjoyed. (d.1.3.9)

The quotation is significant for two reasons. First, Peter makes clear that, for Augustine, "referring" everything to God – that is, having God as the

---

ordered to their needs." The language of treating human beings "as moral ends" is, of course, not Peter's. It is more reminiscent of Kant, reflecting his emphasis upon moral autonomy and the realm of ends in his *Groundwork of the Metaphysics of Morals* and the famous axiom: "Act so that you treat humanity . . . always as an end and never as a means only." See also Philipp Rosemann, *Peter Lombard* (Oxford: Oxford University Press, 2004), 59.

object of our enjoyment, does not imply that we cannot love created things as intrinsically valuable and for their own sake (*propter se*). Second, the virtues are to be "used": they are not our ultimate concern (to use more modern language to rephrase the notion of "enjoying God"). Nevertheless, through them, by referring them to God we come to enjoy God. Peter does not entertain the idea that we enjoy and use virtues; for him, we use virtues, and through their use we come to enjoy God. The same applies to the humanity of Christ: through "using" it we can come to enjoy God. This explains why Peter treats the humanity of Christ and the virtues together in Book III. In both cases we are dealing with "things" that can be loved for their own sake, and yet in our "use" of them we come to enjoy God.

Let us finally and by way of summary, return to the structure of Peter's *Sentences*:

Book I: God – Things to be enjoyed.
Book II: Creation – Things that enjoy and use: angels and men (dist. 1–11 and 16–44).
– Things to be used: the world and its things (dist. 12–15).
Book III: Christology and Virtues. – Things to be used through which we come to the enjoyment of God.
Book IV: Signs or Sacraments.

In short, Peter only distinguishes between using things and enjoying God. Of course he does grant that we can "use things" in a way that allows us to enjoy *God*. But we are still using, not enjoying them. This, however, does not imply that we cannot regard them as intrinsically meaningful or valuable. In the first book, then, Peter deals with things to be enjoyed – that is, God. In the second book, Peter deals mainly with things that enjoy and use – that is, angels and men. In the third book, he deals with things to be used, although through our use of them we enjoy God. The final book deals with signs.

In what follows I mainly discuss Books I and IV. I do not attempt to survey all the issues Peter raises but instead focus on a limited number that proved either influential or controversial. In doing so I also hope to illustrate the way in which Peter Lombard's approach inaugurates a "systematization" of theology.

BOOK I: THE MYSTERY OF THE TRINITY

The first book deals with the doctrine of the Trinity. Peter deals with issues such as the scriptural witness to the unity and Trinity (d.2); the knowledge of the Trinity through creatures, which is insufficient without revelation (d.3); generation of the Son (d.4–7); and the procession and names of the Holy Spirit (d.10–18). Peter also pays major attention to the necessity of using proper theological language about the Trinity, discussing such questions as: Can we use the expression "the Father alone," given the fact that the three Persons are inseparable (d.21)? What does it mean to appropriate names (d.22)? What is the meaning of the word "person" (d.23, 25) and "hypostasis" (d.26)? After these more complex Trinitarian issues Peter concludes the first book with a discussion of God's knowledge (d.35–41) and God's will (d.42–48). Given the nature of the book, a mere summary of it would be a tedious affair. Instead, I examine a limited number of issues that have a particular significance in light of later debates.

It is fair to say that Peter's *Sentences* draw almost exclusively on the Church Fathers, especially St. Augustine. With the exception of distinction 2, the reader will not encounter any in-depth engagement with the Scriptures. Later scholastic theologians (especially Thomas Aquinas in his *Summa Theologiae*) will rectify this. In the third distinction, Peter raises the question whether traces of the Trinity can be discerned in creation. He states that "a sufficient knowledge of the Trinity cannot and could not be had by a contemplation of creatures, without the revelation of doctrine or inner inspiration" (d.3.1.9). And yet "we are aided in our faith in invisible things through those things which were made" (ibid.) – an illustration of the fact that Peter adopts the Victorine sacramental understanding of the world.

It is in this distinction that Peter examines the image of the Trinity in the soul. Peter believes he follows an Augustinian line here by arguing that memory, intelligence and love (will) offer a proper similitude of the three divine Persons. Memory, intellect and will are distinct and yet they exist substantially in the soul (d.3.2.8). Now Peter (d.3.2.6) understood memory, intellect and will in terms of three faculties or powers of the mind (*tria naturales proprietates seu vires*). This interpretation, which proved rather influential, was in danger of resulting in a static interpretation of our image-character (i.e., merely in terms of three faculties), and was later explicitly corrected by Thomas Aquinas in *ST* 1.93.7 *ad* 3. Peter is, however, well aware of the dissimilitude between the image (the soul) and its archetype (the Trinity). While we *have* memory, intellect and will, in God the three divine Persons *are* God. In us, "the person is neither memory, nor intelligence, nor love, but has all three. It is the one person who has these three things, but he is not these three" (d.3.3.1). Similarly, while each of us is a person with three faculties, God is not a person but is three Persons. Peter mentions another similitude, again following Augustine – namely, mind, knowledge and love. This is a more dynamic understanding than the one in terms of three faculties. Answering the question why mind is taken for the Father, knowledge for the Son and love for the Holy Spirit, Peter summarizes and passes on the Augustinian doctrine in the following terms:

The mind (*mens*) is, as it were, the parent, while its knowledge (*notitia*) is, as it were, its offspring: "For the mind, as it comes to know itself, begets knowledge of itself and is the sole parent of its knowledge" [St Augustine, *De Trin.* IX.12 (18)]. The third is love (*amor*), which proceeds from the mind itself and knowledge, when the mind, coming to know itself, loves itself; indeed, it could not love itself, if it did not know itself. It also loves its offspring, which it finds pleasing, namely its knowledge; and so love is an embrace of parent and offspring. (d.3.3.5; trans. pp. 25–26)

As the Father generates his Word as his offspring, and the Holy Spirit proceeds as their love, so too the mind generates knowledge, which it loves.

In distinction 5, Peter addresses the question whether the Father generated the divine essence, or whether an essence generated the Son. It is characteristic of the personalism of his Trinitarian theology that Peter rejects both claims.[4] For Peter, the Person of the Father generates the Son; there is no divine essence or nature "behind" the Persons. The main reason why Peter rejects the claim that the Father begets his essence is as follows. We do not say that the Father is wise because he begets wisdom; but in God to be and to be wise is the same. Therefore, the Father did not generate the essence by which he is: "Just as he did not beget the wisdom by which he is wise, he did not beget the essence by which he is" (d.5.1.4, trans. 31). Similarly, we cannot say that the divine essence generates the Son. For that would imply that the Son, who is the divine essence, would be that from which he is generated – that is, the same thing would generate itself (d.5.1.6).

Before Peter examines in detail how we can distinguish the three Persons, he discusses some properties of the divine nature or essence shared by the Persons. The first property he discusses is simplicity (d.8). Drawing mainly on Augustine, Peter makes the point that there is nothing accidental or composite in God (d.8.8.2). Whereas we have truth, wisdom and goodness, God *is* truth, wisdom and goodness, and these perfections are one in God: his goodness is the same as his wisdom or truth (d.8.4.3). In

---

[4] Personalism in this context refers to giving precedence to the three divine Persons over the divine nature or essence.

short, there is "nothing in God which is not God" (d.8.8.1). Given the simplicity of the being or essence of God, God is not subject to change or mortality (d.8.2).

When discussing the distinction of the Persons, Peter proposes some important and controversial views in relation to the Holy Spirit. In this section Peter argues that "the Holy Spirit is the love of Father and Son by which they love themselves mutually and us, but also the love by which we love God" (d.10.2.3; trans. 60). The first half of the claim is not all that controversial. Again drawing his inspiration from Augustine, Peter distinguishes between a substantialist view of love (i.e., the whole Trinity can be called love), and a view that attributes love to the Holy Spirit, as the love between Father and Son. The second half of the claim – in which the Holy Spirit is identified with the love by which we love God and neighbor – was considered more problematic. Let me consider this in more detail.

Following Karl Rahner, it is a commonplace in theology to claim that the immanent Trinity is the economic Trinity, and vice versa. Rahner's axiom implies that all our statements about the inner nature of the Trinity (= the immanent Trinity) have to be based on how this same Trinity reveals itself in the history of salvation (= the economic Trinity). Peter Lombard would agree. He argues that there are, for instance, two sendings or missions of the Son: one from all eternity (which we call "generation" from the Father), and another one, which occurs in time, and which is twofold: first, in the Incarnation, when the Word assumed flesh; second, when the Son begins to abide in holy souls (d.15.7). Similarly, there is a double procession of the Holy Spirit – namely, "an eternal one, which is ineffable and by which he proceeds from the Father and the Son; and a temporal one, by which he proceeds from the Father and the Son to sanctify the creature" (d. 14.1.1; trans. 73). This gift of the Holy Spirit is the love of God that is being poured into our hearts (cf. Rom. 5:5). As Philipp Rosemann writes, summarizing Peter's position: "the human love of God and neighbour is nothing but the unmediated presence of the Holy Spirit in the soul."[5] Thus, for Peter:

the very same Holy Spirit is the love or charity by which we love God and neighbour. When this charity is in us, so that it makes us love God and neighbor, then the Holy Spirit is said to be sent or given to us; and whosoever loves the very love by which he loves his neighbor, in that very thing loves God, because that very love is God, that is, the Holy Spirit. (d.17.1.2; trans. 88)

[5] Rosemann, *Peter Lombard*, 87.

Peter is aware that his view is controversial, and he deals with a range of objections in some detail (d.17.5 and 6).[6] If charity is the Holy Spirit, does that imply that the Holy Spirit can increase, given the fact that charity can increase? That would seem to clash with the immutability of God. Similarly, how can charity (or the Holy Spirit) be given to somebody who did not as yet have it, seeing that God is omnipresent anyhow? Peter answers these objections by stating that "the Holy Spirit or charity" is entirely unchangeable in himself, but he is "increased or diminished in a person, or better, for a person" (d.17.5.3; trans. 92). In other words, when we say that charity increases, or begins to be in somebody, we mean to say that the disposition to receive charity has grown. Again, if Holy Spirit and charity are being identified, then are we not compelled to say that the Holy Spirit is "an affection of the mind and a movement of the spirit" – a view that appears to clash with the immutability of God and blurs the distinction between creature and the transcendent God? Peter grants that charity can be called a movement of the spirit (*motus animi*), "not because it is itself a motion or affection or power of the spirit, but because through it, as if it were a power, the mind is drawn and moved" (d.17.6.7; trans., 97). Later theology would argue that the Holy Spirit creates the virtue of charity in us, thereby safeguarding the distinction between God and creature. Thomas, for instance, explicitly rejects the view of Peter Lombard in *ST* 11–11.23.2. Thomas claims that Peter's view, by downplaying the distinction between God and charity, effectively does away with the voluntary nature of charity. We effectively become mere instruments of the Holy Spirit, in an entirely extrinsic manner. As Thomas interprets Peter's position, *we* no longer love but it is, rather, the Holy Spirit in us who loves. To him this view simply clashes with the nature of love as an act of the human will.

As Rosemann rightly points out, Peter's view is perhaps the more spiritually appealing. "The idea that the love of God and neighbor is the very presence of the Holy Spirit in our midst is of a powerful beauty."[7] Thomas's position, on the other hand, better safeguards the integrity of our created nature and the distinction between the transcendent God and his creation.

In the remainder of Book 1, Peter pays considerable attention to theological language about the Trinity. Some names refer to a [personal] property, such as Son, Word or Gift (cf. d.18.2). Other words refer to the

---

[6] See d.17.6.1: "that he [= the Holy Spirit] is also the charity by which we love God and neighbour is denied by many."

[7] Rosemann, *Peter Lombard*, 89.

divine unity, such as wisdom, power or truth (d.22.2). Words or names that apply to the divine unity are used in an absolute sense (i.e., not relative, not implying a reference to the relations between the divine Persons) and are used in singular. For instance, "the Father is powerful," or "the Son is powerful," or "God is powerful." This is an example of substantialist use. Substantialist names are usually used in the singular. For instance, we say that the three Persons are Truth; we do not say that there are three Truths (as this would smack of tritheism) (cf. d.22.5). Names that belong to one specific person are used relatively (i.e., "the Second Person of the Trinity is the Word") – that is, they are used for one of the Three in light of the divine processions. Thus, the first Person is called "Father" as he is the fountainhead of the other Persons; similarly, the one the Father generates is called "Son" – and this name only applies to the second Person. The exception to this is the name "person" itself. It is used in a substantialist way – it applies to each of the three – and yet, unlike other substantialist names, it is used in plural. While we do not speak of three Goodnesses we speak of three Persons (d.23).

Peter continues to discuss the personal names of the divine Persons, further illustrating his concern for the use of proper theological language. Proper names, designating personal properties, are Father; Son, Word and Image; and Holy Spirit and Gift. Apart from the three properties (fatherhood, sonship and procession) Peter also mentions a number of "notions" or characteristics – that is, names that apply to one of the Persons only but are yet distinct from the properties mentioned. An example is "unbegotten." This is different from fatherhood and is not necessarily implied in fatherhood, but it too only applies to the first person of the Trinity (d.28.1.1). Later scholastic theology was to summarize these teachings in the following terms: there are two emanations (the Son from the Father, and the Holy Spirit from the Father and the Son), three hypostases (or subsistent realities, i.e., Father, Son and Holy Spirit), four relations (fatherhood, sonship, spiration, procession) and five notions or distinguishing characteristics (unbegottenness, fatherhood, sonship, spiration and procession).[8]

After this technical discussion of language about the Trinity, Peter concludes Book 1 by examining what we can say about the divine unity or substance. He discusses issues such as divine foreknowledge, omnipresence, providence, omnipotence and predestination (d.35ff.). In relation to the latter, he mentions Augustine's early view, according to which God

---

[8] See Bonaventure, *Brevil.* 1.3.

bestowed his grace upon those who would have faith in him (d.41.2.1). But he is aware that Augustine retracted this view (which makes God's bestowal of grace dependent upon our decision whether or not to receive it), and he concludes, with Augustine: "God elected whom he willed by a freely given mercy, not because they would be faithful in the future, but so that they might be faithful; and he gave grace to them not because they were faithful, but that they might become so" (d.41.2.7; trans. 228).

BOOK II: ON CREATION, AND BOOK III: ON THE INCARNATION OF THE WORD

I will not discuss Books II and III of *The Sentences* in detail. After the first, introductory distinction (in which Peter defines creation and explains how it differs from "making" something[9]), distinctions 2–11 discuss angels while distinctions 12–15 treat of the creation in six days (hexameron). In distinctions 16–18 Peter deals with the creation of man and woman, followed by a discussion of the Fall (d. 21ff.), free choice (d. 25) and how the will relates to grace (d.26 and 29), virtue (d.27) and evil and sin (d.30–44).

In Book III, Peter develops his Christology and soteriology, as well as his theological ethics, with a discussion of the theological and cardinal virtues (d. 23–32). While surveying different "opinions" on how to conceive of the hypostatic union (d.6) Peter landed himself in theological controversy.[10] Some of his critics alleged that Peter had aligned himself with the so-called theory of Christological nihilianism – that is, the teaching that Christ, insofar as he is human, was "nothing" (d.10). The question Peter attempts to answer is "whether Christ, according to his being man, is a person or something else." Now, the things of this world are either substances or persons. But Christ, qua humanity, cannot be a person (for his person is the divine Word). But if he is a substance, and assuming we exclude the view that Christ is an irrational substance, we are back to the notion of person. After all, Boethius had defined person precisely as "a rational

---

[9] Peter's ability to unpack complex theological issues in accessible theological language is evidenced by how he characterizes creation in d.1.2 of the second book (trans. 3–4): "A creator is one who makes some things from nothing, and, properly speaking, to create is to make something from nothing; but to make is to produce something not only from nothing, but also from matter."

[10] The three "opinions" are – in scholarly terms – the *homo assumptus* or two supposit theory, the subsistent person or composite person theory and the *habitus* theory. For a discussion of these, see Marcia Colish, "Christological Nihilianism in the Second Half of the Twelfth Century," in *Recherches de théologie ancienne et médiévale* (1996), vol. LXIII, 146–55.

substance." Peter concludes: "But if, according to his being man, he is the third person of the Trinity, then he is God" (d.10.1.2; trans. 41). This conclusion contradicts the teaching of the Church (and the view that the divinity and humanity of Christ are distinct). Therefore, "some say that Christ, according to his being man, is not a person or anything else" (ibid.). As this last quotation suggests, in *The Sentences* Peter himself does not explicitly espouse Christological nihilianism. Some critics (John of Cornwall and Walter of St. Victor), however, claimed that he did. Pope Alexander explicitly rejected the doctrine that Christ was not something insofar as he was man in AD 1177, and it is clear that he had Parisian schoolmasters in mind. Partly because Peter had not explicitly espoused Christological nihilianism in *The Sentences*, this controversy did not halt the dissemination of the work.

BOOK IV: THE DOCTRINE OF SIGNS

One of the achievements of 12th-century theology is the development of sacramental theology. Peter Lombard is one of the first to identify only seven sacraments: baptism (d.2–6), confirmation (d.7), the Eucharist (d.8–13), penance (d.14–22), unction of the sick (d.23), ordination (d.24–25) and marriage (d.26–42). The Lateran Council in 1215 adopted and confirmed the view that there are only seven sacraments. The choice to limit the sacraments to seven is the result of centuries-long reflection and is a genuine innovation of the medieval period. In the 6th century, Isidore of Seville, for instance, when writing about sacraments in the strict sense (i.e., rites used in a liturgical setting), had only distinguished two major sacraments – namely, "baptism and unction, and the Body and Blood [of the Lord]."[11] Isidore was writing at a time when baptism and chrism (unction) were still considered one sacrament. Indeed, to this day the Orthodox Church initiates people by dipping them into water, anointing them and allowing them to participate in the Eucharist. This reflects the older tradition in which the baptismal rite, usually performed at Easter, involved immersion into water, anointing by a priest of the head, laying of hands by the bishop and anointment by the bishop with another oil, and communion. After infant baptism had become universal practice, in the Latin West the traditional multifaceted baptismal rite had gradually been narrowed to "an intinction, that is, an exterior washing of the body made

---

[11] *Etymologies* VI.xix, 39–40.

under a prescribed form of words" (d.3.1.2). Anointing (by the bishop) became confirmation as baptisms did not necessarily take place around Easter anymore, and bishops were not always at hand to perform the anointing of the newly baptized.[12]

As I noted in a previous chapter, Hugh of St. Victor had used a rather broad notion of "sacrament." Peter Lombard will operate with a more focused – or narrower – understanding of sacrament. He defines a sacrament as "a sign of God's grace and a form of invisible grace in such a manner that it bears its image and its cause. And so the sacraments were not instituted only for the sake of signifying, but also to sanctify."[13] A number of aspects of this definition deserve to retain our attention. First, sacraments do not merely signify but also cause grace, and thereby sanctify us. As we will see, different sacraments signify different mysteries, but all of them are a cause of grace. Following Peter, later scholastics will put it succinctly: "Sacraments effect what they signify."[14]

Sacraments sanctify in different ways. Baptism, for instance, is a remedy against sin and confers helping grace (*gratia adiutrix*); marriage, in Peter's view, only confers a remedy, while the Eucharist fortifies us with grace and virtue (d.2.1.1).

Second, Peter believes that sacraments had to be instituted. But he admits that not all sacraments were directly instituted by Christ himself although all sacraments derive their power from the death and passion of Christ (d.2.1.2). Marriage stands out as a sacrament that was instituted as a sign by God in the Garden of Eden before the Fall. Only after the Fall did it serve as a remedy for sin under the new law. The other sacraments were instituted under the new law. Some of these, such as baptism (Matt. 3:16) (d.3.5.3), Eucharist (Matt. 26:26) (d.8.3) and penance (John 11:44) were instituted by Christ; others, such as the sacrament of extreme unction, were instituted by the apostles (cf. James 5:14–15) (d.23.3.1).

Following Hugh of St. Victor, Peter argues that the sacraments were instituted for a threefold reason.[15] First, it is an exercise in humility: while in sinful pride our first parents had scorned divine things, we now have to

---

[12] For a helpful history of the sacraments, see Joseph Martos, *Doors to the Sacred: Historical Introduction to Sacraments in the Catholic Church* (Liguori, MS: Liguori Publications, 2001).

[13] See d.1.4.2. Translation by Giulio Silano from Peter Lombard, *The Sentences: Book IV. On the Doctrine of Signs* (Toronto: Pontifical Institute of Medieval Studies, 2010). I use this translation in what follows.

[14] Cf. *ST* III.62.1 *ad* 1: *efficiunt quod figurant*. In d.4.1.2 Peter mistakenly attributes this phrase to Augustine, talking about the elect: "*Sacramenta in solis electis efficiunt quod figurant* [Sacraments effect what they signify only in the elect]." He uses the phrase again in d.22.2.4.

[15] *De Sacr.* 1, part 9, chapter 3.

find salvation through material elements below us. Second, it involves a useful process of instruction, nurturing in us a sense of the divine in material things. Through the sacraments we learn how to perceive the invisible in the visible. Finally, the sacraments were instituted for the sake of exercise and restoration of the mind. Here Peter only gives a brief summary of Hugh's key insight: through sin we had become splintered and fragmented, losing ourselves in manifold distractions and diversions. Through the different sacraments, however, God leads us back to unity and wholeness (d.1.5).

Let me now briefly discuss Peter's views on each of the sacraments.

Baptism

Baptism was instituted by Christ for the forgiveness of sins. When Christ allowed himself to be baptized by St. John, he did so not to be cleansed (for he was free from sin), but in order to confer his regenerative powers on the waters (d.3.5.3). As I mentioned earlier, Peter defines baptism as an immersion of the body in water under a prescribed form of words – that is, an invocation of the Trinity (cf. Matt. 28:19) (d.3.1.2; d.3.2). Water is to be used because it symbolizes cleansing: as water cleans the body, so too baptismal water cleanses the soul. Peter has already informed us that the sacraments obtain their healing and sanctifying power from the passion of Christ, and he duly refers to John 19:34 (the water and blood flowing from Christ's side) to explicate this link (d.3.6; d.3.9.2).

In previous chapters, I have alluded to the distinction medieval theology drew between the thing or reality (*res*) and the sacrament (*sacramentum*). This distinction allows Peter to offer a nuanced theology of baptism (d.4).

The thing or the reality of baptism is justification, remission of sins, or inner cleanness (*interior munditia*). For baptism has as its goal "a renewal of the mind" (*innovatio mentis*) (d.3.9.1). Now some people receive both sacrament and thing. People who, with faith and the right intention, are baptized in accordance with the proper rite (words and water) will receive the sacrament and the thing. This includes infants who may not have a personal faith: through the faith of their sponsors they receive the saving power of the sacrament.[16] Adults who receive baptism without faith or genuine contrition receive the sacrament but not the thing (*res*).

---

[16] More specifically, the guilt of original sin is forgiven, and they also receive operating and cooperating grace as a gift, not in use (d.4.7.5).

Interestingly, there are also those who receive the thing, but not the sacrament (d.4.4). Those who, without being baptized, suffer for Christ or who have genuine contrition (such as the thief who was promised that he would be with Christ in paradise) receive the thing but not the sacrament.[17] Thus it can also happen that people receive the thing (i.e., justification and inner conversion) before they receive the actual sacrament of baptism (d.4.7). This illustrates that Peter does not endorse a kind of "mechanical" or "magical" understanding of the sacraments. The sacraments derive their saving power from Christ, not from the ritual performed as such. This power, then, can work its effects (e.g., faith, inner renewal) before one undergoes the actual rite of baptism.

Confirmation

Peter's discussion of confirmation is a mere two pages (d.6). He mentions that in principle it can only be administered by the bishop. Through it we receive the power of the Holy Spirit and increase in holiness and virtue. Like baptism, it bestows a character or indelible imprint on the soul, and should therefore not be repeated.

Eucharist

The Eucharist is "a remembrance and representation of the true sacrifice . . . made on the altar of the cross."[18] It was instituted by Christ (Matt. 26:26–28) for the growth of charity and as a medicine for our infirmity (d. 12.6.1). In it we receive Christ, the fount and origin of all grace in a most intimate manner (d.8.1). It was prefigured in the manna from heaven in the desert (Ex. 16:4): "this heavenly food brings the faithful to heaven as they cross the desert of this world" (d.8.2.2). After a brief discussion of the form of the sacrament (i.e., the words to be pronounced to change the bread and wine into the body and blood of Christ, cf. Matt. 26:26–28) Peter turns his attention to the distinction between sacrament (*sacramentum*) and thing (*res*).

Partly in response to Berengar of Tours' challenge, Hugh of St. Victor and others had developed a sophisticated theology of *sacramentum* and *res*, according to which the sacrament of the Eucharist can be both figure and

---

[17] Cf. Luke 23:43, cited in d.4.4.3.
[18] Cf. d.12.5.1. Again he refers to John 19:34, the blood flowing from the side of Christ on the Cross (cf. d.8.2.3).

truth.[19] Hugh had distinguished between a number of possibilities: first, there are those who receive the sacrament and the *res* (the thing, or substance) of the sacrament. They are the people who do not just partake in the bread and wine (the sacrament), but do so in faith and love, and through this communion they become incorporated into Christ (this is the *res*). There are others who only receive the sacrament – that is, they eat the bread and drink the wine, but they do not receive the substance of the sacrament (*res*) because they lack faith and love. Again, there are those who receive grace (*res*) even though they do not participate in the Eucharist (a possibility Peter Lombard will not examine).[20]

Hugh had made clear that the sacrament of the altar contains three components: (a) the visible appearance (of the bread and wine), (b) the truth of body and blood of Christ (which is invisibly present under the visible appearance of bread and wine) and (c) spiritual grace contained in the body and blood.[21]

Peter's outline is fairly similar to that of the Victorines, with a number of qualifications.[22] He distinguishes between (a) the sacrament – namely, the bread and wine. Second is the thing (res), which is twofold: first is what he calls (b) "the thing contained and signified," which is the body and blood of Christ. A second component of the *res* is (c) "the thing signified and not contained": this is "the unity of the Church," the Church (or community of believers), united in faith and charity as the mystical body of Christ (d.8.7.1–2). So, (a) there is the visible appearance of bread and wine, and this is the sacrament (and not the thing); there is (b) the body and blood of Christ, which is the sacrament and the thing; and, finally (c), there is the mystical flesh, which is the thing (and not the sacrament) (d.8.7.2). The second (b) and third (c) elements both belong to the *res*. The difference is that (b) is contained and signified by the visible species of bread and wine, while (c) is signified by but not contained in the bread and wine. Behind this fledgling scholastic terminology one can detect echoes of Augustine's Eucharistic theology and ecclesiology: the body of Christ can refer to the consecrated bread and wine, or it can refer to the Church as the community of believers united in faith and love (the Church as the mystical body of Christ).

This twofold understanding of the *res* of the Eucharist has an important advantage for Peter's theology. It allows him to explain that people who

---

[19] *De Sacr.* 11.8.6.   [20] Ibid., 11.8.5.   [21] Ibid., 11.8.7.
[22] Apart from Hugh, Peter is also influenced by the *Sententiae Divinitatis* and *Summa Sententiarum*. For an in-depth discussion of the theological context of Peter Lombard's Eucharistic theology, see Colish, *Peter Lombard*, 551–83.

partake in the Eucharist in an unworthy manner do receive the real body and blood of Christ (the first aspect of *res*), but they do not receive the spiritual communion (the second aspect of *res*). "They receive, under the visible species, the flesh of Christ derived from the Virgin, and the blood shed for us, but not the mystical flesh, which pertains only to the good" (d.9.2.1). They do receive the genuine body and blood but to no avail and without saving effectiveness.

After a strong affirmation of the real presence of Christ in the Eucharist in d.10, Peter turns to the manner of the change of bread and wine into the body and blood of Christ in d.11. Peter argues that the substances of bread or wine are turned or converted into the body and blood of Christ. After the consecration only the species of the bread and wine remain – that is, the way they look and taste remain the same, but their substance is changed into the substance of the body and blood of Christ. This theory was developed by later scholastics, using Aristotelian categories, into the doctrine of transubstantiation: the substances of wine and bread are changed into the substances of the body and blood of Christ respectively, while the accidents remain.[23] Peter rejects the theory that the substances of bread and wine continue to exist after the consecration – a view known as consubstantiation (d.11.1.10 and d.12.1.1).

Before I conclude my discussion of Peter's outline of the theology of the Eucharist, I want to briefly draw attention to Peter's sensitivity toward the symbolic nature of the Eucharistic rite. The fact that the Eucharist is offered under a double species reveals the wholeness of our redemption: bread and wine are taken to represent our body and soul respectively, which Christ assumed and restored in their entirety (d. 11.4.1). The wine is to be mixed with water, as this symbolizes the intimate union between Christ (the wine) and his people (the water) (d.11.5.1). Again, the bread must be made of wheat, for Christ compares himself to a grain of wheat (John 12:24) (d.11.5.3). And the breaking of the bread represents, of course, Christ's broken body on the Cross (d.12.4.2). Finally, Peter proves himself rather impatient with futile speculations, such as the vexed question of what a mouse receives when it eats the consecrated bread: "What does it eat? God knows!" (d.13.1.8).

Penance

The early Church knew only public confession of sins. The medieval penitential system (private, repeated confession to a priest, followed by

---

[23] Cf. *ST* III.75.

acts of penance) finds its remote origins in the penitential system of Irish monks. Their penitential books detailed the offences and the appropriate remediation. This led to a transformation of penitential practices in the West, and Peter Lombard's extensive treatment of the sacrament of penance reflects this theological reflection of the previous centuries.

Penance is described as "the second plank after shipwreck": after baptism, penance is a second remedy (d.14.1.1). It can even be considered superior to baptism, for while baptism is a sacrament only, penance also involves a virtue of the mind – that is, a contrite heart (d.14.1.2). He defines penance as "a virtue by which we bewail and hate, with the purpose of amendment, the evils we have committed, and we will not to commit again the things we have bewailed" (d.14.3.1).

Peter identifies three central aspects in penance – namely, contrition of heart, confession of the mouth and satisfaction in deed (d.16.1.1). Peter applies the distinction between *res* (thing), *sacramentum* (sacrament) and *sacramentum et res* to these elements of penance. The sacrament alone refers to outward penance, the sacrament and the thing is inward penance, and the thing without the sacrament is remission of sins (d.22.2.5).

The threefold dimension of penance also leads to a number of probing questions, such as (d.17): Can sin be remitted without confession? Is it sufficient to confess to God alone (or is it necessary to confess to a priest)? Can we confess to a layperson if there are no priests around? While Peter gives a balanced answer to these questions, his overall position leans toward a qualified "contritionism."

As in baptism, remission of sins can be obtained without the sacrament. Outward penance and confession are, strictly speaking, not necessarily required for the forgiveness of sins – namely, when they are not possible. Peter quite plausibly argues that we can hardly claim to be truly repentant if we do not have the intention to confess. But remission of sins, and even the very desire to confess and repent, are gifts from God. Confession and acts of repentance reveal that we have been forgiven; they are not the instruments through which we can, in a mechanical or transactional manner, obtain forgiveness from God. Peter states: "And so it is necessary for a penitent to confess, if he has the time; and yet, before there is confession by the mouth, if there is the intention in the heart, remission is granted to him" (d.17.1.13). Similarly, "if the opportunity exists," we must involve a priest in the confession of our sins (d.17.3.8).[24] But in

---

[24] If no priest is available, we can have recourse to a neighbor or a friend (d.17.4.2).

principle we can obtain forgiveness of sins through contrition only. This is why scholars call Peter's position "contritionism."

This stance confirms that Peter does not subscribe to a mechanical view of the sacraments. Going through the motions of the rite will not do. What matters is inner penance, contrition and humility of heart. Contrition, confession and acts of penance are the effect of God's gift of grace, not the cause. If, because of circumstances (such as geographical remoteness), we do not have access to a priest or cannot engage in confession or satisfaction, contrition is what matters and our sins will be forgiven. Indeed, the very fact that we are remorseful is, for Peter, an indication in its own right that we have received God's forgiveness.

The reader may perhaps be wondering: What then is the point of confession? Peter himself raises this question: "And so, if it is asked for what is confession necessary, since the sin is already blotted out in contrition, we say: because it is a kind of punishment for the sin, as is satisfaction in deed" (d.17.5). Peter means that through confession itself we become more humble and careful.

Peter's account of the sacrament of penance is refreshing. For him, the very fact that we feel remorse is already a sign that God has forgiven us.[25] This is a liberating, not oppressive theology of penance. Consider the following passage:

For no one truly has compunction for sin, having *a contrite and humbled heart* [cf. Ps. 51:17], except in charity. Now he who has charity is worthy of life. But no one is simultaneously worthy of both life and death, and so he is not then bound by the debt of eternal death. For he ceased to be a son of wrath from the moment when he began to love and repent; and so, from then on, he is absolved from wrath. .... Therefore, it is not afterwards, through the priest to whom he confesses, that he is freed from eternal wrath; he was already freed from it by the Lord, when he said, *I shall confess* [cf. Ps. 31:5]. (d.18.4.6, trans. 108)

Rosemann aptly summarizes Peter's balanced views: "God's charity wipes out our sins, and the forgiving love announces itself in inner remorse, which in turn gives rise to the desire to make a confession and to engage in works of atonement."[26] It is because charity is at the heart of Peter's vision of the sacrament of penance that his theology of penance is so liberating.

---

[25] Peter's contritionism implies that the sacramental power of the priest is limited. Peter affirms unequivocally that God alone remits sins. God confers upon priests the power to absolve from sin ("the power of the keys"). Peter explains this by drawing an analogy with the priests of the Old Covenant who merely discern which lepers are clean and which unclean (d.18.6.1–3).

[26] Rosemann, *Peter Lombard*, 167.

The Sacrament of Extreme Unction

While Peter's discussion of penance was highly extensive, his treatment of unction of the sick is very short. Peter reminds us that it was instituted by the apostles (James 5:14–15) for the remission of sins and relief of bodily infirmity (d.23.3.1–2). The sacrament is the outer anointing; the thing (*res*) of the sacrament is the inner anointing (through the remission of sin and the increase of virtue). In Peter's view the sacrament is repeatable (d.23.4).

Ecclesiastical Orders

Peter's discussion of ecclesiastical orders is more elaborate. He identifies seven degrees or orders of spiritual offices but pays most attention to the priesthood.[27] Priests receive a spiritual character – that is, a mark by which spiritual power is granted (d.24.13.1). Later scholastics such as Thomas Aquinas were to develop this theology of the spiritual character in much greater detail. The office of bishop and pope is not considered an order or sacrament (d.24.15–16). Peter shows little interest in the role of the pope. He dedicates a mere three lines to it.

Marriage

Marriage is the only sacrament that was instituted before the Fall, so as to safeguard the procreation of the human race. In a sinful world it then also acquired a remedial function – that is, it became a vehicle for chastity ("to avoid illicit stirrings" [d.26.2.1] of a sexual nature).

Marriage is "a good thing," instituted by God between Adam and Eve (Gen. 2:24) and endorsed by Christ at the wedding of Cana (John 2:2–10) (d.26.5). It is a sacred sign of the joining of Christ and the Church. There is a twofold dimension to this signification: "For just as there is between the partners to a marriage a joining according to the consent of souls and the intermingling of bodies, so the Church joins herself to Christ by will and nature" (d.26.6.1). The consent of the partners signifies the spiritual joining of Christ and the Church, which occurs through charity. Sexual intercourse signifies the union of the human and divine natures in the Incarnation (d.26.6).

---

[27] The others are doorkeepers, lectors, exorcists, acolytes, subdeacons and deacons.

The first aspect, consent, constitutes a marriage, which is why the marriage of Joseph and Mary (which was not consummated) is considered valid.[28] Their marriage was perfect in holiness but not in signification (d.30.2.3). It lacked in signification because its asexual nature failed to symbolize the incarnational aspect of the union between Christ and his Church. The marriage of Mary and Joseph did involve the threefold good of marriage – namely, faith (i.e., the fidelity of the spouses to one another), offspring ("that children should be lovingly received and religiously educated") and sacrament ("that the marriage be not severed" – i.e., the indissolubility of marriage, reflecting the union between Christ and his Church) (d.30.2.4 and d.31.1.1).

In short, marriage cannot be reduced to either mere cohabitation or sexual relations. It is "the joining of husband and wife of lawful standing, maintaining an undivided manner of life" (d.27.2).

Peter concludes his work with a discussion of the last things, such as resurrection of the dead, suffrages for the dead and the last judgment (d.43–50).

CONCLUSION

Peter Lombard's achievement in *The Sentences* is considerable. In historical terms it became the standard textbook throughout the Middle Ages and beyond. His selection of topics to be discussed and the responses he includes to the questions raised are always balanced and judicious. His *Sentences*, although deeply influenced by patristic thought (especially Augustine), as well as by some of his contemporaries (such as the Victorines), proved a milestone in the history of theology, leading to a greater systematization of theological thinking. He can be rightly called the father of scholasticism.

BIBLIOGRAPHICAL NOTE

The Latin text of Peter Lombard's *Sentences* has been published as *Magistri Petri Lombardi Sententiae in IV libris distinctae*, ed. Ignatius Brady, 2 vols. Spicilegium Bonaventurianum 4 and 5 (Grottaferrata: Editiones Collegii S. Bonaventurae Ad Claras Aquas, 1971, 1981).

---

[28] Consent is central to the establishment of the marital bond. Peter discusses in detail possible scenarios of invalid consent, which provide grounds for annulment. This need not detain us.

For an excellent English translation (which I have used in this chapter), see Giulio Silano, *Peter Lombard:* The Sentences, 4 vols. (Toronto: Pontifical Institute of Medieval Studies, 2007–10).

The best commentaries on Peter Lombard are Philipp Rosemann, *Peter Lombard* (Oxford: Oxford University Press, 2004) and (more detailed): Marcia Colish, *Peter Lombard*, 2 vols. (Leiden: Brill, 1994).

PART IV

The 13th Century

CHAPTER 13

Introduction
Mendicant Orders, Universities and Islamic Scholarship

The 13th century witnessed major changes in economic and social circumstances, above all the growth of towns that accompanied greater economic activity, and the rise of universities (Oxford, Paris, Cambridge, Bologna, Salamanca), usually out of cathedral schools, as independent centers of learning. Influential nation-states, especially France, rose in Europe at the expense of papal power. Governments were increasingly centralized and professionalized.

The 13th century represents the flowering of medieval culture. The confidence and religious fervor of the 13th century found superb expression in Gothic architecture, which, although dating from the 12th century, was perfected throughout the 13th. The "French Style" (as medievals called it) became the most popular architectural style throughout Europe, from Sicily to Scandinavia, from the British Isles to Poland. The Reims cathedral was begun in the 1220s; the Sainte-Chapelle in Paris was built during the fifth decade of the 13th century. It was one of the defining architectural styles of European culture. With its pointed arches, searing heights and shimmering light, Gothic architecture draws the gaze of the worshipper up to heaven. It is an architectural expression of the self-transcending dynamic of the medieval mind.

In religious terms, the 13th century reflects the societal changes that were taking place. New religious orders were founded, and two were to leave an indelible mark on the intellectual history of the late medieval period: the Franciscans and the Dominicans. The Dominican Order was founded by an Augustinian canon called Dominic. The main aim of the order was to disseminate the truth of the Christian faith through preaching while assuming the simplicity of the apostolic life. The Dominicans focused on academic centers in Europe, such as Paris and Bologna. One of their greatest luminaries is, of course, St. Thomas Aquinas.

Francis was the son of an affluent cloth merchant of Assisi. At the age of twenty-four he gave up all his wealth in order to lead a radical apostolic life of renunciation and radical poverty. The Franciscans put a distinct emphasis on piety and living a life of poverty. Many of the most important 13th- and 14th-century thinkers were Franciscan: St. Bonaventure, John Duns Scotus, Peter Aureoli and William of Ockham.

Both orders grew rapidly. It is estimated that around AD 1300 there were twenty-eight thousand Franciscans and twelve thousand Dominicans.[1] The attraction of the friars was diverse: to poor people becoming a friar meant security and respectability; to the rich it meant freedom from the scramble for ecclesiastical preferment and an opportunity for prolonged theological study and teaching.

The intellectual transformation of the Latin West in the 13th century centered around the incipient universities. Their curriculum, in turn, was profoundly shaped by the gradual assimilation of Aristotle's entire oeuvre and the Islamic commentaries that facilitated this reception. The Latin West in the 13th century was by no means a closed society. It benefited immensely from non-Christian sources, especially Islamic and Jewish scholarship. Christian thinkers such as Albert and Thomas delighted in engaging with Islamic scholarship because it assisted them in absorbing the thought of Aristotle, whom they considered the greatest philosopher of all time. Such an engagement with non-Christian scholarship – pluralist and ecumenical even by 21st-century standards – should not surprise us. It was because there was a fairly cohesive worldview in the 13th century (itself inherently plural in origin – i.e., the fruit of the Judeo-Christian tradition of the first millennium, seasoned by Greek and Roman thought) that engagement with Islamic scholarship could take place so serenely. Furthermore, the Islamic scholarship the Latin West was exposed to at the end of the 12th century and the beginning of the 13th was equally fascinated by Greek philosophy. The difference was, simply, that Islamic thinkers had enjoyed access to Aristotle's key writings long before Western scholars had.

The writings of Latin luminaries such as Albert the Great and Thomas Aquinas are littered with references to Avicenna, Averroes (whom they call "The Commentator") and other Islamic thinkers, especially when they are discussing issues of metaphysics, physics, ethics or psychology rather than theology in the strict sense. Still, philosophical insights have repercussions for theological debates. Let us, by way of example, consider a highly contentious issue that preoccupied the minds of the greatest Latin thinkers throughout the 13th century. In what is perhaps the most disputed passage in his entire oeuvre (*De Anima* 430a13ff.), Aristotle makes a distinction between the passive or

---

[1] See Richard Southern, *Western Society and the Church in the Middle Ages* (Harmondsworth: Penguin, 1990), 272–99.

potential and active aspects of the intellect, and he appears to hold that the active dimension of the intellect is separate from human thinkers. In Thomas Aquinas's reading, however, the function of the passive intellect is to receive the intelligible forms (actually thinkable objects) that our active intellect abstracts from material things in the world. (I perceive a dog because my active intellect has abstracted the intelligible species of "caninehood" from the material thing I perceive.) Arabic commentators generally argued (probably quite correctly) that for Aristotle the active intellect does not belong to the human soul but to a separate intelligence. Averroes, for instance, believed that the Aristotelian so-called active intellect was one and separate from the human person. This view is known as monopsychism. Our (philosophical) happiness on earth, so Averroes argued, was to occur when our own material or possible intellect conjoined the separate active intellect. Thomas rejected this first on philosophical grounds: it would imply that proper thinking no longer occurs in the human person as such. We would not be thinking but thinking would occur to us, in an almost extraneous manner. Second, there was a theological consideration: if we ourselves do not have a proper active intellect (which is incorporeal and universal in range, according to Thomas), it will become impossible to argue for the immortality of the human soul.[2] Albert the Great also contended that the active intellect is ours but he would retain the notion of "conjunction" of our intellect with separate intelligences in which, according to Albert, supreme happiness on earth consists. Other theologians, often with more Augustinian leanings, claimed that the active intellect was God's intellect: they combined a peripatetic reading of the active intellect as separate with the Augustinian doctrine of illumination. Roger Bacon, for instance (in his *Opus Majus*, Part 11, chapter 5), accepted that the active intellect is the divine intellect.

This discussion illustrates that philosophical issues (e.g., how we know and the status of the active intellect) have major repercussions for our understanding of the soul, its potential immortality and the nature of happiness, both here on earth (as with Albert's espousal of the possibility of philosophical happiness through "conjunction") and in the afterlife (where, according to Thomas, an illumination by God through the light of glory does take place, in contrast to our earthly ways of knowing, which are invariably dependent on the senses as their primary source). There were

---

[2] The assumptions are that incorporeal things are not subject to decline; for the soul to be able, in principle, to cognize all things (including material things), it itself needs to be immaterial. To use an analogy: if you want to see all the colors around you, you should wear neutral (non-colored) glasses. Similarly, the soul, which in principle can know all things, including material things, cannot itself be material.

other major issues, aside from the status of the active intellect and the
immortality of the individual soul it involves, such as: the question of
whether the world is eternal or created with a beginning in time; the
relation between theology and philosophy, and faith and reason (itself
a burning and long-established problem in Islamic thought); and whether
God exerts providential care over his creation.

The gradual exposure of the Latin West to the major writings of
Aristotle (*Nicomachean Ethics, Metaphysics, De Anima, Physics*, etc.) was
to occur via two channels.[3] First, through its trade Venice was in close
contact (and at times conflict) with the Byzantine Empire. As early as the
middle of the 12th century James of Venice provided a (literalist) translation into Latin of the Greek text of Aristotle's *Posterior Analytics, Physics*
and *De Anima*.

The Iberian Peninsula, with the south still under Muslim rule and
influence (it was not until 1492 that the Spanish Reconquista was finally
completed), proved a fertile soil for intellectual exchanges. In Toledo
a number of scholars translated works from Arabic into Latin, including
Dominicus Gundissalinus (d. ca. 1190) and, somewhat later, Michael Scot
(d. 1232) who also produced translations of Averroes's *Commentaries* on
Aristotle. One of the major figures in Toledo was Gerard of Cremona (d.
1187), who translated Euclid's *Elements of Geometry* and Aristotle's *De Coelis*,
as well as *The Book of Causes* (*Liber de Causis*) from Arabic into Latin. The
Liber de Causis offers an illuminating example of the crisscross intellectual
exchanges I alluded to earlier. Gerard translated a book from Arabic under
the title *The Book on the Exposition of the Pure Good*, which was generally
attributed to Aristotle, despite its strong Neoplatonic character. The text
Gerard translated, later known in the West as *Liber de Causis* was, as it
happened, an Arabic compilation from *The Elements of Theology* by a Greek
philosopher of late antiquity, Proclus (d. AD 485). William of Moerbeke (d.
1286), a celebrated Flemish Dominican who provided the definitive Latin
translations of key works from Greek philosophy (including new translations
of *Politics* and *Poetics* and revisions of older translations of Aristotle's
writings), made a full translation of Proclus's *Elements*. When he shared

---

[3] For a lucid overview, see Russell Friedman, "Latin Philosophy, 1200–1350," in John Marenbon (ed.),
The Oxford Handbook of Medieval Philosophy (Oxford: Oxford University Press, 2012), 192–219,
especially 194–96; and Bernard Dod, "Aristoteles Latinus," in Norman Kretzmann, Anthony Kenny
and Jan Pinborg (eds.), *The Cambridge History of Later Medieval Philosophy* (Cambridge: Cambridge
University Press, 1982), 45–79; see also Dag Nikolaus Hasse, "Influence of Arabic and Islamic
Philosophy on the Latin West," *Stanford Encyclopedia of Philosophy* (spring 2020 edition), ed.
Edward N. Zalta. https://plato.stanford.edu/archives/spr2020/entries/arabic-islamic-influence

his work with his famous fellow Dominican, Thomas Aquinas, the latter immediately realized that *Liber de Causis* could not possibly have been an Aristotelian work but consisted of excerpts from Proclus's *Elements*. Such a discovery mattered tremendously for it allowed Thomas to gauge better how the authentic Aristotle differed from the (Neo)Platonism he had become associated with throughout the centuries.

The translations of the works of Avicenna and Averroes had an enormous impact on the Latin intellectual and cultural scene, and I conclude this section by giving a brief sketch of their achievements, even though their influence made itself felt more immediately in philosophy than in theology.

Ibn Sina (AD 980–1037), or Avicenna as he was known in the Latin West, was born near Bukhara, in what is today Uzbekistan. Unfortunately, the details of Avicenna's rather colorful life cannot be discussed within the constraints of this chapter. His philosophical thought (which included metaphysics, psychology, natural science, logic and medicine) benefited from an earlier translation movement in the 9th century in which the major Greek philosophical and scientific writings had been translated into Arabic. At the center of this movement, in Baghdad in Persia, al-Farabi (ca. 870–950) became one of the most celebrated philosophers in the peripatetic tradition, and his thought had a major impact upon Avicenna's own interpretation of the Aristotelian oeuvre. His major work is *Kitāb al Shifa'* (*The Book of Healing*), part of which proved highly influential in the Latin Middle Ages. Of particular importance was the distinction he made between essence and existence, the notion that being is what our intellect grasps first, the metaphysical proof of God's existence (for Aristotle, physics, rather than metaphysics, proved God's existence), and his decision to define the subject matter of metaphysics in terms of existent qua existent.[4] Anyone familiar with Thomas Aquinas's writings will discern Avicenna's influence on Thomas's metaphysical outlook.

Averroes (Ibn Rushd) (1126–98) was born in Cordoba, Andalusia. Averroes acted as judge and physician but dedicated most of his free time to philosophy. Scholars identify three periods in his philosophical output: after an initial period in which he mainly worked on logic, he wrote middle commentaries on Aristotle's works and produced a treatise that has received considerable attention from scholars today – namely, the so-called *Decisive*

---

[4] Amos Bertolacci, "Ibn Sīnā (d. 428/1037). 'Metaphysics of the *Shifā*,'" in Khaled el-Rouayheb and Sabine Schmidtke (eds.), *The Oxford Handbook of Islamic Philosophy* (Oxford: Oxford University Press, 2017), 143–68 and Jon McGinnis, *Avicenna* (Oxford: Oxford University Press, 2010).

Treatise on the relation between Islamic law and philosophy. In a final period he wrote long commentaries on Aristotle's most important works, such as *Metaphysics*, *Physics* and *De Anima*, amongst others.[5] These writings, which were quickly translated into Latin, secured for Averroes the title of "the Commentator" on Aristotle's oeuvre. In the *Decisive Treatise* Averroes propounds a harmonious relation between philosophy and religion. This treatise, however, was not known in the medieval West. As a consequence, Latin authors erroneously came to associate Averroes with the view that theology and philosophy have their own truths, which can be opposed to one another. I have already commented on Averroes's view that the active intellect is one for all human beings. According to Averroes, when the human intellect acquires all intelligibles and becomes an "acquired intellect" (*intellectus adeptus* in Albert the Great's writings), it is able to think in virtue of the active intellect as its form. In full "conjunction" our intellect is joined with the (separate) agent intellect as its final form, and it is in this that human felicity on earth consists.[6]

The view that philosophical and theological truths can be in tension with one another, as well as the notion that philosophical contemplation on earth is the most secure route to happiness, came to be associated with "Latin Averroism." It provoked the important condemnations of 1277, discussed in Chapter 19.

The religious fervor of the 13th century also found expression outside the standard ecclesial channels. One of the most striking examples of a religious movement on the fringes is the so-called beguine movement. The term *beguine* refers to a woman who lives a religious life without taking vows. The beguines have left us beautiful spiritual texts, often deeply Christocentric, and mostly written in the vernacular. Key examples are Hadewijch, Beatrijs van Nazareth (both Flemish), Marguerite Porete (from Hainault) and Mechthild von Magdeburg (Germany). In this part I focus primarily on the main scholastic thinkers of the period, but I commence by considering the mystical theology of two beguines, if only because in theological terms the early beguines were indebted to the Cistercian tradition (discussed in Chapter 8), with which they often enjoyed strong ties.

---

[5] Catarina Belo, "Averroes (d. 1198), The Decisive Treatise," in Rouayheb and Schmidtke, *Oxford Handbook of Islamic Philosophy*, 278–95.
[6] Matteo di Giovanni, "Averroes and Philosophy in Islamic Spain," in Marenbon, *Oxford Handbook of Medieval Philosophy*, 106–29.

CHAPTER 14

Two Beguines
Mechthild of Magdeburg and Hadewijch

The beguine movement was a unique phenomenon in the medieval period. It consisted of mostly women who decided to lead a life of devotion but who declined to take official religious vows. They provided for themselves, usually living in a small community. This was a strikingly independent move. To have women living in the world, fending for themselves, who were neither married nor a member of a religious order, but who still led a life of devotion, struck their contemporaries as disturbingly innovative.

The movement flourished from the beginning of the 13th century to the first decades of the 14th century in parts of the Low Countries and the west of Germany, after which it declined. It is difficult to account for the trend. Undoubtedly, this area was one of the most advanced areas of medieval society at that time (in terms of trade, prosperity and urbanization).[1] Another contributory factor may have been the surplus of women (due to warfare and the attractions of monastic life for men). This is evidenced by the fact that the demand for places in convents far surpassed availability. It appears that especially Cistercian nunneries grew dramatically. As Bernard McGinn reminds us, there were close links between the houses of beguines and the Cistercian convents. Often beguines became Cistercian nuns.[2] Many Cistercian nuns claimed to have visions and led lives of profound holiness. They managed to acquire prestige and influence due to the protection of monks or friars who vouched for their sanctity, and who often wrote their biographies. The beguines' contemporary male admirers wrote dozens of *Lives* of devout women. Thomas of Cantimpré (born in 1200 and joined the Dominicans in 1232) wrote five such *Lives*,

---

[1] The other highly advanced area was northern Italy (especially Tuscany and Umbria). In both Flanders and northern Italy we find women writing religious treatises in the vernacular.

[2] Bernard McGinn, *The Presence of God: A History of Western Christian Mysticism. Vol. III. The Flowering of Mysticism: Men and Women in the New Mysticism, 1200–1350* (New York: Herder and Herder, 1998), 160.

including *The Life of Christina the Astonishing* (of St. Truiden in the eastern part of present-day Flanders), *The Life of Margaret of Ieper* and *Lutgard of Aywières* (Flemish and born in Tongeren). These *Lives* and others like them were written in Latin by men. But some women also wrote their own treatises in the vernacular. One of the earliest of these is Beatrice of Nazareth, whose short treatise *The Seven Manners of Loving* is one of the first surviving religious treatises written in Dutch.[3]

The central themes in beguine literature are an intimate encounter with Christ, a profound Eucharistic theology, feats of holiness and a pursuit of – and at times abandonment by – Love or *Minne* (about which I say more later in this chapter). As indicated, from a purely literary point of view these writings by women are amongst the first written in vernacular languages during that high medieval window of opportunity before the Renaissance, after which classic Latin became more prestigious again.[4] It allowed people outside the circuit of "high" theology to read spiritual writings – that is, those who did not necessarily know Latin, the language of theological learning. In this manner, these vernacular writings constitute one of the ways in which the barrier between people of learning and ordinary folk was broken down in the late medieval period. It would be incorrect to see this in terms of an opposition between religious and laypeople: many religious (especially nuns) did not know any Latin. Devotional literature written in the vernacular would strongly appeal to all (religious or lay) with an interest in devotional literature but whose command of Latin was deficient.

MECHTHILD OF MAGDEBURG

Mechthild of Magdeburg lived most of her life as a beguine. She enjoyed the protection and support of influential members of the Dominican Order. Toward the end of her life (around 1270) she joined a Cistercian convent at Helfta, at which she remained until her death in 1282 (or 1294?). Mechthild is remembered for a work written in German entitled *Das Fließende Licht der Gottheit* (*The Flowing Light of the Godhead*), consisting

---

[3] She was born in Leuven and became a Cistercian nun in 1216. Twenty years later she became the prioress at the convent of Nazareth near Lier, where she resided until her death in 1268. The reader can find a summary in McGinn, *The Flowering of Mysticism*, 166–74.

[4] Beatrice and Hadewijch wrote in Middle Dutch, Mechthild of Magdeburg (1207–82) wrote in medieval German, and Marguerite Porete from Hainault wrote in French her (*Miroir des Âmes Simples et Anéanties*),for which she was censored, resulting in her being burned at the stake in 1310.

of seven parts.[5] She worked on it for a number of years, roughly between 1250 and 1280. Dominican friars translated the first six of the seven parts into Latin as *Lux Divinitatis* in 1290. *The Flowing Light* contains a variety of literary forms, from poetry, prayers and dialogue between the soul and Lady Love or God, to mini-plays. The title of the book illustrates a remote Neoplatonic influence: God could not contain himself and simply bubbled over in his erotic desire to create the world, the soul in particular: "When God could no longer contain himself, he created the soul and, in his immense love, gave himself to her as her own" (1, 22). Scholars have traditionally identified two kinds of love: agapeic love (which is utterly gratuitous and selfless, not dependent on the needs of the one who bestows it or on the characteristics of the recipient, and therefore universal in nature) and erotic love (which includes sexual love, amongst others). Erotic love is grounded in the needs of the one who loves, takes into account the qualities of the beloved, and is therefore particular or preferential, not universal. Some scholars, usually from Lutheran provenance, argue that God's love for us is profoundly agapeic. Mechthild, however, clearly attributes a strong erotic dimension to God's love.

She expresses this erotic dimension in daring sexual metaphors. Bernard of Clairvaux and other Cistercian authors had undoubtedly portrayed the encounter with God using metaphors of kissing and embracing. Mechthild's favorite metaphor to describe the union of God and soul is sexual union. Consider the following dialogue between Christ and the soul from Book 1, 44:

> Our Lord speaks: "Stay, Lady Soul."
> "What do you bid me, Lord?"
> "Take off your clothes."
> "Lord, what will happen to me then?"
> "Lady Soul, you are so utterly formed to my nature
> That not the slightest thing can be between you and me.
> Never was an angel so glorious
> That to him was granted for one hour
> What is given to you for eternity.
> And so you must cast off from you
> Both fear and shame and all external virtues.
> Rather, those alone that you carry within yourself
> Shall you foster forever.
> These are your noble longing

---

[5] In what follows I use the translation by Frank Tobin from *Mechthild of Magdeburg: The Flowing Light of the Godhead*. Classics of Western Spirituality (New York: Paulist Press, 1997).

And your boundless desire.
These I shall fulfill forever
With my limitless lavishness."
"Lord, now I am a naked soul
And you in yourself are a well-adorned God.
Our shared lot is eternal life
Without Death."

Then a blessed stillness
That both desire comes over them.
He surrenders himself to her,
And she surrenders herself to him.
What happens to her then – she knows –
And that is fine with me.
But this cannot last long.[6]

While adopting sexual imagery, the passage echoes the theme from Luke's gospel story (Luke 10:42) where Mary's choice to dwell near the Lord (choosing "the better part") is praised over the exterior activity of her sister Martha. Mechthild suggests that love and desire are more fundamental than external works and virtuous behavior. The burning desire of Christ and the soul converge into a union of bliss that, however, cannot continue for long. Indeed, scholars have noted a progression throughout the seven books of *The Flowing Light*: by the time Mechthild writes the seventh book, the theme of bridal union has faded. She complains that, in her old age, she has become "cold as to graces." All that remains for her is to be "joyfully patient and trust in God alone." When in her discouragement she complains to God, he replies that in her childhood she was the playmate of the Holy Spirit, her youth was spent as bride to his humanity, and in her old age she is now a housewife of his Godhead (VII, 3).

If the delights of the bridal chamber have faded, suffering itself still offers a medium of communication with Christ. Christ carries her suffering, and Mechthild is asked to stand with Christ, in union, so as to allow Christ to carry her burdens with her (VII, 11). As Bernard McGinn aptly summarizes: "While Mechthild delights in the joys of being a bride of the Trinity . . . it is clear from the emphasis on the necessity for accepting pain and even estrangement from God that it is the kenotic Christ on the cross, suffering, dying, and emptying himself of all things, who is her deepest love."[7]

---

[6] Tobin, *The Flowing Light*, 62.   [7] McGinn, *The Flowering of Mysticism*, 242.

The mystical journey culminates in a transformation of the mystic. This transformation can be best captured in the concepts of detachment and involvement. Detachment means radical selflessness – that is, a disposition in which we relate to the world in an utterly non-possessive manner. It is exactly this disposition of selflessness that allows us to engage with the world in an open and non-self-centered manner – that is, authentic involvement with the world implies detachment of self and its possessiveness. The theme (and the language in which it is framed) was to have a profound influence on Meister Eckhart, as the following passage from Book 1.35 illustrates:

> You should love nothingness,
> You should flee somethingness.
> You should stand alone
> And should go to no one.
> You should not be excessively busy
> And be free of all things . . .
>
> You should restore the sick
> And yet should have nothing yourself.
> You should drink the water of suffering
> And ignite the fire of love with the kindling of virtue:
> Then you are living in the true desert.[8]

The metaphor of the desert evokes biblical connotations of the place where we encounter God, usually after a period of purification and self-abnegation. Through detachment (love of nothingness, freedom from all things) we can engage with the world, heal the sick, suffer for Christ and practice virtue. The themes we encounter in Mechthild's book had already been developed somewhat earlier by Hadewijch, whom McGinn quite rightly considers "one of the greatest medieval mystics."[9]

HADEWIJCH

We know nothing of Hadewijch's life except for what is revealed in her own writings. They suggest she was a beguine of noble stock, although the possibility that she was a Cistercian nun cannot be ruled out altogether.[10] On the other hand, if she had been a Cistercian nun it stands to reason that

---

[8] Tobin, *The Flowing Light*, 55–56.   [9] McGinn, *The Flowering of Mysticism*, 200.
[10] Rob Faesen, *Lichaam in Lichaam, Ziel in Ziel. Christusbeleving bij Hadewijch en haar tijdgenoten* (Baarn: Ten Have, 2003). We cannot date her writings accurately either. In one of the manuscripts a "List of Perfect" is included, which lists fifty-seven persons (the majority of which [thirty-three]

her writings would not have suffered the fate of oblivion as they did, for communities were at pains to preserve the memory and the writings of their saintly members. Hence, for now, scholars are happy enough to accept that Hadewijch was indeed a beguine. If Hadewijch was of noble descent her choice to adopt the ambiguous state of a beguine would in all likelihood have met with fierce resistance, even abandonment, by her family. It is therefore perhaps not surprising that the theme of abandonment by God and people is a recurrent one throughout her oeuvre, which is of the highest literary and spiritual quality.

Hadewijch had clearly enjoyed an excellent education. She effortlessly incorporates and translates extracts from William of St. Thierry in her own writings. Her high social background is also attested to by the fact that she adopts the idiom of courtly literature, especially in her *Poems*, while recasting it in a religious vein in terms of service to and abandonment by divine Love. What distinguishes her writings from those of her contemporary male counterparts, aside from their literary superiority, is their more existential tone with themes such as burning desire and love for God, intimacy with Christ in the midst of abandonment and personal participation in the life of the Trinity figuring prominently. These are some of the topics that will retain our attention.

The Nature of Love (Minne)

As will have become clear, one of the characteristic themes of medieval theology and spirituality is that of radical theocentricity. Throughout her writings Hadewijch describes the utter gratuitousness of love, which is always to be pursued for its own sake. As she puts it in *Letter* 22: "Charity does not seek her own (1 Cor. 13:5) and Love applies herself only to herself. Therefore, let anyone lose himself if he wishes to find God and to know what he is in himself (*Daer omme verliese hem selven, die gode vinden wilt ende bekinnen wat hi es in hem selven*)."[11] In other words, bestowing Love

---

incidentally are women), including "a beguine killed by Master Robert (Robbaer) because of her true love." This appears to be a reference to Dominican Robert le Bougre, a papal inquisitor who executed around 260 heretics in northern France and the Low Countries in 1236–39. The problem is that we are not sure that this List was compiled by Hadewijch herself. It may be a later insertion into the manuscript and her writings may therefore predate 1239. I owe this information to Rob Faesen.

[11] In the Dutch text "what he is in himself" could refer to both God (most likely) or the human person, who (in that reading) can only come to know himself (herself) when he (she) comes to know God. I use the edition by Paul Mommaers, *De Brieven van Hadewijch* (Kok: Kampen, 1990). In what follows I include references to the translation by Mother Columba Hart, *Hadewijch: The Complete*

requires a shedding of all calculations and self-centeredness. It demands utter abnegation and loss of self. Hadewijch, like Augustine before her, argues that it is only through losing ourselves that we can find ourselves and know God more intimately.

Especially in her *Poems* Hadewijch has given a most penetrating sketch of the nature of Love and burning desire for God. Love (*Minne*) is "possessed in violent longing" (*Poems in Stanzas* 20, 6); it is "the substance of her joy" (*Poems in Stanzas* 22, 3). In colorful language she describes a kind of amorous struggle (*orewoet*) between her soul and God, which affects every aspect of her being, including her sensuality. This is a characteristic passage, from *Vision 7*:

On a certain Pentecost Sunday I had a vision at dawn. Matins were being sung in the church, and I was present. My heart and my veins and all my limbs trembled and quivered with eager desire and, as often occurred with me, such madness and fear beset my mind that it seemed to me I did not content my Beloved, and that my Beloved did not fulfil my desire, so that dying I must go mad, and going mad I must die. ... The longing in which I then was cannot be expressed by any language or any person I know; and everything I could say about it would be unheard-of to all those who never apprehended Love as something to work for with desire, and whom Love had never acknowledged as hers. I can say this about it: I desired to have full fruition of my Beloved, and to understand and taste him to the full.[12]

Love (*Minne*) is a multifaceted and highly rich concept in Hadewijch's writings. It can refer to divine Love, Christ the Bridegroom (usually called *Lief*), the Love that is the Holy Spirit and our love for God. It is generally portrayed as a religious life force, both transcendent and ever-elusive, and immanent, eliciting incessant desire. In her *Poems* Hadewijch borrows particularly from *trouvère* (troubadour) poetry to describe her desire for and abandonment by Love. In doing so, she reverses gender roles. After all, in courtly literature it is the knight who usually serves his fair Lady and laments his separation from her. Hadewijch effectively assumes the role of the knight who goes to great lengths to acquire intimacy with Love or *Minne*. In *Poems in Stanzas* 22, 4 she writes in characteristic vein:

> I do not complain of suffering for Love:
> It becomes me always to submit to her,

Works. Classics of Western Spirituality (New York: Paulist Press, 1980) unless I make my own translation.

[12] Hart, *Hadewijch*, 280. For a Dutch edition of the *Visions*, see Imme Dros and Frank Willaert, *Hadewijch. Visioenen* (Amsterdam: Bert Bakker, 1996).

> Whatever she commands, softly or loudly.
> A full knowledge of her is beyond me.
> She remains an unfathomable mystery,
> Which has touched my heart,
> And left me wandering in a desert wild.

It must be admitted that Hadewijch does complain of suffering for Love, more than once. An example of such a lament over Love can be found in *Poems in Stanzas* 26:

> Although day and season are drear,
> God blesses them all.
> We shall soon behold better.
> It is in you, my Love, that I find my delight;
> You being apart from me
> Is a source of constant sorrow.
> But it is only right:
> The light of my heart,
> That should illuminate my life's path,
> Is always searching for you.
> See what must befall me:
> Nothing is left to me,
> But longing.
>
> Oh, what does anything but you,
> My love, matter to me?
> Yet, my lot it is not to possess you entirely.[13]

This could easily be misunderstood as a secular love poem in which the lover (Hadewijch) mourns the absence of a full union with her beloved. As it happens, the poem goes on to describe how we should utterly surrender to divine Love in the very midst of our inability to do so (as finite beings). It is, in other words, a deeply *theological* love poem even though it borrows the idiom of courtly literature.

Divine Transcendence and Christocentrism

In Hadewijch's mystical theology an emphasis upon the elusiveness and transcendence of God is counterbalanced by an all-pervasive Christocentric focus. *Letter* 22, in which she describes the paradox of God's utter transcendence and immanence, illustrates this. The *Letter* is

---

[13] My translation. For the *Poems in Stanzas* I use the edition by Herman Vekeman, *Hadewijch, Het Boek der Liederen. Vol. 1. Tekst en Vertaling* (Budel: Damon, 2005), 197.

inspired by the hymn "Alpha et Omega," attributed to Hildebert of Lavardin (d. 1133). She outlines how God is "above all and yet not remote" (*boven al ende onverhauen*) (which translates the line *super cuncta, nec elatus* of the hymn). Hadewijch suggests that the very transcendence of God's nature is the reason why he cannot be remote or distant: "Since he himself is what he has (*heeft*), he does not exalt himself and remains unelevated." Hadewijch is drawing here on Augustine's insight (*De. Trin.* VI.4.6; XV.4.22) that the divine nature is simple and that the properties God has coincide with his very being.[14] She appears to suggest that the very otherness of divine simplicity is the foundation of his nearness. Because God is so radically different from creaturely things, we cannot begin to say how he differs from everything else; the dialectic of divine transcendence and immanence is therefore the condition of possibility of our encounter with God (*Letter* 22 [69–74]).

Hadewijch then outlines how the transcendent God makes himself freely and concretely available. First, in relation to eternity and time: God bestows "to us in Love the eternal time that he himself is." In loving God with bottomless affection and unfathomable mind, in a deep interiority, we become one spirit with God and enjoy a foretaste of divine eternity here and now. The second way in which God makes himself known is in the human person, who has been made in the image of the Trinity, with our three faculties mirroring the three divine Persons. This theme, Augustinian in provenance and mediated through the Cistercian authors of the 12th century (especially William of St. Thierry), will be retained by all authors in the Flemish school after Hadewijch. The third consists in the self-gift of the substance of his Body, initially on the Cross and then in the Eucharist as our food and drink. As she suggests in *Vision 7*, the Eucharist is one of the ways in which she can attain "a union without difference" with God. Through receiving the Body and Blood of Christ Hadewijch attains an intimate union with – or even apparent transformation into – Christ crucified.[15] The fourth and final gift is "the relaxation of time": God has "inclined himself toward us, in time," giving us the freedom and scope to respond to him.

All four ways, and not just the third one, have a Christological dimension. While God's eternal transcendence is the foundation of his presence in the world it is more specifically through the Incarnation that eternity has

---

[14] R. Vanneste, "Over de betekenis van enkele abstracta in de taal van Hadewijch," *Studia Germanica* (1959) 1: 9–95 (here p. 24).
[15] Faesen, *Lichaam in Lichaam*, 63.

entered into time, and by being one spirit with Christ we come to taste something of his eternity here and now. The Christocentric dimension also comes to the fore in that one of our faculties is enlightened by the Word. Again, the "relaxation" of time appears to refer to the fact that God, "with arms outstretched" (a reference to the beams of the Cross) has "inclined himself to us, in time, ... in order that he may be with us in Love and fruition."[16] Christ's death on the Cross is the moment when the Holy Spirit, or Love, is released through which we can come to enjoy God.

It is a key idea of Hadewijch that the encounter with Christ, human and divine, shapes Christian existence. As she writes in her *Letter 6*: "With the humanity of God you must live here on earth, in the labour and sorrows of exile, while within your soul you love and rejoice with the omnipotent and eternal divinity in sweet abandonment. For the truth of both [i.e., the humanity and divinity of Christ] is one single fruition."[17] Indeed, elsewhere in her writings Hadewijch appeals to the theological view that Christ enjoyed the vision of God in the midst of his suffering to defend her claim that joy and suffering are not mutually exclusive but rather coexist at the heart of our lives. From a Christocentric perspective she comes to know that she can experience "sweet love, embraces and kisses" in the midst of "suffering, pain, and misery."[18]

As indicated, she comes to know this concretely through a radical identification with the man Christ. Hadewijch desires to know in her own humanity and at the core of her existence what it was like for Christ to be human.[19] As she puts it in *Vision 7*: "I desired that his humanity should to the fullest extent be one in fruition with my humanity." In this *Vision* she meets Christ, first as a child who offers her the Eucharistic Bread and Wine, and then in the form of a Man, and again he offers himself in Bread and Wine. She then writes:

After that he came himself to me, took me entirely in his arms, and pressed me to him; and all my members felt his in full felicity, in accordance with the desire of my heart and my humanity. So I was outwardly satisfied and fully transported. Also then, for a short while, I had the strength to bear this; but soon, after a short time, I lost that manly beauty outwardly in the sight of his form. I saw him completely come to nought and so fade and all at once dissolve that I could no longer recognise or perceive him outside of me, and I could no longer distinguish him within me. Then it was as if we were one without difference.[20]

---

[16] *Letter* 22 (155–64); Hart, *Hadewijch*, 97.   [17] *Letter* 6; Hart, *Hadewijch*, 59.
[18] *Vision* 7; Hart, *Hadewijch*, 280.   [19] Faesen, *Lichaam in Lichaam*, 60.
[20] *Vision* 7, Hart, *Hadewijch*, 281.

The erotic undertones are obvious, yet like the Song of Songs the erotic points to and underscores the theological. Through receiving the Body and Blood Hadewijch attains an intimate union with or even apparent transformation into Christ. This is not, however, a union with Christ as such but with Christ crucified, which explains why she could only bear this for a short while.[21] Through the sacrament of the Altar Hadewijch acquires a deeper Christocentric orientation and comes to know how Christ experienced his humanity.

The encounter with Christ, human and divine, is therefore of central importance for the way Hadewijch conceives of our transformation and union with God. Through radical identification with the God-man she experiences joy in affliction and vice versa, in a dialectical disposition we can perhaps best characterize as "reconciliation." Hadewijch is therefore one of the first authors writing in the vernacular who consistently develops the theme that through suffering and the identification with Christ it implies we can come to know in a truly embodied manner the transcendent God.

Trinity

For Hadewijch this God is always the Trinitarian God: identification with the God-man leads to participation in the life of the Trinity. Hadewijch sees the divine nature in dialectical terms – that is, in terms of a fruitive unity on one hand and the activity of the Persons on the other. God is "enclosed and yet overflowing," as she reiterates in *Letter* 28 (101). Elsewhere (*Letter* 22 [279–344]) this "overflowing" is described in terms of a genuine Trinitarian kenosis in which the Father pours himself out in creation and in the processions of his Son and Holy Spirit who in turn empty themselves out in the Incarnation, life and death of the Son, and the sanctification of the world through the Holy Spirit. Yet this outpouring is always counterbalanced by a pull back toward divine fruition. At the heart of the Deity, "there never was and never can be any other work than that one fruition."[22] Similarly, we are encouraged to be active and yet fruitive, involved and detached. As she puts it in *Letter* 28 (26): "Whenever it [the soul] is in this contemplation, it is needful that it remain in repose of heart (*in rasten van herte*), even if it is busy outwardly."[23] This *Letter* – one of the

---

[21] See Faesen, *Lichaam in Lichaam*, 63.   [22] *Letter* 17 (74); Hart, *Hadewijch*, 83.
[23] Hart, *Hadewijch*, 109.

most elusive texts written by Hadewijch – concludes with a remarkable description how the soul, reposing in God, attains wholeness. Here the dialectic of detachment and involvement, of drawing in and flowing out, is rephrased in terms of wholeness and particularity: "I have integrated all my diversity, and I have individualised all my wholeness." This integration is the time of bliss and fruition. She continues in poetic vein, describing how the soul is beyond all things and yet in the middle of them. "I called this the time of bliss. I remained there, standing above all things and yet in the midst of all things, and I looked out above all things into the glory without end."[24]

In conclusion, Hadewijch has developed a mystical theology in which the transcendence of God (which elicits a burning desire for union, which will never be fully fulfilled in this life) is qualified by a profound Christocentricism, which in turn invites us to a life of detachment and involvement that mirrors the Trinitarian dynamics of flowing out and drawing in: "Pouring out and keeping back are the pure divinity and the entire nature of Love."[25] Jan van Ruusbroec will adopt this theme (which has its roots in the Neoplatonic dynamic of *exitus* and *reditus*) and develop it in an even more explicitly Trinitarian manner.

BIBLIOGRAPHICAL NOTES

The writings of Mechthild of Magdeburg and Hadewijch are available in English translation in the Classics of Western Spirituality series: Mother Columba Hart, *Hadewijch: The Complete Works* (New York: Paulist Press, 1980) and Frank Tobin, *Mechthild of Magdeburg: The Flowing Light of the Godhead* (New York: Paulist Press, 1998).

Excellent short introductions to Hadewijch and Mechthild can be found in Bernard McGinn, *The Presence of God: A History of Western Christian Mysticism. Vol.* III. *The Flowering of Mysticism: Men and Women in the New Mysticism, 1200–1350* (New York: Herder and Herder, 1998), 199–244. In German there is Kurt Ruh, *Geschichte der abendländischen Mystik. Vol* II. *Frauenmystik und Franziskanische Mystik der Frühzeit* (Munich: C. H. Beck, 1999), 160–224 and 247–92. For a discussion of Hadewijch's theological vision the publications by Rob Faesen deserve special mention. A helpful introduction in English to Hadewijch is Paul Mommaers, *Hadewijch: Writer, Beguine, Love Mystic* (Leuven: Peeters, 2004).

[24] *Letter* 28; Hart, *Hadewijch*, 113.   [25] *Letter* 17 (24); Hart, 82.

CHAPTER 15

Early Franciscan Theology
Robert Grosseteste, Roger Bacon and the Summa Halensis

As indicated in Chapter 13, during the early to mid-13th century, the intellectual and spiritual renewal the Western Church enjoyed was inextricably bound up with the emergence of two new religious orders – namely, the Franciscans and Dominicans.[1] Members of these two mendicant orders quickly established themselves as leading theologians and philosophers at the two greatest universities of the 13th century: Oxford and Paris. The most famous of the early Franciscan and Dominican theologians are of course Bonaventure, Albert the Great and Thomas Aquinas, who will be discussed in subsequent chapters. Little studied but foundational for the later medieval Franciscan and Dominican schools, however, is the generation of mendicant thinkers who preceded them. This chapter focuses upon some of the very earliest contributors to Franciscan intellectual and spiritual tradition, Oxford scholars Robert Grosseteste and Roger Bacon, and their Parisian contemporaries Alexander of Hales and John of La Rochelle – the authors of the famous *Summa Halensis*.

Although highly diverse in terms of their academic styles and points of interests, each of these scholars played a fundamental role in shaping the early Franciscan intellectual vision with regards to its theological outlook as well as its significant contribution to fostering the nascent disciplines of academic philosophy and scientific inquiry. In particular, I look at how these early Franciscans laid the basis for many of the innovations in Christology, Trinitarian theology and the understanding of faith and reason articulated by later generations of Franciscans, in particular Bonaventure and John Duns Scotus. As will be shown, the seeds of many of the highly innovative doctrines for which Bonaventure and Duns Scotus are rightly famed – such as the former's famous description of the Trinitarian procession's being founded in the self-diffusive nature of

---

[1] This chapter was written by Dr. William Crozier and revised by Rik Van Nieuwenhove.

the good, and the latter's argument for the absolute predestination of Christ irrespective of the Fall – are found in the very earliest generation of Franciscan thinkers.

ROBERT GROSSETESTE

Life and Works

One of the most remarkable figures of the early Middle Ages, and perhaps the most celebrated of the 13th-century cleric scientists, Englishman Robert Grosseteste played a pivotal role in shaping the intellectual and spiritual developments of the 13th-century Franciscan tradition. Whilst Grosseteste himself never became a Franciscan friar, his connection with the early Franciscan academic communities, both at Oxford and at Paris, was nonetheless deep and long-lasting. Grosseteste helped not only train and promote several of the very earliest Franciscans studying at Oxford and Paris, most notably Alexander of Hales, Adam Marsh and Thomas of York, but he also took an active role in the educative program of the Franciscan convent at Oxford, being formally appointed its *lector* in 1229–30. Indeed, so deep was Grosseteste's affection for the Oxford Franciscans that upon his death in 1253, he bequeathed the entirety of his vast library to the Oxford convent, where we know it remained until Duns Scotus's day.

Like with many of his contemporaries, our knowledge of Grosseteste's life and whereabouts is often patchy. Born to a poor Anglo-Norman family sometime around 1168 in the south of England, Grosseteste seems to have received his early education in the liberal arts at Hereford through his connection to the city's bishop, William de Vere. That Grosseteste entered de Vere's episcopal *familia* and studied there is suggested by a letter addressed to de Vere by Gerard of Wales, who, seeking to commend Grosseteste to the bishop's care, praises the young Robert as "a man of wide reading" and possessing a solid "foundation in the Liberal Arts."[2] However, in 1198 William de Vere died and our knowledge of Grosseteste's whereabouts becomes vague, with only a few references to him found. We begin to pick up the thread of Grosseteste's life again in 1225, when he is recorded as being installed as deacon at the church of Abbotsley by the then bishop of Lincoln, Hugh of Wells.

---

[2] Cf. Richard Southern, *Robert Grosseteste: The Growth of an English Mind in Medieval Europe* (Oxford: Clarendon, 1992), 65.

In the year 1228–29, Grosseteste's life took a decisive turn when he was invited by Agnellus of Pisa, minister provincial of the newly founded English Franciscan province, to take up teaching duties at the Franciscan convent in Oxford. In 1235, Grosseteste was elevated to the bishopric of Lincoln, the largest see in England, which at that time incorporated Oxford, thereby securing his continued influence at the university and his connection with the Franciscan community there. As bishop, Grosseteste committed himself with great vigor to the reform of his diocese and did much to implement many of the dictates of the Fourth Lateran Council (1215) and the Second Council of Lyons (1245), famously even refusing to appoint the pope's nephew to a canonry at Lincoln's cathedral in 1253 on account of the latter's inexperience.

During his academic and episcopal career, Grosseteste produced a large and varied corpus of scholarly, pastoral and spiritual writings. These range from short *dicta* (i.e., personal reflections on various issues) and his delightful allegory about the drama of sin and redemption entitled *Château d'Amour* (*Castle of Love*) (in which the ransom theory occupies a central role), to his extensive and highly important theological works, many of which take the form of extended biblical commentaries and sermons. His most notable theological works include his *De Decem Mandata* (*On the Ten Commandments*), *De Cessatione Legalium* (*On the Cessation of the Laws*) and his much-celebrated *Hexaemeron* (*On the Six Days of Creation*). It is, however, for his many highly original scientific writings that Grosseteste is perhaps best known today. The most important of these include his *De Luce* (*On Light*), *De Iride* (*On the Rainbow*), *De Sphera* (*On the Sphere*), *De Cometis* (*On Comets*) and *De Colore* (*On Color*), to name but a few. Aside from his own scientific works Grosseteste also produced extensive commentaries on Aristotle's *De Physica* and *Posterior Analytica*, as well as several works devoted to philosophy and metaphysical issues, including his *De Veritate* (*On Truth*).

During his own lifetime, however, it was as a translator that Grosseteste achieved most prominence. Late in life, Grosseteste took the highly unusual step of teaching himself Greek, believing that it was only by returning to the original language of the ancient texts that they could be accurately interpreted. As Grosseteste repeatedly pointed out, much of the translations of Greek works, in particular those of Aristotle, had come from Arabic translations rather than the original Greek. The result, so he complained, was that these translations were often highly inaccurate, confused or simply incomprehensible. Going to great lengths to acquire original Greek manuscripts, seemingly using his contacts with Franciscan missionaries in the East to do so, Grosseteste was the first to translate the

entirety of Aristotle's *Nicomachean Ethics* into Latin and thereby open up
the fullness of the Stagirite's moral philosophy for Western thinkers.
However, Grosseteste's translation efforts were not restricted to translating
philosophical works. He also translated many Greek spiritual and theological texts, including the writings of Pseudo-Dionysius and the pseudo-
epigraphical *Testament of the Twelve Patriarchs*. Far superior to the earlier
translations of Pseudo-Dionysius, Grosseteste's translation and commentaries on the Pseudo-Dionysian corpus were to prove central to the spiritual and mystical renewal of the 13th and 14th centuries.

Grosseteste on the Nature of Theology

The increasing awareness of Aristotle's concept of "science" during the early
decades of the 13th century led theologians to ask whether theology, like the
lower philosophical disciplines, could be legitimately described as a science
(*scientia*). According to Aristotle's *Posterior Analytics* – which, as noted
earlier, Grosseteste produced an extensive commentary on – a science is an
academic discipline or sphere of reasoning that proceeds, by way of demonstration, from incontrovertible "first principles" or "axioms." These first
principles are knowable to the light of reason and, on account of their logical
necessity, provide the foundational certainty needed for the science to reason
correctly. Thus, to take an example from Grosseteste's *On the Liberal Arts*,
music possesses something of the quality of a *scientia* because it has as its first
principles the unchanging mathematical rules of harmony and dissonance.
What sounds pleasant or unpleasant, and what in turn promotes the desired
emotional response, derives from mathematical ratios. To this extent, music
is – as later scholastics such as Bonaventure and Thomas Aquinas would put
it – a "subalternate science": it derives its first principles from a higher, more
certain science, in this case mathematics.

Whereas some of Grosseteste's contemporaries, both Franciscan and
Dominican, were willing to subscribe to the idea that theology is a *scientia*,
Grosseteste disagrees with this position, arguing that theology neither
complies with the Aristotelian definition of a science, nor should any effort
be made to apply the term *science* to it.[3] This is so because "science" most

---

[3] Cf. James McEvoy, *Robert Grosseteste* (Oxford: Oxford University Press, 2000): "Here [in the *Hexaemeron*] he is at pains to avoid placing theology, that is, the revealed word of God and its appreciative study, under the generic concept of science. *Sapientia* (wisdom) is his preferred designation of sacred science; the very name privileges it and underlines its transcendence with regard to all purely human knowledge" (p. 124).

properly denotes a discipline that proceeds from axioms open to natural reason. As such, a science is said to be founded solely upon unaided rational inquiry. The term *science* in Grosseteste's opinion can thus be legitimately applied to philosophical disciplines (i.e., logic, optics, metaphysics, etc.) that argue from first principles discoverable by the human intellect without the assistance of faith. Theology, by contrast, does not derive its first principles from natural reason, nor is it founded upon human ingenuity. Instead, it is based upon faith, which in turn is a product not simply of the intellect but also of the affections insofar as they become inflamed by the supernatural *habitus* of charity (*caritas*). Therefore, pertaining both to the intellect and to the affections, theology is best described as wisdom (*sapientia*), rather than a science:

The subject of this wisdom is neither known in its own right, nor received through science: it is only accepted and believed, through faith (*sed sola fide assumptum et creditum*). Nor can it be understood, unless it is first believed. For it does not fall under, nor is it included in, any division of the existent that is used by human philosophy in dividing the existent. It is not the Creator alone, nor is it the creation alone. . . . The subject of this wisdom, then, as has been said, is received only by faith (*sola fides accipit*). For this reason the things that belong to this wisdom are things believable rather than things knowable. Hence it should start with things believable rather than with things knowable without faith.[4]

Given the fact that theology is founded upon faith rather than reason, Grosseteste insists that it proceeds by way of authority rather than by way of demonstration. Taking as its starting point the revealed truths of Scripture, which as divinely given are not only infallible but our sole source of knowledge about God's inner Trinitarian life, Grosseteste insists that theology offers a far superior description of reality, both human and divine, than can be achieved through reason alone, be it at the level of physics or the superior science of metaphysics. In the propositions of Scripture, so he tells us, God speaks directly to humanity and summons us to receive his revelation through the gift of faith and the indwelling of charity: "For the things that in this wisdom are believable, properly speaking, are believable on account of the authority of the one who speaks (*quaedam vero propter dicentis auctoritatem*)."[5] To this extent, drawing a fairly sharp distinction between the light of reason and that of revelation, it is clear that for Grosseteste, theology, as *sapientia*, stands significantly apart from all other disciplines.

[4] *Hex.* part 1, chapter 2, translation by C. F. J. Martin (Oxford: Oxford University Press, 1996), 48–49.
[5] Ibid., 49.

Like all modes of inquiry theology has its own proper "subject." "Each science, and each kind of wisdom," Grosseteste writes, "has a matter and a subject on which its attention is turned (*circa quod eiusdem versetur intentio*)."[6] What this subject is, he tells us, theologians disagree upon. In his own opinion, however, the proper subject of theology is "the whole Christ" (*Christus integer*).[7] Theology derives its unity and cohesion from its focus on Christ and his different unions – that is, his union with the divine nature in the Trinity, the union between the Word and the human nature of Christ (hypostatic union) and the union between Christ and his Church, which finds its supreme expression in the Eucharist. The Eucharist, therefore, as the real presence of Christ in the church, and therefore, next to Scripture, the key source of nourishment for theological practice and piety, is, in the wayfaring state at least, the supreme moment of "return" or *reditus* that the *exitus* of the eternally predestined Incarnation (see later in this chapter) set in motion. Insofar as theology reflects and facilitates this *reditus* to Christ, and through him to the Trinity, by disclosing something of the state of glory, it has deeply eschatological and practical dimensions.[8]

All of this points to the fact that for Grosseteste, in the person of Jesus Christ all reality, both human and divine, is woven into one coherent whole. As he puts it in his *On the Cessation of the Laws*, through the Incarnation of the Word "all creation has been led back to the fullness of unity" and "led back into a circular fulfilment."[9] For Grosseteste, Christ thus stands at the center of the dialogue between God and the world, and is thus fittingly described as the primary object of theological study. It is through looking to Christ, the author of all wisdom, and specifically through our desiring and loving him, that we as theologians access all perfect wisdom, truth and virtue. Moreover, it is in Christ that we are bound in union with God and made deiform: "To this conformity and deiformity we are led by the mediator, Christ, God and man, with whom we form one Christ."[10] For Grosseteste, theology, and in turn the spiritual life, are thus radically Christocentric enterprises. In this respect, his thought strongly prefigures the highly Christocentric thought of many of his Franciscan disciples, in particular Bonaventure.

---

[6] Ibid., chapter 1 (p. 47).   [7] Ibid.

[8] Christian Trottmann, *Théologie et Noétique au XIIIe Siècle. A la Recherche d'un Statut* (Paris: Vrin, 1999), 105.

[9] *On the Cessation of the Laws*, trans. Stephen M. Hildebrand, The Fathers of the Church: Medieval Continuation (Washington, DC: Catholic University of America Press, 2012), 167.

[10] *Hex.*, part. 1, chapter 1 (p. 47).

Grosseteste's conviction that theology is founded upon belief and authority rather than human ingenuity led him to mistrust some of the innovations introduced into theological learning during the early decades of the 13th century. During the mid-1220s, Grosseteste's former *socius* (academic pupil), Alexander of Hales, by then a noted theology master at Paris, began the practice of using Peter Lombard's *Sentences* as the primary tool of theological education. Until Alexander's innovation, theology lectures had been largely devoted to exploring passages of the Bible. In Grosseteste's opinion, the practice of lecturing on Lombard's *Sentences* rather than the Bible represented a significant departure from the proper order of theological inquiry. It is the Bible, and it alone, which is the principal object of theological reflection, for it is in the Scriptures that the wisdom of God is found. So concerned was Grosseteste with the new trend in theological education that, upon hearing that his former colleagues at Oxford, Dominican Richard Fishacre and Franciscan Richard Rufus of Cornwall, had begun to compose their own commentaries on the *Sentences*, he used his episcopal jurisdiction in a letter written to the regent of the University of Oxford to warn the theology faculty against such a practice.[11]

The Critique of Natural Philosophy

Despite his great affection for scientific and philosophical study, Grosseteste was by no means blind to the gulf that separated medieval Christian thought from the pagan worldview. Alongside figures like William of Auvergne, he was amongst the first to recognize some of the dangers at work within Aristotle's philosophy, including the latter's claim that the world was eternal and thus uncreated. Appealing to the authority of earlier Greek Christian thinkers who had been familiar with Aristotle's works, most notably Basil of Caesarea, Grosseteste argued that it is clear from the study of his *De Physica* that Aristotle believed that the world had no beginning and thus had always existed. In particular, he took issue with

---

[11] McEvoy, *Grosseteste*, 163–64: "Therefore, because we wish that you do all things uprightly and in order, as the Apostle commands [1 Cor. 14:40], we ask, warn, and exhort you in the Lord Jesus Christ, with all the affection and devotion of which we are capable, to draw all your ordinary lectures at the morning hours from the New or the Old Testament. We want you to be like fathers of families, indeed to be such, bringing out of your treasures new things and old [Mt. 13:52] – not, however, things other than the New or the Old; no intermediary, not even the edifices built by the Fathers upon the teaching of Scripture, can be substituted for the study of the foundations; some other time can be more fittingly set aside for such teaching."

the efforts of figures like Alexander of Hales and Albert the Great who, seeking to excuse Aristotle's errors, claimed that he had not in fact argued that the world was eternal, but merely spoke about the existence of the universe as covering the whole span of time and not the act of creation itself, thus meaning he did not, strictly speaking at least, teach that the world had no beginning. The error of believing that the world was eternal, so Albert argued, was not originated by Aristotle, but rather by his Islamic commentators, in particular Averroes. For Grosseteste such efforts to exonerate Aristotle on this issue were both foolish and dangerous. Not only is it manifestly clear that Aristotle did indeed believe that the world had no beginning and therefore possesses no external Creator, but, more worrying, by seeking to reconcile his opinions with Christian thought, those who would defend Aristotle or reinterpret him opened themselves up to charges of heresy:

We have cited all these texts against certain modern writers who, in the teeth of Aristotle himself, and his commentators, and the sacred commentators too, strive to make Aristotle's view, which was heretical, a Catholic one. . . . They should not deceive themselves and toil away at making Aristotle into a Catholic, or they will fruitlessly use up their time and strength of mind, and while they make a Catholic of Aristotle, will make heretics of themselves.[12]

As we will see, the controversy surrounding the works of Aristotle was to continue throughout the 13th century, and many of Grosseteste's assertions about the dangers of "Aristotelianism" were picked up and reaffirmed by some of his Franciscan disciples, most notably Bonaventure.

Aspectus *and* Affectus: *The Primacy of Charity*

Perhaps one of Grosseteste's most influential contributions to early 13th century theology was his emphasis on the role desire and, in turn, the theological virtue of charity, plays in shaping the intellect's horizon. Echoing Bernard of Clairvaux, William of St. Thierry and Thomas Gallus, Grosseteste argued that the scope of our mental vision, and thereby the scope of our souls as a whole, is dictated by the limits of our affections.[13] Our mental vision (*aspectus mentis*), Grosseteste asserts, can only extend as far as our mind's desire (*affectus mentis*) permits it to go. As Southern puts

---

[12] *Hex.*, part. 1, chapter 8 (p. 59).
[13] For the role of *affectus* in Thomas Gallus, see the important study by Boyd Taylor Coolman, *Knowledge: Love and Ecstasy in the Theology of Thomas Gallus* (Oxford: Oxford University Press, 2017).

it, for Grosseteste, "the mind's range of vision cannot extend beyond its range of love."[14] Critical here, Grosseteste tells us, is the impact of the Fall. Corrupted as it is by sin, the fallen mind – at least prior to its acceptance of faith – can extend its mental vision only so far as its fallen desires allow. These, however, on account of the mind's disposition toward concupiscence, are turned toward the creature and not the Creator, thereby meaning that the fallen soul is blind to the reality of the divinity and imagines it in creaturely terms. The *affectus mentis*, can, however, be restored to its proper dignity and orientation through the infusion of charity. Charity heals the *affectus* by enflaming it with a love for God rather than creatures, thereby allowing the *aspectus mentis* to imagine God properly and thus read the book of creation properly, that is to say, not simply as an object of scientific study but as a vestige of its Trinitarian maker.

According to Grosseteste, the clearest witness to the limitations our intellect suffers through charity's absence is found in the errors of the pagan philosophers, in particular Aristotle and his belief in an eternal world. It was because Aristotle's *affectus* was distorted by a concupiscence for creatures that his thinking about creation went astray and he made the fatal error of believing that the world is eternal. His imaginative faculty was so limited by his fallen *affectus* that he failed to understand God properly, and thus mistakenly attributed eternity – a property of the divinity alone – to creation:

> It was necessary for the philosophers to fall into this error because no one can be scientifically freed from the error of the perpetuity and infinity of movement and of time, past and future, except one who is able to understand the simplicity of eternity. But the *aspectus* of the mind (*mentis aspectus*) or intelligence cannot ascend higher (*superius ascendere*) than its *affectus* or its appetite ascends. The *affectus* of the philosophers, however, were joined more with transitory realities than with eternal ones. Indeed, their apprehension, detained as it was within the phantasms of mutable things, was not able to reach the simplicity of eternity.[15]

For Grosseteste, therefore, it is clear that the study of nature, be it at the level of physics (i.e., the study of material reality) or at the deeper level of metaphysics (i.e., the study of being), can succeed only when our desires are cleansed and our imaginative faculties strengthened by the supernatural *habitus* of charity. It is charity, in conjunction with the gifts of wisdom and

---

[14] Richard Southern, "Introduction," in Gunar Freibergs, Aspectus et Affectus: *Essays and Editions in Grosseteste and Medieval Intellectual Life in Honour of Richard C. Dales* (New York: AMS Press, 1993), 3–16, here 7.

[15] Cf. *Comm. Phys.*, in Richard. C. Dales (ed.), *Roberti Grosseteste Episcopi Lincolniensis Commentarius in* VIII *Libros Physicorum Aristotelis* (Boulder: University of Colorado Press, 1963), 147.

understanding, that allows the *affectus* to reach beyond the purely literal word of creation and thus read the book of nature (*liber naturae*) properly.

Metaphysics of Light

Perhaps the doctrine for which Grosseteste is most famous today is his thinking on light. Often described as offering a "metaphysics of light," Grosseteste argues that the creation of light is foundational to the entire act of creation. It is, in essence, the basic principle from which all other creatures are fashioned. Articulated most clearly in his *De Luce* (*On Light*), Grosseteste argues that light (*lux*) is the "first corporeal form."[16] It is "not a form subsequent to corporeity, but is corporeity itself" (*sed est ipsa corporeitas*).[17] As such, it is that from which all matter and subsequent forms derive their being, at least on a creaturely level. To understand what Grosseteste means by this, it is necessary to grasp that for him light exists at two distinct levels.[18] First, there is metaphysical light (*lux*), which, although a corporeal reality, is so rarefied and so primitive in the schema of created being that it is almost non-being. Second, there is visible light (*lumen*). Properly speaking, this is the light emitted by self-luminous bodies and by whose agency we are able to see the world. At the first moment of creation, so the *De Luce* tells us, God created a single point of metaphysical *lux*. This single point of light was the first and the original principle of all matter and thus the very fabric of all creation itself.

Given that light naturally extends itself instantaneously in all directions, and does so perfectly and completely, it is clear that at the very instant God created this single point of primordial light it immediately expanded in all directions, and through doing so defined the limits of the created universe itself, giving rise to a perfect sphere. Crucially, however, given that *lux* is the form of corporeity, through its instantaneous self-diffusion this primordial *lux* extended the matter of the universe itself, "drawing it out along with itself into a mass the size of the world machine" (*mundi machina*).[19] As this primordial light expanded, it reached a certain limit of its rarefication and then began returning to the central point from which it originated. However, as it returned back to its primordial center, the density of its

---

[16] *On Light*, trans Neil Lewis in John Flood, James R. Ginther and Joseph W. Goering (eds.), *Robert Grosseteste and His Intellectual Milieu* (Toronto: PIMS, 2013), 239.

[17] Ibid., 240.

[18] Here Grosseteste is clearly influenced by Islamicate scholar Avicenna. Cf. Jon McGinnis, *Avicenna* (Oxford: Oxford University Press, 2010), 104–05.

[19] *On Light*, 240.

materiality increased, thereby explaining why at the outermost edges of the "world machine" – the celestial spheres – matter is hyper-rarefied and transparent, whilst toward the sublunar earth matter is dense, tangible and generally opaque. As many scholars have noted, *De Luce*'s creation hypothesis anticipates key elements of the modern big bang theory according to which the universe started from a single point of energy and in an instant expanded in all directions.

Whilst Grosseteste's metaphysics of light does not appear to have been taken up by many of his immediate contemporaries, his notion of light as the "first corporeal form" finds particular expression in Bonaventure's thought, as well as that of his Oxford associate Richard Rufus of Cornwall.

Incarnation and Passion

Perhaps Grosseteste's most important – though largely overlooked – contribution to the theological debates of the 13th century is found in his Christology. Of particular note is Grosseteste's understanding of the motivations that led to the Incarnation. In his *On the Cessation of the Laws*, Grosseteste inquires whether the Incarnation would still have taken place even if Adam had not sinned. Are the Incarnation and Christ's work of salvation dependent upon Adam's Fall, or do they serve a much broader purpose?[20] Grosseteste argues that there are several convincing reasons why we should hold that Christ would have become incarnate even if the satisfaction for sin was not necessary for human salvation. The central thrust of the arguments that Grosseteste advances is that without the Incarnation creation itself would have been fundamentally incomplete, and many of the essential features of the world would have been missing.[21] Based upon the belief that God's infinite goodness means that he cannot withhold goodness from that which is capable of receiving it, Grosseteste contends that the Incarnation was predestined to take place irrespective of Adam's sin.[22]

---

[20] *On the Cessation of the Laws*, part 3, chapter 1 (p. 155): "Nevertheless, whether God would become man even if man had not fallen, none of the sacred writers determine in the books of theirs that I have previously looked at, unless my memory fails me. But rather, they seem to imply that if man had not fallen, God would not have become man. There seem, nevertheless, to be valid reasons to show simply that God would have become man even if man had never fallen. On account of this, we will omit for the moment those reasons by which the sacred writers prove that God must become man in order to restore lost man and will ask whether God would have become man even if man had not sinned."

[21] Ibid., part 3 throughout, especially pages 167–69.

[22] Cf. McEvoy, *Grosseteste*, 127–30; *On the Cessation of the Laws*, part 3, chapter 1 (p. 156).

If Christ had not become incarnate, then the world, so Grosseteste reflects, would have lacked a perfection that it is clearly capable of – namely, union with the divine essence through the Incarnation of God.[23] Similarly, it is clear that this perfection cannot arise from the devil's contrivance but must instead come from the divine goodness itself. After all, how can we believe that the crowning of creation – the coming of the Incarnate Word – arose as a result of sin and the devil's trickery in Eden rather than the eternal, superabundant and perfect providence of the goodness of divine love?[24] Although the question of whether Christ would have become incarnate irrespective of the Fall had been tentatively raised earlier by a Benedictine, Rupert of Deutz (1075–1129), it was Grosseteste who first considered the topic in any real systematic depth and gave it theological legitimacy. Moreover, as we will see, Grosseteste's thought on the subject influenced many of his immediate Franciscan disciples – most notably Alexander of Hales and John of La Rochelle – and serves to provide the horizon for the celebrated discussion on Christ's predestination offered by John Duns Scotus.

Perhaps Grosseteste's most striking contribution to medieval Christology, however, is found in his thought on Christ's passion, specifically his belief that the wounds Christ suffered on the cross, and thereby the cross itself, were not sufficient to explain his death.[25] Using his extensive scientific and medical knowledge, Grosseteste denies that the wounds described in the Gospels would have been sufficient to drain Christ's body of its blood and thereby cause his death. Furthermore, the fact that a significant amount of blood flowed from the dead Christ's side when pierced by the centurion's lance confirms that Christ still possessed enough blood and vital humors to have kept him alive.[26] In Grosseteste's opinion we are therefore led to conclude that Christ's death – that is to say the

---

[23] *On the Cessation of the Laws*, part 3, chapter 1 (pp. 155–56, 167–69).

[24] Ibid., 157: "In addition, the corruption of guilt and of punishment is not an essence, but the privation of an essence. But how could the privation of an essence, which certainly is evil, be the cause of so great a good as the capacity to be assumed by the Word of God or to be united with the word of God?"

[25] McEvoy, *Grosseteste*, 131–32; *On the Cessation of the Laws*, part 3, chapter 6 (pp. 189–90).

[26] *On the Cessation of the Laws*, part 3, chapter 6 (pp. 189–90): "For the piercing only of his hands and feet could not empty his blood from his heart and innards in so brief a time, nor could it extinguish so quickly the vigor of life of a strong, young, and healthy man. There is testimony that he did not die on account of a great loss of blood through the nail-wounds: when his side was opened with the lance after he died, blood came out from his innards (although dead bodies even without the loss of blood, if they are wounded after death, do not usually flow blood because the blood is cooled and coagulated). In addition, he shouted with a loud voice when he expired; his shout was not an inarticulate groan, but a loud extension of the voice, literate, meaningful, and humbly praying to God the Father, when he said, 'Into your hands I commend my spirit.'"

separation of his soul from his body – arose not from the torture of the cross itself, which, of course, Grosseteste in no way seeks to diminish, but rather from Christ's own divine will, for only a divine power is sufficient to separate the soul from the body, at least when the latter is still capable of supporting life.[27] In adopting this position, Grosseteste seems entirely unique.

Trinity, Imago Dei *and the Christian Life*

Whilst Grosseteste uses various models to explain God's inner Trinitarian life, perhaps his most interesting explanation of the Trinity stems from his thought on light.[28] As alluded to earlier, light in Grosseteste's opinion is supremely self-diffusive. Light (*lux*) multiplies or "begets" itself immediately and expands in all directions. Through doing so it gives birth to its *splendor*, which is the visible light (*lumen*) that illumines the world. This *splendor* is an outpouring of the fecundity of the original point of light and is therefore inseparable from it: the two are "locked in a mutual embrace."[29] It is in this relationship between the begetting *lux* and the begotten *splendor* of *lumen* that we find an analogy of the Father's eternal begetting of the Son, for the Son is the outpouring and *splendor* of the Father's majesty and luminosity. Grosseteste adds, however, that we observe within nature that the "mutual embrace" between *lux* and *splendor* gives rise to a third property – namely, warmth (*fervor*). This *fervor* is "breathed forth" by *lux* and *splendor* and is in turn inseparable from them, for warmth exists only where there is light and its radiation. In this mutual production of *fervor* by *lux* and *splendor* we find an analogy of the eternal breathing forth of the Spirit from the Father and the Son:

From the fact that God is a trinity of persons, it follows that God is light (*sequitur quod Deus est lux*); not bodily light but non-bodily light. Or rather, perhaps, neither bodily nor non-bodily, but beyond either (*sed supra utrumque*). Every light has by nature and essence this characteristic, that it begets its splendour from itself (*quod de se gignit suum splendorem*). The light that begets and the splendour that is begotten necessarily are locked in a mutual embrace (*amplectuntur mutuo*) and breathe out their mutual warmth (*spirant de se mutuum fervorem*).[30]

Whilst the use of the analogy of *lux-splendor-fervor* reflects the various Trinitarian Persons and their processions, it also bears witness to the fundamental unity of the Godhead. Light may express itself in different

[27] Ibid.   [28] *Hex.*, part 8, chapter 3 (p. 224).   [29] Ibid.   [30] Ibid.

forms and may in turn give rise to different properties, but it nonetheless retains its essential unity. The *splendor* that is begotten and the *fervor* that it co-spires are united in essence for they derive from the same fundamental self-diffusive *lux*. In the same way, the Son and the Holy Spirit are united with the Father for they all derive from his self-diffusive essence:

There remains, then, that the begotten is not something different from the begetter, but only someone different; and the same argument applies to the breather and the breathed (*de spirante et illo qui spiratur*). There is in God, then, someone (*unus*), and someone else (*aliter*), and a third someone (*tertius*), each of whom is an individual substance of rational nature: thus, three persons (*et ita tres persone*). Nor can there be, or even conceived of, a fourth (*quatuor*) here. For what fourth could be added to the begetting light and the begotten splendour and the mutual warmth proceeding from both?[31]

Whilst God's Trinity is something that is discoverable only through faith – for unaided philosophy can never discover God's Trinitarian being – Grosseteste nonetheless believes that once we have faith, thereby ensuring the expansion of the *aspectus mentis* through the infusion of charity, we can discover within creation seemingly endless testimonies to the divine Trinity. "Each creature," he writes "is a mirror from which a likeness of the creator shines" (*Omnis creatura speculum est de quo resultat similitudo creatoris*).[32]

As the highest sublunar intelligence, the human soul is stamped with a particularly vivid Trinitarian likeness: "Human beings are in all things God's closest likeness in resemblance."[33] This is so because the soul is an "image" (*imago*) and, when reformed through the healing touch of charity, a "likeness" (*similitudo*) of the divine Trinity. It has within itself, through its tripartite faculties of memory, intelligence and will, cognitive and affective processions that reflect the intrapersonal relations of the Father, Son and Holy Spirit.[34] Indeed, the belief that the soul is endowed with the *imago Dei*, Grosseteste remarks, is one of the most profound and fertile aspects of Christian doctrine. Through its restoration via charity, it frames the very nature, pattern and direction of the Christian life itself as through it we not only participate in our original prelapsarian identity but are also taken up into the economy of God's own Trinitarian life. So central is this Trinitarian dimension of human life that if the "fertility" of the *imago Dei* had to be "written down piece by piece," the world would not have room for the books that would have to be written.[35]

---

[31] Ibid.   [32] *Dicta* 60.   [33] *Hex.*, part 8, chapter 1 (p. 222).   [34] Ibid., chapter 5 (p. 228).
[35] Ibid., chapter 1 (p. 221).

For the grasp of the Trinity is supremely needful for us (*Maxime enim necessaria est nobis Trinitatis comprehensio*). The love of the Trinity is the health (*salus*) of the soul, and there is no health of the soul without this love (*et sine huius amore nulla est salus anima*). And it is loved to the degree in which it is grasped by the understanding or by faith. For it is the beauty that catches up the grasp that the believer or the understander has, into love of itself.[36]

ROGER BACON

Born around 1214, English Franciscan friar Roger Bacon – the *Doctor Mirabilis* – is perhaps the most well-known and authentic defender of the theological, philosophical and scientific tradition pioneered by Robert Grosseteste. Although it is unclear whether Bacon ever met Grosseteste, what is certain, however, is that Bacon regarded the bishop of Lincoln as his principal teacher and mentor, unapologetically describing him as one of the few wise men of his day. One of the 13th century's most curious and controversial figures, Bacon is perhaps most famous today for his efforts to promote the study of "experimental science" and his interest in optics, linguistics and alchemy. Once described as one of the fathers of the modern empirical method, Bacon, as a *magister* in the arts faculty, never taught theology and never produced any strictly theological works. Instead he invested his energies into the pursuit of philosophy and science. Indeed, according to tradition, he is to be credited with having produced a recipe for gun powder and even the elixir of life itself – that is, the fabled "philosopher's stone" (*lapis philosophi*). An avid student of all spheres of natural knowledge, Bacon earned the degree of master of arts sometime around 1240, either at Oxford or at Paris, and was lecturing on Aristotle in the Paris arts faculty during the 1240s, even though during this period the public study of Aristotle was officially banned at the university.

Whilst at Paris Bacon also produced several important commentaries on Aristotle's works, including *De Physica*, *De Metaphysica* and *De Sensu et Sensato*. Sometime around 1247–50, however, Bacon retired from his lectureship at Paris and traveled to Oxford, where he embarked on some twenty years of extensive study, spending a small fortune – nearly £2,000 – on acquiring books and scientific instruments.[37] During his time at

---

[36] Ibid., 226.
[37] Cf. David C. Lindberg, *Roger Bacon's Philosophy of Nature: A Critical Edition, with English Translation, Introduction, and Notes,* of De Multiplicatione Specierum *and* De Speculis Comburentibus (Oxford: Clarendon, 1983), xviii.

Oxford, Bacon's affinity with the Franciscans increased, and – unlike Grosseteste – he decided to join the order, probably around 1257. His time as a Franciscan, however, was not an entirely smooth one. Not only did his interest in natural science provoke suspicion from his superiors, but his scathing remarks about some of his colleagues, especially those who were well-respected theologians, both at Oxford and at Paris, led him into conflict with many of his brothers – one need only consider the remarks he made about his Franciscan confrere Richard Rufus of Cornwall, a celebrated theologian and philosopher in his own right. According to Bacon, Rufus – just like Albert the Great – was the "worst" and "most stupid" of men.[38] He deserved such a title on account of his ignorance about experimental science and his introduction of many useless subtleties and logical extravagances into theology.

The Proposed Reform of Christian Education

Bacon's most famous work is his *Opus Majus* (*The Great Work*), which he wrote at the request of Pope Clement IV, with whom, despite his caustic personality, he had managed to foster good relations. The purpose of the *Opus Majus*, and the slightly later *Opus Minus* and *Opus Tertium*, which were also sent to the pope, was to offer a plan for a total reworking of the Christian education system. Addressing the pope directly, Bacon lamented what he saw as the corruption and dilution of Christian wisdom by the proliferation of useless errors promoted by the theologians and philosophers of his day. Intellectual progress, he argued, was being seriously hindered by the foolishness and pointless debates being introduced into philosophy, both at Oxford and at Paris, by figures such as Rufus and Albert the Great. Lacking any true wisdom, either in philosophy or theology, these authors purported to be masters of their field, yet in truth they pursued useless subtleties and needless distinctions.

---

[38] Bacon wrote: "The one I knew best was the worst and most stupid of them all. He was the inventor of these errors. His name is Richard of Cornwall, very famous amongst the stupid masses, but the wise thought he was absurd. And he was rejected at Paris for the errors he had invented and promulgated, while lecturing there on the Sentences solemnly from the year 1250 onwards, after he had lectured on the Sentences at Oxford. From that time, 1250, on, therefore most people persistently followed this master in his errors, and it has mainly weakened Oxford, where all this nonsense started." Bacon makes these remarks in his *Compendium Studii Philosophiae*. Translation from Peter Raedts, *Richard Rufus of Cornwall and the Tradition of Oxford Theology* (Oxford: Clarendon, 1987), 1–2.

Bacon lists a number of capital sins of the scholastic theology of his day in his *Opus Minus*. These include the fact that purely philosophical problems (e.g., the nature of matter, form, etc.) and themes are being discussed at length in theology. A second sin is the sheer ignorance of sciences that would be genuinely useful in explaining the Scriptures, such as knowledge of Hebrew and Greek, or ethics and physics. A third sin is the undue regard in which some contemporary masters are held (such as Alexander of Hales amongst the Franciscans, whose *Summa* Bacon caustically lamented was "as heavy as a horse," or Albert amongst the Dominicans). A fourth sin consists in the fact that the masters have replaced the study of and commentaries on the Bible with commentaries on Peter Lombard's *Sentences*. The fifth sin is the corruption of the biblical texts: because the Latins do not have the required linguistic skills, Bacon laments, they cannot detect faulty readings. This results in a sixth sin – namely, improper exegesis of the literal and spiritual senses. Finally, there is ignorance of the nature of things mentioned in the Scriptures themselves. Without a proper experiential knowledge (i.e., one based on immediate observation of things and an immediate application of reason to the data of experience), our knowledge of the literal sense of the Scriptures will be inherently flawed and it will prove impossible to make the transition from the literal to the spiritual interpretation.[39]

Bacon's critique is not limited to the theological discipline of his day. At the opening of his *Opus Majus* Bacon identifies four causes of error that prohibit true philosophical wisdom from emerging. Each of these, he argues, must be overcome if there is to be any hope of intellectual progress and a recovery of the wealth of Christian wisdom. The first is the appeal to dubious and unsuited authority (*fragilis et indigne auctoritatis exemplum*). Students of philosophy, in other words, prefer to look to false authorities instead of investigating things for themselves. Second, there is the problem of the long duration of custom or tradition (*conseutudinis diuturnitas*). Those studying philosophy, Bacon maintains, prefer to accept tradition without questioning whether a better understanding is possible. Third, there is the opinion and sheer prejudice of the unlearned crowd (*vulgi sensus imperiti*). Here the assumption is made that because a truth is held "by common belief" – that is, a great many people – it must necessarily be true. Finally, intellectual progress is hindered by the fact foolish men "conceal" (*occultatio*) their own ignorance by fostering the appearance of

[39] Roger Bacon, *Opus Minus*, ed. J. S. Brewer, *Fratri Rogeri Bacon Opera Quaedam Hactenus Inedita* (London: 1859), vol. 1, 2, p. 357 and Trottmann, *Théologie et Noétique*, 70–71.

wisdom. So pervasive are these four causes of error that Bacon judges them to threaten the very fabric of the Church itself, for it is through them that the Anti-Christ promotes ignorance within the church and weakens its adherence to divine wisdom.

Moreover, all the evils of the human race come from these deadly plagues; for the most useful (*utillisa*) and the greatest and most beautiful instances of wisdom and the secrets of all the sciences and arts are ignored (*et omnium scientiarum et artium secreta*); but what is even worse, men blinded by the mist of these four arguments do not perceive their own ignorance, but cover and conceal it with all caution so that they find no remedy for it; and finally, what is worst of all, they think they are in the full light of truth when they are in the densest shadows of error.[40]

The cure to these ills is found in the use of empirical knowledge or science (*scientia experimentalis*). Instead of simply accepting the authority of others, we should actively engage with the world ourselves, observing it and testing ideas against it. For Bacon, therefore, speculation takes us only so far in ascertaining truth. It is only through the "path of experience" (*via experientiae*) that fact is distinguished from fiction: "Therefore reasoning does not suffice, but experience does" (*ergo argumentum non sufficit, sed experientia*).[41] Thus a person may guess that fire burns and causes pain if he places his hand within it, "but when he has had actual experience of combustion his mind is made certain and rests in the full light of truth."[42] This appeal to experience, Bacon argues, is the sole weapon students of nature have to drive back the darkness of ignorance, "since without experience nothing can be sufficiently known" (*quia sine experientia nihil sufficienter scire potest*).[43]

The Primacy of Theology and the Unity of Wisdom

Whilst Bacon, like Grosseteste, may have criticized the introduction of the practice of commenting on Lombard's *Sentences* as a tool of theological education, he is nonetheless clear, just like Grosseteste, that he does not see

---

[40] *Opus Majus*, trans. Robert Belle Burke, 2 vols. (Philadelphia: University of Philadelphia Press, 1928), Part I, chapter I, p. 4.

[41] *Opus Majus*, Part VI, chapter I, p. 583.   [42] Ibid.

[43] Ibid. As an example of a falsity disproved by *experientia* Bacon notes is the widespread misconception concerning the male beaver. Many of his contemporaries, Bacon tells us, believed that the male beaver, commonly hunted for the fragrant musk supposedly produced by its genitals, deliberately castrates himself upon hearing the hunter's horn in order that it may avoid pursuit by the hunter's dogs. Empirical observation, however, Bacon argues, disproves this: the male beaver neither castrates itself upon hearing the hunter's horn, nor does it produce musk from its genitals; rather this comes from glands beneath its tail (p. 584).

any tension between philosophy and theology. Indeed, as we saw earlier, one of the fundamental "sins" of the theology of Bacon's day was, in his view, the fact that it did not employ other sciences to interpret the Scriptures. On one hand, Bacon claims that theology is the superior of all sciences and he affirms the Bible as the principal source of wisdom. In the Scriptures, he tells us, is found not only the fullness of all revealed truths necessary for salvation and theological erudition but also a description of creation far superior to anything that philosophy can offer. "The power of all philosophy," Bacon remarks, "is contained in the sacred writings; and this is especially clear, since the Scriptures far more certainly (*certius*), better (*melius*), and more truly (*verius*) comprehend the creatures than philosophical labor would know how to define them."[44] On the other hand, whilst theology may be the mistress of sciences, she is nonetheless utterly dependent on her handmaidens, the lower sciences, to help her elucidate, defend and promote the data of divine writ. The interdependence is hinted at in this quotation:

I say, therefore, that one science is the mistress of the others (*una scientia domin-atrix aliarum*), namely, theology to which the remaining sciences are vitally necessary; and without which it cannot (*non potest*) reach its end. The excellence of these sciences theology claims for her own law, whose nod and authority the rest of the sciences obey. Or better, there is only one perfect wisdom (*una tamen est sapientia perfecta*), which is contained wholly in the sacred Scripture, and is to be unfolded by canon law and by philosophy.[45]

The claim that the lower sciences are "vitally necessary" to theology is striking. Aristotle had argued that metaphysics, as the science that bestows its principles and most fundamental categories upon lower sciences, is the highest or architectonic science. Christian theologians contended that theology is, if not the highest science (as alluded to, and as will be explained more fully later, they disagreed on the scientific status of theology), nonetheless the highest wisdom. In Bacon's view, however, the perspective is partly reversed: it is the *scientia experimentalis* that furnishes its findings and knowledge of things to the other sciences, and ultimately to theology.[46] Furthermore, metaphysics is no longer the supreme philosoph-ical science. In a break with tradition, Bacon argues that the most supreme philosophical science is moral philosophy, "the end of all branches of philosophy."[47] Bacon characterizes moral philosophy in Part VII of the *Opus Majus* as concerned with "our salvation to be perfected through

[44] *Opus Majus*, Part II, chapter 8, p. 50.   [45] *Opus Majus*, Part II, chapter 1, p. 36
[46] Trottmann, *Théologie et Noétique*, 75.   [47] *Opus Majus*, Part VII, chapter 1, pp. 635–36.

virtue and felicity" and therefore intimately connected with theology. At any rate, the claim that moral philosophy trumps metaphysics as the highest philosophical science reveals Bacon's broadly pragmatic bias; moreover, it sets him apart from many of his contemporaries.

Above ethics there is Christian theology. Bacon, however, uses the term *theology* not just as synonymous with the truths of biblical revelation but, given the way he conceives of the porous relation between theology and philosophy, rather as natural theology. He can therefore summarize some of its core teachings in a number of theses which he considers accessible to human reason. Those theses include the claim that God exists and can be known as the most excellent, wise and good; that God is one and yet triune; that God exerts providential care over creation and deserves to be worshipped; that we are in need of revelation (itself therefore being rendered a datum of reason) and a mediator of God and mankind, "a human God," as it were; that our ultimate happiness consists in sharing in the divine bliss in the afterlife, and so forth.[48] Bacon does not, of course, claim that natural reason can have a full understanding of the dogma of the Trinity. He does claim, however, that ancient philosophers, especially those of Platonic provenance, had an inkling of this doctrine.

This kind of natural theology should provide the resources to establish a reconciliation amongst the different nations and denominations,[49] including those that do not accept the authority of the Scriptures: "Wherefore we must seek for reasons in another way which is common to us and unbelievers, namely, philosophy."[50] Whereas philosophy is the forerunner of religion and disposes people to it, Christianity is the only true religion.[51]

For Bacon, the harmony between (Christian) theology and philosophy is grounded in the fact that all wisdom – both supernatural and natural – has God as its author. Like theological wisdom, philosophical knowledge is achieved through God's "illumination" of the mind. As suggested, this was the case even with the ancient pagan philosophers: "Although in some measure the truth may be said to belong to the philosophers, yet for possessing it the divine light first flowed into their minds (*primo lux divina influxit in animos eorum*), and illuminated them from above."[52] To this extent, it is clear that "the power of philosophy is not foreign to the wisdom of God, but is included in it."[53] Moreover, "all philosophy (*tota philosophia*)

[48] Ibid., 638–59.   [49] Trottmann, *Théologie et Noétique*, 76–78.
[50] *Opus Majus*, Part VII, part 4, chapter 1, p. 793.   [51] Ibid., 807–08.
[52] *Opus Majus*, Part II, chapter 5, p. 43.   [53] *Opus Majus*, Part II, chapter 3, p. 39.

was manifestly given and revealed by God" (*a Deo datum et revelatam*).[54] The "philosophy" Bacon has in mind here is nourished and shaped by Christian revelation and was implicitly shared and anticipated by pre-Christian thinkers.

In short, for Bacon the boundaries between theology and philosophy are not only rather fluid, but in some cases perhaps blurred. Philosophical sciences offer key findings (often of an "empirical" nature) to theology; theology, in turn, exceeds philosophy insofar as it is nourished by revelation. Christians, as such, should not be worried about engaging with philosophy and the empirical study of nature – including the writings of ancient pagan philosophy. Instead they should harvest the fruits they contain and use them freely for the promotion of Christian wisdom. Bacon's vision of theology and philosophy – in particular his belief that even the wisdom of the ancient pagan philosophers was acquired through some sort of divine illumination – appears to blur the distinction between the natural and supernatural orders of human cognition. It undoubtedly stands at notable variance with the interpretations proffered by many of his contemporaries, including Bonaventure, Albert and Aquinas. Still, this section illustrates that Bacon, just like Grosseteste, represents a particularly unique contribution to the early Franciscan school and is a clear witness to its great intellectual creativity and resourcefulness with regards to theology and philosophy, as well as science.

THE *SUMMA HALENSIS*

Contemporaneous with Robert Grosseteste and Roger Bacon, the earliest Franciscan theology masters at Paris – Alexander of Hales and John of La Rochelle, as well as their little-studied successors, Odo Rigaldus and William of Middleton – played a fundamental role in shaping the early Franciscan intellectual tradition. Like their famous pupil Bonaventure, the early Parisian Franciscan masters did not, however, share Grosseteste's and Bacon's disdain for the introduction of the new dialectic method into theological studies; nor, in turn, did they accept the latter's harsh rejection of the practice of commenting on Lombard's *Sentences* as the primary tool of theological education. Instead, they actively embraced and promoted it: as noted earlier, it was Alexander of Hales who, much to Grosseteste's displeasure, introduced lecturing on Lombard's *Sentences*, rather than the

---

[54] *Opus Majus*, Part II, chapter 6, p. 48.

Bible, as the basis of his teaching activities. Moreover, unlike their Oxford counterparts, the early Parisian Franciscan masters appear to have had little if any real interest in pursuing the scientific lines of inquiry pioneered by Bacon and Grosseteste. We have no concrete examples of any scientific texts by Alexander and his Parisian disciples, nor have they left us commentaries on Aristotle.

Alexander was born in 1186 in Shropshire, England. The dates of Alexander's studies under Grosseteste as his *socius* are not clear, but it seems likely he took up his chair in theology at the University of Paris around 1220–21, having already completed the master of arts degree sometime before 1210. Most of Alexander's surviving academic works date from prior to his entrance into the Franciscan Order in 1236–37, when he was aged around fifty. These include his famous *Glossa* on Lombard's *Sentences* (1222–29) and his vast corpus of *quaestiones disputatae* (the so-called *Quaestiones Disputatae Antequam Esset Frater*). Highly detailed and often very original, these cover a wide range of subjects, from Christ's knowledge, prophecy and the Trinity, to the sacraments, God's knowledge and the nature of the heavens. Born around 1200, John of La Rochelle entered the Franciscan Order on an uncertain date, yet what we do know is that he became a master of theology at Paris sometime after Alexander, thereby bestowing on the Franciscans a second chair of theology. Although there is some manuscript evidence that John produced a commentary on Lombard's *Sentences*, his most important works are his *Tractatus de Divisione Potentiarum de Animae* (ca. 1233–35) and the more well-known *Summa de Anima* (1235–36).

Perhaps the clearest witness to the desire of early Parisian Franciscans to explore Christian belief in a rigorously systematic and dialectic way is the *Summa Fratris Alexandri* (*The Summa of Brother Alexander*), also known as the *Summa Halensis*. Commenced sometime around 1240, this massive, largely neglected Franciscan *summa theologiae* represents a collaborative effort on behalf of Alexander and his associates to produce a comprehensive summary of the key areas of Christian doctrine. The most extensive and systematic example of early Franciscan theology, its purpose was to articulate a distinctly Franciscan theological vision, but also to form the basis of a Franciscan theological textbook that could be used to teach successive generations of friars. Primarily the work of Alexander himself and of John of La Rochelle, the *Summa*, as it has been handed down to us, follows the basic fourfold pattern of Lombard's *Sentences*. Book one discusses God as unity and Trinity; book two examines the creation of the world and the Fall, and book three addresses the Incarnation. Book four is devoted to the sacraments.

In 1245 both Alexander of Hales and John of Rochelle died, leaving the *Summa* incomplete. Despite their best efforts, Alexander and John had only managed to complete books one to three of the *Summa* while the envisaged discussion of the sacraments and the last things in the projected book four was missing. Several years later, however, Pope Alexander IV wrote to William of Middleton, who had taken over from Alexander and John as the Franciscan *magister* at Paris, and asked him to complete the *Summa* by producing the missing fourth book. This William duly did by using extracts from his own extensive *Quaestiones de Sacramentis* and, seemingly, by borrowing much material from his successor at Paris, Bonaventure. In particular William drew upon Bonaventure's thought concerning prayer, fasting and almsgiving. Indeed, the questions pertaining to the latter in the fourth volume of the *Summa* (currently not included in the Quaracchi edition) are almost certainly versions of disputed questions Bonaventure conducted during his regency of 1254–57; that this is so is confirmed by the fact that they closely match the unedited *quaestiones* on prayer, fasting and almsgiving attributed to Bonaventure in a Vatican manuscript.[55]

The Nature of Theology in the Summa Halensis

Whilst Alexander of Hales and John of La Rochelle may have embraced a notably different approach to theological inquiry than the one Grosseteste and Bacon endorsed, on the question of whether theology ought to be classified as a "science" and how it relates to the lower philosophical disciplines, they nonetheless share many of the key ideas of their Oxford counterparts. Theology, the *Summa* argues, is more appropriately characterized as wisdom rather than as a science, and this for a number of reasons. First, according to Aristotle, one of the characteristics of higher sciences is the fact that it is being pursued for its own sake (*sui gratia*). Given the fact that theology considers the highest Cause (i.e., God) in its own right, it is not subject to any other science but is being pursued for its own sake. For this reason it should be called "wisdom" rather than merely "science." Second, theology concerns more the affections and the

---

[55] Cf. Balduinus Distelbrink, *Bonaventurae Scripta Authentica Dubia Vel Spuria Critice Recensita* (Rome: Instituto Storico Cappuccini, 1975), 13–14; Victorine Doucet, "De quaestionibus S. Bonaventurae adscriptis in Cod. Vaticano Palatino lat. 612," *Archivium Franciscanum Historicum* 26 (1933), 487–96. These *quaestiones* are therefore of great importance for those working on Bonaventure, especially given that we have only a handful of *quaestiones* from Bonaventure's time as Franciscan regent master and that they are not included in his *Opera Omnia*.

promotion of piety than the intellect and the acquisition of knowledge. Theology is wisdom as it moves the soul "towards the good through the principles of love and fear [of the Lord]."[56] To this extent, theology is primarily an affective and practical discipline. It helps "perfect the soul by way of affection" and thereby strengthens its adherence to God.[57] Sciences, by contrast, merely perfect the intellect. Moreover, deriving from divine revelation rather than from our own intellectual efforts (*inspirata, non acquisita*), theology stands above all the lower philosophical sciences and must not therefore be confused or equated with them in any way. "Theology is not like any other science (*non est sicut alia scientia*), nor should it be listed among them. Nor is it under (*supponatur*) any part of philosophy."[58]

Therefore, theology, which perfects the soul by way of affection, moving it towards the good through the principles of fear and love, is more appropriately and mainly wisdom. First philosophy, which is philosophers' theology [i.e., metaphysics] and deals with the cause of all causes, perfects our cognition by way of skill and reasoning, and is less appropriately called wisdom. As for the rest of the sciences, which are about subsequent [levels of] causes and about the effects, they should not be called "wisdoms" but sciences [strictly speaking].[59]

This affective nature of theology leads the Summists to argue that theology proceeds differently from the lower sciences, particularly at the level of "experience." Where speculative sciences derive their certainty solely from intellectual axioms and deductions, theological wisdom, by contrast, whilst it may still utilize rational inquiry, derives its certainty primarily through the "certitude of affection" and appetitive cognition that comes through the spiritual senses and their adherence to God through charity.

There is a certitude of speculation and that of experience. In addition to those, there is a certitude of intellect and a certitude of affection. Also, there is a certitude as far as the spiritual [part of the] soul and a certitude as far as the animal [part of the] soul is concerned. I say, then, that the theological approach is more certain by the certitude of experience, by the certitude of affection, which is by way of taste . . . but not more certain as far as intellectual speculation goes, which operates by way of seeing. Also it is more certain to a spiritual man but less certain to an animal man.[60]

---

[56] *Summa Hal.*, Lib. 1, Tract. Intro., q.1, c.1 (p. 2).   [57] Ibid.

[58] *Summa Hal.*, Lib. 1, Tract. Intro., q.1, c.2 (p. 5).

[59] *Summa Hal.*, Lib. 1, Tract. Intro., q.1, c.1 (p. 2). Translated in Oleg Bychkov, "The Nature of Theology in Duns Scotus and His Franciscan Predecessors," in *Franciscan Studies* 66 (2008): 64–65.

[60] *Summa Hal.*, Lib. 1, Tract. Intro., q.1, c.4, a.2 (p. 9). Translation from Bychkov, "The Nature of Theology," p. 73.

The last sentence should be understood in light of 1 Corinthians 2:14. This affective characterization of theology was shared by most theologians in the 13th century, not just Franciscan but also Dominican – for example, Albert the Great. As we will see, however, Thomas Aquinas was to disagree: for him, theology is primarily theoretical rather than practical or affective.

Trinity in the Summa Halensis

Containing one of the most detailed expressions of early Franciscan Trinitarian speculation, the *Summa Halensis* offers a rich, dynamic and highly systematic analysis of Trinity, one that plays a decisive role in shaping Trinitarian theology of later Franciscan thinkers, in particular St. Bonaventure.[61] The *Summa's* Trinitarian thought has at its heart the Pseudo-Dionysian notion that the good is self-diffusive (*bonum diffusivum sui*) and thus naturally wishes to bestow itself upon another. For the *Summa Halensis*, God, as the supreme and most perfect being, is the highest and most perfect good (*bonitas*). Given that the good is naturally self-diffusive, it is clear that the goodness of the divinity, being the highest of all possible goods, must not only be self-diffusive but must be supremely so; and it is this supremely self-diffusive nature of the divine *bonitas* that explains why there is a plurality of divine Persons: "The highest good is as the principal cause (*principalis causa*) of this multiplication in God" (*multiplicationis in divinis*).[62]

The wellspring of the divine goodness, the *Summa Halensis* argues, is found in the Person of the Father (*Pater*), who is the root and source of the divine being itself. The fecundity of the Father's goodness entails that it must be shared with another Person, one who is equal in divinity to the Father and who shares in his infinite eternity; this of course is the Son (*Filius*), who is the eternal outpouring of the Father's goodness and the Word (*Verbum*) of his eternal wisdom (*sapientia*). The fecundity of the divine goodness shared by the Father and the Son is, however, capable of a higher state of self-diffusion; it is for this reason that both the Father and the Son breathe forth the Spirit (*Spiritus*), who through a process of joint love (*condilectio*) is the shared object and delight of the Father and Son. With an explicit reference to Richard of St. Victor, the *Summa* argues that

---

[61] For a lucid and very helpful overview, see Boyd Taylor Coolman, "The Comprehensive Trinitarianism of the *Summa Halensis*," in Lydia Schumacher (ed.), *The* Summa Halensis: *Doctrines and Debates* (Berlin: De Gruyter, 2020), 107–40.

[62] Lib. 1, part. 1, inq. 2, tract. un. q.3, c.5, resp. (p. 465).

it is therefore "required that the one who loves most highly and the one who is loved most highly" – namely, the Father and the Son – "seek out one who is co-beloved, and who is loved mutually by both with an equal will."[63]

According to the *Summa*, there are two modes by which the self-diffusive goodness of the Father proceeds. The first is according to nature (*natura*), the second is according to will (*voluntas*). In order for the Godhead to be the highest good, both modes of procession are necessary in it (*ergo in summo bono necesse est ponere utrumque modum diffusionis*).[64] For if only one were present, then the self-diffusive nature of the *bonitas summa* would be lacking perfection, and that is clearly impossible; as such, both must be posited within the Godhead. It is the Son, so the *Summa Halensis* argues, who proceeds according to nature (*secundum naturam*) for he is the outpouring of the Father's own nature as the fount of superabundant goodness. Whereas the Holy Spirit proceeds according to will because he arises from the love the Father and Son share, love is clearly an act of the will and not the intellect:

For there are two principles of diffusion in things, namely by nature (*natura*) and by will (*voluntas*). The most perfect diffusion of nature is that which is by generation (*per generationem*), whereas the most perfect diffusion of the will is that which is through love or delectation (*per amorem sive per dilectionem*); and this is that which is praiseworthy of the goodness in things (*in rebus*). More praiseworthy, however, is that good which diffuses itself according to both modes rather than simply according to one or the other. Therefore, if that which is praiseworthy (*laudabile*) and perfect (*perfectum*) cannot be absent in the highest good, then it is clear that in the highest good, which is God, there must be a diffusion of generation, upon which the difference between generator and generated (*differentia gignentis et genit*), that is the Father and the Son, is consequent, and there must also be a diffusion through the mode of delectation, which we speak of as the procession of the Holy Spirit.[65]

The notion that the Son and Holy Spirit are generated *per modum naturae* and *per modum voluntatis*, respectively, points to the fact that the *Summa Halensis*, very much like later generations of Franciscan thinkers, regards the constitution of the individual Trinitarian Persons as being realized through their origins as opposed to their relations. Where later 13th-century figures like Thomas Aquinas and successive generations of Dominican scholars were to follow St. Augustine, and in turn Boethius, in believing that the divine Persons are primarily constituted through their

---

[63] Lib. I, part. I, inq. 2, tract. un. q.I, tit. 2, c.I (p. 439).   [64] Ibid.   [65] Ibid., 438.

relationships to one another (i.e., the Father is the Father because he is the Father of the Son, etc.), the *Summa*, by contrast, prefers to follow the opinion of Richard of St. Victor that the Persons are primarily constituted through their origins – that is, according to the order of their emanations from one another.[66] In doing so, the *Summa* established a tradition that later Franciscan thinkers – Bonaventure in particular – were to follow with relative faithfulness, and that, as Russell Friedman has observed, served to characterize much of 13th-century Franciscan Trinitarian speculation, right up until the thought of Duns Scotus.[67]

Prefiguring Bonaventure's strongly Christocentric theology of the Trinity, the *Summa Halensis* argues that the Son is the "middle" person (*persona media*) between the Father and the Holy Spirit.[68] To understand how this is so we need to recognize the distinctly linear model of the Trinity that is at work within the *Summa* and how, in turn, it arises from its definition of the good as self-diffusive. If the Father is the fount (*fons*) or beginning (*principium*) of the divine *bonitas*, then it is clear that he receives his goodness from no one, and is thus said to be a purely active principle. By contrast, the Son is said to be both active and passive, for he both receives his goodness from the Father and, in conjunction with the Father, is responsible for breathing forth the goodness of the Holy Spirit. The Holy Spirit, in turn, is purely passive, for he is the recipient and manifestation of the overflowing love between the Father and the Son, but, crucially, he is not responsible for bestowing goodness upon either the Father or the Son; instead, he is merely the recipient and manifestation of their shared love (*condilectio*). From this perspective, the Son thus occupies a middle position between the purely active agency of the Father and the purely passive agency of the Spirit, for he is both active and passive in the diffusion of the divine goodness. The following text summarizes the discussion well:

There is one Person from whom all the others come, but who is not himself from another; and there is one Person who is from the others but who does not himself produce another Person; and, finally, there is one Person who is the middle between the one which is from another and the one from whom the others come. And the Person from whom the others come but who is not from another,

---

[66] For later Trinitarian accounts, see Russell L. Friedman, *Medieval Trinitarian Thought from Aquinas to Ockham* (Cambridge: Cambridge University Press, 2010) and *Intellectual Traditions at the Medieval University: The Use of Philosophical Psychology in Trinitarian Theology among the Franciscans and Dominicans, 1250–1350*, 2 vols. (Leiden: Brill, 2013).

[67] Friedman, *Intellectual Traditions at the Medieval University*, 1.341–416.

[68] Lib. 1, part. 1, inq. 2, tract. un., q.4 (p. 476).

is the Person of the Father; the Person who is from the others but from whom no other Person comes is the Person of the Holy Spirit; however, the middle Person is the Person of the Son; he, therefore, is from the Person of the Father and from him is the Person of the Holy Spirit, who is solely from the other Persons.[69]

Trinity and the Transcendentals: Unity, Truth and Goodness

The *Summa Halensis*'s rich Trinitarian theology does not exclude a detailed analysis of God's unity and simplicity (*De Deo Uno*). Crucially, however, its discussion of the divine unity contains many key elements designed to show how the divine unity, specifically the nature of the divine qualities, leads seamlessly into the Trinitarian nature of God. It is thus clear that although the *Summa* formally separates its discussion of the divine unity (*De Substantia Divinae Unitatis*) from its Trinitarian speculation (*De Pluralitate Divinae Trinitatis*), the two are very much intertwined; indeed, it is impossible to understand its rich theology of the Trinity and its Trinitarian reading of creation without retracing these back to its understanding of the divine unity, in particular the notion of the self-diffusive nature of the good.

This becomes clear when we consider the *Summa Halensis*'s discussion of transcendentals, which can be defined as the fundamental properties that characterize all things, such as being itself, oneness (every thing is distinct from something else), truth and goodness.[70] Medieval thinkers argued that being, truth and goodness are convertible: all things are truthful and good insofar as they are. This may strike the modern reader as odd: for most (post) modern thinkers, the being of things no longer radiates an inner splendor of truth and goodness. In the medieval worldview, however, which is deeply sacramental, teleological and nonmechanistic, God has bestowed an inherent intelligibility and goodness upon all things.[71]

In ontological terms, when a being is distinct from other things and undivided in itself, it expresses being as "one" (*unum*). When we consider beings in relation to other things "according to a difference" being(s) can be characterized as "true." This may at first appear an obscure statement. It needs to be understood in light of the exemplarist teaching that all things

---

[69] Ibid.

[70] See Rik Van Nieuwenhove, *Thomas Aquinas and Contemplation* (Oxford: Oxford University Press, 2021), 50–51.

[71] For a masterful study, see Jan Aertsen, *Medieval Philosophy and the Transcendentals: The Case of Thomas Aquinas* (Brill: Leiden, 1996).

have their own species, which allows us to distinguish them truthfully from other things. Finally, as a being is considered in relation to fittingness or order (*secundum convenientiam sive ordinem*), it is "good," for *bonum* refers to that to which something is ordered. In short, all things, insofar as they are, have their own integrity or oneness. Their truth is based on the inherence of an intelligible form, while their goodness has a teleological orientation.

The *Summa* continues his discussion by showing how this ontological analysis of the being of things (*esse rerum*) is, in turn, embedded in Trinitarian causality, which is threefold: efficient, formal or exemplar (*formalis ut exemplar*) and final. Although divine causality is shared by the entire Trinity, efficient causality is appropriated to the Father (the Origin of the Trinity), exemplar or formal causality to the Son (the Word, in whom all things have their exemplarist archetype in accordance with John 1:3) and final causality is associated with the Holy Spirit (who proceeds as Goodness from the Father and the Son by way of Love). Created being, then, acquires a threefold imprint that conforms it to the threefold divine cause: efficient causality bestows unity (*unitas*) and distinct integrity or indivisibility (*indivisum*) upon things; formal exemplar causality is the foundation of truth in thing: "as the exemplarist cause is the first art of truth (*causa exemplaris est ars prima veritatis*), so too every creature (insofar as possible for it), is made in imitation of this art, and this is what it means to have truth."[72] The exemplar or archetype of all things is the divine *ars*, or Word. All things reflect this divine blueprint. Thus, the exemplarist ontology of the *Summa Halensis* finds its theological foundation in the Word. Finally, beings receive a third imprint that bestows goodness on them. Every created being has an orientation and conformity toward the highest good (*inclinatio et conformitas ad summam bonitatem*), and this very conformity constitutes its goodness. In short, the goodness of things is inherently teleological, and this teleology has a Trinitarian foundation: it reflects the goodness of the Holy Spirit who bestows final causality upon things.

The *Summa Halensis* thus offers us a splendid vision in which every being reflects the triple causal operation of the divine Persons, bestowing oneness, truth and goodness upon the core of every being. It then proceeds to make one more move by establishing a connection between this discussion of the transcendentals (and their Trinitarian foundation) on one hand, and theological anthropology on the other. The human person is

---

[72] Lib. 1, part 1, Inq. 1, tr. 3. q.1, m.1, c.2 (p. 115).

predisposed through her three faculties toward relating to the oneness, truth and goodness inherent in all things. There is, in other words, a fitting harmony between theological anthropology and Trinitarian ontology:

The being of things can be compared to the soul in a triple manner, namely insofar as things are retained in memory, perceived by the intellect, and loved by the will. In every being there is oneness due to the efficient cause, in virtue of which it is ordered and preserved in memory. . . . Again, from the exemplary cause there is truth in all things, in virtue of which it is understood by the intellect. Finally, from the final cause there is goodness, by virtue of which it is loved and affirmed by the will.[73]

Here the *Summa Halensis* articulates an important insight shared by most scholastics of the 13th century: the human mind (and its faculties) enjoys a preestablished harmony with core aspects of reality. This explains why medieval authors are reluctant to discuss epistemological issues independently from ontological ones, thus preempting modern dualist problems as to how the mind can relate to or even affirm the existence of the world "out there." Hence, when medieval authors define truth as the *adaequatio intellectus et rei*, this phrase should not be translated as "correspondence of mind and reality" as if there were two parallel tracks – mind and reality. It should rather be understood as the "convergence" or even "assimilation" of mind and reality.[74] Whether their epistemological stance is more Augustinian or Aristotelian, according to medieval authors, the inherent intelligibility of the world (based on its forms) harmoniously coheres with the mind that receives or abstracts these forms for its cognitive activity.

In summary, each of the divine essential attributes finds analogous expression in the unity, truth and goodness of creatures, which are participated "vestiges" of the divine unity, truth and goodness. "In God there is a certain triad, which shines forth and is represented in every creature, and in this way a creature is called a vestige, and this is noted in three ways: one, true, good."[75] In rational creature we find an even more expressive imprint, for we have been made as image of the Trinity, reflected in our faculty or power, wisdom and will. According to the *Summa*, the triadic identity of the divine essence thus finds manifestation, in different degrees, within the creatures produced by it. In all of this the *Summa Halensis* gives an eloquent expression to the sacramental worldview of the medieval period.

---

[73] Lib. 1 part 1, Inq. 1, tr. 3. q.1, m.1, c.2 (p. 115).
[74] Van Nieuwenhove, *Thomas Aquinas and Contemplation*, 30–31.
[75] Lib. 1, part 1, inq. 1, tr. 3, q.3, cap. 3 (p. 172).

Incarnation in the Summa Halensis

Given the close connection between Alexander of Hales and Robert Grosseteste, it should come as no surprise that many of the innovations introduced into Christological speculation by the bishop of Lincoln, particularly regarding the predestination of the Incarnation independent of the Fall, find clear echoes in Alexander's thought, and indeed that of his disciples.[76] Amongst his many early *quaestiones disputatae*, Alexander raises the question "whether the Incarnation would have had a certain usefulness if there were no passion?"[77] Alexander's response is an affirmative one. He advances several arguments in favor of the idea that the Incarnation would have taken place even if humanity had not fallen – one of which is clearly indebted to his theology of the self-diffusive nature of the good. If God is the supreme diffusive good, Alexander argues, then it is necessary that his goodness be diffused to the highest degree possible not only within his own internal Trinitarian processions but also within creation itself, which, after all, is the outpouring of his self-diffusive goodness. The supreme *bonitas* God could bestow upon creation, Alexander asserts, would be the union of God with his creation through his Incarnation and taking on the form of the highest creature; hence the coming of the Word in human flesh.

A similar line of argumentation is found in book three of the *Summa Halensis*. Crucially, however, the *Summa* introduces several arguments not found in Alexander's *quaestiones* or his *Glossa*. The most novel of these is an argument derived from an observation made by St. Bernard of Clairvaux. The *Summa* notes how, in his commentary on John 1:12, St. Bernard explains that the devil's foreknowledge of the Incarnation was the reason for his procuring the Fall.[78] Driven by envy that humanity should receive such a blessing, the devil sought to thwart the union of divine and human natures by corrupting the latter through sin. The fact that the devil knew of the Incarnation prior to its realization, proves – so Bernard reasons – that the Incarnation of the Word had been predestined prior to the Fall and is not, as such, a consequence of it. For if it were, then this would make the Incarnation a product not of divine volition and design but rather of the devil's malice. The *Summa* endorses Bernard's reasoning and affirms that Christ's Incarnation was both predestined and fitting, irrespective of sin.

---

[76] See also Justus H. Hunter, "The Contribution of the *Summa Halensis* to the Reason for the Incarnation," in Lydia Schumacher (ed.), *The* Summa Halensis: *Doctrines and Debates* (Berlin: De Gruyter, 2020), 141–52.

[77] *Quaestiones Disputatae Antequam Esset Frater*, q. 15, dist. 2, mem. 4. (Quaracchi: 1960), vol. 1, 207–09.

[78] *Summa Hal.*, Lib III, inq. un., tr. 1, q.2, tit. 2, resp. (p. 42).

Robert Grosseteste

A Latin edition of the *Hexaemeron* can be found in R. Dales et al. (Oxford: Oxford University Press, 1989) and an English translation by C. F. J. Martin as *Robert Grosseteste: On the Six Days of Creation. A Translation of the* Hexaemeron (Oxford: Oxford University Press, 1999). Stephen M. Hildebrand produced a translation of *De Cessatione Legalium* as *On the Cessation of the Laws* (Washington, DC: Catholic University of America Press, 2012). There is a translation of *De Luce* by Neil Lewis in John Flood, James R. Ginther and Joseph W. Goering (eds.), *Robert Grosseteste and His Intellectual Milieu* (Toronto: PIMS, 2013), 239–47. The attractive allegory *Castle of Love* (*Château d'Amour*) has been translated by Evelyn A. Mackie as "Robert Grosseteste's Anglo-Norman Treatise on the Loss and Restoration of Creation, commonly known as *Le Château d'Amour*: an English Translation," in Maura O'Carrol (ed.), *Robert Grosseteste and the Beginnings of a British Theological Tradition* (Rome: Istituto Storico de Cappucini, 2003), 151–79. A fine introduction to his work and thought remains James McEvoy, *Robert Grosseteste*. Great Medieval Thinkers (Oxford: Oxford University Press, 2000). Also see Richard W. Southern, *Robert Grosseteste: The Growth of an English Mind in Medieval Europe* (Oxford: Clarendon, 1992). Online one can profit from Neil Lewis, "Robert Grosseteste," *Stanford Encyclopedia of Philosophy* (summer 2019 edition), Edward N. Zalta (ed.), https://plato .stanford.edu/archives/sum2019/entries/grosseteste.

Roger Bacon

A Latin edition of *The Opus Majus of Roger Bacon* was edited by John Henry Bridges in 1879 and reissued in 2010 in the Cambridge Library Editions in two volumes. The translation by Robert Belle Burke, *Roger Bacon: Opus Majus*, 2 vols. (Philadelphia: University of Philadelphia Press, 1928) has also remained in print. For an introduction to his life and reforms, see Amanda Power, *Roger Bacon and the Defence of Christendom* (Cambridge: Cambridge University Press, 2013).

Summa Halensis

The Latin text of the *Summa Halensis* can be found in *Alexandri de Hales Summa Theologica*, 4 vols., ed. Bernardine Klumper, Constantinus Koser,

Pacificus Perantoni and Bonaventura Marrani. (Ad Claras Aquas, Quaracchi, Collegium S. Bonaventurae 1924–48). Lydia Schumacher (ed.), *The* Summa Halensis*: Doctrines and Debates* (Berlin: De Gruyter, 2020) contains great essays, including the ones by Boyd Taylor Coolman and Justus Hunter already referred to. Lydia Schumacher has also edited a sister volume, entitled *The* Summa Halensis*: Sources and Context* (Berlin: De Gruyter, 2020). Oleg Bychkov and Lydia Schumacher (eds.) have also published translations of extracts in: *A Reader in Early Franciscan Theology: The* Summa Halensis. Medieval Philosophy: Texts and Studies (New York: Fordham University Press, 2021), which is a great resource.

CHAPTER 16

Bonaventure

INTRODUCTION

Bonaventure was born in Bagnoregio, probably in 1217, about ninety kilometers north of Rome. He initially studied at the Parisian university under Alexander of Hales. From 1248 he lectured on the Bible, and from 1250 to 1252 he lectured on Peter Lombard's *Sentences*. Bonaventure's profoundly Franciscan theology draws on Augustinian, Pseudo-Dionysian and Victorine elements, as well as on his immediate predecessors (incl. *Summa Hal.*). In 1257, when he became the minister general of the Franciscan Order, Bonaventure's formal academic career ceased. His works written after that time are more pastoral and spiritual than strictly scholarly. His works are usually divided into two categories: first, there are his more theoretical works, such as his *Commentary on the Sentences* (*Sent.*), the *Breviloquium* (a wonderful summary of the Christian faith), *Disputed Questions on the Mystery of the Trinity* (*Myst. Trin.*) and *Disputed Questions on the Knowledge of Christ*. But there are also his more devotional works such as *The Soul's Journey into God* (*Itinerarium mentis in Deum*), *The Tree of Life* and *The Life of Saint Francis*, amongst many others. Bonaventure has also written biblical commentaries, such as *On John*, *On Ecclesiastes* and *On Luke* – a particular voluminous and profound one. A work, addressed to his fellow friars, which reveals some of the central concerns of Bonaventure (including the significance of the theology of the Trinity for our understanding of the world), is the *Collations on the Hexameron* (*Hex.*). It dates from the final period of his life, when he was involved in a number of controversies, such as the status of the mendicant orders and the influence of radical secularist Aristotelian interpretations (Latin Averroism) on the Parisian intellectual scene. Bonaventure, having been appointed a cardinal in 1273, died on July 15, 1274, and was buried in Lyons, where he was attending the Council convened to bring about the reconciliation between Latin Catholicism and Greek Orthodoxy.

Few theologians in the West have been imbued with such a strong sense of the splendor of the Trinitarian God. I discuss his theology of the Trinity in some detail. First, however, I deal with the way he sees the relationship between theology and philosophy, faith and reason.

SAPIENTIAL THEOLOGY

In Bonaventure's view, merely relying on the natural light of reason is nothing but a dangerous, self-inflicted tutelage. Philosophy has to subject itself to theology if it is to flourish. Only faith can separate light from darkness (Gen. 1:4) while a presumptuous, supposedly autonomous philosophy will only lead to error. These views may, at first, not appear all that different from Thomas's. Thomas too had expressed concerns about the fallibility of philosophy, and had emphasized the need for *sacra doctrina*. A closer examination, however, brings out the differences.

Bonaventure was deeply concerned about the growing influence of peripatetic philosophy at the expense of Augustinianism. As Bonaventure sees it, because Aristotle rejected exemplarism and the theory of ideas he fell into a triple error: he affirmed the unity of the intellect and the eternity of the world, and he denied the immortality of the soul (*Hex.* VI.1–4). In contrast, Bonaventure asserts, "This is the sum total of our metaphysics: emanation, exemplarity, and consummation, that is, to be illuminated through spiritual rays (*illuminari per radios spirituales*) and return to the Supreme Being (*reduci ad summum*). And in this you will be a true metaphysician" (*Hex.* 1.17). It is useful to discuss these elements in turn.

Emanation for Bonaventure does not refer to the fact that the world flows from God (as in some Neoplatonic authors). Rather, for Bonaventure, it is above all a Trinitarian concept. Within the Trinity, the fruitfulness of the Father generates his Word, while the Holy Spirit proceeds as their Bond of Love. Bonaventure states that the whole of creation is a material extension, freely willed by God, of these intra-divine processions – a view shared by Thomas (*ST* 1.34.3 and 45.7). For both Bonaventure and Thomas the created world is a vast expression, a symbol (in the sense that it represents, or makes present) of the Trinity, and as such it is caught in the dynamism of *egressus* and *reditus*.[1]

---

[1] Zachary Hayes, *The Hidden Center: Spirituality and Speculative Christology in St. Bonaventure* (New York: Franciscan Institute, 2000), 12–13.

In *Breviloquium* II.12.1 Bonaventure writes that "the created world is a kind of book, reflecting, representing, and describing its Maker, the Trinity, at three different levels of expression: as a vestige, as an image, and as a likeness."[2]

From the fact that the inner Trinitarian life of God grounds and is reflected in the world, Bonaventure, unlike Thomas, concludes that a philosopher who examines it from the perspective of natural reason will fail to perceive its most fundamental dimension. Philosophy is therefore a deeply ambivalent enterprise for Bonaventure. He links its pursuit with the Genesis story (the tree of the knowledge of good and evil) claiming, moreover, that philosophers are in danger of changing wine into water, bread into stones, "a most miserable miracle" indeed.[3]

Exemplarity, the second aspect of Bonaventure's metaphysics, refers to the view that things have their true reality in the divine ideas. These divine ideas are located in the Word, the Second Person of the Trinity, the eternal archetype through whom God eternally expresses himself in all things, and without whom we cannot understand the most fundamental truths:

From all eternity, the Father has generated a Son who resembles him [in whom] he expressed himself. ... He has expressed everything he can do and above all everything he wanted to do, and he has expressed all things in him, the Son, as in a medium and as in his art. This is why this medium is the Truth ... and this is why no truth whatsoever can be known except through this Truth.[4]

Thus, for Bonaventure the Word is the true reality of created things, and it is only in the Word, as the metaphysical center (*medium metaphysicum*) that we can know things properly (*Hex.* 1.17).

But how do we share in the divine truth of the Son? This brings us to his theory of illumination, which also finds its origins in the thought of Augustine, and which will also play a major role in Bonaventure's spirituality. Bonaventure does not claim that we have a direct knowledge of divine ideas. As a matter of fact, he adopts a version of the Aristotelian abstraction theory to explain how the intellect gathers its data. However, this occurs only at the lower level of the epistemological scale, so to speak. In order to attain truth, these "data" need to be evaluated in light of the divine ideas, the eternal standards of truth, which we simply intuit and which we cannot in turn evaluate. As Christopher Cullen puts it: "The eternal art is that by which we judge, even though it is not the object of cognition. It illumines

---

[2] All translations from *Bonaventure: Texts in Translation Series, vol.* IX, *Breviloquium*, ed. Dominic V. Monti (New York: Franciscan Institute, 2005).
[3] See *Hex.* XIX.14; XVII.27.   [4] *Hex.* 1.13; see also III.4.

our judgements, even if it does not provide the objects of those judgements."[5] Thus, the divine ideas are not the *obiectum quod* of human knowledge – not *what* we can perceive – but rather the *obiectum quo* – that is, that *through* whose influence we can attain certainty. In a famous quotation from *De Scientia Christi* 4, Bonaventure explains: "For certain knowledge, the eternal reason is necessarily involved as the regulative and motivating principle (*ut regulans et motivans*), but certainly not as the sole principle nor in its full clarity. But along with the created reason, it is contuited by us in part as is fitting in this life."[6] Contuition refers to an indirect and implicit awareness of the divine ideas, which make our truthful judgments possible in the first place.[7]

In order to appreciate how Bonaventure's stance differs from that of Thomas Aquinas, it is important to remember that illumination, as the condition of possibility of our intellectual processes, is situated somewhere between the order of nature and that of grace.[8] It is only in light of his emanationist, exemplarist and illuminist views that Bonaventure's claim that philosophical reason is in radical need of divine assistance (and cannot operate properly at the ordinary, natural level) becomes intelligible. For Thomas, natural reason, in its pursuit of truth, may be fallible and in need of guidance. But it is not *intrinsically* inadequate without God's assistance. For Bonaventure, it is.

When it comes to theological reason, even more assistance is required – namely, an infusion of grace. Theology, as a kind of wisdom (*sapientia*), is both knowledge (*cognitio*) and love (*affectum*). Theology is "an affective habit" or disposition (*habitus affectivus*) with both speculative and practical dimensions. For Bonaventure it is mainly practical – namely, "that we become good."[9] For Thomas, it is just the opposite: theology is more speculative than practical.[10] Bonaventure's sapiental understanding of theology implies a closer link between theology and spirituality than we find in Thomas: "There is no sure passage from science (*scientia*) to wisdom (*sapientia*); a medium must be provided, namely holiness (*sanctitas*)" (*Hex.* IXX.3). This is the reason why Bonaventure, quoting Wis. 6:18, argues that

---

[5] Christopher M. Cullen, *Bonaventure* (Oxford: Oxford University Press, 2006), 85.

[6] Bonaventure, *Disputed Questions on the Knowledge of Christ*, ed. and trans. Zachary Hayes (New York: Franciscan Institute, 2005), 134.

[7] See Charles Carpenter, *Theology as the Road to Holiness in St. Bonaventure* (New York: Paulist Press, 1997), 81–93.

[8] *Unus Est Magister Noster Christus*, no. 16.

[9] See Bonaventure, 1 *Sent* Prooem q.3 concl. See also Carpenter, *Theology as the Road to Holiness*, 24–27.

[10] *ST* 1.1.4.

a scholastic discipline needs to be complemented by a monastic one: "It is not solely by listening but also by obeying that we attain wisdom" (*Hex.* 11.3).

Thomas valued the integrity of the philosophical search in its own right[11] and argued that theologians could make use of philosophical arguments in their theological endeavors.[12] The mature Bonaventure rejects the first claim, which has major implications for the second. Given the fact that Thomas allows for a certain integrity to philosophy as a discipline in its own right (albeit ranked lower than theology in the hierarchy of science), it is hardly surprising that Bonaventure is often portrayed as an alternative to the Thomist synthesis, which, in the eyes of some of its critics, has ceded too much to a secularizing outlook. Gregory LaNave, for instance, writes, "Bonaventure has seemed to many to hold our hope either for a salutary corrective or even a very different methodology."[13] I refrain from deciding which perspective is the most appropriate to respond to the (post)secular climate in which we find ourselves. I suggest later, when dealing with the famous Condemnations of 1277, that the Bonaventurean stance may unintentionally have led to the separation of faith and reason it had set out to abolish. In a sense this is not entirely surprising: there can only be a genuine encounter between faith and reason, or theology and philosophy, when the integrity of both is respected.

THEOLOGY OF THE TRINITY

The devout and loving disposition I outlined in the previous section is crucial to make sense of Bonaventure's theology of the Trinity. It will prove essential, for instance, to see how he deduces the threeness of God from the divine unity. A quotation from *Breviloquium* 1.2.3 makes Bonaventure's stance clear:

Since faith is the source of our worship of God and the foundation of that doctrine which is according to piety (cf. 1 Tim. 6:3), it dictates that we should conceive of God in the most elevated and most loving manner. Now our thought would not be the most elevated if we did not believe that God could communicate himself in the most complete way, and it would not be the most loving if, believing him so able,

---

[11] *ST* 11–11.167.1 *ad* 3 ("the study of philosophy is in itself lawful and commendable").

[12] *ST* 1.1.8 *ad* 2.

[13] Gregory LaNave, *Through Holiness to Wisdom: The Nature of Theology according to St. Bonaventure* (Rome: Istituto Storico dei Cappuccini, 2005), 13. He refers, amongst others, to Hans Urs von Balthasar, who is deeply influenced by Bonaventure.

we thought him unwilling to do so. Hence, if we are to think of God most loftily and most lovingly, faith tells us that God totally communicates himself by eternally having a beloved and another who is loved by both (*condilectum*). In this way God is both one and three.[14]

This passage – especially the use of the word *condilectus* – echoes the theology of Richard of St. Victor. Before I discuss this, I would like to point out that according to Bonaventure one needs a certain mindset, informed by grace, to approach the mystery of the triune God. Today we would say that one needs a kind of religious receptivity, an openness – not unlike the openness needed to appreciate great works of art. The fact that we revert to aesthetic categories is no coincidence: for Bonaventure, the created world is like a piece of art that reflects and reveals the splendor of its triune Creator.

This is not a fideist stance. Clearly, Bonaventure never ceases to emphasize the limitations of reason when it mistakenly deems itself self-sufficient or autonomous. In his view, reason attains its perfection only when supplemented by faith: "Although it may not be credible from reason alone that God is a Trinity, yet it is credible for reason aided by grace and by the light poured in from above. What is credible in this way is not believed irrationally since the grace and light infused from above do not pervert reason but rather direct it" (*Myst. Trin.* q. 1, a.2 *ad* 3, p. 134; also *ad* 8). As we saw earlier, when Bonaventure claims that it is necessary to cultivate a certain mindset in order to interpret reality properly, he does so because reality itself is Trinitarian. Hence reason needs to be supplemented by faith in order to perceive reality properly (III *Sent.* d.24 a.2 q.2).[15]

Divine Oneness and Threeness, Simplicity and Primacy

We need to keep in mind this hermeneutics of devotion when evaluating Bonaventure's arguments, for instance when he makes a case for the existence of God by appealing to Anselm's argument: If God is "that than which nothing greater or better can be conceived," it follows that God exists: "No one can be ignorant of the truth that 'the best is the best,' and no one can think this is false. But that which is best is the most complete being, and every being that is complete to the highest degree by that very fact exists in actuality. Therefore, if the best is the best, the best

[14] Translation by Dominic V. Monti from *Works of St. Bonaventure, vol. IX: Breviloquium.* Bonaventure Texts in Translation (New York: Franciscan Institute, 2005), 30–31.
[15] See "Introduction" by Hayes to *Myst. Trin.* 79.

exists. It can be argued in a similar way: If God is God, then God exists"
(*Si Deus est Deus, Deus est*) (*Myst. Trin.* q.1 a.1, arg. 29, p. 113).

The same reasoning is used to argue for the oneness of the divine nature:
if the word *God* signifies the first and highest principle, it follows that the
divine nature is one (*Myst. Trin.* q.2 a.1). But how can divine unity coexist
with the threeness of the divine Persons?

Following the *Summa Halensis*, Bonaventure argues that the divine
nature is love and therefore shares itself. This view is inspired by both
the biblical witness (1 John 4:8, 16) and the Pseudo-Dionysian notion that
goodness is self-diffusive (*bonum diffusivum sui*) and wants to share itself.
Aristotle had distinguished between three types of emanation – namely,
fortuitous, natural and voluntary (in *Meta.* 6.22, 1032a12–13). Given the
fact that we can exclude fortuity in God, Bonaventure concludes that there
must be two modes of emanation in God: by nature (*per modum naturae*)
and by will (*per modum voluntatis*):

Since the perfect production, emanation and germination is realized only through
two intrinisic modes, namely by way of nature and by way of will, that is, by way of
the word and of love, therefore, the highest perfection, fontality, and fecundity
necessarily demands two kinds of emanation with respect to the two hypostases
which are produced and emanate from the first person as from the first producing
principle. Therefore, it is necessary to affirm three persons. (*Myst. Trin.* q. 8, concl.
p. 263)

Bonaventure argues that the divine nature of the Father is fruitful goodness
that has to share itself, and it does so in two ways, by way of nature and by
way of love. Before discussing these two processions in the next section,
I would like to draw attention to another aspect of Bonaventure's thought –
namely, how he harmonizes belief in the divine oneness with belief in the
threeness of the Persons by emphasizing the notions of divine simplicity
and primacy. "By reason of *simplicity*, the Essence is communicable and
able to be in more. By reason of the *primacy*, the (first) Person is naturally
bound [*nata est*] to produce Another from himself" (1 *Sent.* d.2 a. un, q.2
concl.).

The emphasis upon the divine *simplicity* allows Bonaventure to develop
the theological notion of divine perichoresis, thereby avoiding the charge
of tritheism. Oneness and threeness coexist in God because of the simplicity of the one divine nature shared by the three Persons: "Since the divine
nature is entirely indivisible and without any matter, therefore it is not
multiplied or numbered by division or partition. Therefore it is entirely
one in the produced and in the producer. But because no one can produce

himself, it is necessary that there be a plurality at the level of person" (*Myst. Trin.* q. 2, a. 2, concl. p. 152). For Bonaventure, therefore, the issue is not a choice between emphasis upon oneness of the divine nature on one hand and threeness of the divine Persons on the other. In his understanding, the one divine love is shared amongst the three Persons, and oneness and threeness do not exclude but rather strengthen one another. It is only *in* the divine Persons that we find the unity. There is nothing but the Persons and each of these Persons is of one essence, which is utterly simple. Bonaventure proves himself an heir to what Lewis Ayres has called the Augustinian "grammar of simplicity." "In using the grammar of simplicity to articulate a concept of Father, Son, and Spirit as each God, and as the one God, we find that the more we grasp the full reality of each person, the full depth of being that they have from the Father, the more we are also forced to recognise the unity of their being."[16]

In relation to *primacy*, Bonaventure claims that the Father, as the First Principle, by the very fact that he is First (i.e., most perfect, most actual, most fruitful), is the origin of the Trinity. Because of the divine simplicity we can hold the belief that there are three Persons in one shared nature. It is now time to examine in more detail the two processions.

The Generation of the Son and the Procession of the Spirit

Like Richard before him, Bonaventure distinguishes the divine Persons through their origin: while the Father is without origin, the Son is from the Father. The Father, in the fruitfulness of his loving nature, produces the Son, and from their mutual loving contemplation the Holy Spirit proceeds as their Bond of Love.

The Love, who is the Holy Spirit, does not proceed from the Father, inasmuch as he loves himself, nor from the Son, inasmuch as he loves himself, but inasmuch as the One loves the Other, because it is a nexus: therefore the Holy Spirit is the Love, by which One loving tends unto the Other: therefore there is a Love both from Another and unto Another. (1 *Sent.* d.13, a.1, q.1 fund.4)

The Father and the Son tend to one another in a mutual love that is freely bestowed by them on a third Person. Thus, while the Son is generated through the fecundity of the divine nature, the Holy Spirit proceeds by way of will or love: *per modum voluntatis* rather than *per modum naturae*.

---

[16] Lewis Ayres, *Nicaea and Its Legacy: An Approach to Fourth Century Trinitarian Theology* (Oxford: Oxford University Press, 2006), 379–80.

Itinerarium VI.2 offers a good summary. "Good is said to be self-diffusive; therefore the highest good must be most self-diffusive." Now, unless "a beloved and a co-beloved were present, i.e., the generated Son and the spirated Holy Spirit, God could not be considered the highest good."[17] He concludes:

> If, therefore, you can behold with your mind's eye
> the purity of goodness,
> which is the pure act
> of a principle loving in charity
> with a love
> that is both free and due and a mixture of both,
> which is the fullest diffusion
> by way of nature and will,
> which is a diffusion by way of the Word,
> in which all things are said,
> and by way of the Gift, in which other gifts are given,
> then you can see
> that through the highest communicability of the good,
> there must be
> a Trinity of the Father and the Son and the Holy Spirit.
>
> (*Itinerarium* VI.2)[18]

This quotation resounds with Richardian elements: the Father as the Origin of the Trinity freely bestows his Love out of the fecundity of the divine nature (by way of nature); the Son receives this Love and in turn freely co-bestows it with the Father on the Spirit who is Love received or due (by way of love or will). As this quotation suggests, a discussion of the generation of the Son and the procession of the Spirit brings us to the topic of personal names (Word, Gift).

The Personal Names

Bonaventure's indebtedness to Richard's model has an interesting implication – namely, that the origin of the Persons is the basis of incipient mutual distinctions even before they are properly constituted in their personhood. Thus, paternity (the personal property of the Father) presupposes the act of generation: the first Person is Father because he generates, and not the other way around (as Thomas Aquinas was to argue). Thomas will raise

---

[17] Translation by Ewert Cousins in *St. Bonaventure: The Soul's Journey into God. The Tree of Life. The Life of St Francis*. Classics of Western Spirituality (New York: Paulist Press, 1978), 103.
[18] Ibid., 104.

a legitimate objection. How can there be an action (such as generation) without an agent (the Father)? To negotiate this issue, Bonaventure argues that unbegotteness itself is a positive concept, affirming the paternal plenitude of divine fruitfulness.[19] The First Person is called "Father" because he is the Unbegotten one, the Principle who proceeds from no other (*principium non de principio*). In short, Bonaventure could be seen to be moving toward "an absolute property theory," which is associated with the early Duns Scotus. In this view, the divine Persons have properties in their own right that distinguish them from the other Persons before they are considered distinct through the way they relate to each other. I briefly return to this issue in Chapter 20.

The main personal names of the Second Person are Son, Image and Word. "Word" is even richer in meaning than "Son," for while "Son" only expresses the relationship of the Second Person with the First, from whom he proceeds, "Word" also expresses a link with creatures (exemplarism), Incarnation (the utterance of the divine mystery as Word), the teaching he communicated in revelation and so forth (*Comm. on John* 1.6). In expressing his Word, the Father has expressed his full nature and all things that he could and wished to create, which have an eternal existence in his Word (*Hex.* 1.13). Since the Father brings forth the Son, and through the Son and together with the Son brings forth the Holy Spirit, God the Father through the Son and with the Holy Spirit is the principle of everything created. For if the Father did not produce (*producere*) the Son and the Spirit from all eternity, he could not, through them, produce creatures in time (*Myst. Trin.* q. 8, reply 7, p. 266).

The Son takes a central role in the theology of the Trinity. He is the *Middle Person* (*persona media*), not just between the Father and the Holy Spirit within the Trinity but also between the Father and the created world, both in its creation and its redemption through his Incarnation.[20] The Son is at the middle of the Trinity because he is between the Father (who communicates his being to the Son) and the Holy Spirit (who only receives). The central role the Son occupies in the Trinity is reflected in Bonaventure's theology of creation, epistemology (theory of illumination), Christology, soteriology and eschatology (*Hex.* 1.11–39)). This is one of the major attractions of the scholastic theology of the Trinity: it posits an intimate link between the intra-Trinitarian processions of Son and Holy Spirit, on one hand, and the creation and sanctification of the world, on

---

[19] *Brevil.* 1.3.7: *innascibilitas in Patre ponit fontalem plenitudinem.*
[20] See Gilles Emery, *La Trinité Créatrice* (Paris: Librairie J. Vrin, 1995), 199; III *Sent.* d.1 a.2 q.3 *ad* 1.

the other. "As the Word is the inner self-expression of God, the created order is the external expression of the inner Word."[21] The fecundity at the heart of the Trinity finds therefore further expression in the creation and sanctification of the world.

As we have seen, the Son is generated from the fruitfulness of the divine nature of the Father (*fecunditas naturalis*), while the Spirit proceeds *per modum voluntatis* (1 *Sent*. d.6 a.u. q.2 resp.). Adopting Richard's model, Bonaventure argues that the Spirit proceeds as the *Love* between the Father and the Son (1 *Sent*. d.10 a.1 q.1 fund. 1). However, the whole Trinity can also be called Love ("God is Love"). Therefore, in order to make clear the meaning of "Love" as a *personal* name for the Holy Spirit, Bonaventure draws an original comparison between the love of husband and wife (1 *Sent* d.10 a.2 q.1 resp.). "Love" can therefore be used in three ways: it can refer to the whole Trinity (God is Love); it can refer to the love between Father and Son (this is a notional use in the sense that it is this love by which the third Person becomes known); and, finally, it can be used as a personal name for the Holy Spirit, who proceeds as Love from the Father and the Son. The love between husband and wife is compared to the notional love between Father and Son, while their love for their child is compared to the Love that constitutes the Spirit as a Person.[22]

Another personal name for the Holy Spirit is "Gift"– the *Gift* in whom all gifts are given. Again I need to make a number of distinctions. After all, the whole Trinity could be called a Gift (this is an "essential" under-standing – that is, it refers to the self-giving nature of God as such), or both Son and Holy Spirit could be said to be given in the Incarnation and at Pentecost respectively, but as a personal name it specifically applies to the Holy Spirit only as the one who has been bestowed by the Father and the Son, and it is this bestowal that constitutes the Spirit as a distinct Person. As all things are contained and virtually produced in the Word, so too all the gifts of grace are contained in the Gift that is the Holy Spirit. "In the beginning was the Gift," Bonaventure writes, adapting the opening of John's Prologue. "Before the production of things at the beginning there was the Word; therefore before the conferral of graces at the beginning was the Gift" (1 *Sent*. d.18 a. un, q.2 contra 5 (fund. 5).[23] As the Son is the exemplar of the production of creatures in that he himself emanates as Exemplar or Image, so too the Holy Spirit is the archetype of created gifts in that he himself is Gift in a personal manner. Just as every emanation of

---

[21] Hayes, "Introduction," 47.   [22] See ibid., 55–56; Emery, *La Trinité Créatrice*, 203–04.
[23] Emery, *La Trinité Créatrice*, 207–08.

creatures is contained in the Son as their first principle, every gift given to creatures is contained in the Spirit who proceeds as Gift.[24] This brings out, once again, an attractive aspect of Bonaventure's theology of the Trinity (and of that of the Schoolmen in general): it establishes a close connection between the intra-Trinitarian processions of Son and Holy Spirit on one hand, and creation and their missions in the economy of salvation on the other.

Theology of the Trinity and Spirituality

This brings us to the relevance of Bonaventure's theology of the Trinity for spirituality. As the previous section made clear, according to Bonaventure our creation and our sanctification cannot be understood without reference to the processions of Son and Holy Spirit. The Holy Spirit, for instance, as the Uncreated Gift in which all gifts are bestowed, is the archetypal principle of all gifts, including the economy of grace, which results in our sanctification. But Bonaventure also develops a Trinitarian anthropology and this too brings out the significance of his theology of the Trinity for Christian spirituality.

Bonaventure draws on Augustine's intrapersonal model when considering the soul as made in the image of the Trinity. In contrast to modern scholarship, Bonaventure does not seem to oppose it with the Richardian interpersonal model. I have already quoted a passage from *Itinerarium* VI.2, which illustrated the interpersonal approach. The following quotation, also from *Itinerarium*, is characteristic of the intrapersonal approach:

From memory, intelligence comes forth as its offspring, since we understand when a likeness which is in the memory leaps into the eye of the intellect in the form of a word. From memory and intelligence love is breathed forth as their mutual bond. These three – the generating mind, the word, and love – are in the soul as memory, understanding and will, which are consubstantial, coequal, and coeval, and interpenetrate each other. If, then, God is a perfect spirit, he has memory, understanding and will; and he has the Word generated and Love breathed forth. ... When, therefore, the soul considers itself, it rises through itself as through a mirror to behold the blessed Trinity of the Father, the Word, and Love: three persons, coeternal, coequal and consubstantial. (*Itinerarium* III.5 trans. 84)

This may at first seem a somewhat static understanding of our image character, positing merely a parallel between memory, intellect and will

---

[24] Ibid., 211.

on one hand and the three Persons on the other. However, Bonaventure's understanding of the relation between the Trinity and its image (the human soul) is more dynamic than an initial reading might suggest. The human soul only becomes image of God in the full sense when memory, intelligence and will turn toward God and conform to him (1 *Sent.* d.3 p.2. a.1 q.2, concl.). If the soul only takes itself as object, it remains only a potential image. Through knowledge and love of God we begin to fully mirror the processions of Son and Holy Spirit.

SANCTITY AND LEARNING

In a short treatise entitled *On the Reduction of the Arts to Theology*, Bonaventure has attempted to demonstrate how all human disciplines have an inner Trinitarian focus and dynamic.[25] He is arguing that all disciplines can only be properly understood if their theocentric focus is acknowledged. Bonaventure's text is indebted to Hugh's *Didascalicon* but is more explicitly Trinitarian. Like Hugh, Bonaventure adopts a broad notion of the arts. It includes the mechanical arts (e.g., weaving, agriculture, medicine, dramatic arts), which provide for our basic human needs, as well as philosophy and its subdisciplines (rational, natural and moral philosophy).[26] In each case, Bonaventure highlights the Trinitarian aspect. The production of artifacts (in mechanical arts), for instance, implies a Trinitarian dimension insofar as we conceive of things in our mind and proceed to produce them accordingly. This mirrors the way all things have been made through the divine Word. Even the processes of perception display a Trinitarian dynamic. According to medieval psychology of perception, sense objects stimulate the cognitive faculty only if a kind of similitude or image proceeds from the object and moves our senses.

This mirrors, once more, the generation of the Word from the Father. These analogies may perhaps strike the modern reader as far-fetched. Bonaventure's universe is, however, a deeply symbolic or sacramental one in which creaturely things are the vestiges of the Trinitarian God. It is only with the eyes of faith that we can truly perceive this inner depth of creation. Bonaventure continues to show how the higher arts can be "led back" to theology. Natural philosophy, for instance, considers our material

---

[25] St. Bonaventure, *Works of St. Bonaventure, vol. 1: On the Reduction of the Arts to Theology*, trans. Sr. Emma Healy and Zachary Hayes (New York: Franciscan Institute, 1996).

[26] Rational philosophy is in turn subdivided into grammar, logic and rhetoric. Natural philosophy is divided into physics, mathematics and metaphysics.

world, which is, for Bonaventure, the expression of the divine exemplars. Moral philosophy concerns our ultimate fulfillment, which we can only hope to reach when our spiritual faculties have become transformed by divine truth and goodness. Bonaventure concludes that "the manifold wisdom of God, which is clearly revealed in sacred Scripture, lies hidden in all knowledge and in all nature . . . It is clear how the divine reality itself lies hidden within everything which is perceived or known. And this is the fruit of all sciences, that in all, faith may be strengthened."[27] For Bonaventure, all knowledge is a form of enlightenment that finds its ultimate source in the light of God. All knowledge and all disciplines have an inner dynamic that points to their ultimate source: God.

Few theologians have been imbued with such a strong sense of a unified theological and spiritual vision, which is both Christocentric and Trinitarian. It leads to a deeply sacramental approach to the created world, which is seen as a ladder by which we can ascend to God. No theologian has captured the ecstatic character of the Christian life as well as Bonaventure: "Since happiness is nothing other than the enjoyment of the highest good (*fruitio summi boni*) and since the highest good is above, no one can be made happy unless he rise above himself" (*supra semetipsum ascendat*).[28]

Given this radical theocentric focus that permeates every aspect of Bonaventure's thought, it is hardly surprising that he was deeply worried about the consequences of the intrusion of Aristotelian thought into Christian doctrine, especially in its Averroist forms, in which Aristotle's thought was being studied in its own right without due regard for the truths of faith. It is not accurate to call Bonaventure anti-rationalist, anti-intellectual or even anti-Aristotelian. He is, however, deeply concerned about an independent Aristotelian philosophy, not guided by the light of faith. As he puts it in *Hex.* VII.13: "only faith 'separates the light from the darkness' (cf. Gen. 1:4) . . . Faith, with hope and love and its works, heals the soul and, thus healed, purifies it and renders it deiform." Again, in *Hex.* II.7 he writes: "It is a very great abomination that the most beautiful daughter of the king [namely, wisdom] is offered to us as a bride, and we prefer to fornicate with a base servant-maid and resort to a prostitute." It is revealing that Luther was to echo these sentiments. For Bonaventure's skepticism of Aristotelian philosophy (in its Averroist version) proved influential in the Condemnations of 1277, and those, in turn, would lead to a further separation of faith and reason, and philosophy and theology.

---

[27] *On the Reduction*, no. 26 (trans., 61).   [28] *Itinerarium*, I.I.

It is out of this intellectual climate that the modern period would emerge. I consider the nature and the impact of the Condemnations in more detail in Chapter 19.

BIBLIOGRAPHICAL NOTE

The critical edition of Bonaventure's *Opera Omnia* is known as the Quaracchi Edition published by Collegium S. Bonaventurae (Ad Claras Aquas, 1882–1902). The Franciscan Institute at New York's St. Bonaventure University is publishing English translations of Bonaventure's works as *The Works of St. Bonaventure* under the general editorship of Robert Karris. There is a literalist translation of Book 1 of the *Commentary on the Sentences* by Alexis Bugnolo as *Opera Omnia of S. Bonaventure. Tome I. Commentaries on the First Book of the Sentences. On the One & Triune God* (Wesminster, MA: Franciscan Archive, 2014).

There is a fine introduction to Bonaventure's thought in Christopher Cullen, *Bonaventure* (Oxford: Oxford University Press, 2006). Readers will find the collection by Jay Hammond, Wayne Hellmann and Jared Goff (eds.), *A Companion to Bonaventure* (Leiden: Brill, 2013) a useful resource.

CHAPTER 17

Albert the Great

Albert of Cologne, known since the middle of the 14th century as Albertus Magnus (Albert the Great), was born around AD 1200 into a family of nobility in Lauingen (diocese of Augsburg).[1] In his twenties he spent some time in northern Italy and is said to have studied in Padua. As a young man Albert met Jordan of Saxony, the master general of the new Order of Preachers, founded by St. Dominic in 1215. The encounter with the charismatic Jordan strengthened Albert in his resolve to join the Dominican Order (in 1223 or 1229). (The exact year and the place [Padua or Cologne] remains a matter of dispute amongst scholars.)

Albert is reported to have commenced his teaching career in Hildesheim (as *Lector* on the Bible) before going to Freiburg (or Freiberg?), Regensburg, Strasburg and Paris. Early in his career he wrote some important theological and philosophical works (*De Sacramentis, De Incarnatione, De Resurrectione, De iv Coaequaevis, De Homine* and *De Bono*).[2] In Paris Albert lectured on Peter Lombard's *Sentences* and may have embarked on commentaries on the Pseudo-Dionysian corpus (or perhaps only after his move to Cologne).

When Albert taught in Paris he numbered amongst his students a young, somewhat taciturn Italian called Thomas Aquinas. Albert was deeply impressed by him, and famously remarked: "We call him the dumb ox but one day he will make such a bellowing that it will resound throughout the entire world." Prophetic words indeed.

The Dominican Order sent Albert to Cologne (accompanied by Thomas) to open a *Studium Generale* (a study center to educate Dominican novices). Here Albert worked on his commentaries on the Pseudo-Dionysian oeuvre and introduced the *corpus Dionysiacum* into the

---

[1] I am grateful to Professor Katja Krause for critical comments on a previous draft of this chapter. All errors remain my responsibility.

[2] The four coevals are matter, time, the empyrean heaven and angelic nature.

study of theology at the *Studium*. A copy of these lectures, in the handwriting of his student Thomas Aquinas, survives to this day.

The arts faculty of the Parisian university had allowed the study of Aristotle's works in March 1255. Even before this date, Albert enthusiastically embarked on a massive project – namely, to write commentaries on all of Aristotle's works, starting with a *Commentary on Physics* in 1251. In doing this he drew significant inspiration from the writings of Islamic peripatetic scholars (Avicenna, Averroes). In his *Commentary on Aristotle's Metaphysics*, Albert expresses the view that, in order to be an accomplished philosopher, one had to engage with the thought of both Plato and Aristotle. As he himself informs us in his *Commentary on Physics*, his aim was to follow the order and thought of Aristotle's writings, to set out his ideas and demonstrate their veracity, dispel doubts of interpretation by elaborating certain points, and even add entire parts of books that Aristotle left unfinished or that were lost in time.[3] This was an important task because Aristotle's worldview appeared to clash with Christian thought on a number of important issues. Aristotle does not hold that the world is created out of nothing; he does not seem to believe in the immortality of the individual soul (especially if read through the lens of Averroes, who argued that the active intellect pertained to God, and not the human person); he knows nothing of the beatific vision and is only concerned with this-worldly happiness, and so forth. Albert had to outline the thought of Aristotle without doing violence to the text. This was a complex task, not helped by the fact that scholars mistakenly attributed writings to Aristotle, such as the *Liber de Causis* (*The Book of Causes*), which were actually Neoplatonic in inspiration.[4] Albert's project proved very important in historical terms, if only because the reception of Aristotle remained deeply controversial, both in the university setting and even in the Dominican Order itself.

The fact that in Albert's thought the two most important streams of ancient philosophy (Platonism and Aristotelianism) converge in a sophisticated, complex and evolving synthesis explains why it defies easy summary. Moreover, Albert's interests were extremely broad: they included what we would today call systematic theology, philosophy, botany, astronomy, medicine, mathematics and biblical exegesis (with scriptural commentaries on the four gospels, on Job, Jeremiah, Isaiah, etc.).[5]

---

[3] *Physica*, I, t. 1, c. 1, 1, 23–41.

[4] It fell to his student, Thomas Aquinas, to prove that the *Liber de Causis* was drawn from Proclus's *Elements of Theology*.

[5] The ongoing critical edition of his *Opera Omnia*, commenced in 1951 by the Albertus Magnus Institute in Cologne, is set to amount to forty volumes.

Given this extraordinarily broad range of interests and expertise, it is little wonder that he was considered a genuine miracle of his time, acquired the title of *Doctor Universalis*, and was declared the patron saint of scientists. At the end of his life he embarked on writing a new theological synthesis, entitled *Summa Theologiae sive de Mirabili Scientia Dei* (*Summary of Theology or on the Wondrous Knowledge of God*). The work remained unfinished at the time of his death (November 15, 1280).

The extent of Albert's philosophical, scientific and theological output is all the more remarkable given his active engagement with his Order and the Church. He served as prior provincial from 1254 to 1256; in 1260 he was appointed bishop of Regensburg until 1262, when he was released from this onerous burden. Later he was asked to act as vicar general for the archdiocese of Cologne. All these responsibilities would have required Albert to travel widely.

In what follows, I discuss Albert's early views on the nature of theology (and its relation with philosophy), introduce some themes of his theology of the Trinity and Trinitarian anthropology, and discuss his notion of mystical theology.

TRINITARIAN THEOLOGY AND THE SOUL AS IMAGE

I restrict this discussion to Albert's *Commentary on the Sentences* (a work Aquinas knew well) and leave out of consideration his later *Summa Theologiae*, in which Albert often defends very different views from his earlier *Commentary on the Sentences*. Albert started working on his *Commentary on the Sentences* in 1243 and finished it six years later. Book I considers the theology of the Trinity, Book II deals with creation, Book III discusses the Incarnation and Book IV addresses the sacraments and eschatology. I focus on the prologue and the first three distinctions of this work.[6]

The short *Prologue* (only three pages) to the entire work illustrates how Albert discovers profound riches in a short biblical extract (Eccles. 24:5–6) and creatively organizes the structure of the four books of Peter Lombard's *Sentences* around it.[7] It also touches upon some important Trinitarian themes in his theology.

---

[6] These have been critically edited by Maria Burger as *Alberti Magni Opera Omnia, Vol. 29, part 1. Super I Librum Sententiarum. Distinctiones 1–3* (Monasterii Westfalorum in Aedibus Aschendorff, 2015), abbreviated as Ed. Col.

[7] "I came out of the mouth of the most High, the firstborn before all creatures; I made that in the heavens there should arise light that never faileth, and as a cloud I covered all flesh."

Albert interprets the first part of the quotation from Ecclesiasticus ("I came out of the mouth of the most High") as a reference to the generation of Wisdom from the Father. A word, however, cannot be emitted from a mouth without a movement of breath. Drawing on St. Augustine's *De Trin.* Book IX (where Augustine argued that a word that is being issued is a knowledge intrinsically connected with love [*notitia cum amore*]), Albert takes the verse from Ecclesiasticus to imply that the expression of the Word from the mouth of the Father will also involve the procession of the Holy Spirit.[8] Whereas the Father as the most High is the principle without principle (or origin), the Son is the principle from the principle, who, with the Father, co-spirates the Holy Spirit who is not a principle of another divine Person but only of created things. In brief, the distinction between the divine Persons and the generation of the Word and the procession of the Holy Spirit – the topic of the first book of the *Sentences* – are captured in the short quotation from Ecclesiasticus.

"The firstborn of all creatures" encapsulates the topic of the second book of the *Sentences*, which deals with creation. Two aspects come to the fore. In the notion of "the firstborn" Albert discovers the *exitus*, or going out, of all created things from their First Cause – namely, God. In quoting Psalms 32:9 ("For he spoke and they were made") in this context, Albert draws an intimate connection between the generation of the Word and the creation of all things. Faithful to the Augustinian doctrine of exemplarism, Albert says that all things exist in the Word, which is the artwork or craft (*ars*) of the Father, containing the archetypes (*rationes*) of all things. This preexistence of things in the Word is both epistemologically and ontologically relevant: in terms of knowledge, for the Word in which things exist in an archetypical manner is a medium of knowledge (*in medio cognoscendi*); and in ontological terms, for the created being of things corresponds to their archetypal existence in the Word. This mirrors the fact that the Father both knows and causes creation through the Word. Albert then throws in another biblical quotation, this time from John 1:3–4 ("All things were made by him ... In him was life, and the life was the light of man"). He explains that things are light insofar as they have an intelligibility manifest to the knowledge angels enjoy. As life they flow out (*effluunt*) from the Word, and thus come to be in their own right. Even this brief summary reveals Albert's indebtedness to Neoplatonic Christian exemplarism, which he evidently develops in an authentically Trinitarian manner: the creation of all that is must be regarded in light of the generation of the Word, the firstborn of all creation.

[8] In Latin *spiritus* (spirit) retains connotations of breath.

Here, however, Albert signals a problem. If there is such an intimate connection between the generation of the Word and creation, does this imply that the Word and creation have something in common? To claim that Creator and creation have something in common (*aliquod commune*) appears rather troubling. In the following chapter I discuss in greater detail the notions of analogy, univocity and equivocity. For now, it suffices to say that Albert clearly rejects a univocal relation between God and creation. They have nothing in common in a univocal sense. The relation between Word and creation is that of Cause and what-is-caused, eternity and temporality. The Word and creation do have something in common, albeit only in an analogical sense – namely, "receptivity." The receptivity of the Word (who receives everything from the Father) precedes the receptivity that characterizes all created things. (In support, Albert quotes Greek Church Father Basil of Caesarea: "To receive is common to the Son and all created things.") Of course, the nature of this "receptivity" differs essentially when applied to the Son and to created things.

Albert uses Ecclesiasticus 24:6 ("I made that in the heavens there should rise light that never faileth") as a key to unlock the third book of the *Sentences*. The rising light refers to Christ, the sun of justice, and the illumination he brings "through the sacrament of his Incarnation and passion" (in the first part of Book Three); and as an unfailing light Christ bestows his grace of virtues, gifts and commandments (the topic of the second part of Book Three). The reference to light echoes perhaps some of Grosseteste's insights. Albert links it with a quote from Luke 1:78–79 and James 1:17, suggesting a theme of descent and flowing out, which is a major subject in his thought. For Albert, references to "light" and "illumination" evoke a metaphysics of light characterized by emanation, hierarchy, participation and order, as well as an epistemology.

Finally, Albert interprets the contents of Book Four of the *Sentences* in light of the final part of the quotation from Ecclesiasticus: "And as a cloud I covered all flesh." The obscurity associated with a cloud symbolizes the grace of sacraments hidden in material elements. Borrowing an idea we encountered in Bernard of Clairvaux, Albert suggests that our return to God as sinful beings occurs through material things (i.e., oil, water, bread, wine). The very materiality that proved a source of inappropriate attraction to our first parents (Adam and Eve eating the forbidden fruit from the tree of knowledge) also functions as an instrument of our return to God. This is so because of the Incarnation of the Son: the sacraments ultimately signify and point to the glory of Christ's resurrection in which we are called to share.

This brief overview of the *Prologue* to his *Sentences Commentary* reveals some of Albert's main themes of his theology of the Trinity, such as the appropriation of the Augustinian model of the Trinity (incl. the *Filioque*), the intimate link between the generation of the Word and the creative act, the theme of *exitus* and *reditus* through grace, and so forth.

I now consider Albert's Trinitarian anthropology, in which Aristotelian and Platonic elements converge in creative tension. This becomes evident in his very definition of the human soul. Albert characterizes the soul in general terms both as "a self-sufficient substance" and as "the form of a living body." The first characterization is broadly Platonic in inspiration and suggests that the soul, as intellect, is what makes us characteristically human (*homo solus intellectus*) and can subsist on its own, without the body; the second one is more Aristotelian and implies that the soul informs the body in an intimate union.

In what follows I restrict the discussion to Albert's Trinitarian anthropology – that is, how he conceives of the human person as the image of God. In his *Commentary on the Sentences*, Albert considers our image character from a threefold perspective. The image of creation refers to our intellectual nature, *mens* (mind) or *ratio* (reason). The image of likeness expresses the correspondence between the uncreated exemplar (the Trinity of the divine Persons) and the faculties of *memoria* (memory), intellect and will.[9] The image of recreation, then, refers to our transformation through grace – that is, through the bestowal of the three theological virtues, faith, hope and love, the intellect, *memoria* and will become perfected.[10]

Memoria is not used here in the Aristotelian sense of the sensible power of remembering (which other animals enjoy as well and which is therefore not typically human, thus ruling it out as a constitutive part of what it means to be in the image of God). Albert uses it, rather, in the Augustinian sense, as a power that can transcend temporality in terms of past, present and future (as the intellect can do as well).[11] Memory relates to things beyond the succession of time, and in this manner (which somehow mirrors God's own eternity) it preserves time. Albert continues:

Memory is nothing else but the power of the rational soul, according to its highest part, to retain within itself the *habitus* of truth and goodness, which it is according to its own nature, and the *habitus* of truth and goodness, which is God. Or rather,

---

[9] The mind (*mens*) does not coincide with *memoria*. Rather, *mens*, as the superior part of the soul, contains the three faculties. Albert refers to this threefold understanding of *imago Dei* in *De iv Coaequaevis* 4.69.3.3 (p. 705a) and *De Homine*.

[10] 1 *Sent.* d. 3, c. 2 (p. 99a).   [11] 1 *Sent.* d. 3, c. 2 (p. 96b).

which is perhaps closer to Augustine's meaning, [it is the power] to retain within itself knowledge through the presence of the essence (*per praesentiam essentiae*), and not the *habitus*, of truth and goodness, which the soul is through its nature.[12]

This is an elusive but suggestive passage. *Habitus* is a technical Aristotelian term that refers to a stable disposition. Albert seems to be suggesting that memory is a power that relates to truth and goodness, which inhere in the very being of the soul and are divine. Albert is not claiming that the core of the soul, *memoria*, is divine; he is, however, suggesting that it has an ever-present, innate orientation toward truth and goodness at the very core of its being. As a human power its act does not consist in doing things but rather, as Albert puts it, in retaining "the presence of knowledge in the essence" (*praesentiam notitiae in essentia*) of the soul. This alludes to a passage from St. Augustine's *De Trin*. x, 10 [16] where Augustine had argued that we come to a proper knowledge of ourselves, not by engaging with exterior things but by becoming attentive to ourselves "through some inner, non-simulated but true presence" (*vera praesentia*), "for nothing is more present to the soul than itself."

Similarly, the *intelligentia* as part of the image of likeness refers to the intellect insofar as it relates to innate knowledge of God in the soul. The will, third, is taken as the fundamental orientation toward itself or to God.

In these admittedly obscure remarks about our three faculties Albert is hinting at a profound insight inspired by Augustine: at the core of our being we are ontologically constituted as a relation to God, and through reflection (or reorientation) of memory, intellect and will upon ourselves we approximate the presence of God who is more intimate to us than we are to ourselves. When memory, intellect and will relate to the truth and goodness of the soul in which God dwells, they come to actualize their image character and can be drawn into God: "I say thus, that the soul through intellect, memory and will can be carried without intermediary into God (*immediate ferri in deum*), and then it imitates and is genuinely formed by the Trinity and the Unity."[13] In a later section I consider in greater detail Albert's views on how the soul can become one with God. First, however, I examine how Albert defends the scientific nature of theology.

THEOLOGY AS A SCIENCE

With the arrival of the entire Aristotelian corpus in the early 13th century in the Latin West theologians were faced with the question of to what extent

---

[12] Ibid. [13] I *Sent*. d. 3, c. 2 (p. 99b).

theology could be considered a "science" (*scientia*) in the Aristotelian sense.[14] This was a challenge, if only because Augustine had in *De Trin.* XII. 21–25 drawn a negative contrast between *scientia* as a lower, practical knowledge of created things with wisdom (*sapientia*), the contemplation of things eternal. Moreover, according to Aristotle, a science concerns itself with universal truths, not knowledge of particular facts. An example will clarify this. A mother may know through her own personal experience that her child, when agitated, responds well to Mozart's piano concerto no. 23. This is a singular case (one mother, one child) and does not amount to causal knowledge or science. In contrast, neuroscientific research has shown exposure to classical music to be conducive to the positive development of the mental capacities of children. The latter is acquired through knowledge of causes that is universal in scope (it concerns all children). Experience without causal knowledge is mostly had of particulars, whereas science includes causal knowledge that is had of universals. In short, Aristotle's claim in *Metaphysics*, Book 1, chapter 1 that we do not have scientific knowledge in the proper sense without universality and knowledge of causes creates difficulties for theology, and this for at least two reasons. First, theology appears to be concerned with particular issues and events (e.g., the Fall, the Passion, Pentecost). Second, given his unfathomable nature, we can hardly claim to understand God as the ultimate Cause of all things.

Albert deals with these issues in his *Commentary on the Sentences* and in his late *Summa Theologiae*. There are some considerable differences between the answers given in these works, and I only consider the first of these works. Albert discusses the subject matter of theology, its unity, its practical and theoretical character, and its mode of proceeding. In relation to the first point, Albert subscribes in a general sense to Peter Lombard's distinction between *res et signa* (things and signs) to outline the subject matter of theology, at least insofar as they assist us in attaining a share in perfect happiness. Theology considers things and signs insofar as they are instrumental in our orientation toward union with God. In a more specific sense, Albert considers that which is worthy of belief (*credibile*) to be the subject matter of theology (such as the Creed). In a third sense, God is the subject matter (as the etymology of the very word *theologia* suggests), as well as all things insofar as they relate to God. Albert qualifies this by saying that God is not the subject matter of theology in an absolute sense

---

[14] See Mikolaj Olszewski, "The Nature of Theology According to Albert the Great," in Irven Resnick (ed.), *A Companion to Albert the Great* (Leiden: Brill, 2013), 69–104 and Hannes Möhle, *Albertus Magnus* (Munster: Aschendorff, 2015), 29–49.

(presumably in light of his unknowability) but only insofar as he is the origin and end of all things.

If *res* and *signa* constitute its subject matter, how, then, can theology's unity be defended? Usually, the subject matter of a science consists of things of the same kind (the same genus, in Aristotelian terms) – but things and signs do not belong to the same genus.[15] Albert argues that the unity of theology is derived from the fact that its ultimate focus or end is our beatification. The concern with our ultimate happiness bestows on theology its unity and universality. Metaphysics (which considers being as being, undertaken with the ultimate goal of knowing its principles and causes, chief among which is God[16]) and theology (which considers our ultimate happiness) are universal in the sense that the subject matter of neither is restricted. Botany, for instance, studies plants, and zoology studies animals. Metaphysics, however, studies the most fundamental constituents of reality, and is therefore truly universal in nature. The same applies to theology, which looks at all different kind of things from the perspective of salvation. Like metaphysics, theology is therefore a universal and not a particular science.

It should have become clear, however, that the "universality" of theology is rather different in kind from that of metaphysics. All things share in being (the subject of metaphysics, which can therefore offer the foundational principles to the lower sciences), but not all things can be considered from the perspective of our beatific happiness. Metaphysics, therefore, appears to be the more genuinely universal of sciences. Perhaps it is not surprising that Albert effectively gives up on theology's claims to universality in his later *Summa Theologiae*.[17]

Trying to defend the universality of theology by appealing to its focus on our beatification has an important implication: theology is not primarily a theoretical science but is effectively "an affective science" (*ista scientia proprie est affectiva*). In 1 *Sent.* d. 1, a. 3 Albert appeals to Titus 1:1, where Paul invokes "the truth which is according to godliness" (*secundum pietatem*) to argue this point. *Affectus* (affectivity) is a notoriously elusive concept. In broad terms we can characterize it as an existential orientation that involves our fundamental longing and affectivity. So when Albert calls theology "an affective science," he is suggesting that theology includes not just contemplation of truth but our

---

[15] 1 *Sent.* d. 1, c. 1 (p. 12b). A symbol of a person (for instance on a road sign) is obviously different in kind from a real person.

[16] See Bruno Tremblay, "Albert on Metaphysics and Most Certain Philosophy," in Resnick, *A Companion to Albert the Great*, 561, with a reference to his *Commentary on Metaphysics*, 1.1.2 (Ed. Col. 16/1.3) and 4.1.2 (Ed. Col., 162–63).

[17] *Summa Theol.* tr. 1, q. 3, c. 4 (Ed. Col., p. 13b–14): theology is neither universal nor particular.

fundamental orientation toward ultimate fulfillment in God. In other words, theology appeals to heart and mind. Our intellect, *affectus* and the core of our being (*substantia*) are to be joined with that which is our beatifying end.[18] This beatifying end cannot be found amongst created things. Philosophers may have dealt with created truth and goodness in separate disciplines, but they could not conceive of a discipline oriented toward an end in which uncreated good and truth coincide.[19]

Seeing that theology concerns the pursuit of a beatifying, affective truth (*veritas affective beatificans*), it is being pursued for its own sake (we want to know God for himself). Thus, the radical theocentric focus that characterizes theology renders it genuinely free (*libera*) and more leisurely than any other discipline.[20] It should therefore not be reduced to ethics (as thinkers were prone to do in the 18th century). Albert explains that becoming a good person is merely an aid in attaining our goal of participation in God's beatitude. In its orientation toward the beatifying, affective truth theology transcends ethics, which "attends to," or serves it.

Interestingly, Albert's characterization of theology as an affective science, which considers truth as intimately bound up with goodness, results in two distinct modes of engaging in theology. First, following Titus 1:9, it should "exhort in sound doctrine" and, second, it should "refute those who raise objections." Albert associates Titus's term "exhortation" with the four senses of the Scriptures (historical, allegorical, moral and anagogical). This corresponds to one task of the theological master: to lecture on the Scriptures. Insofar as its goal is "to refute objections," theology operates in a different mode – namely, by setting out the truth and exposing erroneous views. In this mode, it appeals to fitting arguments from authority (Scriptures and Fathers), or from natural reason. This mode reflects the more systematic-theological activities of the theological master (as when he writes a commentary on Peter Lombard's *Sentences*). In this distinction we detect the first evidence of an incipient gap between scriptural exegesis and systematic theology, which characterizes theology to this day.

UNION WITH GOD AND HAPPINESS

It is fair to say that Albert attributes a greater autonomy to philosophy and other sciences than his pupil Thomas. Albert views theology and philosophy

---

[18] 1 *Sent.* d. 1, c. 1 (p. 14).
[19] Ibid.; Olszewski, "The Nature of Theology According to Albert the Great," 78.
[20] 1 *Sent.* d. 1, c. 1 (p. 14b).

not merely as distinct (as Thomas does) but as separate. Given this perspective on the relation between theology and the other sciences, as well as his different anthropology, Albert offers a rather optimistic account of our capacity to attain philosophical happiness on earth. This is one of the main themes from the two commentaries Albert wrote on Aristotle's *Nicomachean Ethics*, the first one around 1250–52, the second one around 1262 in Orvieto at the court of the pope.

Perhaps partly reacting to earlier Christianized readings of partial translations of Aristotle's oeuvre, Albert considers the *Nicomachean Ethics* strictly a work of philosophical ethics. Jörn Müller claims that there is a connection between Albert's notion of earthly fulfillment and his Neoplatonic anthropology that identifies the human person with her intellect (*homo inquantum homo solus estintellectus*) rather than with the composite of soul and body.[21] By perfecting our intellect through theoretical studies – a perfecting Albert (following Islamic sources) calls "the acquired intellect" (*intellectus adeptus*) – we have immediate access to immaterial beings without having to rely on sense perceptions.[22] Müller summarizes: "Albert seems ready to recognize a genuinely worldly happiness, a *felicitas in via*, to be realized by man's own intellectual achievements. By so doing, he reinstates philosophy as a distinct way of life and a road toward true happiness."[23] A similar ideal of philosophical happiness was advanced and developed by Siger of Brabant and others at the arts faculty in Paris, eliciting the Condemnations of 1277. Let me examine this in more detail.

The question of the nature of human happiness (on earth or in heaven) was a highly charged one throughout Albert's career.[24] On January 13, 1241, William of Auvergne, a distinguished theologian and bishop of Paris (since 1228), issued a condemnation of a number of theological propositions. The first of these concerned the beatific vision of God. The theological thesis that was singled out for censorship stated that "the divine essence will not be seen in itself by either any human being or by any angel." A number of different influences had contributed to this view, which, in William's

---

[21] Jörn Müller, "*Duplex Beatitudo*. Aristotle's Legacy and Aquinas's Conception of Human Happiness," in Tobias Hoffmann, Jörn Müller and Matthias Perkams (eds.), *Aquinas and the Nicomachean Ethics* (Cambridge: Cambridge University Press, 2013), 57.
[22] Ibid., 58.   [23] Ibid.
[24] On these matters, see the comprehensive classic study by Christian Trottmann, *La Vision Béatifique. Des Disputes scolastiques à sa définition par Benoît XII* (Rome: École française de Rome, 1995) and more recently, Katja Krause, *Thomas Aquinas on Seeing God: The Beatific Vision in His Commentary on Peter Lombard's* Sentences *IV.49.2* (Milwaukee, WI, Marquette University Press, 2020), which contains an illuminating "Editor's Introduction" (pp. 3–69).

opinion, dramatically undermined the Christian hope for salvation. A first contributing factor was the appearance in the Latin West of a brand of radical apophaticism inspired by Greek theology (and some of its Latin counterparts, such as in the writings of Scotus Eriugena, deeply influenced by the Pseudo-Dionysian writings).[25] Second, there was the attempt to apply newly discovered peripatetic epistemological categories to the issue of our knowledge of God. Aristotle had argued that in an act of knowing, the intellect and that which it understands become one. (In grasping what a tree is, my intellect must assimilate a form of "tree-ness." Hence, Aristotle argued in *De Anima*, 430a10–15 that the intellect "can become everything" in intentional terms.) If this peripatetic teaching of assimilation is invoked in an unsophisticated manner, it will be difficult to avoid accusations of pantheism and autotheism (as soon as we think or God, our intellect becomes divine), as David of Dinant had already learnt some decades earlier when his views were condemned in 1210–15.[26]

So how does Albert negotiate these issues? Let's first consider how Albert describes the attainment of philosophical happiness. Albert's account is shaped by elements from Aristotle, Averroes and Christian Neoplatonism. A passage from 1 *Sent.* d. 2, c. 1 where Albert explains what is needed for truth to occur, illustrates this. He first distinguishes between the possible intellect, which is purely receptive; the agent intellect, "by whose light the abstraction occurs of the forms in which the truth or the particular truth resides"; the reality itself, which receives light from the agent intellect and gives the possible intellect the light of a specific truth; and the principles or axioms. The crucial illuminist element (alluded to already in the *Prologue* of the *Sentences Commentary*) lies herein that Albert does not consider the light of the agent intellect sufficient by itself, but it needs to be "directed by the light of the uncreated intellect":

This can happen in two ways, depending on whether there is simply a twofold light or whether there is a threefold light. The light is twofold if the mind is joined (*coniunctio*) to the light of the uncreated intellect, and that light is "the interior teacher." But sometimes the mind is joined to an angelic light as well as to the divine ... and this is what some philosophers call "the link-up of intellects" because they too said that nothing is seen except by way of the first light.[27]

---

[25] This radical apophaticism may not have been faithful to its Greek sources, as Krause argues, 13–42.

[26] "In an unsophisticated manner": Aristotle's notion that the intellect can assimilate the species of things needs to be understood in an intentional, not a real-ontological manner. As the scholastics put it: "*Non lapis in anima*" ("A stone is not [literally] in the soul").

[27] 1 *Sent.* d. 2, c. 1 (p. 48). I use the translation by Simon Tugwell, "Introduction," in *Albert and Thomas: Selected Writings*. Classics of Western Spirituality (New York: Paulist Press, 1988), 57.

This complex passage illustrates that Albert attempts to combine peripatetic and Neoplatonist elements. In contrast to Averroes, Albert holds that the active and potential elements belong to the human soul. In the passage I am discussing he associates the active intellect with the abstraction of forms from the sensual data we acquire through perception. These forms are then bestowed upon the possible intellect to enable to soul to think. This is broadly peripatetic in inspiration. The quotation (and the reference to Augustine's treatise *The Teacher*) makes clear, however, that Albert introduced an illumination theory into this framework, whereby the intellect is dependent on the influx of the divine light. "The light of the active intellect does not suffice on its own but requires the assistance of the light of the uncreated intellect, just as the light of the sun illuminates the stars."[28] In short, Albert is associating the active intellect with the Augustinian higher part of the soul that is receptive to divine illumination.[29]

The end of our passage reveals Albert's further indebtedness to Averroist elements. What Simon Tugwell translates as "the link-up of intellects" (*continuationem intellectuum*; *coniungi*) is the highest instance of happiness on earth and therefore the ultimate goal of philosophy.[30] Despite his critique of his monopsychism (i.e., the Averroist notion that the active intellect is one for all human souls and extraneous to them), Albert draws on Averroes to develop this idea. Averroes had claimed in his *Long Commentary on De Anima* that the agent intellect could act as form, and not just as the principle of actualization of thinking.[31] Albert adopts the terminology of conjunction or linking up to characterize the acme of philosophical happiness, and he concurs with Averroes that genuine philosophical happiness in this world is possible by a kind of intellectual deification. As he writes in a later work: "This makes it evident that the contemplation of wonderful truths is the highest delight and the most natural occupation in which people's whole human nature, precisely as such, blossoms, particularly in the contemplation of the things of God. . . . This reveals how it is by study that the intellect takes possession of itself."[32]

---

[28] I *Sent.* d. 2, c. 1 (p. 48b).

[29] See Markus Führer, "Albert the Great and Mystical Epistemology," in Resnick, *A Companion to Albert the Great*, 137–60, here 149.

[30] Alain De Libera, *Métaphysique et Noétique. Albert le Grand* (Paris: Vrin, 2005), 301ff.

[31] De Libera, *Métaphysique et Noétique*, 302; Averroes [Ibn Rushd] of Cordoba, *Long Commentary on De An. of Aristotle* III, 36: "Assurance of the possibility of the conjoining of the intellect with us lies in explaining that its relation to a human being is a relation of form and agent, not a relation of form alone," translated by Richard Taylor (New Haven, CT: Yale University Press, 2009), 401.

[32] Tugwell, *Albert and Thomas*, 59, from *De Intellectu et Intelligibili* II, 8–9.

Albert's student Thomas Aquinas was to disagree with the claim that philosophical happiness is possible on earth by a "linking" of our intellect with separate substances. Indeed, it stands to reason that Thomas was implicitly distancing himself from Albert's views when explicitly criticizing the views of Averroes and the notion of *continuatio*.[33] Such a conjunction of divinizing form and intellect was, in Thomas's opinion, to be reserved to the beatific vision when the light of glory will illuminate and elevate the intellect to enjoy an immediate vision of God.

Despite the fact that Albert operates with a fairly strong dichotomy between theology and philosophy, his account of the nature of mystical union with God is not altogether different from the way he describes philosophical happiness. In order to see this, we need to examine his commentaries on the Dionysian corpus, and on *The Mystical Theology* in particular.

The purpose of the teaching in *The Mystical Theology*, Albert claims, is not merely that we should acquire knowledge or that we should become good, as in ethics, but that we should attain everlasting salvation, "where we shall encounter openly and without veil what is at present hidden from us about God by way of negations."[34] Through negations we shed our all too creaturely understandings of God because God's perfections are infinitely beyond created perfections.

In contrast to sciences that rely on first principles that our reason can understand mystical theology begins rather with a kind of divine light, "which is not a statement by which something is affirmed; it is a kind of reality which convinces the understanding (*res convincens intellectum*) to adhere to it above all else."[35] Modern commentators (having read William James's *The Varieties of Religious Experience*) might be tempted to interpret Albert's outline of union in terms of an immediate, affective mystical experience of God, but this would be a mistake. Albert is clear that not even Moses enjoyed an immediate union with God.[36] Rather, union with God refers to our transformation in which our intellect is raised through an encounter with divine "theophanies" or manifestations, leaving our understanding dazzled and without clearly defined knowledge.[37] On earth, this

---

[33] See *ScG* III, 43 and 44 [no. 5]: "It is clear that Aristotle, whose views the aforementioned philosophers try to follow, did not think that our ultimate felicity is to be found in such a connection (*in tali continuatione*)."

[34] Tugwell, *Albert and Thomas*, 136 (Ed. Col. p. 454). All references from Ed. Col. refer to Albertus Magnus, *Super Mysticam Theologiam Dionysii, Alberti Magni Opera Omnia*, Vol. 37/2, Simon (ed.), Munster, 1978 (pp. 451–75).

[35] Tugwell, *Albert and Thomas*, 139 (Ed. Col. p. 455).   [36] Ibid. (Ed. Col. p. 464a).

[37] Albert writes: "In the case of God all our natural ways of knowing . . . lapse. He is not known per se, as first principles are, nor do we know 'why' he is, because he has no cause, nor do we know 'that' he

encounter is always mediated by faith. Once more, Albert compares this encounter with light. Light does not give us specific knowledge of anything in particular, but it renders things visible. Similarly, this light does not yield additional knowledge; rather, it assists us in perceiving better the contents of faith and its mysterious truths (which we know from the Scriptures).

The ultimate reason our intellectual encounter with the divine reality remains deeply apophatic is that God is not a thing amongst others. God transcends every genus: "God is not categorized with other things that exist, as if he formed a class with them."[38] God is utter simplicity, and our knowledge of God in mystical theology will reflect this darkness.[39] The reader will have noticed that Albert borrows a key term from Eriugena – namely, *theophanies*.[40] In this life we do not grasp God directly, but we contemplate him through theophanies or divine manifestations that express his goodness: "We ought to cleave to the divine lights, that is, illuminations sent us by God, but not as they were our object; we should regard them as the medium in which our object is seen."[41]

It is in the beatific vision, when grace is replaced with the light of glory, that we will enjoy an immediate vision of God by becoming "joined to God." "The substance itself of God will be known by the blessed in an immediate manner through conjunction (*per coniunctionem*), in such a way that God gives himself as object to our intellect."[42] Then we will be able to say with the Apostle: "I shall know even as I am known" (1 Cor. 13:12). The vision of God in heaven differs, however, in a threefold way from the way we know God on earth:

The two kinds of knowledge are different, because in heaven God is seen directly, whereas in this life he is contemplated in the effects of grace and light which flow from him into the soul. Also in heaven the vision will free us perfectly from wretchedness, and this does not happen here. Finally, in heaven we shall know God by being in a state of glory (*per habitum gloriae*), whereas here we know him by being in a state of grace.[43]

is, because he produces no effect which is proportionate to himself. Instead our minds receive a certain divine light, which is above their own nature and raises them above all their natural ways of seeing things, and this is how our minds come to see God, though only in a blurred and undefined (*confuse et non determinante*) knowledge 'that' he is. This is why it is said that God is seen by not-seeing: he is seen by the absence of natural seeing" (ibid., 172; Ed. Col. 37/2, p. 466b).

[38] Ibid., 147 (Ed. Col. p. 457b).   [39] Ibid., 148 (Ed. Col. p. 457b).
[40] For Albert's different understandings of theophany, see Krause, *Thomas Aquinas on Seeing God*, 59.
[41] Tugwell, *Albert and Thomas*, 157 (Ed. Col. p. 461a).   [42] 1 *Sent.* d. 1, c. 2 (Ed. Col., p. 29b).
[43] Tugwell, *Albert and Thomas*, 163 (Ed. Col.p. 463a).

Albert's thought drew on a broad range of sources (e.g., Platonic, Aristotelian, Augustinian, Islamic) and often evolved. The variety and richness of his thought could therefore bear fruit in highly diverse ways. His views on the autonomy of philosophical sciences, for instance, may have, according to some, contributed to Latin Averroism, while his more spiritual writings came to fruition in the school of the German mystics.

Albert had a number of important students and followers, some of whom remained closer to his insights than his most celebrated student, Thomas Aquinas. These include Hugh Ripelin of Strasburg (d. 1267), who wrote a highly influential *Compendium of Theological Truth*[44]; Ulrich of Strasburg (his favorite pupil, d. 1277), who wrote a *Summa de Summo Bono* (*A Summa on the Highest Good*); and Dietrich of Freiberg (d. 1318), whose range of interests almost matched those of Albert himself. Dietrich (a fierce opponent of Thomas Aquinas's views) wrote an important treatise on the beatific vision. As suggested, it is within the context of Albert's German Dominican followers that the daring mystical theology of Meister Eckhart and the Rhineland school should be understood.

BIBLIOGRAPHICAL NOTES

The critical edition of Albert's works is ongoing (*Alberti Magni Opera Omnia*. Editio Coloniensis, Albertus Magnus Institut, Munster 1950ff). For works that have not been critically edited we continue to rely on the so-called Borgnet edition, edited by Auguste Borgnet in Paris (1890–99), totaling thirty-eight volumes. There are disappointingly few translations of Albert's writings, especially in English. There are at present four volumes in The Fathers of the Church series (Washington, DC: Catholic University of America Press) – namely, *On the Resurrection* (2020), translated by Irven Resnick and Franklin Harkins; *On Job* (2020) and *On the Body of the Lord* (2017), translated by Sr. Albert Marie Surmanski, and *Questions Concerning Aristotle's On Animals*, translated by Irven Resnick and Kenneth Kitchell (2008).

Most of the secondary literature focuses on his philosophy and is written in German or French. An excellent and highly recommended introduction (in German) is Hannes Möhle, *Albertus Magnus. Zugänge zum Denken des Mittelalters*. Band 7 (Munster, Aschendorff, 2015). The writings of Alain de Libera (in French) also offer important insights, especially his book

---

[44] *Compendium Theologiae Veritatis*, available in Volume 34 of the Borgnet edition of the *Opera Omnia* by Albertus Magnus.

Métaphysique et Noétique. Albert le Grand (Paris: Librairie Philosophique J. Vrin, 2005). In English there is a comprehensive collection of essays in Irven Resnick (ed.), *A Companion to Albert the Great: Theology, Philosophy, and the Sciences* (Leiden: Brill, 2013). Simon Tugwell's *Albert and Thomas: Selected Writings in* the Classics of Western Spirituality series (New York: Paulist Press, 1988) includes a translation of Albert's *Commentary on Dionysius's Mystical Theology* (pp. 131–98) as well as a superb "Introduction."

CHAPTER 18

Thomas Aquinas

LIFE AND WORKS

Sometime around 1224 or 1225, Thomas Aquinas was born in Roccasecca (midway between Rome and Naples) into an aristocratic family.[1] As the youngest of their sons, Thomas was sent by his parents as an oblate to the Benedictine monastery of Monte Cassino for study. Thomas entered the monastery at the age of five or six. In 1239, when he was about fourteen or fifteen, Thomas left the monastery and went to Naples, where he studied the arts and philosophy. It is here that Thomas came into contact with the Dominican Order, which he was to join in 1244, despite severe opposition by his parents, who had hoped for a more illustrious order (such as the Benedictines). Having overcome the disagreements with his parents, Thomas went to Paris (1245) and then to Cologne (1248), where he studied with Albert the Great, who lectured on Aristotelian thought. In 1252, Thomas was sent to Paris to teach. It is here Thomas wrote his first major theological work as part of the curriculum to become a Master in Theology: his *Commentary on the Sentences* of Peter Lombard. In 1256, Thomas was granted the *Licentia docendi* by the chancellor of the Parisian university. In the period 1256–59 Thomas wrote *De Veritate* (*On Truth*), a wide-ranging work that covers topics such as truth, providence, predestination, the human mind and knowledge of Christ (qq. 1–20), and goodness and the will (in qq. 21–29). Thomas returned to Italy and lectured in Orvieto (1261–65), where he also finished his first original theological synthesis, the *Summa contra Gentiles* (*ScG*), which consists of four parts. The First Part deals with God, the Second with Creation and the Third with Providence. Only in the Fourth Part does Thomas deal with "truths

[1] I am following Jean-Pierre Torrell, *Saint Thomas Aquinas, vol. 1: The Person and His Work* (Washington, DC: Catholic University of America Press, 1996).

inaccessible to reason" – that is, the Trinity, the Incarnation, the sacraments and eschatology. Unlike his other main theological works, the *ScG* is written in a format different from the scholastic question-and-answer template. During this time he also wrote a *Commentary on Job*, in which he focuses on the literal meaning of the text, in striking contrast to Gregory the Great's approach. In 1265–68 we find Thomas working in Rome in a Dominican *Studium*. It is here he embarked on his most important theological masterpiece, the *Summa Theologiae* (*ST*), a "summary of theology" (as the title indicates). The First Part, dealing with God, was finished in Rome. While working on the *Summa*, Thomas also wrote a *Commentary on Aristotle's De Anima*. For reasons that are not entirely clear, Thomas returned in 1268 to Paris, which was embroiled in heated discussions on the influence of Aristotelian philosophy (Averroism), as well as the role of the mendicant orders in the university. During this time Thomas also wrote a profound *Commentary on St. John's Gospel, Disputed Questions on Evil* (*De Malo*) and more commentaries on Aristotle, including massive commentaries on the *Nicomachean Ethics* and *Metaphysics*. The engagement with Aristotle's material assisted him in writing the Second Part of the *Summa Theologiae*. In the Second Part, Thomas first discusses the ultimate end of human life (beatitude), and then he examines in great detail the means of attaining this end. The first part of the Second Part (*Prima Secundae*) considers human acts, the passions of the soul and virtues and vices in general. In the second part of the Second Part (*Secunda Secundae*), Thomas treats of the theological (faith, hope, love) and cardinal (prudence, justice, temperance, fortitude) virtues and concludes with a discussion of the different states of life, including the active and contemplative lives. Thomas spent the final period of his career in Naples (1272–73), where he was in charge of a new center of teaching. It is here Thomas may have taught a course on *The Epistle to the Romans*; he also pursued the composition of the Third Part of the *Summa Theologiae* (which deals with Christology and sacraments), but he never finished it. It ends in the middle of the treatise on penance. On December 6, 1273, while celebrating Mass, Thomas underwent a major transformation, and he ceased writing. He explained to his friend and secretary Reginald of Piperno: "I cannot do any more. Everything I have written seems to me as straw in comparison with what I have seen."[2] The *Summa Theologiae*, the greatest theological work in the history of the West, was to remain incomplete. At the beginning of 1274, when he set out to Lyons for

---

[2] See Torrell, *Saint Thomas Aquinas*, 289.

a council convoked by Pope Gregory X, he suffered an accident (he hit his head against a branch), and shortly afterward he fell ill. The monks at the Cistercian abbey of Fossanova cared for Thomas in his last days. He died on March 7, 1274. He was canonized in 1323 by John XXII and declared a Doctor of the Church in 1567.

In this brief overview I have listed some of Thomas's main works, but his output is much larger. Apart from the three major theological syntheses there are commentaries on the Gospels (Matthew, John) and on letters of the New Testament (Paul's letters, Hebrews), as well as important Old Testament commentaries (Job) and expositions (Isaiah, Jeremiah, Psalms). Apart from the commentaries on Aristotle's works there are commentaries on the Neoplatonic *Book of Causes*, as well as on Pseudo-Dionysius's *The Divine Names*. He also wrote a commentary on Boethius's *De Trinitate*. Finally, he wrote many *Disputed Questions* on a whole range of topics (On Truth, On the Power of God, On the Soul, On Evil and On the Virtues) and many other smaller works, including a popularizing overview of theology, dealing with Faith, Hope and Love. It is called the *Compendium of Theology* but it too remained unfinished. This overview indicates some of the major sources of Thomas's theology: first and foremost, the Scriptures, and second, St. Augustine, whose key theological teachings Thomas had deeply absorbed, and other Church Fathers, A third source is Greek philosophical thought (both Aristotelian and Neoplatonic).

In this overview I focus mainly on the *Summa Theologiae*. An in-depth discussion of this work is of course impossible. I concentrate on the following topics: the nature of theology, the Five Ways, analogy, the Trinity, the Christian life and soteriology.

THOMAS AND THE "SCIENCE" OF THEOLOGY

The exact nature of theology in Thomas Aquinas, and its relation with philosophy in particular, is a controversial issue. The discussion is often obscured by our modern (Cartesian or Kantian) understanding of philosophy and reason in terms of autonomy – a view as alien to Thomas Aquinas or Bonaventure as to thinkers of antiquity (for whom rationality was unthinkable in separation from its constituting tradition).

Some have argued, quite rightly, that Thomas's two *Summae* are theological works to the core. Thomas himself explicitly states in *ST* 1.1.7 that God is the proper subject matter of theology. That is not to say that he does not deal with other issues, such as "things and signs" (an obvious reference to Peter Lombard's structuring principles of his *Sentences*). But the theologian treats of these other things only "insofar as they have a reference to God" (*secundum ordinem ad Deum*) (*ST* 1.1.7).

While Thomas Aquinas's *theological* status is beyond dispute, some scholars (e.g., Eugene Rogers or Nicholas Healy) have made the case that Thomas actually shuns philosophical arguments altogether. Others have discovered in Thomas's works philosophical arguments that have validity without recourse to revealed truth.[3] It seems to me that these divergent readings partly reflect our contemporary (post-Kantian and Barthian) concerns, and I doubt whether these concerns offer the most nuanced perspective from which to interpret properly Thomas's own texts. As Thomas sees it, a theologian is somebody who has a theocentric focus – but that does not mean, as we shall see, that a theologian cannot use arguments (e.g., "the Five Ways") that have a claim to philosophical validity. The readings of those scholars who deny that Thomas allows for a demonstration of the existence of God by the natural light seem therefore unconvincing. Although it remains subject to theology in the hierarchy of sciences, philosophy (similar to any other discipline) has its own remit and claims to validity.[4]

When Thomas calls theology a "science," he does not use the word "science" in the modern, Western sense of the word. For us, "science" involves observation, experimentation, formation of hypotheses, their verification and so forth. *Scientia* for Thomas is the discovery of reasons in light of first truths that are necessary. Thus, in sciences we demonstrate something unknown from principles that are known or at least assumed to be correct. Just as at the basis of logic there are some self-evident principles (e.g., the principle of non-contradiction), so too the articles of faith lie at the basis of Christian theology.

In contrast to principles or axioms from logic, the articles of faith are not self-evident. How, then, can Thomas argue that theology is a proper science? He distinguishes between two kinds of science: sciences that start from self-evident principles (such as logic), and sciences the principles of which can be retraced to a higher science (e.g., today's molecular biology is based on chemistry). Christian theology is a science of this sort. It takes its principles directly from God's knowledge (*scientia*) through revelation

---

[3] For a lucid overview of divergent readings of Thomas on a range of issues, including faith and reason, see Fergus Kerr, *After Aquinas: Versions of Thomism* (Oxford: Blackwell, 2002).

[4] For a more in-depth discussion, see Rik Van Nieuwenhove, *Thomas Aquinas and Contemplation* (Oxford: Oxford University Press, 2021), 98–125.

(and not from any of the other sciences). The articles of faith reveal something of the mystery of God who allows us to share in his self-knowledge (*scientia*) through his revelation, especially in Christ.

The fact that theology "borrows" its principles – it is a science only fully known by God – explains the peculiar nature of the virtue of faith of the Christian believer; it is between science and opinion (as Hugh of St. Victor had argued). It is *intrinsically* more certain (in its cause) because it is founded on divine Truth itself, and yet it is less certain *for us* because for us, matters of faith are above the human intellect.[5]

For Thomas, theology (*sacra doctrina*) and philosophy have a different focus. As he explains in *Summa contra Gentiles* II.4, whereas the philosopher focuses on creatures first and is then led to a consideration of God, the first consideration of the theologian is God, and she examines creatures only in relation to God. But why do we need Christian theology in the first place? Thomas explains that it was necessary for our salvation that there should be a body of knowledge revealed by God, in addition to philosophical research. There are a number of reasons for this: first, because the Christian understanding of God as Trinity and other core truths of the Christian faith are beyond the grasp of human reasoning; second, "even as regards those truths about God which human reason could have discovered, it was necessary that we should be taught by a divine revelation; because the truth about God such as reason could discover, would only be known by a few, and after a long time, and with the admixture of many errors."[6]

Thomas's understanding of theology remains indebted to the Anselmian *fides quaerens intellectum*: theology uses human reasoning, not to prove faith, but to make manifest some implications of its message. Natural reason should assist faith "as the natural bent of the will ministers to charity."[7] Thomas therefore sees philosophy and theology in harmonious terms, although the scope of theology is more universal and broader than any of the other sciences. Theology is distinctive in that it looks at things from the perspective of God's self-revelation. There are many things that theology does not explicitly deal with and that are the subject of other disciplines.[8] The theologian can sometimes use arguments from other disciplines (e.g., philosophy) to illustrate a theological point, just as a philosopher can use arguments of other disciplines (e.g., physics) to

---

[5] *ST* II–II.4.8.
[6] *ST* I.1.1. All translations by the Fathers of the English Dominican Province as *St Thomas Aquinas: Summa Theologica*, 5 vols. (Westminster, MD: Christian Classics, 1981).
[7] *ST* I.1.8 *ad* 2.   [8] See *ScG* II.4.

make his (philosophical) point. Similarly, philosophy can be used to demonstrate the preambles of faith (such as that God exists), or it can be used to refute assertions that are contrary to the faith by showing them to be false or lacking in necessity.[9]

All sciences are part of a hierarchy that is crowned by theology (the most universal and noble science). The very idea of a hierarchy of sciences implies that the other sciences cannot truly teach something that is in contradiction to the Christian faith.[10]

While Thomas sees the relation between philosophy and theology in harmonious terms, he is emphatic in stating that we should resist any attempt to reduce theology to philosophy: it would be an error to include "the content of faith within the bounds of philosophy, as would happen should somebody decide to believe nothing but what could be established by philosophy. On the contrary, philosophy should be brought within the bounds of faith, as the Apostle says in 2 Cor. 10:5: 'We take every thought captive to obey Christ.'"[11] Responding to the criticism that his views on the harmonious relation between theology and philosophy may appear to be mixing water with wine (Bonaventure's point) – that is, mingling philosophical doctrines with sacred teaching, Thomas retorts that "those who use the works of the philosophers in Sacred Doctrine, by bringing them into the service of faith, do not mix water with wine, but rather change water into wine."[12] For Thomas, this is nothing but an application of his foundational theological stance that grace does not destroy nature but perfects it.[13]

We saw earlier that theology borrows its principles from the *scientia* of God himself. It does not aim at demonstrating its principles, but it advances from them to prove other things, which were not yet known (e.g., from the resurrection of Christ and his communion with us, we can deduce the resurrection of all). This has important consequences for our

---

[9] See Thomas Aquinas, *Commentary on Boethius*, q.2, art. 3, trans. Armand Maurer, in *Thomas Aquinas: Faith, Reason and Theology. Questions I–IV of the "Commentary on the De Trinitate" of Boethius* (Toronto: Pontifical Institute of Mediaeval Studies, 1987), 49.

[10] Thomas also states (in *ST* 1.1.6 *ad* 3) that theology can judge the principles of other sciences. Theology therefore does not simply judge the conclusions but also the principles of other sciences.

[11] Aquinas, *Commentary on Boethius*, q.2, art. 3, trans., 49. [12] Ibid., q.2, art. 3 *ad* 5; trans. 50.

[13] Ibid., q.2, art. 3; trans. 48–49: "The light of faith, which is imparted to us as a gift, does not do away with the light of natural reason (*lumen naturalis rationis*) given to us by God. . . . Now just as sacred doctrine is based on the light of faith, so philosophy is based on the natural light of reason (*lumen naturale rationis*). So it is impossible that the contents of philosophy should be contrary to the contents of faith, but they fall short of them. . . . If anything is found in the sayings of the philosophers contrary to faith, this is not philosophy but rather an abuse of philosophy arising from faulty reasoning."

dealings with those people who reject some or all of these principles. We should not try to prove the basic truths of revelation (e.g., God as Trinity, the Incarnation) in a rational manner, although we can argue from revealed truths, if our opponent admits some of them. If she does not admit any revealed truths, we can only refute her objections, but we will not be able to prove in a positive fashion the truth of revelation. However, we should remember that Thomas has more confidence in human reason when it comes to establishing the "preambles of faith" than most post-Kantians would: he holds, for instance, the view that we can prove the existence of God from the created world.[14] Before I examine this, I discuss the final article of Question 1, which deals with the senses of Scripture.

Thomas discusses the four senses in *ST* 1.1.10. The article gives us a good insight in Thomas's power of synthesis; it also allows us to examine the structure of a scholastic article. Thomas raises a question: "Whether in the Holy Scripture a word may have several senses?" First, a number of *objections* are listed. The first objection contends that many different senses will only result in confusion; the third objection states that the four senses are not complete, for it does not appear to accommodate the *sensus parabolicus* – that is, metaphorical sense, such as when we say "the arm of the Lord." After these objections, Thomas always quotes an *authority* (the Bible, a Church Father, or, occasionally, a philosophical authority) who gives a view different from the objections (*Sed contra*), and which supports the main thesis. In this case, he quotes Gregory the Great (*Mor.* xx.1): "Holy Writ by the manner of its speech transcends every science, because in one and the same sentence, while it describes a fact, it reveals a mystery." He then gives his *main response* (*Respondeo dicendum*). This is the full response Thomas gives to this particular question:

The author of Holy Writ is God, in whose power it is to signify his meaning, not by words only (as we also can do), but also by things themselves. So, whereas in every other science things are signified by words, this science has the property, that the things signified by the words have themselves also a signification. Therefore that first signification whereby words signify things belongs to the first sense, the *historical* or *literal*. That signification whereby things signified by words have themselves also a signification is called the spiritual sense, which is based on the literal, and presupposes it. Now this spiritual sense has a threefold division. For as the Apostle says (Hebrews 10:1) the Old Law is a figure of the New Law, and Dionysius says (*Coel. Hier.* 1) "the New Law itself is a figure of future glory." Again, in the New Law, whatever our Head has done is a type of what we ought to

---

[14] *ST* 1.2.2 and 2.3.

do. Therefore, so far as the things of the Old Law signify the things of the New Law, there is the *allegorical* sense; so far as the things done in Christ, or so far as the things which signify Christ, are types of what we ought to do, there is the *moral* sense. But so far as they signify what relates to eternal glory, there is the *anagogical* sense. Since the literal sense is that which the author intends, and since the author of Holy Writ is God, Who by one act comprehends all things by his intellect, it is not unfitting, as Augustine says (*Confess.* xii), if, even according to the literal sense, one word in Holy Writ should have several senses.[15]

A number of observations need to be made. First, for Thomas, God is the author of the Scriptures, which explains their inspired nature and multi-layered meaning. Whereas words usually signify things, in a nonliteral or spiritual reading things refer themselves to other things. For instance, manna from heaven, which fed the Israelites in the desert (cf. Exod. 16:15–16; 16:31) can, in a spiritual sense, refer to the Eucharistic Bread. Or the tree in the Garden of Eden can refer to the tree of the Cross. Within these spiritual senses, Thomas goes on to define the allegorical sense. Quoting Hebrews, he defines it as a kind of typology in which things of the Old Testament signify things of the New (e.g., the manna prefigures the Eucharist). The meaning of the moral sense, clarified with an allusion to the Pauline notion of the union between Christ, the Head, and his Body, the Church, refers to how we should act as members of Christ's Body. The anagogical sense, illustrated with a quotation from Pseudo-Dionysius, has an eschatological thrust.

Having put forward his own view, Thomas finally *replies* to the objections. For instance, he argues against the first objection (*Ad primum*) that multiplicity of senses does not result in equivocation or confusion, as all senses are based on the literal sense. He also makes the point that "nothing necessary to the faith is contained under the spiritual sense which is not elsewhere put forward by the Scriptures in its literal sense" (*ST* 1.1.10 *ad* 1). This stance illustrates Thomas's skepticism toward more daring spiritual interpretations.[16] In reply to the third objection (*Ad tertium*), Thomas makes clear that metaphors can be part of the literal sense. Thus, as God obviously does not have a corporeal arm, the metaphor "the arm of the Lord" refers to the divine power, and this is part of the literal sense, in which words ("arm") refer to things ("power").

---

[15] *ST* 1.1.10 (my italics).

[16] It is little coincidence that his *Commentary on Job*, in marked contrast to that of Gregory the Great, sticks to the literal sense only. Nevertheless, in his own *Commentary on John*, for instance, Thomas has adopted many spiritual interpretations, usually inspired by St. Augustine or John Chrysostom.

This overview of the structure of one of the articles of the *ST* reveals the dialogical nature of scholasticism. Often the "objections" are powerful, and they assist the reader in looking at the issues from an alternative and critical perspective.

Having discussed the nature of theology in question 1 (in ten articles), Thomas goes on to discuss the existence of God in question 2.

GOD'S EXISTENCE AND OUR GOD-TALK

For Thomas, the so-called Five Ways do not belong to the Christian faith itself: they are part of the preambles of faith. A lot has been made of these Five Ways, although they occupy a very minor place in the whole of Thomas's *Summa Theologiae* (*ST* 1.2.3 – one article only!). The arguments are based on a perception of the goodness and intelligibility of the world.[17]

First, there is the argument based on *change* or motion, inspired by Aristotle: "Anything in process of change is being changed by something else. This cannot go indefinitely; hence there must be a First Mover." Second, there is the argument from *efficient causality*: "If there were no first cause there would be no causes at all" (inspired by Plato's *Timaeus*). Third, there is the argument from *necessity*: contingent things do not exist of necessity but are caused. Only that which necessarily exists has no cause outside of itself. Contingent things have a cause external to them, because if they did not, they would not exist. Therefore, ultimately there is a First Necessary Being, which we call God (= God does not owe his existence to anything other than himself). Fourth, there is the argument of gradations of goodness and truth: there are *degrees* of goodness, truth and beauty in the universe. We could not make comparative judgments ("A is better than B") unless we possessed a standard of absolute goodness, beauty and goodness. The argument is Augustinian in inspiration and is central to the thought of St. Bonaventure. Finally, there is the argument of design and *telos*. This is the teleological argument: there is order in the universe: everything acts because of a goal (*omne agens agit propter finem*).[18] There has to be a First Intelligence that directs this goal-oriented activity of all things.

---

[17] For an excellent discussion of the Five Ways, and the ways they have been interpreted, see Kerr, *After Aquinas*, 52–72.

[18] The notion of teleology is of paramount importance in Thomas's worldview. It finds a beautiful expression in *ST* 1.65.3: "The entire universe, with all its parts, is ordained towards God as its end, inasmuch as it imitates, as it were, and shows forth the divine goodness, to the glory of God. Reasonable creatures, however, have in some special and higher manner God as their end, since they can attain to him by their own operations, by knowing and loving him."

Brian Davies observes that behind these arguments another argument is operative, what he calls the *Existence* argument.[19] We find it in *ST* 1.65.1. Here Thomas teaches that the fact that there are actual things in this world ultimately means that something exists independently of any cause outside itself, and accounts for the existence of everything else. The argument hinges on a key insight inspired by Avicenna: in created things, there is a distinction between essence and existence. You can know the essence of something (i.e., you can give a definition of it) even if it does not exist (or no longer exists). You can, for instance, define a unicorn. In created things essence and existence do not coincide. From this it follows that the existence of things cannot be deduced from what they are by definition (i.e., their "essence"). Created things *have* existence but they *are* not their existence. The question then arises: Why is it that things have existence in the first place? Why is there anything rather than nothing? The answer cannot be that things cause themselves to exist. For this would imply that they preexist themselves, which is impossible (for to cause existence implies existence). Nor can we argue that there is an infinite regress of things that in turn depend on other things that depend for their existence upon other contingent things. (If each cause of Henry's existence were itself in need of a cause of its existence, then no cause of Henry could exist, and Henry himself could not exist.) In short, there must be a cause the existence of which is not itself in need of a cause. And this is God, in whom existence and essence coincide (*ST* 1.3.4). It belongs to God's essence to exist. All things that exist participate in Existence itself, which is God: "All beings apart from God are not their own being, but are beings by participation" (*ST* 1.44.1). Creatures "have" existence; God is Existence itself – that is, is not created.

The "Existence argument" that forms the foundation of the Five Ways makes clear that we should not (mis)interpret the arguments from motion and causality in a "horizontal" manner. Rather, they can only be properly understood in light of the "vertical" Existence argument. For Thomas, God is not the First Cause in a horizontal series of causes; rather, when Thomas calls God the First Cause he means that God is the one who bestows being upon all creatures and makes possible their own creaturely activity and causality. Understanding God in terms of horizontal efficient causality is a Deist understanding of God: God merely sets the world in motion. Thomas's view is vertical or transcendental (i.e., it refers to the condition of possibility of creation) – that is, it assumes that God bestows

[19] Brian Davies, *The Thought of Thomas Aquinas* (Oxford: Oxford University Press, 1993), 31–33.

being upon all things. A metaphor will perhaps clarify the distinction between horizontal and vertical understandings of causality. Imagine a room full of dominos nicely placed beside one another. If you push the first domino, all the other dominos will fall over. In a Deist (or horizontal) understanding of divine causality, God is seen as the first domino, which causes the other dominos to fall over. In a vertical understanding, God is not the first domino; he is the One who puts all the dominos there in the first place.[20]

The history of the disputes on the status of the Five Ways reflects the history of the debate about the relation between faith and reason during the past seven centuries. According to some, such as Norman Kretzmann, Thomas's proofs are meant to appeal to all those rational beings who may or may not share his theological beliefs. In other words, in this interpretation Thomas would be putting forward a purely philosophical argument for the existence of God. After all, the Five Ways belong to the "preambles" of faith, not to faith as such. They are part of so-called natural theology, which is not particularly theological at all.

The possibility and desirability of natural theology was severely criticized by Karl Barth in the 20th century. This has led to a reevaluation of the status of the Five Ways in Thomas's theology. According to a second interpretation, the Five Ways are not meant to be a rational proof for the existence of God, but they are deeply theological pointers that will only appeal to those who already believe in God anyway. In other words, they must be seen in the context of "faith seeking understanding." Thomas, so it is argued, is not a philosopher but a theologian, and this also applies to his proofs for the existence of God.

The Barthian rereading of Thomas allows us to rescue him from the clutches of a rigid view on natural theology, such as, for instance, (allegedly) promoted by Vatican I. However, it must be said that it is somewhat implausible. Thomas makes perfectly clear that the Five Ways are preambles to faith, not part of faith itself. They have a different status than, let's say, the articles of the Creed. Moreover, and more important, it was actually a common view amongst gentile ancient writers, as well as Christian thinkers, that the existence of God could be proved. Aristotle accepted the existence of the First Mover on philosophical grounds, and it

---

[20] That this is the correct interpretation of the Five Ways can be illustrated by the fact that Thomas does not believe that we can give a conclusive rational or philosophical argument for the creation of the world in time (cf. *ST* 1.46.2). In a "horizontal" reading of the Five Ways – if one were to assume the validity of that reading – the non-eternity of the world would be implied.

seems implausible to attribute a deeper skepticism to Thomas than to Aristotle in this regard.

A third – and more interesting – position in this discussion has been put forward by Denys Turner. According to Turner, the Five Ways are an attempt to prove the existence of God. However, in doing so, we do not know what it is that we are proving. Ultimately, the Five Ways are five rational routes that point to the existence of a Mystery that grounds our own existence: "Reason gets us to where unnameable mystery begins."[21] As he continues: "For Thomas ... reason's powers, pushed to their limit, open up into the territory of *intellectus*: and they do so ... precisely in the proofs of the existence of God. In those proofs, we could say, reason *self*-transcends, and by its self-transcendence, becomes 'intellect.'"[22] The bafflement of reason is not done away with by faith: even through the revelation of grace we do not know what God is in this life, and so by grace we are made one with God "as to one unknown" (*ST*, 1.12.13 *ad* 1). Turner comments:

For Thomas, faith deepens everything that reason knows, including the "darkness" of its knowing. The believer has a stronger sense of mystery than the philosopher, not a weaker. For even if in truth Christians do know by grace and revelation what the philosopher can never know – and they do – such knowledge as faith teaches us can serve only to draw us into a darkness of God which is deeper than it could possibly be for pagans; it is deepened, not relieved by the Trinity, intensified by the incarnation, not dispelled.[23]

This is an attractive reading, which ties in nicely with the nature of the "Existence argument" discussed already. It makes clear that faith opens up a deeper dimension of our existence. The broader, self-transcendent nature of reason echoes Richard of St. Victor's discussion of the nature of reason and intellect. Thomas shares these views.[24] Turner suggests that reason can point toward the existence of the divine, but he denies that either reason or faith give us a clear understanding of God. Turner's reading therefore avoids two one-sided positions: the naive philosophical view that we can rationally prove the existence of God *and* that we have a clear understanding of God; and the view that reason (because of its fallenness) is totally inadequate, leading to a deep chasm between faith and reason, theology and philosophy.

---

[21] Denys Turner, *Faith, Reason, and the Existence of God* (Cambridge: Cambridge University Press, 2005), 121.
[22] Ibid., 87.   [23] Ibid., 43.
[24] See his *Commentary on Boethius' De Trinitate*, q. 6, art.1 and *ST* 1.79.8.

But how, then, do we talk about God? Thomas discusses this issue in *ST* 1.13. It is here we find his teaching on analogy. Thomas Aquinas's teaching on analogy can be interpreted in at least two, not mutually exclusive manners: a semantic one and an ontological one. Let's start with the semantic one. Here we are mainly concerned with words and their meaning.

First we need to make an important preliminary remark. Thomas is a profoundly negative or apophatic theologian. In *De Pot.* 7.5 *ad* 14 we find, for instance: "Because our intellect falls short of the divine essence, this same divine essence surpasses our intellect and is unknown to us: therefore, we reach the highest point of our knowledge about God when we know that we do not know him, inasmuch as we know that that which is God transcends whatsoever we conceive of him."[25] Similarly, in *ST* 1.3 he states, before dealing with God's simplicity, that "we cannot know what God is, but rather what he is not." In short, throughout his writings (e.g., *De Pot.* 7.5; *ScG* 1.30 and III.49; *De Ver.* 2.1 *ad* 9) he reiterates that we cannot know what God is (*quid est*) but only that he is (*an est*). A quiddative knowledge (knowing what God is by grasping his form) would imply that we somehow can grasp God's essence. Given his sense of divine otherness and transcendence Thomas rules this out altogether. Nonetheless, this negative knowledge does yield some insight. For instance, if you do not know what a human being is, but you know that a human being is not inanimate, your knowledge increases, even though you still do not know what a human being is (cf. *ScG* IIII.49.10). It is the same with our knowledge of God. We can say that God is not composite, not temporal, not changeable and so forth, although a quiddative knowledge of God (what God is) will elude us in this life. Within these parameters of apophatic or negative theology, Thomas discusses God's non-composite nature – that is, his simplicity (*ST* 1.3), his perfection (*ST* 1.4), his goodness based on his perfection (*ST* 1.6), infinity (*ST* 1.7), immutability (*ST* 1.9), eternity (*ST* 1.10) and unity (*ST* 1.11). These attributes are indeed disguised negations. For instance, God's perfection is based on the fact that he lacks potentiality (*ST* 1.4.1). In *ST* 1.13 Thomas addresses the issue as to how we can name God, developing his teaching on analogy. The theory of analogy tries to explain how we can speak of God while respecting his transcendence. For the acknowledgment that we cannot grasp God's essence does not mean that we cannot say anything truthful about God. For instance, "God is

---

[25] The work has been translated as *On the Power of God* by English Dominican Fathers (London: Newman Press, 1932). For this passage (with translation modified), see vol. III, p. 33.

just" is a true statement. The problem is, however, what does it mean? What happens to language when we apply it to God?

There are three possibilities. Given the fact that God radically transcends our creaturely limitations, it may be that our language, when applied to God, becomes equivocal. An example of equivocal use of language is "This note pierced my heart," where "note" can refer to a written text or a musical note. If our terms, when applied to God, acquired such a radically different meaning, this would result in a most radical agnosticism. We would, quite literally, not know what we are saying (cf. *ScG* 1.33.6; *ST* 1.13.5). Another possibility is univocal use of language. This will not do either. For in that case creaturely terms (e.g., "wise" or "just") retain exactly the same meaning when applied to God. This would result in a grossly anthropomorphic understanding of God. Thomas identifies a third possibility, which holds the middle between pure equivocation and simple univocation (*ST* 1.13.5). This is analogical use of language. Analogy is not a philosophical tool that allows us to bypass the rigors of negative theology, thus allowing us to adopt a natural philosophical stance (as Barth erroneously interpreted it). Analogy is not a springboard that permits us to jump from a consideration of creaturely perfections to a theory about God's nature; rather, it is a theory that explains what happens to our language when we apply it to God.

In order to explain analogical use of language in more detail, we need to make a distinction between what Thomas calls (*ST* 1.13.3) the *res significata* (the perfections being signified, such as goodness or justice) and the *modus significandi* (the mode of signification). What this distinction alludes to is that perfections ascribable to God and creatures differ in the way they are being actualized. Brian Davies, to whom I am indebted for this account, gives an illuminating example.[26] Consider the following statement: "X is faithful." This is a meaningful statement, even if we do not know who or what "X" is – somebody's husband or somebody's dog. Brian Davies summarizes. "The point that Aquinas is getting at here is that one can understand something of what is meant when a thing is said to be thus and so without understanding exactly what it is like for the thing itself to be thus and so."[27] In short, the term "faithful" has meaning regardless of what or who is being called faithful. When we call God "goodness," the term "goodness" does not mean exactly the same (univocation) as when we call a human being "good." Nor does it mean something totally unrelated (equivocation). We can apply the term analogously, and call

[26] Davies, *The Thought of Thomas Aquinas*, 65.   [27] Ibid., 65–66.

God "goodness" even though we do not fully understand how goodness is actualized in God (or what it means for God to be good).

So far, I have explained analogy in terms of the changing meaning of words when applied to God. Here we are in the area of predication. Analogy describes what happens to our concepts (such as goodness, justice or wisdom) when applied to God. As I indicated earlier, there is another way of interpreting analogy – namely, in terms of an analogy of being.[28] Here we are in the realm of ontology. There is a hierarchy of being and perfection (*ST* 1.4.2 *ad* 3; *ST* 1.89.1). A stone has less being or actuality than a horse, and a horse has less actuality or being than a human. God is all-perfect being, pure actuality (*ST* 1.4.2). This interpretation of analogy of being does not imply, however, that God and creatures are somehow in the same genus – namely, being. This would do away with God's transcendence, and Thomas, as a negative theologian, explicitly rejects this (*ST* 1.3.5).

The two approaches are not mutually exclusive: God is the apex of being (approach 2), and because of the divine simplicity God's perfections can only be described in analogous language (approach 1). For Thomas, God's simplicity implies that, despite the hierarchy of being, our language of God always falls short. It is not untruthful, but it is inadequate – that is, only analogous. This applies to all of Thomas's language about God: God as Cause, God as omnipotent, merciful, omnipresent. In short, all the divine attributes Thomas discusses in the first twenty-six questions of the *ST* are merely analogous because of the corrosive effect of divine simplicity.

Given the simplicity of God we cannot philosophically evaluate the adequacy or inadequacy of the perfections we ascribe to God. We ascribe them to God (to whom they primarily belong; cf. *ST* 1.4.2) because God is the cause of creation and as creatures we have a real relationship to God as the source of our being. But we cannot rationally examine the adequacy or otherwise of our descriptions of God's perfections. We could only do so if we could adopt a bird's-eye perspective that would allow us to compare how, for instance, faithfulness is actualized in creatures, and in God. Now, while we have knowledge of the former, we do not have knowledge of the latter: we do not know what it is like for God to be faithful, for we cannot pry into the divine essence (*ST* 1.12.11). Thus, while Thomas has shown that God is good, eternal and immutable, using reasoned arguments, it is a matter of *faith*, not reason, how these attributes are analogously predicated of God. This remark has a bearing upon those who argue that

---

[28] See John Wippel, *The Metaphysical Thought of Thomas Aquinas* (Washington, DC: Catholic University of America Press, 2000), 73ff. for a more in-depth discussion of this aspect.

Thomas develops a "philosophy of God." Even if we were to grant that Thomas uses philosophical arguments to describe the perfections of God, these arguments end up in *theological* conclusions. This illustrates, again, the self-transcendent dynamic of human reason and, by extension, philosophy. This approach may strike moderns as odd, but it made sense in an intellectual climate such as Thomas's, in which theology and philosophy, although distinct, were not separate.

Having discussed the divine substance and its names or perfections, Thomas goes on to examine God's operations – that is, his knowledge (*ST* 1.14–17) and will (*ST* 1.19ff.), including providence (*ST* 1.22), predestination (*ST* 1.23) and the power of God (*ST* 1.25). He concludes this section by examining God's beatitude (*ST* 1.26). He then goes on to discuss the doctrine of the Trinity (*ST* 1.27–43). This will be followed by a treatise on creation (*ST* 1.44–74), including a treatise on man (*ST* 1.75–102). An examination of the governance of created things (*ST* 1.103–19) concludes the First Part. I now discuss Thomas's theology of the Trinity.

TRINITY

Processions

Let me start with a text that captures Thomas's mature teaching on the Trinity well. Having reiterated his point that there are inner or immanent processions in God (cf. John 8:42;15:26), Thomas goes on to say:

Such action in an intellectual nature is that of the intellect, and of the will. The procession of the Word is by way of an intelligible operation. The operation of the will within ourselves involves also another procession, that of love, whereby the object loved is in the lover; as by the conception of the word, the object spoken of or understood is in the intelligent agent. Hence, besides the procession of the Word in God, there exists in him another procession called the procession of love. (*ST* 1.27.3)

A number of comments should be made. First, the passage is deeply indebted to Augustine's theology of the Trinity, and more specifically to Augustine's so-called psychological model. Second, it is important to remember that this is a case of analogy. Thomas does not consider the psychological analogy a proof, nor is it univocal use of language (*ST* 1.32.1 *ad* 2). As we saw earlier, analogy means that our creaturely language, when applied to God, changes in meaning without, however, becoming utterly equivocal. So the psychological analogy is just that: a mere analogy. When we think of something, there is a kind of inner movement in our mind, and the divine procession of the Word is somewhat like this (but with the difference that there is never a "moment" that the Father is without his Word while we can abstain from thinking about something). Third, readers often miss the point that Thomas's concern is soteriological: we can only come to a personal relation with God if the Son and the Holy Spirit are truly divine (quoting 1 John 5:20 and 1 Cor. 6:19). But if the Son and the Holy Spirit are truly divine, this raises questions about the nature of the one God – questions answered by arguing that there are immanent processions in God, one of knowledge and one of love. In other words, biblical exegesis invites metaphysical considerations.[29]

It is not just the desire to make sense of the biblical words about God that lead Thomas to develop his theology of the Trinity. There is a more spiritual dimension to it as well. As we have been made in the image of God (Gen. 1:26), we actualize our image character most supremely when we know and love God. As Juvenal Merriell has shown, Thomas's presentation is much more dynamic than the standard medieval reading of Augustine, which effectively sees the analogy of the human soul with the Trinity in terms of the three faculties – that is, the three faculties (memory or mind, intellect and will) mirror the divine triad. Thomas prefers a more dynamic understanding that focuses on the two processions (of Word and Love) rather than on the three Persons.[30] When we truly know God and love him rightly, we share in and most resemble the intra-Trinitarian processions of Word and Love (*ST* 1.38.1). As he puts it:

As the uncreated Trinity is distinguished by the procession of the Word from the Speaker, and of Love from both of these (cf. *ST* 1.28.3); so we may say that in rational creatures wherein we find a procession of the word in the intellect, and a procession of the love in the will, there exists an image of the uncreated Trinity. (*ST* 1.93.6)

Thomas, of course, allows for a gradation of the image character in the human being. As created beings, every one of us has a natural aptitude or

---

[29] Matthew Levering, *Scripture and Metaphysics: Aquinas and the Renewal of Trinitarian Theology* (London: Blackwell, 2004), 154.

[30] See D. Juvenal Merriell, "Trinitarian Anthropology," in Rik Van Nieuwenhove and Joseph Wawrykow (eds.), *The Theology of Thomas Aquinas* (Notre Dame, IN: University of Notre Dame Press, 2005), 123–42. See also Rik Van Nieuwenhove, "In the Image of God: The Trinitarian Anthropology of St. Bonaventure, St. Thomas Aquinas and the Blessed Jan van Ruusbroec," *Irish Theological Quarterly* 66 (2001): 109–23 and 227–37.

potential for understanding and loving God; when we actually know and love God in this life in response to grace, we actualize this potential, albeit only imperfectly. Only in the afterlife will our image-character be fully realized (*ST* 1.93.4). It is here that the significance of the "psychological" analogy becomes fully clear. Unlike Richard's model (and present-day social Trinitarian thinkers), the psychological model allows for a very fruitful connection between the theology of the Trinity and theological anthropology and spirituality. Put in a slightly different manner: there is an intimate link between the intra-divine life and the understanding of the human being as made in the image of God. The implications for Christian spirituality are far-reaching, for all aspects of human life can be seen in the context of "knowing and loving God."

Let me summarize. Thomas argues that in order to do justice to biblical revelation, we need to allow for processions within God, and this without compromising monotheism. There has to be real difference between Father, Son and Holy Spirit without implying that Son and Holy Spirit are created. Thomas has identified two processions: the procession of the Word from the Father, and the procession of the Holy Spirit in Love from the Father and the Son. The latter is a more outgoing or ecstatic aspect of the Trinity: the procession of the Holy Spirit is "by way of impulse and movement" toward an object (*ST* 1.27.4). Thomas recaptures something of the biblical connotation of *pneuma* (or breath) when he writes that the word "spirit" expresses "a certain vital movement and impulse" (*vitalis motio et impulsio*).

Relations and Personhood

Having established that there are two immanent processions, Thomas goes on to treat of the relations. This is a crucial discussion because it further drives home the point that the Persons do not compromise the divine unity. The relations imply a "relative opposition" according to origin (*ST* 1.28.3). Thomas distinguishes four relations:
- paternity (the relation of the Father to the Son)
- filiation (the relation of the Son to the Father)
- active spiration (the relation of the Father and the Son to the Holy Spirit)
- passive spiration (the relation of the Holy Spirit to the Father and the Son).

These four relations constitute three Persons:

```
                          paternity

            Father            →                    Son

                          filiation

                             ←


                  active ↓ ↑ passive spiration




                          Holy Spirit
```

Thus, the two processions lead to four ways of relating to one another (the arrows) (cf. *ST* 1.28.4). But these four ways of relating result in only three Persons (not four) because Father and Son are not constituted as distinct Persons in the active spiration of the Holy Spirit but only through paternity and filiation. (Because active spiration is common to Father and Son it does not constitute them as distinct Persons.) The Holy Spirit is constituted as a distinct Person by passive spiration (*ScG* IV.24.8).

For Thomas, the relations are identical to the divine essence. However, because of the relative opposition they imply, relations allow us to distinguish the three Persons from one another. Hence, in *ST* 1.28.2 Thomas can write that "relation really existing in God is really the same as his essence." And he can also state (in *ST* 1.28.3), "as in God there is a real relation there must also be a real opposition," and this implies distinction. All of this may sound rather abstract. What it means is this: the Father is God, the Son is God, the Holy Spirit is God, and yet Father, Son and Holy Spirit are distinct (through their "relative opposition"). As he puts it in *ST* 1.28.4 *ad* 1, "although paternity, just as filiation, is really the same as the divine essence, nevertheless these two in their own proper idea and definitions import opposite respects. Hence they are distinguished from each other."

For Thomas, it is "relation" that allows us to develop the doctrine of three Persons in one God. The being (*esse*) of the divine relation is the same being as the divine subsistence; but as relation as such (*ratio*) it implies "opposition" or distinction (*ST* 1.28.2). These two aspects of relation (as identical to the essence, and as implying distinction) are crucial in his understanding of personhood. Thomas, by defining personhood in terms of subsisting relation, manages to harmonize the relational and essential understanding of Personhood the tradition had bequeathed to him. In this way, by defining a divine Person in terms of a relation as subsisting (*Persona divina significat relationem ut subsistentem*), Thomas harmonizes the essentialist and relational understandings of personhood.

It is clear that Thomas uses the word "Person" when applied to God and humans in an analogical sense (*ST* 1.29.4 *ad* 4). Thomas, unlike Richard, is happy to adopt the Boethian definition of person as "the individual substance of a rational nature." But the word "person" changes in meaning from when applied to a human (such as Jack – i.e., an individual human being) to when applied to God. In the latter case, the word "substance" in the definition refers to the hypostasis and not to the essence (*ST* 1.30.1 *ad* 1). In other words, it acquires a relational dimension (more specifically, a subsisting relation) that creaturely substances do not have.

Before I discuss how Thomas conceives of personal names I would like to signal some important differences between Thomist and Bonaventurean Trinitarian doctrine. It will have become clear that, according to Thomas, personal distinction within the Trinity is based upon the opposition of divine relations. His Trinitarian thought can therefore be characterized as "a relational account." Bonaventure's theology of the Trinity, influenced by Richard of St. Victor, is more "emanational." When confronted with the issue whether the Father is Father because he generates the Son, or whether he generates because he is the Father, their divergence of views becomes evident. Bonaventure argues that the Father is Father because he generates (*ideo Pater, quia generat*).[31] Thomas rejects this. He argues, plausibly, that in order for generation to occur in the first place, there needs to be a Father: because he is Father, he generates.[32] Thus, for Thomas, the constitution of the Persons takes conceptual (not temporal) precedence over emanation because relations have an existence of their own prior to the emanations of the Persons. In Bonaventure's thought, emanations have priority.[33]

---

[31] 1 *Sent.* d. 27, part 1, a. un. q. 2 sol.   [32] *ST* 1.40.4.

[33] See Russell L. Friedman, *Intellectual Traditions at the Medieval University: The Use of Philosophical Psychology in Trinitarian Theology among the Franciscans and Dominicans 1250–1350* (Leiden: Brill, 2013), 72–89.

Personal Names

The main personal name of the First Person is "Father." The Father is the principal of the whole Godhead (*ST* 1.39.5 *ad* 6). But indirectly he is, of course, also the Father of all created beings. Like other scholastics before him, Thomas establishes a close link between the intra-divine processions and the extra-divine activity (creation and sanctification): just as an architect first conceives of the plan of a house in his mind before he builds it, so too the Son of God first proceeds from the Father before the world is created (cf. *ST* 1.33.3 *ad* 1).

When discussing the personal names of the Son, Thomas examines "Word" and "Image." The personal name "Word" (understood here as the inner word or concept formed by the intellect, not a vocalized word) goes to the heart of Thomas's theology of the Trinity as it is intimately linked with his understanding of the generation of the Son in terms of an intellectual emanation (*ST* 1.34.2). Again Thomas explicitly draws out the link between the generation of the Word and the creation of the world. "Because God by one act understands himself and all things, his one only Word is expressive not only of the Father, but of all creatures" (*ST* 1.34.3). Because God's knowledge is creative, there is an intimate connection between the generation of the Word from the Father and the creation and redemption of the world.[34]

The main personal names Thomas examines when dealing with the Holy Spirit are Love and Gift. The connection between the intra-divine processions and the economy of salvation is alluded to in a passage that offers a good summary of some of the main elements I have discussed:

As the Father speaks himself and every creature by his begotten Word, inasmuch as the Word begotten adequately represents the Father and every creature; so he loves himself and every creature by the Holy Spirit, inasmuch as the Holy Spirit proceeds as the love of the primal goodness whereby the Father loves himself and every creature. Thus it is evident that relation to creature is implied both in the Word and in the proceeding Love. (*ST* 1.37.2 *ad* 3)

In light of these texts Gilles Emery is surely right to challenge the widespread view that Thomas's doctrine presents an "abstract" approach to the Trinity, a Trinity "locked within itself." As a matter of fact, there is an intimate link between the processions of Word and Love, and the economy of salvation.[35] Indeed, it would be correct to describe Thomas's theology of the Trinity as performing a hermeneutic spiral: building on a profound

---

[34] Gilles Emery, *Trinity in Aquinas* (Ypsilanti, MI: Sapientia Press, 2003), 152–53.   [35] Ibid., 156.

engagement with the legacy of the theology of the Trinity by Augustine and others, which in turn is based on an in-depth engagement with the economy of salvation as testified in the Scriptures, Thomas develops a theology of the Trinity that allows us in turn to see both creation and the economy of salvation and sanctification in light of the intra-Trinitarian life of Word and Spirit.

Moreover, as I have already suggested, Thomas's "psychological" model also allows for a fruitful spirituality: as we have been made in the image of the Trinity, whenever we know and love God we share, albeit in an imperfect manner, in the divine processions of Word and Spirit. I now discuss in more detail how Thomas conceives of the Christian life.

THOMAS ON FAITH

Thomas defines faith as "a habit of the mind, whereby eternal life is begun in us, making the intellect assent to what is non-apparent" (*fides est habitus mentis, qua inchoatur vita aeterna in nobis, faciens intellectum assentire non apparentibus*). Faith is an inchoate participation in God that can grow and fructify every aspect of our life, assisting us "on our journey towards the enjoyment of God" (*ST* II–II.1.1) – which is why Thomas writes that through it "eternal life is begun in us." Faith orients us to God and is a foretaste of heaven in which it will be fulfilled. The main object of faith is the First Truth, or God, and given the fact that this object is unseen in this life, faith relates to things that are not apparent.[36] Thomas understands the act of faith as "the firm adhesion of the intellect" of the believer to non-apparent truths. In the afterlife faith will cease as we enjoy the beatific vision of God.

Because we do not attain the full knowledge of God in faith, our ultimate fulfillment or felicity cannot lie in faith. As a matter of fact, Thomas argues that the knowledge of faith does not bring rest to desire but rather sets it aflame, since all of us desire to see what we believe (Cf. *ScG* III.40.5). Echoing Hugh, Thomas writes that the act of believing is not the same as scientific knowledge (cf. *De Ver.* 14.2); nor is it the same as opinion (you are inclined to go with one view, but you cannot rule out that the

---

[36] Faith is oriented toward God, the First Truth, and God is the formal and material object of faith. The "formal" object refers to the authority of the One who makes us believe. We believe because *God* vouches for revelation (*ST* II–II.1.1). The "material" object of faith refers to the *contents* of our faith. This includes, first and foremost, God, as well as other things that relate to God and the salvation he works for us.

other view might be the correct one) or doubt (where you waver between two contradictory propositions). In short, faith is between opinion and science. Because the act of believing does not attain the perfection of perfect sight (such as in science), it shares some elements with doubt and opinion. The latter dimension (faith is not sight) explains the restlessness of faith (cf. *De Ver.* 14.1 *ad* 5). On the other hand, given the fact that believing implies firmly clinging to one side, it has something in common with certain knowledge or *scientia* (*ST* II–II.2.1).[37]

Although Thomas sees faith as residing in the intellect (as distinct from the will), this is not to say that the will has no role to play in our act of faith. The act of believing takes place by the command of the will, which in turn responds to the stirring of divine grace. You cannot decide for yourself that you will become a believer: it is the result of the operation of God's grace on the will, which stirs the intellect to give its assent. Thomas puts it in his characteristically crisp manner: "The act of believing is an act of the intellect assenting to divine Truth at the command of the will moved by the grace of God" (*ST* II–II.2.9).[38]

We have not discussed the first element in Thomas's definition – namely, faith is "a habit of the mind." Thomas sees faith as a theological virtue. A virtue is a *habitus*, a disposition. The best way to grasp this Aristotelian concept is to think of the English phrase "something is second nature" to somebody. Habits have durability and dispose us toward good or bad acts. In the first case we talk of virtues: they are habits that render human acts good (see *ST* II–II.4.5); in the latter case we speak of vices. Thomas differs from Aristotle in that he claims that some of these dispositions (*habitus*) can be divinely produced, rather than being simply generated by society, upbringing and our own practices (*ST* I–II.51.4). Thomas further distinguishes between intellectual virtues (wisdom, *scientia*, art), moral virtues (temperance, fortitude) and theological virtues (faith, hope and love). The latter are the ones infused by God, who is their object or goal. Faith is thus a theological virtue because it has God as its final end (*ST* II–II.4.7), and it does so, Thomas adds, under the aspect of Truth. This explains why faith resides in the intellect, unlike the theological virtue of love, which resides in the will (God as the object of our love).

---

[37] In claiming that our desire for ultimate fulfillment (felicity) will only come to rest when it meets God face to face – that is, in the afterlife, Thomas radically transforms the Aristotelian legacy (who does not mention the significance of the afterlife in the attainment of happiness).
[38] See Van Nieuwenhove, *Thomas Aquinas and Contemplation*, 106–13.

Avery Dulles has helpfully identified a number of the different models of faith and it may be useful, by way of summarizing this section, to examine how Thomas's definition of faith fits in. A first model is the propositional model, where faith is equated with a set of beliefs. A second model can be called the hermeneutical one, in which faith is seen as a perspective on the world. It is not (just) a set of beliefs but rather it offers us a different perspective on the world. The fiducial model understands faith mainly in terms of obedience and surrender – a view that is stressed in Reformation circles but one that Thomas would associate more with hope. Dulles goes on to discuss an affective-experiential model (which puts a distinct emphasis upon the experience of the Holy Spirit in us), a praxis model (which is concerned with the positive impact of faith on tackling socioeconomic injustices) and a personalist model (which understands faith in terms of a special relationship with a personal God who communicates himself in love).[39] Our exposition of Thomas's understanding of faith allows us to show how he combines several models. For starters, Thomas adopts the *propositional* model. After all, the essence of the things we hope for are contained in the articles of faith (*Comm. on Heb.* no. 557). Thomas's emphasis upon faith as a virtue or disposition that resides in the intellect allows us to link his analysis with the *hermeneutical* model. For Thomas, faith is a way of relating to the world (it is, after all, a *habitus*, a disposition). It allows you to see things that mere reason or a positivistic approach cannot (cf. *ST* II–II.2.3 *ad* 3). There is an element of the *fiducial* model in Thomas's approach, insofar as he emphasizes that it is the will, in response to the stirrings of God's grace, which makes the intellect assent (cf. *ST* II–II.2.9). The *affective-experiential* model is also accommodated in that Thomas sees faith as the beginning of eternal life here and now. Faith purifies the heart (*ST* II–II.7.2). It cannot be reduced to extrinsic agreement with a set of propositions. In relation to the *praxis* approach, Thomas would certainly agree that faith must find expression in charitable works. He would, however, discuss these under the heading of charity rather than faith. For the *personalist* approach, we need to consider his views on charity as well.

Before I do this, I want to briefly consider hope, the second theological virtue. The object of hope is a future good, difficult but possible to obtain (*ST* II–II.17.1). The most supreme future good is eternal fulfillment or beatitude (*ST* II–II.17.2). It is clear that hope, unlike faith, resides in the

---

[39] Avery Dulles, *The Assurance of Things Hoped For: A Theology of Christian Faith* (Oxford: Oxford University Press, 1997), 170–84.

will (*ST* II–II.18.1). Thomas then goes on to discuss the vices of despair and presumption. Both do away with hope and its orientation toward God: despair insofar as it refuses to see God as the source of our salvation (*ST* II–II.20.1); and presumption insofar as it is an inordinate and immoderate claim on God's grace (solely trusting in God's mercy while despising divine justice) or an overconfidence in one's own powers to obtain salvation (*ST* II–II.21.1). In both cases the dynamic orientation toward God, characteristic of our pilgrimage on earth (the *status viatoris* or the state of the wayfarer – cf. *ST* II–II.18.4), is abolished.[40] Let me now turn to the third theological virtue, charity or love.

THOMAS ON CHARITY

Charity as Friendship for God

Thomas's analysis of charity or Christian love is quite original. First, he draws on the Aristotelian analysis of friendship and transforms it so as to describe the nature of Christian love. Second, he draws on the Pauline notion of *communicatio* or fellowship. He also develops a profound analysis of charity in triangular terms. Finally, he details an order of love, in which he pays ample attention to the significance of kinship relations. I explain these topics, and in doing so illustrate that in his discussion of charity the transcendental thrust of Thomas's theology is prominent.

In *ST* II–II.23.1 (the first article on charity) Thomas makes the point that love has the character of friendship, which implies benevolence – that is, we wish good to the other person in her own right. We like wine for our sake, but wine is not our friend because we do not wish wine well. But well-wishing is not yet sufficient to define friendship, "for a certain mutual love is requisite" and this reciprocity is based on "some kind of communication" (*communicatio*). Thomas summarizes:

Accordingly, since there is a communication between man and God, inasmuch as He communicates his happiness to us, some kind of friendship must needs be based on this same communication, of which it is written (1 Cor 1:9): God is faithful: by Whom you are called unto the fellowship of His Son. The love which is based on this communication, is charity: wherefore it is evident that charity is the friendship of man for God. (*ST* II–II.23.1)

---

[40] See Josef Pieper's book *On Hope*, which develops this theological anthropology in greater detail.

Charity as friendship implies both benevolence (in which we wish good to somebody for his sake) and mutuality (made possible by the Incarnation – cf. John 15:15, quoted in the first article on charity), and these in turn are based on a certain "communication" (*aliqua communicatio*) of the person with God. Thomas links the key term *communicatio* with *societas* or fellowship (*koinonia*) through a reference to 1 Corinthians 1:9. Thus, Thomas is synthesizing the Aristotelian thought on friendship with the Pauline notion of fellowship or communion.

This is an extraordinary move, for Aristotle had argued that genuine friendship can only occur amongst equals. We honor the gods and we are grateful to them, in Aristotle's view, but we are not friends with them. Through the Incarnation, there is a sense in which God has graciously established some kind of equality with humanity. In an important contribution, Eberhard Schockenhoff[41] makes clear that *communicatio* refers to a sharing of God's love with humanity through the participation of the faithful in Christ and the vital union of all Christians with the Son (as the quotation from Paul suggests), resulting in an inner transformation of the person: "Thomas's God is neither the unmoved mover nor the highest thought who sees only his own essence in the finite spirit. He is the God of love, who yearns for intimate community with human beings and seeks companionship and exchange with them."[42]

Search for Fulfillment

Before I continue with my consideration of the nature of charity, I would like to pause and briefly examine how Thomas sees our search for fulfillment or happiness. According to Thomas, human beings have a "natural" orientation toward fulfillment or beatitude, which is a supernatural goal (*ST* 1–11.5.5).[43] "Supernatural" in this context means that we cannot attain it through our own efforts. Thus, we have an inbuilt orientation toward something (beatitude in God) that surpasses our nature and that cannot be attained without divine aid. Our

---

[41] Eberhard Schockenhoff, "The Theological Virtue of Charity," in Stephen Pope (ed.), *The Ethics of Aquinas* (Washington, DC: Georgetown University Press, 2002), 244–58.

[42] Ibid., 248.

[43] *ST* 1–11.5.8 *ad* 2: "Happiness may be considered as the final and perfect good, which is the general notion of happiness: and thus the will naturally and of necessity tends hereto (*et sic naturaliter, et ex necessitate voluntas in illud tendit*)." Also, *ST* 1–11.3.6 *ad* 2.

whole existence as pilgrims on earth is determined by this nonpossession of ultimate fulfillment.[44]

The notion that we have a *natural* orientation toward *supernatural* fulfillment is central to Thomas's theological outlook. He would have been extremely uncomfortable with a two-tiered understanding of the world in which the natural and the supernatural are separated from one another. The later separation of the natural from the supernatural would result in "pure naturalism" in the modern period, in which the natural world is seen as self-sufficient and the supernatural as something extrinsic.[45] This view is deeply alien to Thomas, for whom "grace does not abolish nature but fulfils (or perfects) it" (*ST* 1.1.8 *ad* 3: *gratia non tollit naturam, sed perficit*).

In the text from *ST* 11–11.23.1 which I quoted, Thomas wrote that "there is communication between man and God, inasmuch as He communicates his happiness to us" (*quod nobis suam beatitudinem communicat*). The reference to happiness or beatitude in *ST* 11–11.23.1 recalls the beautiful discussion on our search for happiness in the first part of the Second Part of the *Summa Theologiae* (1–11.1–5), one of the most profound examinations of human desire and its search for happiness written in the medieval period. Thomas deals with a whole range of created goods that fail to provide us with ultimate fulfillment or happiness, such as wealth, honors, fame, power, bodily goods, pleasure and goods of the soul (*ST* 1–11.2). The list may have been inspired by Boethius's discussion in his *Consolation of Philosophy*. Like Boethius, Thomas rejects them all as ultimately inadequate. Thomas is very much aware that human desire has an almost infinite, inexhaustible dynamic – and it is for this very reason that only God can fulfill human desire. The key idea, which I hope to explain, is that religion transforms our desires and attachments toward finite things through a desire for the infinite (in which it finds rest) *in* these finite things.[46] Let me examine this in more detail by returning to our topic of charity, more specifically its triangular nature.[47]

---

[44] See *ST* 1–11.5.3: "A certain participation of happiness can be had in this life: but perfect and true happiness cannot be had in this life."

[45] Thomas explicitly rejects extrinsicism in *ScG* 111.54.8. For a more detailed discussion of Thomas's understanding of the relation between grace and nature, and the multifarious (mis)interpretations in, odernity, see Kerr, *After Aquinas*, 134–48.

[46] I have benefited from Jos Decorte's posthumous book *Raak me niet aan. Over middeleeuws en postmiddeleeuws transcendentiedenken* (Kapellen: Pelckmans, 2001), 22–30.

[47] I have developed some of these ideas in "The Religious Disposition as a Critical Resource to Resist Instrumentalization," *Heythrop Journal* (2009): 689–96, especially pp. 691–92.

The Triangular Nature of Love

Not unlike Hugh, Thomas describes love (*caritas*) in triangular terms: our love for neighbor goes via God. The following quotation from *ST* II–II.27.4 illustrates this point eloquently. In this article, Thomas first contrasts our ways of knowing God to our ways of loving God. We know God through other things the way we know a cause through its effects, albeit within the necessary apophatic limitations.[48] Thus our knowledge of God is from the bottom up (beginning from creatures) and mediated. It is different with our love of God. This love is not mediated, and originates from God:

Love ... tends to God first, and flows on from him to other things, and in this sense charity loves God immediately, and other things through God (*dilectio ... tendit in Deum primo, et ex ipso derivatur ad alia: et secundum hoc charitas Deum immediate diligit, alia vero Deo mediante*).[49]

Because humans (other people or ourselves) are united with God as their highest good, they also become worthy of each other's love. Thomas states that it would be wrong to love our neighbor as if he were our last end, but not if we loved him for God's sake, and this is what charity does (*ST* II–II.25.1 *ad* 3). Because our love tends to God first and flows from God to other things (*ST* II–II.27.4), we can even love our enemies, not directly (which would be "perverse"), but insofar as we love God and God loves them. Thomas draws a comparison between our love of enemies on one hand and the love of a friend's children who treat us badly on the other (*ST* II–II.25.8). Similar to what Hugh had argued, the triangular nature of love also extends to ourselves: "God is loved as the principle of good, on which the love of charity is founded; while man, out of charity, loves himself by reason of his being a partaker in the aforesaid good, and loves his neighbour by reason of his fellowship in that good" (*ST* II–II.26.4). In other words, because we love God, we love ourselves and our fellow men.

The triangular understanding of love, which makes clear how we should love our neighbor for the sake of God, is a reappropriation of the notion that only God is to be "enjoyed" – itself an important theme in the Augustinian tradition. In the *Sed contra* of the second article on charity (*ST* II–II.23.2), for instance, Thomas quotes a passage from *De Doctrina*

---

[48] "With regard to knowledge ... we know God through other things, either as a cause through its effects, or by way of pre-eminence or negation as Dionysius states (*Divine Names* 1)."

[49] Given the fact that we must first know whom or what we love, Thomas speaks of "a circular movement," "for knowledge begins from creatures, tends to God, and love begins with God as the last end, and passes on to creatures" (*ST* II–II.27.4 *ad* 2).

Christiana, in which Augustine wrote that by charity he means "the movement of the soul towards the enjoyment of God for his own sake" (*motum animi ad fruendum Deo propter ipsum*).[50] Clearly, for Thomas, charity orients us toward the enjoyment of God. Through charity all our desires and loves become redirected through God. Instead of being immediately focused on finite things, they become diverted to God and from there revert to things finite.

The focus of desire on God is essential if we want to relate to created things properly. If human desire and its infinite dynamic *directly* targets created things, we are in danger of either idolizing them or turning away from them with tedium. In this context Thomas's rejection of wealth is noteworthy. It offers an illustration of the sense of futility we may experience if our desire "invests" itself directly in created goods. Thomas writes that our desire for wealth can be infinite (*ST* I–II.2.1 *ad* 3). In that sense it resembles our desire for God, which is infinite too. However, whereas the desire for God leads to fulfillment (and the more we possess the ultimate Good, the more we find fulfillment in it), the desire for wealth leads to a bad infinity, a never-ending search for more wealth as it fails to grant our desire for fulfillment. Quoting John 4:13 in Reply 3 in *ST* I–II.2.1, he writes: "*Whosoever drinks of this water*, by which temporal goods are signified, *shall thirst again*. The reason for this is that we realize more their insufficiency when we possess them: and this very fact shows that they are imperfect, and that the sovereign good does not consist therein." When we possess riches, we realize that they fail to fulfill us and we seek more. Because the object of human desire is the perfect good, nothing in this created world can satisfy the human will (*nihil potest quietare voluntatem hominis*); only God suffices to fill our hearts (*solus Deus voluntatem hominis implore potest*).[51] Drawing an analogy with interpersonal relations we can say that in erotic terms this bad infinity is represented by the womanizer.

There is also the possibility that our desire zooms in on one specific created good and invests its infinite dynamic on it. When this happens, we relate to it in an improper manner. Thomas considers it a kind of superstition (where divine worship is offered to whom it ought not to be)[52] or even

---

[50] Similarly, in *ST* II–II.27.3 we find Thomas quoting from Augustine's *De Doctrina Christiana*: "To enjoy is to cleave to something for its own sake. Now God is to be enjoyed (*Deo fruendum est*). Therefore, God is to be loved for himself." Again in *ST* II–II.23.8 he makes the point that "the ultimate and principal good of man is the enjoyment of God (*principale bonum hominis est Dei fruitio*) ... and to this good man is ordered by charity."

[51] *ST* I–II.2.8 and *Commentary on John* no. 586.   [52] *ST* II–II.92.1.

(in the broadest sense of the word) idolatry, the gravest of sins.[53] In erotic terms this happens in infatuation, when we idolize the other in highly unrealistic terms. In idolatry the finite becomes the exclusive focus of our desire and finds a momentary rest in it whereas our desire should retain its dynamic toward God in the midst of the finite.

In short, given the almost inexhaustible dynamic of human desire, there is always the danger that human desire rests in a finite object that, so to speak, cannot support this burden or intensity – and then we may end up idolizing something finite. Or else desire turns away in disgust, pursuing another transient object. Religion solves the riddle of human desire by allowing it to maintain its dynamic without, however, pursuing a "bad infinity," wandering from one particular created thing to another in a futile quest for fulfillment in this life. By refocusing our desire toward God our desire for created things is not abolished, but our desire for created things is now mediated through God. Again pursuing our analogy we can compare this to marriage, in which God is present as "the middle term" (to borrow a phrase from Kierkegaard).[54]

Thomas has provided us with a profound analysis of human desire and love. It is only when we refocus human desire on God that we can relate to created things properly. Thomas's analysis of the triangular nature of love does not imply that we cannot attribute intrinsic value to created things. On the contrary, it is only when human desire relates to God as its ultimate focus that we can desist from instrumentalizing or idolizing created things. I return to this theme when I discuss Meister Eckhart's notion of detachment.

The Order of Charity

Finally, I want to conclude this section on charity by pointing out that Thomas's triangular understanding of love does not imply that he adopts

---

[53] *ST* II–II.94.3: "The greatest of all [sins] seems to be for a man to give God's honor to a creature, since, so far as he is concerned, he sets up another God in the world, and lessens the divine sovereignty." Thomas mainly has in mind the worship of inanimate objects or animals, but his remarks have a wider application (see *ST* II–II.94.1 *ad* 4).

[54] See Søren Kierkegaard, *Works of Love* (Princeton, NJ: Princeton University Press, 1998), 106–07: "Worldly wisdom is of the opinion that love is a relationship between persons; Christianity teaches that love is a relationship between: a person – God – a person, that is, that God is the middle term. . . . To love God is to love oneself truly; to help another person to love God is to love another person; to be helped by another person to love God is to be loved." Although Kierkegaard shares the view that Christian love is triangular in nature, his universalist, non-preferential understanding of love differs from Thomas's robust defense of kinship preference.

a universalist, non-preferential understanding of love. When he raises the question of whether we ought to love one neighbor more than another (*ST* II–II.26.6) he begins his response by stating that "there have been two opinions on this question." The first opinion – the non- preferential one – states that we should love all our neighbors equally as regards the affection we feel for them, but not in the outward effects (I bestow more money on my children than on the children in Africa, but I should love them all equally). Thomas considers this view "unreasonable." Charity is from God, but it is *we* who love with charity. Therefore, given these two principles of loving (i.e., God and ourselves), we love those who are nearer to God or to ourselves more: "We must, therefore, say that, even as regards the affection we ought to love one neighbour more than another." Thomas, as an Aristotelian in his moral orientation, will not be tempted by an ethics that downplays our everyday affections.

I hope it has become clear how, in Thomas's view, charity bestows on our desires (and our existence in general) a radical theocentric orientation. Charity is indeed the form of all virtues (*ST* II–II.23.8): it directs other virtuous acts to their final end – the enjoyment of God.[55] However, just as there is "restlessness" at the heart of faith, so too charity orients us toward our final good, although perfect fulfillment or enjoyment is not possible in this life. Hence, our enjoyment of God in this life is imperfect (*ST* I–II.II.4 *ad* 2), and "the movement of our will remains in suspense (*motus voluntatis remanet in suspenso*), although it has reached something" (*ST* I–II.II.3).

CONTEMPLATION

In this section, I want to elaborate on Thomas's notion of contemplation and the priority of intellect it implies.[56] The priority Thomas attributes to the intellect is in contrast with later Franciscan thinkers. John Duns Scotus, for instance, will argue that the will is a superior faculty to the intellect, if only because love of God is more important than knowledge of God. Thomas, incidentally, agrees that love of God is better than knowledge of God, but he argues, not implausibly, that it does not follow from this that the will is superior to intellect (*ST* I.82.3). Thomas teaches that all

---

[55] See *ST* II–II.23.8 *ad* 3: "Charity is said to be the end of other virtues, because it directs all other virtues to its own end. And since a mother is one who conceives within herself and by another, charity is called the mother of the other virtues, because, by commanding them, it conceives the acts of other virtues, by the desire of the last end."

[56] For a book-length treatment, see Van Nieuwenhove, *Thomas Aquinas and Contemplation*.

beings desire happiness or fulfillment, but our happiness does not consist in an operation of the will. In other words, we desire happiness, but this happiness is only attainable if it is made present to us by the intellect. Then our desire comes to an end and finds delight in it. Thomas summarizes. "At first we desire to attain an intelligible end; we attain it, through its being made present to us by an act of the intellect; and then the delighted will rests in the end when attained. So, therefore, the essence of happiness consists in an act of the intellect: but the delight that results from happiness pertains to the will" (*ST* I–II.3.4). Identifying happiness with the pursuit of happiness itself (or with the act of will) is a major mistake, according to Thomas. Just as the object of sight is not vision itself (i.e., the act of seeing) but visible things; so too the first object of the will cannot be its act. "From the very fact that happiness belongs to the will as the will's first object, it follows that it does not belong to it as its act" (*ST* I–II.3.4 *ad* 2).

Thomas, in line with other medieval thinkers, distinguishes between two acts of the one intellective power – namely, *ratio* (discursive reason) and *intellectus* (intellect). The latter is the realm of contemplation. The act of the intellect is "to apprehend intelligible truth; and to reason is to advance from one thing understood to another (*procedere de uno intellecto ad aliud*), so as to know an intelligible truth ... Reasoning, therefore, is compared to understanding, as movement is to rest, or acquisition to possession; of which one belongs to the perfect, the other to the imperfect."[57] Denys Turner draws out the important implication of this view: "We could not be rational if we were not also more than rational; human beings are not rational unless they are also intellectual."[58] Human reason has a self-transcendent dynamic to it, and it comes to fruition in contemplation, in which intellect takes central stage. Our intellect is something we share with angels, who have it in fullness. The act of the intellect is an immediate grasp or intuition of the truth. Usually we have to go through a whole reasoning process to attain this kind of insight; angels have an immediate and timeless grasp.[59] When contemplating, discursive reasoning must be put aside and the gaze of the soul must be fixed on the contemplation of the one simple truth.[60] Thus, contemplation, in the

---

[57] *ST* 1.79.8; see also Thomas's *Commentary on Boethius' De Trinitate*, q.6 a.1, reply to the third question, trans. pp. 70–71 and footnote 36.

[58] Turner, *Faith, Reason, and the Existence of God*, 89.

[59] For the timelessness, see *ScG* II.96.10. ST II–II.180.6 *ad* 2 speaks of a simple intuition (*simplici intuitu*) of the intellect; see also *ST* II–II.180.3 *ad* 1: *contemplatio pertinet ad ipsum simplicem intuitum veritatis*. On this, see Van Nieuwenhove, *Thomas Aquinas and Contemplation*, chapter 2.

[60] *ST* II–II.180.6 *ad* 2.

words of Josef Pieper, is "a type of knowing which does not merely move towards its object but rests in it. The object is present – as a face or a landscape is present to the eye when the gaze 'rests upon it.'"[61] Contemplation concerns a purely receptive approach to reality, disinterested and independent of all practical aims of the active life. It is pursued for its own sake (*contemplatio maxime quaeritur propter seipsam*) and not subject to any other goal (*ST* 1–11.3.5).

Contemplation is thus not in the first place an activity but rather a disposition of theocentric receptivity that permeates every aspect of our life. It is similar to what Simone Weil calls "attention."[62] It is not difficult to draw a comparison between what Thomas as a Christian theologian sees as the highest aspect of life – contemplation – and the aesthetic disposition of disinterestedness. Contemplation as an end in itself resists instrumentalization. It consists, after all, in "a certain liberty of mind" (*libertas animi*) (*ST* 11–11.182.1 *ad* 2), in "leisure and rest" (quoting Ps. 46:10: "Be still and see that I am God" [*ST* 11–11.182.1]). Moreover, it is contemplation that "redeems" the practical life: the practical life is fulfilled in the contemplative life. "The contemplative life is loved more for its own sake, while the active life is directed to something else (*ad aliud ordinatur*)" (*ST* 11–11.182.1). Given our preference for things practical, this view may strike readers from the 21st century as elitist or even unchristian. But Thomas's key point is a perfectly plausible one: after all, the purpose of acts of charity cannot lie within themselves. The alleviation of suffering, for instance, is only a means to an end – that is, creating the conditions in which other people can enjoy a fulfilled life oriented toward God (i.e., a contemplative life). Morality and the life of virtue point to something beyond themselves. The active life is necessary and meaningful, but its meaning is to make possible the happiness of contemplation; it becomes meaningless the moment it sees itself as an end in itself.[63]

The fact that the contemplation is ultimately more meaningful than the active life does not imply that, at times, the urgencies of the active life will not take precedence over contemplation: "In a restricted sense and in a particular case one should prefer the active life on account of the needs of the present life" (*ST* 11–11.182.1). But when we engage in charitable activity ("the active life"), we should attempt to retain a contemplative dimension to this activity (*ST* 11–11.182.1 *ad* 3). Just as our love of neighbor needs to be

---

[61] Josef Pieper, *Happiness and Contemplation* (South Bend, IN: St. Augustine's Press, 1998), 74.

[62] Rik Van Nieuwenhove, "The Religious and Aesthetic Attitude," *Literature and Theology* 18.2 (2004): 160–72.

[63] See *ST* 11–11.182 and Pieper, *Happiness and Contemplation*, 92–95.

referred back to love of God, so too the active life is referred back to the contemplative life (cf. *ST* II–II.188.2). It is in light of this that Thomas at times seems to affirm the primacy of the *vita mixta* (the mixed life) over the exclusively contemplative life: "When a person is called from the contemplative to the active life, this is done by way not of subtraction but of addition" (*ST* II II.182.1 *ad* 3). Or again, in a beautiful text that became the motto of the Dominican Order in which teaching and preaching are of central importance, "For even as it is better to enlighten than merely to shine, so it is better to give to others the fruits of one's contemplation (*contemplata aliis tradere*) than merely to contemplate" (*ST* II–II.188.6). In this Thomas shows himself an heir to some of Gregory the Great's key insights.

THE SAVING WORK OF CHRIST

In what follows, I outline Thomas's soteriology by examining the following themes: the saving significance of the Passion of Christ, the Body of Christ, and the role of the Eucharist.[64] Given the systemic nature of Thomas's theological enterprise, these themes are deeply interwoven.

The Death of Christ, the Universal Cause of Salvation

In his earlier works, Thomas mainly referred to the notion of "making satisfaction" to describe the saving meaning of Christ's death. In *ST* the picture becomes more diverse, and he appeals also to a number of other key categories, including the more biblical notion of "sacrifice."[65] Nevertheless, the notion of making satisfaction remains important for Thomas in his mature works, and it is this notion I examine first.

Thomas is obviously indebted to Anselm's theory of satisfaction, as the following quotation from *CT* 1.200 makes clear:

---

[64] I developed some of this material elsewhere, such as in "'Bearing the Marks of Christ's Passion' – Thomas' Soteriology," in Van Nieuwenhove and Wawrykow, *The Theology of Thomas Aquinas*, 277–302; "St. Anselm and St. Thomas Aquinas on 'Satisfaction': Or How Catholic and Protestant Understandings of the Cross Differ," *Angelicum* 80 (2003): 159–76; "The Saving Work of Christ," in Brian Davies and Eleonore Stump (eds.), *The Oxford Handbook to Aquinas* (Oxford: Oxford University Press, 2011); "Saint Thomas Aquinas on Salvation, Making Satisfaction, and the Restoration of Friendship with God," *The Thomist* 83: 521–45.

[65] In *ST* III.48 Thomas describes how the Passion of Christ effects our salvation by way of merit, by way of making satisfaction, by way of sacrifice and by way of redemption.

If God had decided to restore man solely by an act of his will and power, the order of divine justice would not have been observed. Justice demands satisfaction for sin. But God cannot render satisfaction, just as he cannot merit. Such a service pertains to one who is subject to another. Thus God was not in a position to satisfy for the sin of the whole of human nature; and a mere man was unable to do so. . . . Hence divine Wisdom judged it fitting that God should become man, so that thus one and the same person would be able both to restore man and to offer satisfaction.[66]

While the onus was on humanity to restore the relationship with God, we could not do so, infected as we are by sin. Therefore it was necessary that somebody who was both human and divine (and thus sinless) would restore this relationship (i.e., make satisfaction). I would like to make a number of comments.

As with Anselm, it is a gross misreading to understand "making satisfaction" in terms of retribution and punishment. Thomas repeatedly points out that there are two major differences between punishment and making satisfaction. The first difference is that punishment is inflicted upon the sinner against his will, while making satisfaction is something we *freely* undertake to restore a broken relationship with somebody: grieving for the offense we committed we are anxious to become reconciled with or make satisfaction to our friend (cf. *ST* III.85.3 *ad* 3 and *ST* III.84.5 *ad* 2). Hence, for Thomas, as for Anselm, satisfaction excludes punishment. Incidentally, the language of friendship Thomas uses here suggests that he does not subscribe to a judicial or legalistic paradigm for understanding salvation. This is further confirmed by the link between the satisfaction Christ makes on the Cross and the sacrament of penance (cf. *ScG* IV.72.14).[67] Given the fact that penance is described as "a spiritual healing of a sort" (*ScG* IV.72.1) or "a spiritual medicine" (*ST* III.84.10 *ad* 5) and that sin is called "a sickness of the soul" (*infirmitas animae*) in *ST* I–II.88.1, it is clear that "making satisfaction" too should be understood in medicinal terms. It comes therefore as no surprise to find that Thomas describes Christ as a doctor (in *ST* III.49.1 *ad* 3): these metaphors of course reveal a world of difference: whereas a judge punishes, a doctor heals.

---

[66] *CT* I.200, trans. C. Vollert as *The Light of Faith: The Compendium of Theology* (Manchester: Sophia Institute Press, 1993), 229–30. See also *ScG* IV.54.9 and *ST* III.48.2.

[67] The sacrament of penance consists of three elements: confession, contrition and making satisfaction (see *ScG* IV.72). It is only the element of making satisfaction (*satisfactio*) that applies to Christ's redemptive activity through the union with his members (see *ST* III.48.2 *ad* 1).

The second major difference between punishment and making satisfaction is that one person can make satisfaction for *another* if the two are united in *charity* (*ScG* III.158.7 and *ST* III.48.2 *ad* 1). By drawing on the Pauline notion of the Church as the mystical Body of Christ (*ST* III.49.1; III.48.2 *ad* 1), Thomas argues that Christ's saving activity benefits all the faithful. I will come back to this important point.

Some readers might perhaps be wondering whether Thomas's soteriology is not excessively subjectivist: has the Cross actually made an objective difference in the world? Undoubtedly, as Abelard had done before him, Thomas puts a strong emphasis upon our need to somehow "appropriate" the saving work of Christ: Christ's Passion, which is a kind of universal cause of merit and the forgiveness of sins, needs to be applied to each individual for the cleansing of personal sins (*ST* III.49.1 *ad* 4). Similarly, as a doctor prepares a medicine we still need to apply it through faith, love and the sacraments of the Church (cf. *ST* III.49.1 *ad* 3; *ST* III.49.3 *ad* 1). However, although there is undoubtedly a strong personalist or subjectivist element to Thomas's soteriology, this should not be taken to imply that the saving work of Christ has nothing to do with the restoration of justice in "objective" terms. The order of the world, as created by God, was distorted by sin. This needs to be rectified, and if it had not been for Christ's saving work this distortion and alienation would have been perpetuated indefinitely (an alienation that would involve, according to Thomas, the punishments of hell). In that sense there is something "objectively" changed in the world. Sin cannot have the last word: it needs to be cancelled out by the overarching mercy of God.

The restoration of the order of justice in the world should not be taken to mean, as is sometimes alleged, that God somehow subjects his mercy to his justice in the redemptive work of Christ. In agreement with Anselm, Thomas argues that in the divine self-gift that is the life and death of Christ divine mercy and justice are in perfect harmony with one another (*ST* III.46.1 *ad* 3).[68]

Perhaps the reader might ask: Is it appropriate to attribute saving significance to the suffering of an innocent man? Should we not see the Cross for what it is, a horrible crime inflicted upon a defenseless victim, rather than the way in which God reconciles the world? Thomas, however,

---

[68] Also, when we speak of an "objective" dimension of Thomas's soteriology we mean that something is changed in the world – not in God. Thomas, like other medieval theologians before him, rejects the view that God is somehow "changed" by the life and death of Christ (cf. *ST* III.1.1 *ad* 1): the Cross is the expression and manifestation of God's love, not the cause of it (*ST* III.49.4 *ad* 2).

argues that this is a false dilemma. Given his understanding of providential care and divine causality, which implies that God is such a powerful efficacious Cause that he can attain his goals by genuinely contingent events (cf. *ST* 1.19.8; *ScG* III.72), Thomas suggests that it is not incoherent to state that the slaying of Christ was a most grievous sin, and yet in accordance – on a more transcendent level, if you like – with God's providential plan (cf. *ST* III.47.4 *ad* 2; *ST* III.47.3 *ad* 1).

Of course God could have forgiven us without Christ's saving work, but this would have been less "fitting" (cf. *ST* III.46.1 and 3). Examining the reasons why this is the case reveals a lot about how much Thomas values human dignity and the reciprocity of the relationship between humanity and God: if we had simply been forgiven by a divine *fiat* we would not have been allowed to participate, through Christ and in union with him (as members of his Body), in the restoration of our relationship with God (i.e., making satisfaction) (cf. *ScG* IV.54.8).

At any rate, salvation does not originate from Christ's sufferings as such but rather from what these sufferings reveal: his obedience and love. Thus, not the sufferings per se but the willingness with which Christ took them upon himself are a source of merit that can be shared with all the faithful (see *ST* III.48.1; *ScG* IV.55, 25–26). The emphasis upon the voluntary nature of Christ's saving activity allows Thomas to state in *ST* III.48.4 that making satisfaction needs to be understood in terms of a *gift of self* by Christ (*Christus autem satisfecit . . . dando . . . seipsum*). This is an important observation for two reasons: first, it dispels the specter of a revengeful God and instead reveals a self-giving God (cf. *In Rom.* 5:8–9, no. 399). And second, it teaches us something about the way we should approach our own afflictions – that is, we should refrain from attributing any intrinsic value to them as such; rather, if borne with obedience and love, they can become an occasion for us to become more Christlike. I now discuss this theme of our participation in Christ's redemptive work as members of his Body.

Our Participation in Christ as Members of His Body

The key presupposition governing Thomas's soteriology, and to which I have alluded a number of times, is the intimate union between Christ and his faithful. This element, which Anselm left underdeveloped in his work *Cur Deus Homo*, receives major attention in Thomas's exposition. In *ST* III.48.2 *ad* 1 we read, for instance: "The head and members are as one mystic person; and therefore Christ's satisfaction belongs to all the faithful as being his members" (see also *ST* III.8.1 and a.3). Similarly, in *ST* III.49.1, dealing with the issue of how we have been redeemed from sin by the Passion of Christ, Thomas writes:

For since he is our head, then, by the Passion which he endured from love and obedience, he delivered us as his members from our sins, as by the price of his Passion: in the same way as if a man by the good industry of his hands were to redeem himself from a sin committed with his feet. For, just as the natural body is one, though made up of diverse members, so the whole Church, Christ's mystic body (*mysticum corpus Christi*), is reckoned as one person with its head, which is Christ.

This does not simply mean that Christ is in union with us; it also means that we are in union with Christ. Thus, it is not just the case that Christ suffers for us, but also our own sufferings can be seen as a sharing in those of Christ. Commenting on John 20:21 Thomas writes: "He [= Christ] says *As the Father has sent me, so too I sent you*, which means: as the Father who loves me has sent me in the world to suffer the Passion for the salvation of the faithful . . . so too I love you, and I send you to endure tribulations for my sake" (*Comm. Jn* no. 2527). The view that our own sufferings are a way of becoming more Christlike was a prominent theme amongst the early Church Fathers. As I noted in Chapter 2, Augustine had put it at the heart of his *Exposition on the Psalms* and had even claimed that the risen Christ himself continues to suffer in the members of his Body, the Church. Although Thomas does not go as far as stating that the risen Christ continues to suffer in his members, Thomas does adopt the notion that our sufferings can be interpreted as a means of growing in conformity with Christ. In *ScG* IV.55.28, for instance, when dealing with the objection that it seems odd to claim that Christ saved us while death and other penalties are still with us, he writes that the afflictions that remain allow us to achieve conformity to Christ as members to the head:

It was both fitting and useful to have the penalty remain even when the fault was taken away. First, indeed, to achieve conformity of the faithful to Christ as members to the head; hence, just as Christ bore many sufferings, and thus arrived at the glory of immortality, it was also becoming to his faithful first to undergo sufferings and so to arrive at immortality, bearing in themselves, so to say, the marks of the passion of Christ, in order to achieve likeness to his glory. So the Apostle says: "Heirs, indeed of God, and joint-heirs with Christ: yet so, if we suffer with him, that we might also be glorified with him" (Rom 8:17).[69]

---

[69] *ScG* IV.55.28.

Thus Christ does not take away our afflictions here and now. Rather, we should regard our continuing afflictions as a way of sharing in his saving work, and as a way of becoming more Christlike (cf. *ST* III.49.3 *ad* 3; *ST* III.79.2 *ad* 1; *ST* I–II.85.5 *ad* 2; *ST* III.56.1 *ad* 1; *In Rom.* 8:17 no. 651). Although Thomas does not share the view that the risen Christ continues to suffer in the members of his Body, he does make room for the notion that Christ's saving work continues for all eternity. He does so by developing the idea of Christ's eternal priesthood and by pointing out the significance of the sacramental economy.

The Priesthood of Christ, Sacrifice and the Lord's Supper

As suggested earlier, in the *ST* Thomas retains the notion of making satisfaction, but he now also pays attention to a number of other concepts to describe the saving work of Christ, including "sacrifice" (cf. *ST* III.48.3). This concept has two advantages: it is more biblical, and it allows Thomas to link in a more cohesive manner the sacrifice of Christ on the Cross with the sacramental economy (especially the Eucharist; cf. *ST* III. 83.1, but also *ST* III.63.6 *ad* 1). This connection is strengthened by Augustine's definition of sacrifice from Book x of *De Civ. Dei*, which Thomas repeatedly quotes (*ST* III.22.2; III.48. 3 *obj.* 2; III.60.1; II–II.81.7 *ad* 2): "The visible sacrifice is the sacrament, i.e., the sacred sign, of the invisible sacrifice." This text proves fruitful for a number of reasons. First, as I have already noted, it reiterates the view that saving value is not to be found in Christ's sufferings as such but rather in the obedience and love they manifest: it is not the external but the interior sacrifice that matters. Second, it makes clear how the faithful can share in this sacrifice by offering themselves up, mirroring the self-gift of Christ, as we saw in the previous section (cf. *In Rom.* 12:1–2, nos. 957–67; *ST* II–II.85.2; *ST* II–II.85.3 *ad* 2; *In Eph.* 5:2, no. 270). Third, this offering is continued in the sacrament of the Lord's Supper, which contains "Christ crucified" (*ST* III.73.5 *ad* 2) and is called "Christ's sacrifice" (*ST* III.83.1). Let me examine this connection between Christ's sacrifice on the Cross and during the sacrifice of Mass in more detail.

When discussing the priesthood of Christ, Thomas, again quoting Augustine, points out that Christ was both priest and offering (*ST* III.22.2). A priest is a mediator between God and the people, somebody who bestows divine things upon the people:[70] as priest Christ freely offers himself to suffer on our behalf. Through this sacrifice of Christ we become

---

[70] *Sacerdos* (priest) is derived from *sacra dans*, to give sacred things, as Thomas explains in *ST* III.22.1.

reconciled with God and partakers of the divine nature (*ST* III.22.1).[71] As we will see, Thomas attributes the same benefits to the Lord's Supper.

The notions of sacrifice and priesthood allow Thomas to cover the same material as that covered by the notion of *satisfactio*, and sometimes his terminology reverts to "making satisfaction" when discussing priesthood.[72] All the faithful, for instance, can participate in the priesthood of Christ through faith and love, and by offering themselves up (*ST* III.82.1 *ad* 2).[73] The notions of sacrifice and priesthood, however, open up a number of vistas that had been left unexplored in the theory of satisfaction. Drawing on *The Letter to the Hebrews*, Thomas states, for instance, that Christ's priesthood lasts eternally (*ST* III.22.5) and that the resurrected Christ still carries the scars of his Passion, so as to allow him to intercede on our behalf with the Father for all eternity (*ST* III.54.4). However, it is especially in the Lord's Supper that the saving efficacy of Christ's sacrifice on the Cross is continued.

In a beautiful article (*ST* III.73.4), Thomas makes clear that the Lord's Supper has a threefold significance. In relation to the past it is a *sacrifice*, commemorative of the Passion of our Lord; in relation to the present, it establishes union amongst the faithful through participation in Christ, and is therefore called *communion*; in relation to the future, it is called *Eucharist* or Viaticum: this is the eschatological meaning, referring to the fact that it anticipates the union with God we will enjoy in heaven, a foreshadowing of our enjoyment of God in the afterlife (*hoc sacramentum est praefigurativum fruitionis Dei*). Thus, in the Lord's Supper, we receive grace (*Eucharistia*, meaning good grace, *bona gratia*), the Church as the Body of Christ is constituted (*communio*), and the sacrifice Christ offered on Calvary is reenacted for the forgiveness of sins (*sacrificium*). Through the Lord's Supper the Church as the Body of Christ is established and Christ's saving deeds become universally present. As Thomas puts it in his *Commentary on John*:

Because this sacrament is that of the Passion of our Lord, it contains within itself the suffering of Christ; therefore, all the beneficiary effects of the Passion of our

---

[71] Christ's priesthood fulfills the priesthood of the Old Testament in its threefold aspect – namely, as offerings for sins, peace offerings and burnt offerings (*ST* III.22.2). For an illuminating discussion as to how Christ fulfills the hopes of Israel, see Matthew Levering, *Christ's Fulfillment of Torah and Temple: Salvation According to Thomas Aquinas* (Notre Dame, IN: University of Notre Dame Press, 2002).

[72] For instance, in *ST* III.22.1 we find that Christ in his role as priest is the mediator who "offers up the people's prayers to God, and, in a manner, makes satisfaction to God for their sins" (*et pro eorum peccatis Deo aliqualiter satisfacit*). Similarly, *ST* III.22.3.

[73] See the brilliant contribution by Gilles Emery, "Le Sacerdoce Spirituel des Fidèles chez Saint Thomas d'Aquin," *Revue Thomiste* 99 (1999): 211–43.

Lord reside plentifully in this sacrament. This sacrament is nothing else but the Passion of our Lord that is communicated to us. . . . The destruction of death that Christ has effected by his death and the renewal of life that he effected through his resurrection are also the effects of this sacrament. (*Comm. Jn.* no. 963)[74]

Commenting on John 6:54 Thomas states that through the Eucharistic food we become Christlike; it is the Eucharistic food that transforms us into Christ, makes us members of his Body, deifies us and inebriates us with the divinity (*Comm. Jn.* nos. 972). Because the Word resides in this sacrament according to his divinity and his humanity, it is the cause of our spiritual and bodily resurrection (nos. 972–73).

Conclusion

This is a balanced and beautiful soteriology, utterly faithful to the biblical witness; it does justice to the reality of sin, the need to tackle the disorder it causes and the overwhelming mercy of God. Given the sacramental understanding of Christ, it is Thomas's view that every aspect of Christ's life, death and resurrection has saving meaning. The salvation Christ effected, particularly through his redeeming death, continues to reside in the sacraments, especially in the Lord's Supper, through which the Church is established as one Body. This notion of the Church as the Body of Christ is pivotal in everything Thomas has to say about how we appropriate the salvation Christ accomplished. This suggests the organic unity of Thomas's views on Christ's saving activity and his sacramentology.

BIBLIOGRAPHICAL NOTE

Thomas's *Opera Omnia* are available online at www.corpusthomisticum. org. The Aquinas Institute in Wyoming is in the process of publishing Thomas's *Opera Omnia* in an attractive bilingual edition. It has also made it available online. See https://aquinasinstitute.org/operaomnia. For Thomas Aquinas's *ST*, see Thomas Aquinas, *Summa Theologiae*, Latin Text and English translation, 61 vols. (London: Blackfriars, 1964), which has been reissued by Cambridge University Press. I have used the translation entitled *Summa Theologica* (5 vols.), by the Fathers of the Dominican Province (Westminster, MD: Christian Classics, 1981), widely available online.

[74] My translation. A similar view in *ST* III.73.5 *ad* 2: "The Eucharist is the perfect sacrament of our Lord's Passion, as containing Christ crucified."

An excellent introduction to Thomas's thought is Brian Davies, *The Thought of Thomas Aquinas* (Oxford: Clarendon, 1992). A useful theological reading can be found in Nicholas Healy, *Thomas Aquinas: Theologian of the Christian Life* (Burlington: Ashgate, 2003). A collection of essays covering every aspect of Thomas's theology can be found in Rik Van Nieuwenhove and Joseph Wawrykow (eds.), *The Theology of Thomas Aquinas* (Notre Dame, IN: University of Notre Dame Press, 2005). Also helpful are Brian Davies and Eleonore Stump (eds.), *The Oxford Handbook of Aquinas* (Oxford: Oxford University Press, 2011) and Philip McCosker and Denys Turner (eds.), *The Cambridge Companion to the Summa Theologiae* (Cambridge: Cambridge University Press, 2016).

CHAPTER 19

The Condemnations of 1277

As we saw in Chapter 13, the works of Aristotle were translated (from Greek or from Arabic translations) during the 12th century and the first half of the 13th century in Sicily and Toledo. From the middle of the 13th century, the works of Aristotle were a well-established part of the academic curriculum in Paris and elsewhere, despite initial (and recurring) reservations about Averroism. Some of these concerns were raised in the 1270s.

A first official reaction occurred on December 10, 1270, when Etienne Tempier, the bishop of Paris, condemned thirteen propositions as opposed to the Christian faith. The key issues were monopsychism (the teaching that there is only one intellect for the human race – i.e., the divine intellect); the denial of individual immortality, which follows from monopsychism; denial of freedom of will; the doctrine of the eternity of the world (Aristotle, like other Greek thinkers, was not familiar with the notion of a world created out of nothing); and the denial of God's knowledge of individual things and hence of Providence.

This initial condemnation had little impact, and Pope John XXI requested Tempier to examine the situation at the Parisian university in more depth. Instead of producing a report as requested, Tempier actually issued a condemnation on March 7, 1277 – significantly, three years to the day after Thomas Aquinas's death. The condemnation consisted of 219 erroneous propositions. Apart from a number of specific theses lifted from the work of Averroes, Aristotle, Siger of Brabant and Thomas Aquinas, the document takes issue in general terms with the *Diesseitigkeit* of the new climate and the way the new Aristotelian science threatens Christian faith and theology in general. The first condemned proposition reads, "That there is no more excellent state than to study philosophy." The second claims "That the only wise men in the world are philosophers." The fifth contends "That man should not be content with authority to have certitude about any question." Others state "That happiness is in this life and not in another" (172); "That the Christian law impedes learning" (180);

"That there are fables and falsehoods in the Christian law just as in others" (181); and "That the teachings of the theologian are based on fables" (183). The final erroneous proposition (216) reads: "That a philosopher must not concede the resurrection to come, because it cannot be investigated by reason." The document goes on to comment: "This is erroneous because even a philosopher must bring his mind in captivity to the obedience of Christ (cf. 2 Cor. 10:5)."[1]

In the past, scholars may have exaggerated the impact of the 1277 Condemnations. The view that it caused the decline of Aristotelian influence and paved the way for modern science has been discredited.[2] It was not the first time the use of Aristotle had been condemned in Paris (also in 1210 and 1215), nor did it result in the decline of the influence of Aristotelianism in the schools, as the example of John Duns Scotus makes clear. In short, it has been argued that the Condemnations led to the rise of voluntarism and nominalism and ultimately paved the way for the rise of the modern sciences and our secular world as we know it today. In an important article, however, Peter Harrison has argued that the traditional link between voluntarism and the emergence of science simply does not hold. There were empiricists who were rationalists and voluntarists who were not empiricists. He reformulates the thesis of the link between voluntarism and the sciences as saying something about the limitations of human intellect rather than about the arbitrary nature of God.[3]

This is an important nuance, for it makes clear that the real issue was not voluntarism as such but rather the decline of confidence in reason to engage in metaphysical pursuits. The split between faith and reason as we have come to know it in modernity is not the result of voluntarism and nominalism; it is the other way around: the critique of natural reason (in response to the perceived impact of peripatetic philosophy) led to growing metaphysical skepticism, voluntarism and nominalism. Thus the Condemnations of 1277 both expressed and contributed to a different theological climate in which there was a growing awareness of the limitations of metaphysics in its dialogue with theology. Theologians in the 14th century still use reason and philosophy in their theological writings.

---

[1] Translation from *Philosophy in the Middle Ages: The Christian, Islamic and Jewish Traditions*, ed. Arthur Hyman and James Walsh (Indianapolis, IN: Hackett, 1973), 584–91. For a discussion of the Condemnation and its context, see John Wippel, "The Condemnation of 1270 and 1277 at Paris," *Journal of Medieval and Renaissance Studies* 7 (1977): 169–201.

[2] See Jason Gooch, "The Effects of the Condemnation of 1277," *Hilltop Review* 2 (2006): 34–44.

[3] See Peter Harrison, "Voluntarism and Early Modern Science," *History of Science* 40 (2002): 63–89.

Hence, it is too sweeping a claim that a separation of faith and reason occurs. Nonetheless, there are differences. First, philosophical argumentation becomes more logical and semantic rather than metaphysical. Also, and related to this, theological writings are less systematic but prefer to consider distinct aspects from Peter Lombard's *Sentences*. Finally, reason employed appears decidedly more analytical rather than synthetic-intellective. It is this kind of analytical mindset that at times results in skepticism regarding the claims of theology and a tendency to rely on revelation and faith more than upon philosophical reasoning to determine the truth of theological conclusions.

The condemnation of the use of Aristotle in the Arts Faculty in Paris was repeated ten days later by Robert Kilwardby, Archbishop of Canterbury, at the University of Oxford. John Peckham, a Franciscan successor to Kilwardby, reiterated the condemnation in 1286, targeting the teachings of Thomas Aquinas and his followers (Richard Klapwell), labeling them as "heresies." In an invaluable letter, Peckham allies himself to the thought of Alexander and Bonaventure who, in Peckham's view, remained faithful to the thought of Augustine, in marked contrast to Thomas Aquinas and others. The reference to the Augustinianism of Bonaventure is revealing: those who opposed the influence of Aristotle's new learning aligned themselves explicitly with Bonaventure:

Which doctrine is more solid and more sound, the doctrine of the sons of Saint Francis, that is, of Brother Alexander (of Hales) of sainted memory, of Brother Bonaventure and others like him, who rely on the Fathers and the philosophers in treatises secure against any reproach, or else that very recent and almost entirely contrary doctrine, which fills the entire world with wordy quarrels, weakening and destroying with all its strength what Augustine teaches?[4]

It is certainly ironic that the conservative reaction of 1277 contributed to the double truth theory, which was rejected by Stephen Tempier, and which is very much part of the modern outlook (due to the influence of Kant, which finds a theological response, faithful to the Kantian presuppositions, in the work of Karl Barth and others). In short, I suggest that the Bonaventurean attack upon natural reason had two historical consequences, both unintentional: first, as indicated, his stance, reinforced by other theologians (not all of them Franciscans) after him, resulted in a gradual severing of links between theology and metaphysics – although

---

[4] *Registrum Epistolarum Fratris Johannis Peckham Archiepiscopi Cantuariensis*, 3 vols., ed. C. T. Martin (London, 1882), III.871, quoted in Etienne Gilson, *History of Christian Philosophy in the Middle Ages* (London: Sheed and Ward, 1980), 359.

Bonaventure's explicit goal was just the opposite – that is, to draw philosophy into the ambit of grace and theology. Again, this will lead to a different notion of reason that is less intellective, less porous to faith, more immanent and empirically minded and more concerned with philosophy of language and logic rather than with attempts to build an encompassing theological system. This becomes especially evident amongst English thinkers in the 14th century.

A second unintended consequence, related to this, is the growing separation of spirituality and theology. Scholars have noticed how from 1300 onward few theological scholars are saints, and vice versa.[5] An entirely satisfactory historical account has not been forthcoming. In my view, the growing separation of theology and spirituality should be partly attributed to the skepticism of reason, which finds its origins in Bonaventure's stance against the new peripatetic learning. In a climate in which theology and metaphysics are becoming increasingly disengaged, and in which theology itself becomes more analytical and focused on issues of epistemology and language, voluntarism and a more affective spirituality severed from theological discourse begin to take root. Hence, whereas Bonaventure himself attempts to bring theology and spirituality together, the attack upon natural reason and peripatetic philosophy throughout his later works (such as *Hexameron*) will actually result in the 14th century in the growing separation of spirituality from an allegedly cerebral theology that appears increasingly more concerned with technical and logical (sub)problems rather than with systematic attempts to fathom the mystery of God.

---

[5] See Hans Urs von Balthasar, "Theology and Sanctity," in *Explorations in Theology, vol. 1: The Word Made Flesh* (San Francisco: Ignatius Press, 1989), 181–209.

CHAPTER 20

John Duns Scotus

INTRODUCTION

John Duns Scotus (ca. 1266–1308) is widely regarded as the last major thinker of the golden age of 13th-century scholasticism. In many ways, he is a pivotal figure, both reflecting the end of the classic age of scholasticism and inaugurating some of the new trends that were to come to fruition in the thought of his fellow Franciscan, William of Ockham. We know little enough about his life. As his name suggests, he was from Duns, in the south of Scotland. He was ordained in Northampton on March 17, 1291, which allows us to conclude that he was probably born circa 1266. Around 1298–99, while at Oxford, he prepared a first set of lectures on Peter Lombard's *Sentences*. This set of lectures is known as the *Lectura*. Scotus thoroughly revised this work throughout his short life, and the revised version is known as the *Ordinatio*. Between 1302 and 1303, Scotus lectured in Paris, and student notes on Book 1 corrected by Scotus himself have survived as "The Examined Report of the Paris Lectures" (*Reportatio Examinata Parisiensis*).[1] It is effectively a third version of his commentary on the *Sentences*. Scotus also wrote a *Treatise on God As the First Principle* (*De Primo Principio*), probably written around 1305, as well as commentaries on a number of Aristotle's works. Of these, his *Commentary on Metaphysics* is the most important one. Scotus went to Cologne in 1307, where he died in November 1308.

---

[1] A bilingual edition (Latin-English) of *Reportatio I–A* (a commentary on the first book of the *Sentences*) has been published in two volumes by Allan B. Wolter and Oleg Bychkov (eds.) as *John Duns Scotus: The Examined Report of the Paris Lecture. Reportatio I–A* (New York: Franciscan Institute, 2004 and 2008). As this work represents a relatively late and fairly polished version of Scotus's theology, it is my primary source for some of the material discussed in this chapter, and I use it when quoting.

Reading Scotus is no easy matter. First, until recently critical editions of his major writings were not available. Moreover, as indicated, Scotus repeatedly commented on Peter Lombard's *Sentences*, often revising his views. His early death prevented him from achieving a finished theological synthesis, which further complicates the task of interpretation. Moreover, Scotus was a technical thinker who developed complex metaphysical and theological arguments by rigorously applying Aristotelian logic. His writings can therefore strike the modern reader as dry and overly complex. The fact that Scotus's surviving writings hardly ever directly engage with or quote from the Bible does little to dispel this impression. Another complicating factor is that, throughout his works, Duns Scotus often enters into dialogue with authors who may not be particularly well known today outside a select field of scholars. His main interlocutors are not Thomas Aquinas or Bonaventure but Henry of Ghent, Godfrey of Fontaines and a number of others.

Finally, a proper evaluation of Scotus's contribution is hindered by certain simplifications and presuppositions operative in contemporary theology. John Duns Scotus is often disparaged as the author responsible for the start of the decline of medieval scholasticism, who expressed views that eventually resulted in the modern climate. In Hans Urs von Balthasar's estimation, for instance, Duns Scotus should be regarded as the first of the truly modern authors, whose univocal understanding of being (which I explain shortly) led to the modern, secular, positivist and immanent worldview.[2] Again, as his critics see it, Scotus introduced an arbitrary view of freedom (voluntarism), which was later adopted by William of Ockham. In what follows, I examine Scotus's views on theology and philosophy, his understanding of univocity and his voluntarism. I also briefly discuss some elements of his Trinitarian theology, his Christology and his Mariology (where he made his most influential contribution).

PHILOSOPHY AND THEOLOGY

The thought of John Duns Scotus can be best characterized as "transitional" in relation to the Condemnations of the late 13th century. Unlike 14th-century thinkers, Scotus is not skeptical of the claims of reason within the realm of metaphysics and he does not shy away from metaphysical speculation. On the contrary, he can be rightly called one of the most

---

[2] See Hans Urs von Balthasar, *The Glory of the Lord*, vol. v (San Francisco: Ignatius Press, 1991), 6–28.

metaphysically minded thinkers of the 13th century. But his understanding
of the relation between theology and philosophy is different from that of
Thomas Aquinas. Even more so than Thomas had done, Scotus makes
a very clear distinction, if not separation, between theology and metaphysics. For him, good fences between theology and metaphysics make good
neighbors.

For starters, theology and metaphysics have *a different subject*. The
subject of theology is God; the subject of metaphysics is being.[3] Given
the fact that metaphysics deals with being as being, and theology with God,
a clear distinction, if not separation, between theology and metaphysics is
implied.

Metaphysics does not just have its own distinct subject but it also has
its *own source of knowledge*: metaphysics draws on natural reason while
theology relies on revelation.[4] The contrast with Thomas is more radical
than may appear at first. As we saw in Chapter 18, for Thomas, theology is
scientific insofar as it is based on participation in divine (self-)knowledge
(*scientia*). Thus, for Thomas, theology is a subaltern science – that is,
subordinate to God's own knowledge. Scotus explicitly rejects the
Thomist account. How can theology be a science if it is based on principles
that are accepted only on the basis of faith?[5] Second, Scotus questions the
usefulness of subalternation, arguing that there is no causal link between
the knowledge or theology of the blessed, and "our theology":

The knowledge which the blessed have about God as both triune and one is not
essentially a cause of our theology, because [their knowledge gives us] neither our
intellective power nor the object known to us. For I do not rely on their knowledge
in order to know God to be triune. Hence, the knowledge of the blessed is not
a cause of our science about God. And thus our science does not depend upon
the science of the blessed as subordinate upon a superior science, and no one is
said to know theology because its principles are known scientifically by the blessed.
Indeed, it would be similar if one were to claim: "I know geometry because
I believe that, by virtue of you knowing geometry, I possess the science of
geometry."[6]

William of Ockham was later to express his reservations about the scientific
nature of theology along similar lines.

---

[3] *Rep. Par. I–A*, Prol. q.3 no. 218 (p. 76): "God is not the subject of metaphysics."
[4] *Rep. Par. I–A*, Prol. q.3 nos. 226–27 (pp. 79–80).
[5] See *ST* 1.1.1 and 2: "Sacred science is established on principles revealed by God." *Rep. Par. I–A*, Prol.
q.2 no. 149; *Ox. Prol.* q.1 no. 30; for Scotus's views on how faith and science relate to one another, see
Rep. Par. I–A, Prol. q.2 nos. 173–74.
[6] *Rep. Par. I–A*, Prol. q.2 no. 152 (p. 55).

Theology, insofar as it is based on revelation and not on deductive demonstration, is not a science in the strict sense. As Scotus puts it in *Rep. Par. I–A*, "It does not have the character of science because it does not have such evidence from the object as the scientifically known does through demonstration, which is required per se for the notion of science according to Book I of the *Posterior Analytics*."[7] Theology does not deal with necessary things, which is an essential aspect of Aristotelian science. Creation and Incarnation, for instance, are contingent events and therefore not necessary. Also, given that the object of theology is not evident to our intelligence but to faith, the conclusions drawn from principles of faith are not scientific in the strict sense but belong to the order of faith.[8]

Following Bonaventure, Scotus argues that theology is more practical than speculative.[9] After all, its goal is a loving union with God. Love of God is more important than speculative knowledge of God. This signals a well-known bias of Scotus: the primacy of love and will over intellect.

While allocating theology and metaphysics their own distinct areas of investigation Scotus has nonetheless more confidence in human reason than many later authors would have. He argues, for instance, that we can philosophically prove the existence of God through natural reason. Similarly, metaphysics can demonstrate a number of the divine attributes, such as God's infinity, oneness, supremacy, eternity and goodness. Other attributes, such as God's providence, mercifulness, omnipresence and omnipotence are, however, the object of belief and cannot be shown by natural reason.[10] Before I deal with this I would like to come back to the subject matter of metaphysics – that is, being as being.

METAPHYSICS AND THE UNIVOCAL CONCEPT OF BEING

As we saw in a previous chapter, Thomas's teaching on analogy presupposes a harmonious coexistence of faith and reason, theology and philosophy. For Scotus, writing after the Condemnations of 1277, theology and philosophy are effectively separate. This will have repercussions for the way

---

[7] *Rep. Par. I–A*, Prol. q.2 no. 208 (pp. 73–74). For an outline of the four conditions of science, see *Rep. Par. I–A*, Prol. q.1 nos. 8–14 (pp. 2–4).

[8] Scotus is willing to call theology a science in a derivative sense, insofar as it is certain, and insofar as it uses syllogistic deduction: "Theology is the science of truths contained in the Holy Scriptures and of those truths which can be obtained by way of systematic deduction." But it is not a science in the full sense of the word: *Ordin.* Prol. p. 3 q. 1–3, no. 204.

[9] *Ordin.* Prol. p. 5 q.1–2.

[10] *De Prim. Princ.*, 4.86; for omnipotence, see *Rep. Par. I–A*, d.42 q.1 nos. 13–14 (p. 512).

he views analogy. Indeed, in Scotus's view, analogy (especially in the version that Henry of Ghent proposed) does away with the possibility of metaphysics. If there is no bridge between creation and God, all our metaphysical talk about God becomes invalid. This is why Scotus has to insist on the univocity of being. Let me attempt to clarify this.

For Scotus (*Ordin.* 1 d.3 p.1 q.1–2 no. 26), we have univocity when we cannot affirm and deny something about the same thing. Scotus is inspired by the Aristotelian principle *eadem est scientia oppositorum*: affirmations and their corresponding negations are one and the same knowledge. Something ("p") is univocally predicated when "p" and "not-p" are contradictories. Thus, for Scotus, we have univocity when to affirm and to deny something of the same subject amounts to a contradiction.[11] If "God is being" and "God is not-being" are contradictory statements, then "God" is used in a univocal manner.[12] In short, words are univocal when they have the same meaning.[13]

In accordance with the medieval tradition, Scotus denies that God and being are in the same genus. He does, however, affirm that being is univocally predicated of God and beings. "The concept of being affirmed of God is . . . univocally common to him and to a creature."[14] There is "a common concept" (*aliquis communis conceptus*) that can be affirmed of God and creatures.[15] This concept is being, and "it applies to everything that is not nothing" (*se extendit ad quodcumque quod non est nihil*) – that is, God and creatures.[16] This is an empty, abstract and contentless concept, and it can therefore be "filled in" in radically different ways. The major difference Scotus identifies is between finite (or creaturely) being and infinite (or divine) being. When the univocal concept of being is joined with another notion (e.g., goodness) the resulting notion only applies to God, and is therefore not univocal anymore. As Scotus puts it:

"Being" is a simply simple concept affirmed of God and a creature; this concept, qualified by means of some other equally common concept, such as goodness, actuality, and necessary existence, simultaneously joined to it, is proper to God

---

[11] See Denys Turner, *Faith, Reason and the Existence of God* (Cambridge: Cambridge University Press, 2005), 127.

[12] Compare Richard Cross, *Duns Scotus* (Oxford: Oxford University Press, 1999), 168.

[13] If we delve deeper into the definition it becomes somewhat puzzling. After all, the whole issue of analogy and univocation is not about the same subject but rather about the meaning of perfections when ascribed to two subjects – namely, God and creatures. An example will clarify this. Scotus allows us to say that if "God is Being" and "God is not Being" are contradictories, then "God" is used univocally. A Thomist would object that the real issue of analogy relates to applying a term (such as "goodness") to two subjects (God and creation: "Creatures are good" and "God is good"), not one.

[14] *Rep. Par. I–A*, d.3 q.1 no. 32 (p. 194).   [15] *Rep. Par. I–A*, d.3 q.1 nos. 40–41 (p. 196).

[16] *Op. Ox.* 1 d.3 q.2 no. 4; d. 8 q.3 no. 14.

and inapplicable to any creature (*proprius Deo et nulli creaturae conveniens*): e.g., "a being that is good, pure act and has necessary existence" is God. And this is just about as proper a concept as we can have of him in this life.[17]

"Being" when predicated of God and creatures abstracts from all modes of being and retains only the nature of being as such. In actual existence, however, being is not univocal but analogous: creaturely being is not univocally predicated of God's being.[18] Take the example of wisdom: infinite wisdom is not actualized in God in the same way as wisdom is actualized in creatures. Indeed, wisdom in God and creatures is actualized in an analogous manner, not a univocal manner. Scotus's theory of univocity claims that we need univocal concepts to speak of God. The univocity theory is a semantic or cognitive rather than a metaphysical theory.[19]

Infinite being is a concept that best captures God's nature for us. Infinity is not an accidental addition to being (which would compromise the simplicity of God's being), but it is a mode of being. A comparison will clarify what Scotus has in mind. We can distinguish between different kinds of color (green, red, yellow), which are all different kinds of light. However, we can also increase the intensity of light (weaker or stronger). Infinite being, for Scotus, is an infinite degree or modality of being (infinitely strong light) – but this does not impact the kind of light we understand it to be.[20] What Scotus is trying to make clear is that the modality or degree of being can be intensified (from finite to infinite) without impacting the univocity of the concept of being. "Being" is still used in a univocal manner, just as "light" is used in a univocal manner when speaking of a weak light or an infinitely intense light.

Scotus espouses univocity of being in order to avoid all theological statements becoming equivocal.[21] In his view, denying this univocal core at the heart of analogy can only result in equivocation – that is, our language about God becomes effectively meaningless, which would render both theology and metaphysics null and void.[22]

---

[17] *Rep. Par. I–A*, d.3 q.1 no. 46 (p. 197).

[18] Armand Maurer, *Medieval Philosophy* (Toronto: Pontifical Institute of Medieval Studies, 1982), 228.

[19] Richard Cross, *Duns Scotus on God* (Aldershot: Ashgate, 2005), 254.

[20] As Scotus puts it in *Rep. Par. I–A*, d.45 q.2 no. 34 (p. 549), speaking of the infinity of the divine will: "A specific mode or degree of any whatsoever entity or quiddity does not destroy the notion of this entity, but preserves and accentuates it. Therefore, 'infinity' added to the will does not destroy the latter's formal notion, but indicates a specific degree of its power that is intrinsic to it." See also: *Op. Ox.* 1 d.3 q.1 art. 4 no. 17.

[21] Cross, *Duns Scotus*, 34–35.

[22] *Lect.* 1 d.3 p. 1 q. 1–2 no. 113. It is revealing that Scotus at times seems to identify analogy and equivocation. For instance, in *Lect.* 1 d.3 p. 1 q.1–2 no. 25, he writes: "If a concept attributed to God

Scotus's theory of univocity implies that a number of concepts apply to both God and creatures: first and foremost being, but also other perfections such as goodness, wisdom, justice and so forth. As I pointed out earlier, this does not commit him to the view that being, wisdom and goodness are actualized in a univocal way in God and creatures. On the contrary, their actualization would be a case of analogy: in infinite being and wisdom, for instance, "being" and "wisdom" are used analogously in comparison to finite being and wisdom.

In contemporary theological literature, Thomas's theory of analogy is often favorably contrasted with Scotus's theory of univocity. We need to tread carefully when comparing their views. One can say that existence does for Thomas what univocity does for Scotus: it makes our God-talk possible. The most significant difference between Thomas and Scotus relates to roles occupied by divine simplicity and infinity. Simplicity acts in Thomas's theology, in the words of Thomas Williams, as "an ontological spoilsport for theological semantics." It seriously complicates our language about God; indeed, it means we do not have a very adequate understanding of terms when applied to God. Thomas's understanding of God is more apophatic than that of Scotus, due to the Thomist emphasis upon divine simplicity.[23] For Scotus, the emphasis is different: the theory of univocity and the role of infinity in his metaphysics are the conditions of the possibility of knowing God and using proper language about him. For Scotus, there is "a harmonious cooperation between ontology (what God is) and semantics (how we can think and talk about him)."[24] Thus, Thomas Aquinas's use of analogy allows him to say that "God is wise," but we do not fully know what it means for God to be wise. For Scotus, however, this results in unacceptable equivocation. In my view, the changed dynamics of the relations between reason and faith, philosophy and theology account for this difference of emphasis. A narrower understanding of theological and philosophical reason in Duns Scotus, without the self-transcendent dynamic of reason toward theological discourse (as found in Thomas Aquinas), forces Scotus to espouse a univocal concept of being so as to salvage the claims of metaphysics and theology.

---

and creatures were simply analogous and simply signified two concepts that were radically different, we would know absolutely nothing about God."

[23] Cross, *Duns Scotus*, 44.

[24] Thomas Williams, "John Duns Scotus," published in the online version of the *Stanford Encyclopedia of Philosophy*. See http://plato.stanford.edu/entries/duns-scotus.

GOD'S EXISTENCE AND THE DIVINE ATTRIBUTES

Scotus's proof for the existence of God is highly complex and defies a short summary. Moreover, as Scotus sees it, the proof is part of metaphysics and not of theology. Indeed, while scholars have disagreed fundamentally whether or not Thomas's Five Ways are merely philosophical proofs for God's existence or, rather, theological ways of penetrating deeper into the mystery of God, there has been a broad acceptance that Scotus's arguments are merely philosophical in nature. This reflects the strict distinction, or even separation, of revealed theology and metaphysics after the Condemnation of 1277.

Given these considerations, I therefore merely focus on its most salient aspects. First, Scotus disagrees with Anselm's a priori demonstration of God's existence. We do not have a clear idea of God, and if we had, his existence would not need proof: it would be self-evident, and that is not the case. Like Thomas, Scotus therefore develops an a posteriori argument. Unlike Thomas, however, he does not accept that we can prove the existence of God from simply arguing on the basis of causal effects within the created order. The reason for this is that created beings are contingent (i.e., not necessary) and can therefore yield no certain knowledge. Scotus proposes instead to develop a *necessary* argument that starts from the *possibility* of the causal order: if God had decided not to create the world, it would still be necessarily true that some being can be produced.[25] Scotus then goes on to argue that no infinite succession of "horizontal" causes is possible unless it is founded upon a cause of a different, vertical order:

If there were an infinity of causes ... then the whole collection of what is caused would depend upon some other prior cause that is not part of that collection, for then something would be a cause of itself. For the whole collection of dependents depends, but not upon something that is part of that collection, because everything there is dependent. Consequently it depends upon something that is not part of that totality. And this I call the first efficient. Hence, even if there is an infinity of causes, they still depend upon something that is not part of that infinity.[26]

The key point of Scotus's argument is that the cause of the totality of things cannot possibly be part of this totality: the whole totality of things is dependent, and it is dependent not on anything belonging to that totality, as the quotation suggests.[27] Why can the cause of the totality of being not belong to the totality itself? Because in that case it would be

---

[25] *Rep. Par. I–A*, d.2 p.1 q.1–3 no. 28; see also *De Prim Princ.* 3.6.

[26] *Rep. Par. I–A*, d.2 p.1 q.1–3 no. 21 (pp. 119–20).   [27] See also *De Prim. Princ.* 3.12–13.

caused, and if the cause of the totality of being were caused, it would belong to the totality of caused things. But the cause of all things cannot belong to the totality of caused things, for nothing can be the cause of itself. As Peter King concludes: "Given the totality of essentially ordered caused things, there is some cause that is both the cause of the totality and is not itself caused. It is simply first."[28] Now something that is essentially uncaused and first has to be a necessary existent, and not just a possibility. It is at this stage of the demonstration that Scotus rehabilitates Anselm's argument.[29]

While God is first and foremost infinite being, Scotus also demonstrates a number of divine attributes (such as divine simplicity, intelligence, volition, oneness). In this context, it may be useful to indicate that Scotus does not accept the Thomist view that the divine attributes exist as one and simple in God, whereas our concept of them is multiple (cf. *ST* 1.13.4 *ad* 3 and *ST* 1.13.12). For Scotus, the divine attributes are formally distinct. Scotus uses this notion of formal distinction (*distinctio formalis a parte rei*) throughout his works, and I therefore want to explain it in some more detail.

The formal distinction is midway between a real distinction and a virtual or conceptual distinction. Two persons, for instance, are really distinct. In contrast, the distinction between the morning and the evening star is only virtual or conceptual – they are identical in reality. In case of a formal distinction we distinguish in a thing between two or more formal aspects that are distinct but inseparable from one another.[30] Scotus gives the example of goodness and wisdom.[31] They can be distinguished, even in God, and yet they are one in God because of divine simplicity.

As suggested, Scotus applies this notion of formal non-identity to a number of problems, such as between the soul and its powers, or in his theology of God (as we will see). Another instance in which he uses it is in his discussion of universals. According to Scotus, there is a formal but not a real distinction between the universal "human nature" and the "this-ness" or haecceity (from the Latin *haecceitas*) of an individual person – for example, Socrates.

---

[28] Peter King, "Duns Scotus on Metaphysics," in Thomas Williams (ed.), *The Cambridge Companion to Duns Scotus* (Cambridge: Cambridge University Press, 2003).

[29] See *Rep. Par. I–A*, d.2 p.1 q.1–3 no. 73 (p. 137) and *De Prim. Princ.* 4.65.

[30] Cf. *Rep. Par. I–A*, d.45 q.1–2 no. 32; *Ordin.* 1.d.8. q.1.4 no. 193 and *Rep. Par. I–A*, d.33 q.2 no. 63 (p. 330).

[31] *Rep. Par. I–A*, d.45 q.1–2 no. 32 (p. 548).

In this context, I would like to make two observations in passing, which will prove relevant when discussing the views of William of Ockham. First, as the example given illustrates, Scotus adopts a moderate realist position in relation to universals: universals do exist but they do not exist in separation from the individual entity in which they are instantiated. The distinction is not real but formal. Second, Scotus pays more attention to the individuality of things than any of his predecessors. Thomas Aquinas, following Aristotle, had argued that matter is the individuating principle of things. You and I share a human nature (the universal aspect), but what makes us individuals is the material aspect (our bodies and their distinguishing aspects). This means that our intellectual operations can never really grasp the individuality of things, for our intellect deals with universal things, not individual things that are the subject of sensual perception.[32] Scotus rejects the Aristotelian-Thomist account, which allocates the individuality of things and people to their material dimension. He claims, on the contrary, that there is a formal principle that individuates – namely, haecceity (or "this-ness"). It refers to the ultimate reality of any being, its ineffable and unique character.[33] In Duns Scotus's own words, "the [individuating] entity, therefore, is not the matter or the form or the composite insofar as each of these is a 'nature'; rather, it is the ultimate reality of the being that is the matter or that is the form or that is the composite."[34] This emphasis upon the individuality of things was to have a lasting influence upon his Franciscan followers, especially William of Ockham, with remarkable consequences.

DIVINE FREEDOM, VOLUNTARISM AND LOVE

One of the propositions condemned in 1277 was the claim that whatever God does is done of necessity. Perhaps as a response to this, Scotus puts a particular emphasis upon the unlimited freedom of God. Given the fact that we are created out of nothing, we have no claim over God. "In respect to creatures God has no obligations of any kind."[35] Or again: "God does not owe any creatures any of his perfections, for he makes everything out

---

[32] *ST* 1.86.1. We can know the individual or the singular only indirectly, by turning to phantasms in which we understand the species. In other words, we know the individual only through the image or similitude into which sensory knowledge is converted in the imagination.

[33] Mary Ingham, *Scotus for Dunces: An Introduction to the Subtle Doctor* (New York: Franciscan Institute, 2003), 54 (with a reference to *Ordin.* II.d.3 no. 188).

[34] *Ordin.* II.d.3 no. 188, quoted in Ingham, *Scotus for Dunces*, 163.

[35] *Rep. Par. I–A*, d.41 sol. q. no. 76 (p. 507).

of pure generosity" (*mere liberaliter omnia facit*).[36] This view has led to accusations of arbitrariness in his understanding of God, as if we are dealing with a capricious god who is not bound by any standards (moral or rational). Against this interpretation, a number of scholars, such as Wolter and Ingham, have claimed that God, once he has created, "respects the internal constraints of the created order."[37] One particular analogy scholars often adopt is that of an artist: God is free to write any piece of music he chooses (a symphony, a string quartet), but once he decides to do so, "he owes it to himself that whatever he chooses to create will have a beauty and natural goodness about it."[38]

This sympathetic reading of Scotus has been questioned, in turn, by Thomas Williams in a penetrating essay, arguing that God does not have to act in accordance with right reason.[39] "No other good, apart from God himself, functions as a reason for God's willing."[40] If something is good or right, it is such "not simply on account of the right reason, but insofar as it is willed by God."[41] The will of God is the rule and origin (*regula et origo*) of justice.[42] Williams summarizes: right reason "does not direct God's discussion; it merely reports it."[43] He concludes, alluding to the analogy of God as artist, that there are no standards of evaluation independent of God. God can only be considered an artist if one acknowledges that he makes up the standards that govern his aesthetic output. Hence, Scotus's God is "more like Schönberg than like Bach."[44]

Scotus admits that there are necessary moral truths, such as "You shall have no other gods before me" or, implied in this: "God is to be loved." Thus, God cannot command contradictions, such as the command to hate God. Therefore, not even God could abolish the first two commandments: he cannot permit us to practice idolatry or take the name of the Lord in vain. The status of the third commandment (to keep the Sabbath) is, however, more ambiguous: is it to be kept on a Saturday or a Sunday? Clearly, here an element of contingency is introduced. The other

---

[36] *Rep. Par. I–A*, d.44 q.2 no. 30 (p. 540). Thomas Aquinas too had argued for the gratuity of the creative act (cf. *ST* 1.45.4 *ad* 1), which finds its origin in the divine will. However, he emphasizes more than Scotus the rational character of divine goodness (cf. *ScG* III.97.13).

[37] Ingham, *Scotus for Dunces*, 51.

[38] Allan Wolter, "Native Freedom of the Will as a Key to the Ethics of Scotus," in Marilyn McCord Adams (ed.), *The Philosophical Theology of John Duns Scotus* (Ithaca, NY: Cornell University Press, 1990), p. 158, quoted by Thomas Williams on page 198 of his article "A Most Methodical lover? On Scotus's Arbitrary Creator," *Journal of the History of Philosophy* 38 (2000): 169–202.

[39] Williams, "A Most Methodical Lover," 177.   [40] *Rep. Par. I–A*, d.41 sol. q. no. 55 (p. 502).

[41] *Rep. Par. I–A*, d.44 q.2 no. 31 (p. 540).   [42] *Rep. Par.* IV.d.14. q.1.8.

[43] Williams, "A Most Methodical Lover," 198.   [44] Ibid., 201.

commandments clearly contain contingent moral truths (such as prohibitions of murder, adultery, theft). They can definitely be changed by God
and do not belong to the natural law in the strict sense.[45] This view has the
advantage that it allows us to make sense of those Old Testament passages
in which God dispenses with these prohibitions, such as when he orders
Abraham to sacrifice his son.

But the voluntarism that is undoubtedly present in Scotus's thought
(i.e., God freely decides what is morally good without submitting himself
to external standards) does not mean that humans cannot rely on reason to
discern what is right and wrong – just as we can discern structure and logic
in Schönberg's works.[46] For Scotus, contingent moral truths are immediately accessible to us and we therefore do not necessarily need divine
revelation to inform us of their contents. Murder, for instance, is wrong
because God wants it to be wrong (and not the other way around – that is,
God does not want murder because it is wrong). But contingent truths,
such as the prohibition of murder, are written in our hearts. While they
cannot be justified through discursive arguments (by appealing to considerations of human nature, the common good of society), they can be
intuitively known. Right reason, then, refers to the correct ascertainment
of the relevant moral facts – but the moral facts themselves are freely
established by God's will.[47] Hence, in Scotus there is a delicate balance
between voluntarism on one hand, and right reason on the other. Future
theologians, notably William of Ockham, will also struggle with this
tension.

Generally speaking we can conclude that Scotus's emphasis upon the
gratuity of God's creative act results in what we might call "facticity" –
things simply are the way they are, and we can't give any further reasons for
the way they are (apart from God's will). This emphasis upon facticity is
reflected in a number of issues. For instance, Christ's saving work is only
considered meritorious because God deems it such: just as everything else is
good on account of the fact that God wills it, and not the other way
around, so also merit had as much goodness as it was accepted to have.[48]
The same applies to his understanding of sin (where Scotus adopts
a forensic notion). Similarly, the same "facticity" can be illustrated by
the fact that Scotus refuses to attribute instrumental causality to the

---

[45] *Lectura Parisiensis*. III.37. For Thomas, in contrast, the whole Decalogue belongs to the natural law.
[46] Thomas Williams, "Reason, Morality and Voluntarism in Duns Scotus: A Pseudo-Problem Dissolved," *Modern Schoolmen* 74 (1997): 73–94.
[47] Williams, "Reason, Morality and Voluntarism." [48] *Ox.* III.d.19 q. un.7.

sacraments (occasionalism)[49] or in his rejection of eudaimonistic ethics. This safeguards God's freedom, undoubtedly, and does not result in a random, arbitrary creation (as some of Scotus's critics would have it). But it does mean that we cannot give an ultimate ground for God's creative act or for the structure of creation, apart from God's will.

As I suggested, this divine voluntarism extends to human action. It comes as no surprise that Scotus's anthropology and ethics are equally voluntarist.[50] The freedom of God is reflected in the freedom we enjoy. Now it is the will that is the true seat of human freedom. The assent of the intellect is, after all, determined by its object (when something becomes evident to you, you cannot disagree with it). The assent of the will, however, is in its power.[51] Again, our beatitude is found primarily in loving union with God rather than in our knowledge of him. In relation to ethics: right actions are right because God has freely commanded them and, as suggested earlier, this command finds its roots in the divine will. This perspective signals a significant departure from the Aristotelian-Thomist eudaimonistic virtue ethics. For Scotus, morality is not tied to human flourishing at all, for he does not entertain the idea that moral norms are intimately bound up with human nature and happiness.[52] This moves Scotus's ethics closer to Kant's understanding of morality than to Thomas Aquinas's. Incidentally, the divine command ethic, when secularized, results in a subjectivist ethics, in which we effectively construe values rather than recognize them.[53]

THEOLOGY OF THE TRINITY

I do not provide a detailed discussion of Duns Scotus's theology of the Trinity. Scotus's Trinitarian thought remains indebted to the

---

[49] Scotus refuses to attribute any physical causality to the material element of the sacraments. The principal cause is Christ who acts through the sign. Through divine institution, material sacraments are instruments necessary for the bestowal of grace (cf. *Ox.* IV.d.1 q.5 no. 15). Thomas would, of course, agree that God is the principal cause of sacramental efficacy, but he allows more scope for the role of instrumental causality in the sacramental economy.

[50] For a contrast with how Thomas Aquinas sees the role of will and intellect, see *ST* 1.82.3–4. Here Thomas states that the good as "the good understood is the object of the will, and moves it as an end." Scotus (*Lect.* 11, 25) rejects this account as it does away, in his view, with true freedom of will.

[51] *Rep. Par. I–A*, d.1 sol. q. no.17 (p. 93).   [52] Williams, "John Duns Scotus," pp. 16–17.

[53] This point was recognized by Alexander Broadie in *The Shadow of Scotus: Philosophy and Faith in Pre-Reformation Scotland* (Edinburgh: T&T Clark, 1995), 22: "The modern secular version [of the divine command theory of morality] is to the effect that it is we human beings who create our values by an act of choice; and that, contrary to appearances, we are not merely confronted by our values, as if they had a totally distinct reality, existing independently of our will."

psychological model of Augustine. This does not mean that his account does not differ from that of Thomas Aquinas. In relation to the generation of the Son, for instance, he criticizes Thomas for describing the generation of the Word from the divine intellect rather than from knowledge in divine memory, as Augustine had taught.[54] Unlike Thomas, Scotus rejects the Boethian definition of personhood, and favorably comments on Richard's alternative.[55]

Scotus also disagrees with the Thomist notion (cf. *ST* 1.28.2) that there is only a conceptual distinction between relations really existing in God (such as paternity, filiation, passive spiration) and the divine essence. Take the case of paternity. The divine essence, shared by the Father with the other divine Persons, is obviously communicable. But the relation or property of paternity is itself incommunicable.[56] Hence, the divine properties and relations cannot be simply identical with the divine essence. Nor can there be a straightforward real distinction, as this would jeopardize divine simplicity. Scotus therefore argues that there is a formal distinction between divine relations and divine essence.[57] Similarly, Scotus applies the formal distinction between divine essence and divine attributes (e.g., goodness, wisdom), as I have already noted.[58] Again, there has to be a formal distinction between God's will and God's intellect. If there were no formal distinction, it would be impossible to account for the distinction between the generation of the Word from the Father, and the procession of the Holy Spirit as Love.[59]

The divine Persons themselves are, of course, really and not just formally distinct. But how are they distinct? Are they distinct through their mutual relations (as Thomas argued)? Or can they be distinguished by an absolute (non-relational) property?[60] According to Thomas, only opposed relations (such as paternity, filiation, passive spiration) bring about personal distinction in God. Bonaventure's theology, on the other hand, contained the resources for "the absolute property theory." This means that, on top of the relative properties, the Persons have properties in their own right that distinguish them from the other three Persons. For instance, the Father is

[54] For a probing discussion of the Trinitarian thought of Duns Scotus, Thomas Aquinas, Ockham and other theologians, see Russell Friedman, *Medieval Trinitarian Thought from Aquinas to Ockham* (Cambridge: Cambridge University Press, 2010) and *Intellectual Traditions at the Medieval University: The Use of Philosophical Psychology in Trinitarian Theology among the Franciscans and Dominicans, 1250–1350* (Leiden: Brill, 2013).

[55] *Rep. Par. I–A*, d.23 q. un. nos. 15–16 (p. 19).   [56] *Rep. Par. I–A*, d.33 q.1 no. 24 (p. 316).

[57] *Rep. Par. I–A*, d.33 q.2. nos. 62–63; also: *Ordin.* 1.d.2 p.2 q.1–4 nos. 355–56.

[58] Cf. *Rep. Par. I–A*, d.45 q.1–2 no. 32 (p. 548).   [59] *Ordin.* 1.d.8 p.1 q.4 no. 169.

[60] For a helpful discussion of this topic, see Cross, *Duns Scotus on God*, 195–202.

the unbegotten or innascible source of the Godhead. His innascibility already constitutes him to some extent as Father even "before" he generates the Son. (I put "before" in inverted commas as it is a case of logical priority, not temporal priority as there is no temporal succession in God's eternity.) The generation of the Son by way of nature (or intellect) and the procession of the Holy Spirit (by way of will) are the basis for the distinction between the Persons.[61]

Although he was initially drawn to the absolute property theory, the relation theory was eventually adopted by Duns Scotus.[62] The Father is constituted by a positive relation to the second Person – that is, by paternity, and not by innascibility, for a negation (innascibility or unbegottenness) cannot possibly constitute a person.[63] In what sounds almost a reversal of St. Bonaventure's view, for Scotus, the Father is unbegotten because he is Father, and not the reverse (i.e., it is not the case that he is Father because he is unbegotten, as Bonaventure suggested).[64]

One of the advantages of the relation theory, as Richard Cross reminds us, is that relations are not things, and therefore the relations do not jeopardize the divine simplicity. One of its main problems, however, is that relations are not usually logically prior to the absolute items they relate.[65] It seems logical that we can only begin to speak of fatherhood or sonship if we already have two persons – that is, a father and a son, rather than the other way around (i.e., a person comes into being by becoming a father). Similarly, how can Son and Father be simultaneous in nature if the Father is the origin of the Son? Against this objection to the relation theory Scotus argues that priority of origin (of a father) to another (a son) does not exclude the possibility of the two existing simultaneously. It merely means that the other (the son) gets the existence from the first (the father).[66] Scotus gives the example of Socrates, the father, and his (spiritual) son, Plato:

Socrates, the father, is prior in origin to Plato, the son, for paternity is a relationship of origin – and nevertheless Socrates the father and Plato the son are simultaneous by nature as correlatives. ... Therefore, all the more so can there be in the Father simultaneity of nature with the Son as his correlative, and at the same time a priority of origin, [which means] that he is that from whom the Son is.[67]

---

[61] For Thomas, on the other hand, the Persons, in their relative opposition, logically precede the emanations. For a helpful summary, see Friedman, *Medieval Trinitarian Thought*, 171–73.
[62] See Cross, *Duns Scotus on God*, 201; Friedman, *Intellectual Traditions*, 356.
[63] *Rep. Par. I–A*, d.28 q.2 nos. 31, 53 and 56.   [64] *Rep. Par. I–A*, d.28 q.2 no. 57.
[65] See Cross, *Duns Scotus*, 66; *Ordin.* 1.26 un.no. 38.
[66] *Rep. Par. I–A*, d.26 q.4 nos. 141, L43–44 (p. 119).
[67] *Rep. Par. I–A*, d.26 q.4 nos. 144–45 (pp. 119–20).

Hence the Father can be prior to the Son in origin and yet be simultaneous with the Son in nature.

Scotus's discussion of the *Filioque* warrants our attention. Given the fact that the Greeks accept that the Holy Spirit proceeds from the Father through the Son, he is confident that the disagreements between the Latin West and the Greek East are not fundamental and can be overcome. The ecumenically minded text deserves to be quoted in full:

> In this way, therefore, two wise ones, one Greek and the other Latin, not lovers of speech but of divine zeal, would perhaps find the disagreement not to be real, but one of words, for otherwise either the Latins or the Greeks would be heretics. But who wishes to say that Basil, Gregory of Nazianzus, Gregory of Nyssa, Damascene, Chrysostom and many other excellent doctors are heretics; and for the other part that Ambrose, Jerome, Augustine, Gregory, Hilary, etc. who were excellent Latin doctors, are heretics?[68]

Scotus states that the *Filioque* is an explanation of the Nicene-Constantinopolitan Creed, not an innovation or corruption (*non est corruptio primi symboli, sed explicatio*).[69] He defends the correctness of the "explanation" by arguing that it is implied in the spirative nature of the Father. Thus, the generation of the Son is logically prior to the procession of the Holy Spirit, just as the intellect in operating precedes the will. Now the Father bestows his spirative power unto the Son. The Son can therefore produce the Holy Spirit jointly with the Father.[70] Note that I write "jointly," for there is no talk of "double spiration" in Scotus's theology: Father and Son spirate the Holy Spirit as one principle.[71]

Thomas Aquinas had claimed (*ST* 1.36.2) that the *Filioque* is necessary to distinguish the Holy Spirit from the Son – for the relations cannot distinguish the Persons except inasmuch as they are opposite relations. Scotus disagrees: for him, generation and spiration are distinct as emanations – which is, of course, the Greek view as well. More specifically, the distinction between generation and procession can be reduced to the intellectual and volitional nature of the two emanations.[72] Hence, even if

---

[68] *Rep. Par. I–A*, d.11 q.1 no. 10 (p. 408); also: *Ordin.* 1.d.11 q.1 no. 9.

[69] *Rep. Par. I–A*, d.11 q.1 no. 19 (p. 411).

[70] *Rep. Par. I–A*, d. 11 q.1 nos. 11 and 20 (pp. 408 and 412).

[71] *Rep. Par. I–A*, d.12 q.1 no. 17 (p. 426): "The Father and Son do not spirate the Holy Spirit insofar as they are distinct, or by a concordant love in an elicited act, but insofar as in them there is entirely one will, and as they are joined together in this principle that is totally one, except that in the Father it is from himself, and in the Son it is from another."

[72] *Rep. Par. I–A*, d.13 q. un. no. 35 (p. 447): "The first operation of the Father is to understand and the first action is to speak; the second operation is to will and the second action is to spirate." For a more detailed discussion, see Cross, *Duns Scotus on God*, 191–95.

there were no *Filioque*, we could still distinguish the Son from the Holy Spirit.

CHRISTOLOGY AND MARIOLOGY

Perhaps echoing Grosseteste's views, for Scotus, the Incarnation is a perfection of the world. Indeed, one can even argue that the world has been created for the sake of the Incarnation. The final cause of creation is Christ.[73] In *Ordin.* III d.7 q.3 Scotus puts it as follows:

> It does not seem to be solely because of the redemption that God predestined this [= Christ's] soul to such glory, since the redemption or the glory of souls to be redeemed is not comparable to the glory of the soul of Christ. Neither is it likely that the highest good in the whole of creation is something that merely chanced to take place, and that only because of some lesser good.[74]

Redemption is not the fundamental reason for God assuming human nature. The primary reason was the perfection of creation in Christ, the center of the universe. This implies that the Incarnation would have taken place even if the Fall had not occurred. This view is implied in Scotus's emphasis upon God's freedom and sovereignty. If the Fall were the cause of the Incarnation, God would have been responding to contingent events in the world. Scotus does not accept this.[75] Scotus's view that Christ's Incarnation is primarily the result of God's will to perfect creation rather than to redeem humanity, although not all that original amongst scholastics, proved rather influential in Scotism and beyond.

Scotus's most influential contribution to the development of Catholic dogma is undoubtedly his defense of the Immaculate Conception of Mary, which was declared dogma in 1854. This means that Mary was conceived without original sin. The main objection against the doctrine is as follows. If Mary was free from original sin, she was not in need of redemption. But this undermines the universality of Christ's saving activity: there was at least one person not in need of salvation by Christ – namely, his own mother. This is the main reason Bonaventure and Thomas rejected the doctrine.

How then does Scotus deal with the objection that the Immaculate Conception does away with the universality of Christ's saving activity? He

---

[73] *Lect. Par.* III d.7 q.4 no. 4.

[74] Translation by Allan Wolter from *John Duns Scotus: Four Questions on Mary* (New York: Franciscan Institute, 2000), 25.

[75] See also *Lect. Par.* III d.7 q.4 no. 4.

simply argues that it was Christ who, by the merits of his Passion, preserved Mary from contracting original sin. Hence the objection that the doctrine of the Immaculate Conception jeopardizes the universality of Christ's salvific activity does not hold. Moreover, the doctrine does not diminish the saving efficacy of Christ, on the contrary, "it is a more excellent benefit to preserve one from evil than to permit one to fall into it and then free such."[76]

Still, the reader might object that it seems strange that Mary's Immaculate Conception occurs before the Son assumes human nature. How can she benefit from the merits of Christ before he is born, lives and dies? Scotus answers that the case is not fundamentally different from that of the patriarchs, whose original sin was forgiven before the coming of Christ.[77]

CONCLUSION

John Duns Scotus is often portrayed as the thinker who inaugurates some of the key modern developments. Scholars have paid particular attention to his theory of univocity. This would, allegedly, threaten the transcendence of God and initiate onto-theological developments in the intellectual history of the West. I found these claims untenable. Scotus's theory of univocity is not primarily a metaphysical but a conceptual one. Again, while there is undoubtedly a growing voluntarist and individualist tendency in Scotus (when compared to Thomas Aquinas), it is his Franciscan successors who will draw out the more radical implications of these views. What links John Duns Scotus with the other great scholastics of the 13th century is his constructive approach to theology. But it must be conceded that his theology also contains the seeds of a radically different approach. In order to illustrate this, I must now consider the thought of another great Franciscan thinker: William of Ockham.

BIBLIOGRAPHICAL NOTE

For the *Opera Omnia*, see C. Balic et al. (Vatican City: Typis Polyglottis Vaticanis, 1950–). A bilingual edition (Latin-English) of *Reportatio I–A* (a commentary on the first book of the *Sentences*) has been published in two volumes by Allan B. Wolter and Oleg Bychkov (eds.) as *John Duns*

---

[76] *Ordin.* III.d.3 q.1; *Four Questions on Mary*, 41.   [77] *Four Questions on Mary*, 53.

Scotus: The Examined Report of the Paris Lecture. Reportatio I–A (New York: Franciscan Institute, 2004 and 2008), while *Reportatio ivA* vol. 1, parts 1 and 2 was published by Oleg Bychkov and R. Trent Pomplun in 2016.

The best introduction in English remains Richard Cross, *Duns Scotus* (Oxford: Oxford University Press, 1999). Another useful introduction is Mary Ingham, *Scotus for Dunces: An Introduction to the Subtle Doctor* (New York: Franciscan Institute, 2003). Étienne Gilson's classic study of Duns Scotus has been recently translated by James Colbert as *John Duns Scotus: Introduction to His Fundamental Positions* (London: T&T Clark, 2018) with an afterword by John Milbank. Antonie Vos, *The Theology of Duns Scotus* (Leiden: Brill, 2018) is also warmly recommended.

PART V

The 14th Century and Beyond

Introduction
Upheavals and Pluralism in the 14th Century

Undoubtedly, the 14th century was a period of major turmoil. The political scene was dominated by the conflict between France and England (the Hundred Years' War [first phase: 1337–96]). In economic terms, Europe faced stagnation, leading to starvation (in 1315–17), insurgencies in the countryside (e.g., in Flanders in 1323–28; the French Jacquerie of 1358; England in 1381) and urban rebellions in Ghent (Artevelde, 1338) and Florence (Ciompi, 1378). To make matters worse, the Black Death struck in 1348–51, wiping out an estimated one-third of the population.

The papacy too faced major crises throughout the century. The main problem was the struggle for power with the new nation-states, especially France. When Philip the Fair (d. 1303) effectively took control of the French Church, Pope Boniface (1294–1303) could only make futile claims that the secular power should be subordinated to the spiritual authority of the successor of St. Peter. A major debate raged throughout the century on the relation between secular and spiritual powers. Giles of Rome (*De Potestate Ecclesiastica* [1301]) and James of Viterbo (d. 1308) supported papal claims; John of Paris (d. 1306), William of Ockham (d. 1347) and above all Marsilius of Padua (d. 1343), who wrote an influential treatise on politics, *Defensor Pacis*, disputed them. In England John Wyclif (d. 1384) questioned papal power and appealed to the Scriptures as the arbitrator of truth.[1] His views resonated with the movement known as the Lollards and later influenced the Czech reform movement led by Jan Hus (d. 1415). The interference of the French crown with the papacy became painfully evident during the so-called Babylonian Captivity when the popes resided in Avignon. This exile ended in 1377 when Pope Gregory XI returned to Rome. A year later worse was to follow. In 1378, French cardinals declared

---

[1] For helpful accounts, see Stephen Lahey, *John Wyclif* (Oxford: Oxford University Press, 2009) and Ian Christopher Levy (ed.), *A Companion to John Wyclif: Late Medieval Theologian* (Leiden: Brill, 2011).

that their election of Urban VI in Rome had been coerced by the Roman populace and was therefore invalid. They then proceeded to elect a cousin of the French king as rival pope Clement VII (d. 1394). This situation would only be solved in the second decade of the 15th century by the Councils of Pisa and Constance (1417). The embarrassment of the schism and the decline of papal influence it entailed led to heated discussions as to how papal power should relate to that of the Councils. Conciliarism, although no longer influential in real terms after 1440, must rank as one of the most important expressions of a more general movement toward representative government in Europe in the late medieval period.[2]

The Gothic architecture of the late medieval period did not innovate in any significant degree on the style of the great cathedrals built throughout the 12th and 13th centuries, although they at times surpassed them in height and elegance. Prime examples are the abbey church of St. Ouen in Rouen, the Cathedral of Notre Dame in Rodez and the Cathedral of Notre Dame in Antwerp, all of which were commenced in the 14th century. While the French example proved influential in the Low Countries, the Iberian Peninsula and England, a German Gothic style (structurally less elaborate, often without transept, ambulatory or radiating chapels and with aisles almost as high as the nave) influenced architecture throughout Central and Eastern Europe as far as Poland and the Baltic states.[3] A rather different kind of Gothic style from the French one emerged in Italy. Here the churches of the Dominicans and Franciscans (e.g., Florence's Santa Croce of 1295) displayed "an earthbound weight and solidity contrary to the weightlessness of French Gothic."[4] A stronger emphasis upon structural clarity was more important than soaring naves and light-flooded choirs.[5]

Throughout the 14th century Gothic architecture was also used for civic buildings in the economically most advanced areas of Europe (such as northern Italy, Flanders and northern France): Florence (Palazzo Vecchio, early 14th century), Siena (Town Hall on Piazza del Campo, 1288–1309), Bruges (Cloth Hall and Belfry, 1270–1486), Brussels (Town Hall, 1402), Leuven (Town Hall, 1458) and Arras (Town Hall, 1450).

In Italy, Florentine Giotto di Bondone (d. 1337) has been credited as the person who inaugurated a move away from static Byzantine art toward

---

[2] See Malcolm Vale, "The Civilization of Courts and Cities in the North," in George Holmes (ed.), *The Oxford History of Medieval Europe* (Oxford: Oxford University Press, 1992), 276–323, here 309.
[3] See Pablo de la Riestra, "Gothic Architecture of the 'German Lands,'" in Rolf Toman (ed.), *The Art of Gothic: Architecture, Sculpture, Painting* (Cologne: Konemann, 1996), 190–92.
[4] Barbara Borngasser, "Gothic Architecture in Italy," in ibid., 242.   [5] Ibid.

Renaissance art, characterized by more dramatic and psychological expressiveness. However, initially at least, it did not displace the influence of Byzantine traditions, which, blended with Italian Gothic painting, continued to flourish in the school of Siena (e.g., Duccio, d. 1318 and Simone Martin, d. 1344). Even in Florence, after the rampages of the Black Death, the works of Orcagna (d. 1368) reverted to elements of the Byzantine style.

The major revolution in Western European painting was to originate in Flanders at the beginning of the 15th century with the paintings of Jan van Eyck (d. 1441) and his followers (the Flemish Primitives). In van Eyck's art, naturalism and realistic depictions of everyday events and objects are infused with a profound Christian symbolism. The art of Jan van Eyck and his school represents one of the most moving and supreme expressions on canvas of the Christian worldview.

The ideals of knighthood and courtly love lingered on in the chivalric literature of the 14th and 15th centuries even though society (and warfare) bore precious little resemblance to the 12th century in which courtly literature first blossomed (Chrétien de Troyes, Wolfram von Eschenbach). In the late medieval period, courtly literature found a belated expression in works such as *Sir Gawain and the Green Knight* and *Morte d'Arthur* (Thomas Malory).

In the 13th century, vernacular literature had become established and some of the finest works of medieval literature and spirituality were written in the vernacular in the 14th century. In England, Geoffrey Chaucer (d. 1400) wrote *The Canterbury Tales*, containing colorful stories by a number of pilgrims en route to the shrine of St. Thomas Becket at Canterbury. A somewhat similar collection of stories (*Decameron*) told by ten men and women who fled the plague in Florence, was written in Italian by Giovanni Boccaccio (d. 1375). Also in Italy, Dante Alighieri (d. 1321) wrote *The Divine Comedy*, written in Tuscan vernacular, encapsulating better than any other literary work the late medieval Christian worldview. Guided by Virgil (representing the wisdom of antiquity), the poet visits Hell; at the threshold of Purgatory, Beatrice (representing Christian grace) begins to accompany him, while St. Bernard of Clairvaux (the great mystic) guides Dante toward the glory of Heaven and the contemplation of the Holy Trinity. *The Divine Comedy* weaves theological, political and cosmological themes into a literary masterpiece.

In the same period we also witness a blossoming of spirituality (or mysticism). The major spiritual authors after the death of Meister Eckhart (d. 1328) are his followers Tauler (d. 1361) and Henry Suso (d. 1365) in German-speaking countries, Jan van Ruusbroec (d. 1381) in the Low Countries,

Julian of Norwich (d. ca. 1416) in England and Catherine of Siena (d. 1380) in Tuscany. All these spiritual writers have a number of important elements in common: they wrote their works in the vernacular, they had little or no connection with the world of academic theology, and at least some of them wrote for laypeople as well as religious disciples. In their works we find a keen interest in the individual and his or her relation with God or Christ. In their own way their writings reflect the societal changes that had taken place from the end of the 13th century onward. A similar focus on the layperson can be discerned in the last important religious movement of the Middle Ages, the so-called Modern Devotion or the Brethren of the Common Life, founded by a layman, Geert Grote (d. 1384). Its main exponent would be Thomas a Kempis's *The Imitation of Christ*, a devout but theologically somewhat unsophisticated work.

The most innovative school of thought in the 14th century was nominalism. The main figure associated with it was William of Ockham. As indicated in Chapter 19, Ockham's philosophy was both an exponent and contributing factor to a different intellectual climate: more concerned with detailed analysis of technical problems than with building systematic projects, more oriented toward philosophy of language and semantics than metaphysics, more rational than intellective, and, given all of this, more inclined to appeal to revelation as final arbitrator to determine problems that in the 13th century had been considered to belong to the metaphysical remit.

Ockhamism is not the only exponent of this new analytical approach. The school known as "the Oxford Calculators" (associated with Merton College), after Richard Swinehead's book *Liber Calculationum*, written around 1350, also epitomizes an approach in which logical and mathematical ways of thinking come to prominence. Lucid, rational in the analytical sense of the word, and focused on clearly delineated issues, it produced writings that remain largely unexplored by historians of science and thought. This school also included Thomas Bradwardine, an extraordinary mathematician, geometrist and physicist who also opposed Ockham's theology, in which he suspected Pelagian elements. Bradwardine therefore wrote an important work on grace and predestination, entitled *De Causa Dei contra Pelagium et de Virtute Causarum* (*On the Cause/Defense of God against Pelagius and the Power of Causes*). In short, the 14th century provides a plural scene in which attention shifts from primarily ontological issues to problems involving language and logic, giving epistemology a prominence it had not enjoyed before. In this broader context, Ockham's thought is just one but nonetheless highly significant exponent of these changes. I discuss it in the next chapter.

CHAPTER 22

William of Ockham

Our knowledge of the life of William of Ockham is fairly limited. He was born in Surrey, in the south of England, circa 1288. He joined the Franciscan Order and studied in London and Oxford, where he lectured on Peter Lombard's *Sentences*. In 1324, before he had formally finished his education, charges of heresy were formally brought against him. Ockham traveled to Avignon, where the papal court held residence. Here he remained for four years. The controversy surrounding apostolic poverty – in which the pope adopted a position severely critical of the one propagated by the Franciscans – did little to improve Ockham's views on the papacy of John XXII, especially after Ockham unearthed a document by Pope Nicholas III (1279–81) that supported the Franciscan view. On May 26, 1328, Ockham and a number of other Franciscans fled to the court of Louis of Bavaria. Excommunicated, Ockham was to stay in southern Germany (mainly Munich) under the protection of the emperor until the end of his life (after 1347, perhaps as a victim of the Black Death).

Ockham wrote his most important theological and philosophical works in the 1320s, such as his *Commentary on the Sentences*, a number of works on logic (including his *Summa Logicae*), a commentary on Aristotle's *Physics* and a treatise *On Predestination and Future Contingents, Quodlibetal Disputations*, as well as treatises on the Eucharist. In his German period, he produced mainly political works on the limits of the power of the papacy, such as *De imperatorum et pontificium potestate, Dialogus* and *Opus Nonaginta Dierum*. In those works too he heralds a new age in which the boundaries between the secular and the religious realms are strictly drawn. In what follows I do not focus on the political writings of his later period. Instead, I examine his nominalism and the implications it has for theology.

In popular handbooks of philosophy William of Ockham is best known for "Ockham's razor" – that is, the notion that "beings are not to be multiplied beyond necessity."[1] This exact turn of phrase cannot be found in Ockham's writings, but he does say similar things, such as, "No plurality should be assumed unless it can be proved by reason, or by experience, or by some infallible authority."[2] As we will see, Ockham puts the principle of parsimony (as it is sometimes called) to use throughout his work. I also want to draw the attention of the reader to the three sources of knowledge Ockham mentions here: reason, experience and infallible authority. Although there may not be anything particularly striking about these three, two elements will prove important: first, Ockham's approach is decisively more empirical than that of his 13th-century predecessors. Also, unlike Thomas Aquinas, Ockham simply accepts that reason and experience can clash with revealed truth, in which case we should accept the claims of the latter.

NOMINALISM

A first area in which Ockham employs his razor is in relation to the status of universals. Ockham strenuously argues against the realism his 13th-century predecessors (such as Thomas Aquinas, Bonaventure and John Duns Scotus) shared. They were heir to the realism of Plato and Aristotle, for whom universals are real, and the foundation of universal knowledge. While Plato argued that forms exist in the Realm of the forms or ideas beyond individuals (which share in the forms that "inform" them), Aristotle claimed that forms simply exist within individual things themselves, without having to subscribe to a "separate" realm of forms. Thomas Aquinas later adopted the Aristotelian view. For Ockham, on the other hand, universals are nothing but universal names or concepts. Every mind-independent thing is particular. Only particulars exist in reality. Universality is therefore a feature of signification; it does not refer to the ontological status of things. Universality is a feature of our cognitive acts and does not refer to anything real outside the mind. In the sentence "Eleanor and Henry are human beings" "human being" is nothing but a mental name (*nomen mentale*).[3]

This raises the obvious question: if universals are mere names and do not have any real ontological status, how then can we account for the similarity

---

[1] *Pluralitas non est ponenda sine necessitate.* Cf. Armand Maurer, *The Philosophy of William of Ockham in the Light of Its Principles* (Toronto: Pontifical Institute of Medieval Studies, 1999), 121–29.

[2] *Op. Theol.* IV, p. 290; *Op. Theol.* V, p. 404 and *Op. Theol.* X, pp. 157–58. I refer to Ockham's works in the edition by Gedeon Gal et al., *Opera Philosophica et Theologica*, 17 vols. (New York: Franciscan Institute, 1967–88).

[3] *Quodlib.* IV.35 (trans. p. 388); *Summa Logicae* I, c.14.

between things (such as Plato and Socrates)? After all, Plato and Socrates are more similar to one another than are Plato and a donkey. A realist had no difficulty accounting for this similarity: Plato and Socrates both share the universal form of humanity. But if "humanity" (the universal) is a mere name, how can Ockham account for the similarity between different human individuals? Here Ockham applies his principle of parsimony. He replies that Socrates and Plato are similar, not because they have something else in common (e.g., a universal nature), but because they themselves, are similar.[4] As Marilyn McCord Adams rephrases it: "Thus, similarity is a two term relation between two things and not a three term relation between two things and a common nature."[5]

EPISTEMOLOGY

In Chapter 20 we had occasion to note that medieval schoolmen had difficulties accounting for certain knowledge of *individual* things. Thomas and Duns Scotus had no difficulty accounting for universal knowledge by explaining it in terms of abstraction of the universal form from particular things. They had, however, difficulty explaining how we can attain proper *knowledge* of a particular thing. Duns Scotus's notion of haecceity (*haecceitas*) attempted to give due status to the individual thing in its particularity. Ockham takes Duns Scotus's insight to its extreme, and effectively turns the problem upside down. For Ockham, there are only particular things. His challenge, then, is to explain how we can acquire universal knowledge.

In order to understand Ockham's position it may be useful to outline briefly Thomas Aquinas's epistemological views. According to Thomas, when our senses (e.g., sight) are affected by something – let's say, a dog – we first receive the sensible species of the thing – that is, the specific configuration of color and shape. The cognitive power called "phantasia" receives the sensible species from the senses and transforms it into a phantasm, or mental image. The intellect then abstracts a universal from this phantasm – and it is only now that we "see" or recognize the thing in question as a dog. This is the "intelligible species." The strength

---

[4] *Ord.* 1, d.2 q.6.
[5] Marilyn McCord Adams, *William Ockham* (Notre Dame, IN: University of Notre Dame Press, 1987), 111. One wonders, however, whether Ockham is not simply begging the question – for how can we account for the fact that two things are similar, if not by appealing to something (i.e., a third element within the two things) they have in common and that can only be delineated by referring to what the two things do not have in common?

of Thomas's position lies in the fact that he can easily explain how the intelligible species can be drawn from the (universal) form (e.g., canine-hood) that is really present in the individual thing (e.g., Pluto the dog).

Ockham, however, does not accept there is a universal form in things. There is, therefore, strictly speaking, nothing to "abstract." Given the fact that Ockham rejects universals he has no need for intelligible species either. We have an immediate apprehension of things, a kind of intel-lectual intuition of individual things. Again Ockham applies his razor.[6]

IMPLICATIONS FOR THEOLOGY

Ockham's universe consists of individual things or monads, existing as absolute substances unrelated to one another. This view is strikingly different from that of his predecessors.[7] This has important implications for his understanding of causality. We can observe that there are causes and effects but we cannot account for these causal relations by establishing any kind of intrinsic connection between things.[8] Thus, Ockham interprets causal relations in terms of regular sequences rather than in terms of intrinsic connections. This illustrates his empiricist bias: we can only establish that A is the cause of B by appealing to experience, and not by examining the inner "nature" of A.

This understanding of causality results in a severely diminished natural theology. Strictly speaking, *the existence of the one God* cannot be proven. It is impossible, for instance, to prove that there is not an infinite series of efficient causes, and therefore the proof that there is a first efficient cause is not convincing.[9] Ockham suggests that it is more convincing to develop

---

[6] It is not at all clear, however, that Ockham's position succeeds in providing a more satisfactory account of perception and cognition than either Thomas or Duns Scotus. For a penetrating essay that compares the epistemological approaches of Thomas and Ockham, see Eleonore Stump, "The Mechanism of Cognition: Ockham on Mediating Species," in Paul Vincent Spade (ed.), *The Cambridge Companion to Ockham* (Cambridge: Cambridge University Press, 1999), 168–203.

[7] In the Aristotelian-Thomist view, things have an *entelecheia*, an inner *telos* or goal toward greater perfection or actuality, which mirrors (and participates in) the pure actuality of God. Ockham's universe is a collection of individuals without real community, which leads him to adopt an empirical notion of causality. See Maurer, *The Philosophy*, 182–83.

[8] *Quodlib.* VI.12.

[9] See *Quaestiones in Lib.i Physicorum* q.135: "Someone basing himself on natural reason would deny this reasoning [=the proof based on efficient causality], because he would say that one of the things that are caused is caused by another member of this multitude, and this again by another member of this multitude, and so on *ad infinitum*" (trans. by Philotheus Boehner, *Ockham: Philosophical Writings* [Edinburgh: Nelson, 1957], 120).

the proof for God's existence by appealing to conservation rather than efficient causality:

We cannot go on *ad infinitum* in the order of preservative causes (*in conservantibus*); for everything that conserves something else, be it mediately or immediately, exists at the same time with that which is conserved. ... Hence, though it is possible to admit that we go on *ad infinitum* in the order of productive causes without an actual infinity, nevertheless going on *ad infinitum* cannot be admitted in the order of conservation without an actual infinity.[10]

The chief advantage in arguing from conservation instead of production is that it is easier to claim that an infinite regress is impossible. As Marilyn McCord Adams explains, the key presupposition is that "an actual infinity of distinct things existing simultaneously" is impossible.[11] My parents are the efficient or productive cause of me; they do not have to exist any more for me to continue to exist. With conservative causes it is different. I cannot have existence or being without there being something – or Somebody – who continually bestows being upon me and "conserves" me in existence. To borrow language from previous chapters, Ockham's proof of conservation is more vertical than horizontal.

However, proofs based on the chain of conserving causes only yield the conclusion that there is one or more primary conserving causes – and in a medieval view these could be stars or angels.[12] They do not yield the conclusion that there is only one God. Similarly, divine omnipotence and omniscience cannot be rationally proved either.

It is equally clear that Ockham's view on universals as mere names sits uneasily with the theology of the *Trinity*. For if the divine nature is a mere name or concept, and has no ontological reality, the charge of tritheism (three Persons) seems valid.[13]

Given his rejection of universals, Ockham discards the traditional (Neo) Platonic dynamic of traditional Latin Christian thought. In marked contrast to Thomas Aquinas (an Aristotelian with a strong Neoplatonic bias), Ockham eliminates any traces of Neoplatonism. This becomes particularly evident in his *rejection of divine ideas*. In Latin theology, divine ideas functioned as the exemplars of created beings. It was this aspect of

---

[10] *Quaestiones in Lib. i Physicorum*, q.136, *trans.* 123. [11] McCord Adams, *William Ockham*, 970.

[12] Ibid., 971–72.

[13] For a discussion of the difficulty of trying to square Ockham's theory of universals with the traditional doctrine of the Trinity, see McCord Adams, *William Ockham*, 996–1003. Similarly, his views on relation (and his rejection of relations as real things distinct from absolute things) are in tension with traditional theology of the Trinity as well (McCord Adams, *William Ockham*, 1003–07).

Christian Neoplatonism that allowed authors as diverse as Augustine, Eriugena, the Victorines and Bonaventure to argue for a sacramental world-view, in which creation manifests and embodies divine patterns or ideas. Now, if universals (such as "humanity" or "caninehood") do not have any real ontological status, as Ockham claims, then divine ideas cannot exist either, for they are, of course, universals. For Ockham, divine ideas are not the exemplar or blueprint of creatures. Rather, they are nothing but the creatures themselves. This stance concords with his epistemological minimalism. Just as Ockham simplifies human epistemology – for instance, by getting rid of species in the process of perception and cognition – so too he argues that God has an immediate knowledge of creatures. When creating things, God does not have to think of universals or divine ideas but he immediately thinks of the creatures themselves.[14] In Ockham's opinion, any theory of essences is in danger of jeopardizing the Christian doctrine of divine freedom and omnipotence.[15]

Safeguarding *divine omnipotence and freedom* was of central importance to Duns Scotus. Ockham merely radicalizes this concern. Ockham adopts the distinction between God's absolute and ordained power, which Peter Lombard had already alluded to in his first book of *The Sentences*, dist. 42–43.[16] In the 13th century this distinction became commonplace amongst thinkers (Alexander of Hales, Albert the Great, Thomas Aquinas), although different theologians understood it in somewhat different ways. For Thomas Aquinas, God's absolute power refers to everything God can possibly do, while his ordained power refers to the divine power insofar "as it carries into execution the command of a just will" (*ST* 1.25.5 *ad* 1). Thus, for Thomas, what God actually does coincides with his ordained power. Punishing the Egyptians or raising Lazarus from the dead are acts of God's ordained power. Following Duns Scotus, Ockham interprets the distinction between absolute and ordained power in more legalistic terms. For Duns Scotus, for instance, ordained power refers to acting in accordance with the right law, while absolute power refers to the possibility of acting outside or contrary to this law.[17] Ockham follows Scotus's lead in this more legalistic approach.

---

[14] McCord Adams, *William Ockham*, 1055–57; Maurer, *The Philosophy*, 212–28. In Ockham's view, the notion of divine ideas, as traditionally understood, also clashes with the notion of simplicity of the divine essence.

[15] Maurer, *The Philosophy*, 226.

[16] In 1 *Sent.* d.43 c.5, Peter Lombard makes a distinction between what God reasonably does and all the things he could reasonably do.

[17] See *Ordin.* 1.d.44 q.u. no. 3, quoted by McCord Adams, *William Ockham*, 1190.

After having explained that the distinction between absolute and ordained power should not be taken to mean that there are two powers in God, Ockham goes on to explain their meaning:

The distinction should be understood to mean that "power to do something" is sometimes taken as "power to do something in accordance with the laws that have been ordained and instituted by God," and God is said to be able to do these things by his ordained power. In an alternative sense, "power" is taken as "power to do anything such that its being done does not involve a contradiction," regardless of whether or not God has ordained that he will do it.[18]

The implications of Ockham's understanding of the distinction between absolute and ordained power are subtly different from that of Thomas.[19] In Thomas's view, God selects ("ordains") a limited number of reasonable options (which may very well be infinite in number). Thus, for Thomas, the ordained power is not contingent – only the absolute power is. Once God has made a choice, it acquires a kind of finality. It follows from Thomas's perspective that God's ordained power cannot change. In Ockham's view, the contingency of the absolute power of God extends to ordained power. For there are many things that are in accordance with the right law that God *can* do but does *not* do. This is impossible in Thomas's understanding of ordained power. Again, for Scotus and Ockham, God's ordained power can change, and God can, for instance, issue new moral laws. God can decide that polygamy is acceptable in one era and unacceptable in a later era.

The implications for theological issues such as grace, predestination and acceptance may not be as radical in Ockham's thought as is often alleged – but they do contain the seeds of a full-blown divine command ethics, utterly severed from a natural law ethics.[20] Ockham did not take this step, however. His ethics includes principles of both right reason and the divine omnipotent will, however uneasy this equilibrium between an ethics of right reason and an ethics of obligation might be.[21]

Ockham can argue that "a human being is able by the absolute power of God to be saved without created charity."[22] According to the laws now ordained by God, however, "no human being will ever be saved or be able to be saved without created grace." God freely loves whom he loves.

---

[18] *Quodlib.* VI.I (trans. 491–92). [19] See McCord Adams, *William Ockham*, 1186–1207.
[20] Maurer (*The Philosophy*, 263) summarizes: "Ockham does not portray God as a capricious monarch: his world is ruled by physical and moral laws which give it order and rationality, but they are contingent on his freely establishing them."
[21] Ibid., 539. [22] *Quodlib.* VI.I art.2 (trans. 492).

Ockham allows for the possibility that someone should be accepted by God, or perform meritorious acts without infused charity or grace. This, to his contemporaries, appeared perniciously similar to Pelagian views.[23] It is interesting to note Ockham's reasons for holding this view: "I hold this because of Sacred Scripture and the teaching of the Saints."[24] Again, God, by his absolute power, can "if it so pleases him, remit all guilt ... without an infusion of created grace."[25] Although it may not be fair to claim that Ockham's God, in his ordained power, acts arbitrarily, it is clear that he puts a stronger emphasis than Thomas on God's freedom to act contingently. As a matter of fact, we are not in a position to attribute arbitrariness to God. Only God decides the worth of a person or an action, and nothing is meritorious save by God's acceptance. Between virtue and merit lies divine acceptance, "which can only be awarded freely as a gift, not exacted as a due."[26]

Again, God is not bound by sacraments. They are not even an instrumental cause of grace. Rather, by divine ordinance there is constant conjunction between receiving sacraments (such as baptism) and receiving grace. As McCord Adams explains, "this constant conjunction holds, not because of any power – whether natural or supernatural – inhering in the sacrament, but because God wills to produce grace in the soul whenever the sacrament is thus received."[27] In relation to transubstantiation Ockham argues that the third opinion Peter Lombard discusses in Book Four of *The Sentences*, dist. 11, chapters 1 and 2 – that is, that the substances of bread and wine remain and coexist with the substance of the Body of Christ (consubstantiality) – is more reasonable than the view the Church adopted (transubstantiation), in which it is held that the substances of bread and wine cease to exist, while only their accidents remain, and that the Body of Christ begins to exist under those accidents. He accepts the transubstantialist view "because of the determination of the Church and not because of any argument" (*Quodlib.* IV.30, trans. 370).

Theology is not a science for Ockham. God is, after all, not an object of intuition or empirical observation. Moreover, theological statements are always based on faith (*credibilia*, such as the articles of faith), not on secure knowledge. This is why we cannot call theology a science.[28] Both Thomas and Ockham agree that theology is based on revelation. However, whereas

---

[23] McCord Adams, *William Ockham*, 1279.   [24] *Quodlib.* VI.1 art.2 (trans. 493).
[25] *Quodlib.*VI.4 art. 2 (trans. 500).
[26] Gordon Leff, *William of Ockham: The Metamorphosis of Scholastic Discourse* (Manchester: Manchester University Press, 1975), 473.
[27] McCord Adams, *William Ockham*, 1278.   [28] *Sent.* I, Prol. q.u.I, no. 2.

Thomas argued for the scientific status of theology on the grounds that it is based on principles (of faith) that share in God's own *scientia* or knowledge, Ockham rejects the scientific status of theology precisely because it is based on faith.[29] Echoing and radicalizing Duns Scotus's views, he disparages Thomas's argument that theology is a subordinate science because we somehow share in the *scientia* of God:

> It is absurd to claim that *I* have scientific knowledge with respect to this or that conclusion by reason of the fact that *you* know principles which I accept on faith because you tell them to me. And, in the same way, it is silly to claim that *I* have scientific knowledge of the conclusions of theology by reason of the fact that *God* knows principles which I accept on faith because he reveals them.[30]

OCKHAM AND THE FATE OF SCHOLASTIC THEOLOGY

Before the nominalism of William of Ockham started to exert a major influence, eroding the possibility of a realistic metaphysics, a number of authors, such as Durandus of St. Pourçain (d. 1334) and Peter Aureoli (d. 1322), had already begun to question the scholastic synthesis of reason and faith, emphasizing instead the non-demonstrability of theological claims. Ockham, however, radicalizes these views, and is therefore a controversial figure in the history of medieval theology. Scholars have focused mainly on his nominalist bias, as well as his voluntarist understanding of God. In the eyes of many commentators, Ockham's allegedly arbitrary God will generate the early modern mindset, focused on this world and its realities. The voluntarism of Ockham and others would unintentionally have led to new vistas of scientific discovery and *diesseitlich* humanism. I have already indicated that I am skeptical of this analysis. Indeed, as I see it, voluntarism is not the cause of the modern division between faith and reason, theology and philosophy. I have argued that it is the other way around. The more analytical, less intellective notion of reason and the resultant skepticism toward the marriage between theology and metaphysics nourish growing voluntarism. Again, it is not the alleged capriciousness of Ockham's God that leads to the modern worldview. Ockham's nominalism both illustrates and further contributes to the breakdown of the medieval synthesis of theology and metaphysics, faith and intellect. In a worldview in which

---

[29] Leff, *William of Ockham*, 337.
[30] *Sent.* 1. Prol. q.u. no. 7 (*Op. Theol.* 1.199), quoted and translated by Alfred J. Freddoso, "Ockham on Faith and Reason," in Spade, *The Cambridge Companion to Ockham*, 334.

reason is no longer supported by an *intellective* horizon, reason is bound to become more empirical, immanent, looking for certainties in the external, observable world; it may very well clash with key aspects of Christian faith. I have noted that Ockham accepts that reason and faith can clash (for instance, in the theology of the Trinity). In that case, we should accept the truth claims of faith. An "irenic separatism" of faith and reason allows us to do this.[31]

It is fair to say that the transcendental thrust, so prominent in earlier writers, has all but disappeared from Ockham's intellectual universe. I recall the most significant factors that contributed to this. First, there is the nominalist approach itself, which is inherently individualistic and hostile to a more *intellective* intuition of the broader horizon that grounds our rational engagements with the world.[32] Given his nominalist stance, it is no coincidence that Ockham rejected a key aspect of Christian Neoplatonism – namely, the notion of divine ideas as archetypes through which the world has been created. This undercuts one of the main pillars for the transcendental dynamic that we explored in authors as diverse as Augustine, Eriugena, Anselm, the Victorines and Bonaventure.

Ockham's strong empirical bias further reinforces the anti-transcendental character of his theological outlook. Ockham applies the Aristotelian standard of evidentness to *intellectus, scientia* and *sapientia*.[33] This further illustrates that he is moving toward a reduction of human understanding to mere *ratio* (reason). In earlier chapters we saw that medieval theologians were of the view that to be rational, we had to be intellective. In Ockham's writings, because of a more one-dimensional and empirical approach to human understanding, reason (*ratio*) is no longer framed by *intellectus*. In this more empiricist and logical-analytical universe, theology has become further separated from metaphysics. Thus, empiricism and (analytical) rationalism do not exclude but invite skepticism and a more fideist understanding of theology. In a sense we end up with two worlds: the world of empirical realities and reason, and the world of faith. From this perspective it is clear that Ockham's thought is closer to Luther or Kant than to Anselm or Thomas Aquinas.

---

[31] The term "irenic separatism" is taken from Freddoso, "Ockham on Faith and Reason," 345.

[32] By "intellective intuition" I have in mind a *noetic* mode typical of earlier medieval thinkers (in varied ways), such as Augustinian *intellectus*, Boethius's *intellegentia*, the Victorine *oculus contemplationis*, or Thomas's *intuitus simplex* through *intellectus*, not the intuitive *perception* of individual things in this world.

[33] Ibid., 336.

In short, Ockham inaugurates some genuinely modern approaches – some of which were developed by later Reformers and early modern thinkers. For in early modern times we witness the triumph of reason (*raison, ratio*) over intellect; a more empirical approach to reality, which is nothing but a collection of monads; and, finally, the separation of faith and reason, theology and philosophy.

Without initially leading to the formation of a distinct school, Ockham's ideas exerted an important and critical influence on Augustinian Gregory of Rimini (d. 1358), Nicholas of Autrecourt, John Buridan, Marsilius of Inghen and others. In the 15th century Ockhamism continued to exert an attraction on thinkers such as Gabriel Biel (d. 1495), who influenced Protestant Reformers.

It would, however, be inaccurate to claim that Ockham altogether destroyed scholastic theology. Indeed, his arguments in favor of nominalism were not universally accepted and the end of the 14th century saw Ockhamism as just one of the different schools that continued to flourish, besides, for instance, Scotism, Thomism and Albertism. These schools, however, represented the *Via Antiqua* (the old way); Ockham's was the *Via Moderna*.[34]

I conclude this book by examining two spiritual authors – for it was in mystical theology that the transcendent dynamic of the medieval mind and heart was increasingly channeled during the 14th century.

BIBLIOGRAPHICAL NOTE

Ockham's works have been edited by Gedeon Gál et al. as *Opera Philosophica et Theologica*, 17 vols. (New York: Franciscan Institute, 1967–88). For a brief discussion of Ockham's life, see William J. Courtenay, *Ockham and Ockhamism: Studies in the Dissemination and Impact of His Thought* (Leiden: Brill, 2008), 91–106. The most in-depth surveys of Ockham's thought are Armand Maurer, *The Philosophy of William of Ockham in the Light of Its Principles* (Toronto: Pontifical Institute of Medieval Studies, 1996) and Marilyn McCord Adams, *William Ockham* (Notre Dame, IN: University of Notre Dame Press, 1987). Paul Vincent Spade (ed.), *The Cambridge Companion to Ockham*

---

[34] The revival of Scholasticism in Spain in the late 15th and throughout the 16th century and beyond (e.g., Thomas de Vio [Cajetan], De Sylvestris, Melchor Cano, Molina, Bellarmine, Suarez, John of St. Thomas [d. 1644]) illustrates the ongoing vibrancy of scholastic theology well into the modern period.

(Cambridge: Cambridge University Press, 1999) contains very useful articles, including theological ones.

A number of Ockham's works have been translated: Alfred J. Freddoso and Francis E. Kelley translated the disputations as *William of Ockham: Quodlibetal Questions, vols.* 1 *and* 11 (New Haven, CT: Yale University Press, 1991), which I have used; Annabel S. Brett translated *On the Power of Emperors and Popes* (Bristol: Thoemmes Press, 1998); Marilyn McCord Adams and Norman Kretzmann translated *William of Ockham: Predestination, God's Foreknowledge, and Future Contingents* (Indianapolis, IN: Hackett, 1983). Philotheus Boehner selected a number of Ockham's philosophical writings in *Ockham: Philosophical Writings* (Edinburgh: Nelson, 1957).

CHAPTER 23

Meister Eckhart

INTRODUCTION

Meister Eckhart was a Dominican master (German: *Meister*) in theology, and a popular preacher. He was born in Tambach, Thüringen. The details of his earlier life are somewhat sketchy. It is possible Eckhart met Albert the Great and he may have studied with him shortly before Albert's death. In 1293 he lectured on Peter Lombard's *Sentences* in Paris, but the text has not survived. After acting as prior in a convent at Erfurt and as Dominican provincial in Thuringen, Eckhart returned to Paris to occupy the Dominican chair of theology. His *Parisian Questions* date from this period. A year later we find him back in Germany as the provincial of Saxony – a position he held from 1303 to 1311. From this period date some of his most important Latin writings, including *Sermons* and *Readings on the Book of Ecclesiasticus*, a *Commentary on Genesis* and a *Commentary on Wisdom*. At the bequest of his Order, Eckhart returned to Paris toward the end of 1311. Here Eckhart may have come across the writings of beguine Marguerite Porete, the author of the controversial *The Mirror of Simple Souls*. After two academic years in Paris Eckhart went to Strasbourg, which was an important center of female piety with numerous beguine houses and convents of Dominican nuns.[1] Eckhart's works written in the vernacular (Middle High German) reflect his role as spiritual director.

[1] For all of this, see the excellent book by Bernard McGinn, *The Mystical Thought of Meister Eckhart: The Man from Whom God Hid Nothing* (New York: Herder & Herder, 2001), 2–10. Two volumes in the Classics of Western Spirituality series are dedicated to Meister Eckhart: Bernard McGinn and Edmund Colledge (eds.), *Meister Eckhart: The Essential Sermons, Commentaries, Treatises, and Defense* (New York: Paulist Press, 1981) and Bernard McGinn (ed.), *Meister Eckhart: Teacher and Preacher* (New York: Paulist Press, 1986). M. O'C. Walshe has translated the German works in three volumes: *Meister Eckhart, Sermons and Treatises* (Dorset: Element, 1987). I have tackled Eckhart's thought and compared it with that of Ruusbroec in "Meister Eckhart and Jan van Ruusbroec : A Comparison," *Medieval Philosophy and Theology* 7 (1998): 157–93.

In 1323 we find Eckhart residing in Cologne, which is where an initial examination of the orthodoxy of his writings was to take place. This initial investigation, performed by his fellow Dominican friars, cleared Eckhart. A second investigation was initiated at the instigation of Archbishop Henry of Cologne, and in September 1326 Eckhart was charged with heresy by a diocesan commission.[2] Eckhart strongly refuted this accusation. He pointed out, amongst other things, that heresy is a matter of will, not intellect – that is, erroneous theological views do not make anyone a heretic; only obstinate adherence to error makes heresy.[3] Moreover, while he admitted that, taken at face value, some of his expressions may have appeared false, when properly understood they were not, and they contained "excellent and useful truths."[4]

Eckhart appealed to Pope John XXII and left for Avignon (where the pope resided) sometime in 1327. Less than a year later Eckhart had died, and the official condemnation of his views followed in March 1329, in the papal bull "In agro dominico." The document is not a blank condemnation. It consists of twenty-eight articles or sentences extracted from his writings, and these are roughly divided into two parts. The first group contains sentences considered to bear "the error or stain of heresy"; the second group is labeled as "quite evil-sounding and very rash and suspect of heresy though with many explanations and additions they might take on or possess a Catholic meaning."[5]

Eckhart's works reflect his academic, spiritual and pastoral activities. Apart from a number of sermons and commentaries on scriptural books, written in Latin, an important and highly influential part of his theological output (sermons and treatises) was written in German. *The Book of "Benedictus"* (consisting of "The Book of Divine Consolation" and a sermon "Of the Nobleman") as well as *Counsels of Discernment* are

---

[2] McGinn, *The Mystical Thought of Meister Eckhart*, 15.

[3] As Eckhart puts it in his *Defense*: "They think that everything they do not understand is an error and that every error is a heresy, when only obstinate adherence to error makes heresy and a heretic" (translation by McGinn from *Essential Sermons*, 75).

[4] See *Essential Sermons*, 76. This echoes what he had written many years earlier, in the *General Prologue* to the *Opus Tripartitum*: "It should be noted that at first sight some items from the following propositions, questions, and commentaries will appear strange, doubtful or false. But they will be judged otherwise if they are examined in a more learned and intelligent way" (translation by Armand Maurer) from *Master Eckhart: Parisian Questions and Prologues* (Toronto: Pontifical Institute of Medieval Studies, 1974), 82.

[5] For a translation see *Essential Sermons*, 77–81. It is a historical irony that some of the theological views of the pope who condemned Meister Eckhart were, in turn, censored by his successor, Pope Benedict XII, who, in his Encyclical *Benedictus Deus* (1336) declared that the souls of the just will immediately after death, before the general resurrection, enjoy the vision of God.

amongst the most widely read treatises. Scholars are divided over the question of whether the beautiful treatise *On Detachment* is Eckhart's. With Bernard McGinn, I accept that the treatise eloquently captures one of the central notions of Eckhart's spirituality.

In what follows, I first examine how Eckhart views the relation of God and creation, paying specific attention to his theological anthropology. Then I proceed to discuss his spirituality.

Eckhart's Understanding of God

In the *Parisian Questions*, 1, Eckhart claims that in God's nature understanding is superior to existence. He denies that God understands because he exists but he argues, rather, "that he exists because he understands. God is an intellect and understanding (*Deus est intellectus et intelligere*), and his understanding itself is the ground of his existence."[6] While Thomas Aquinas had argued that God's act of understanding is his being or essence (*ScG* 1.45.2; *ST* 1.14.4), Eckhart appears to drive a wedge between intellect and being. For him, being or existence has first and foremost creaturely connotations.[7] This notion of being is in marked contrast to that of Thomas for whom (divine) being is the fullness of all perfections (*ST* 1.4.2). Eckhart argues that "in God there is no being or existence (*non est ens nec esse*) ... unless of course, you wish to call understanding existence."[8] One of the arguments Eckhart puts forward for this view reveals his profoundly apophatic metaphysics:

Nothing is formally in both a cause and its effect if the cause is a true cause. Now God is the cause of all existence. It follows that existence is not formally present in God. ... Again, a principle is never the same as that which follows from a principle, as a point is never a line. Now God is the principle or cause of existence or being itself; hence he is not the being or existence of his creature.[9]

If a cause did not differ essentially from its effect it would not make sense to speak of cause and effect – for they would be essentially the same. Seeing that God is the cause of being or existence it follows that he cannot be being itself. God, as intellect, is higher than being. God thinks and therefore things are.

---

[6] See Maurer, *Master Eckhart: Parisian Questions*, 45. See also Eckhart's *Commentary on Genesis* no. 11: "God's nature is intellect, and for him existence is understanding" (translation from *Essential Sermons*, 86).

[7] Maurer, *Master Eckhart: Parisian Questions*, 46. See also Sermon 9: "Unsophisticated teachers say that God is pure being. He is as high above being as the highest angel is above a gnat. I would be speaking as incorrectly in calling God a being as if I called the sun pale or black. God is neither this nor that" (*Teacher and Preacher*, 256).

[8] Maurer, *Master Eckhart: Parisian Questions*, 48.   [9] Ibid.

With us it is the other way around: because things are, we can think about them.

I need to explore in more detail how Eckhart describes the nature of intellect, and its universal formlessness or indeterminate nature, for two reasons. First, it strengthens Eckhart's notion that God is beyond being. Second, it is essential for a proper understanding of his theological anthropology and spirituality (the so-called spark of the soul).

Aristotle had argued in *De Anima* II.7 (418b26) and III.4 (430a) that for thinking to occur the intellect has to be "unmixed," separated from matter. The mind has to become what it knows, obviously not materially, but intentionally. In order to think about the tree outside my window, I need to abstract its spiritual form of "treeness" out of its materiality, and my mind has to become the tree intentionally. This is why intellect has to be beyond all things as "a naked and empty tablet."[10] Indeed, in Eckhart's view it even has to be beyond being:

Aristotle says that the power of sight must be colorless so that it can perceive all colors, and that the intellect is not a natural form so that it can know all forms. So also I deny existence itself and suchlike of God so that he may be the cause of all existence and precontain all things.[11]

The analogy of color, which Eckhart borrows from Aristotle, is helpful. I can only perceive distinct colors if the glasses I wear are themselves neutral and non-colored. If I were to wear green glasses, I could not perceive colors properly. Similarly, I can think all things if the intellect is different from all the things it can know – that is, from all the things that are. From this Eckhart will draw the radical conclusion that the intellect is nothing.[12] It is beyond all things material; it is incorporeal, universal, indeterminate, beyond place and time, and it is beyond being:

The intellect, as an intellect, is none of the things it knows; it must be "unmixed with anything," "having nothing in common," so that it might know everything, as the *De Anima* III says. Similarly, sight must be colorless so that it can see all colors. If the intellect, therefore, insofar as it is an intellect, is nothing, it follows that neither is understanding some existence.[13]

---

[10]   *The Book of the Parables of Genesis*, no. 138, translation from *Essential Sermons*, 109.
[11]   Maurer, *Master Eckhart: Parisian Questions*, 50.
[12]   Denys Turner helpfully summarizes the argument. "If to know a thing is to become it intentionally, and if to become something intentionally is not to become it *in re*; and if the mind can know all things, then it follows that the mind cannot be anything at all *in re*. But to say that there is nothing at all that the mind is, is to say that it is *nothing*" (Turner, *The Darkness of God: Negativity in Christian Mysticism* [Cambridge: Cambridge University Press, 1995], 158).
[13]   *Parisian Questions* 2, translated in Maurer, *Master Eckhart: Parisian Questions* 51.

This applies to the divine intellect, but insofar as we are intellect, and given the features of intellect, it applies to us as well – a notion singled out in the papal bull as heretical.[14] This is why the core of our being, "the ground of the soul," is indistinguishable from God. As Eckhart puts it in *Sermon* 2, describing "the spark of the soul": "It is neither this nor that . . . it is free of all names, it is bare of all forms, wholly empty and free, as God in himself is empty and free. It is so utterly one and simple, as God is one and simple."[15] Again, in *Sermon* 69 Eckhart describes five properties of the soul, which, as intellect, is one with God (and more specifically with the Word of God). First, insofar as the soul is intellect it is beyond here and now; second, it shares in the "no-thingness" of God as intellect. "The very fact that this power is like nothing makes it like God. Just as God is like nothing, so this power is like nothing."[16] Third, it is pure and unmixed – a clear reference to the relevant passage from Aristotle's *De Anima*. Eckhart then hints at the spiritual implications of this: if the soul is indistinctly one with God at the core of its being insofar as it is intellect, it needs to become detached. "The soul should be completely without mixture . . . A person who was resting on nowhere and was attached to nothing, if someone were to overturn heaven and earth, would remain unmoved. For he would be attached to nothing and nothing would be attached to him."[17] I will return to this notion of detachment. For now, it will suffice to indicate that it can only be properly understood in light of Eckhart's theological and philosophical anthropology (and his notion of the soul as intellectual in particular). The fourth aspect Eckhart identifies in *Sermon* 69 is the inner dynamic of the soul, "in all ways seeking within itself" for God who dwells within it. The fifth aspect summarizes all the earlier characteristics Eckhart has identified: the soul is an image of the Second Person, the Word or Image. This union is so intimate that the human soul actually participates in the intra-Trinitarian dynamics – that is, the birth of the Word from the Father:

Image and image are so completely one and joined together that one cannot comprehend any distinction between them. . . . The intellect looks inside and surveys all recesses of the Godhead and perceives the Son in the heart and in the

---

[14] "There is something in the soul that is uncreated and not capable of creation; if the whole soul were such, it would be uncreated and not capable of creation, and this is the intellect." For this translation see *Essential Sermons*, 80. In *Sermon* 13 Eckhart had indeed said: "There is a power in the soul, of which I have spoken before. If the whole soul were like it, she would be uncreated and uncreatable, but this is not so. . . . To this power, the intellect, nothing is distant or external." Translation by Walshe, *Meister Eckhart: Sermons and Treatises*, vol. 1, 190.

[15] *Sermon* 2, "Intravit Jesus in quoddam castellum," translated in *Essential Sermons*, 180.

[16] See *Sermon* 69, "Modicum et iam non videbitis me," translated in *Teacher and Preacher*, 313.

[17] Ibid., trans., 314.

ground of the Father and places him in its own ground. The intellect penetrates within. ... It never rests, it bursts into the ground from which goodness and truth come forth and perceives it [God's being] in principio, in the beginning, where goodness and truth are going out, before it acquires any name, before it bursts forth. ... Further, its sister the will is satisfied with God insofar as he is good. But the intellect peels all this away and enters in and pierces through to the roots from which the Son pours forth and the Holy Spirit is blossoming forth.[18]

Given the intellectual nature of the soul, and its indistinctive or indeterminate nature, Eckhart can boldly claim that we share in the intra-Trinitarian dynamics.[19] There is nothing particularly striking about establishing a close connection between the intra-divine generation of the Son and the procession of the Holy Spirit on one hand, and the creation and sanctification of the world on the other: this is traditional fare amongst the scholastics, as we have seen. Eckhart calls the intra-divine emanations "bullitio" (a kind of boiling or bubbling), and the "spilling over" of these emanations into the creative act "ebullitio." What is original, but not surprising (given the indistinction of the intellect), is how we, as intellective beings, share in the intra-Trinitarian generation of the Son. Eckhart not only claims that the Father gives birth to his Son in the soul;[20] he goes even further. He states that we are indistinctly one with the Son whom the Father generates: "The Father gives birth to his Son without ceasing; and I say more: he gives me birth, me, his Son and the same Son. I say more: He gives birth not only to me, his Son, but he gives birth to me as himself and himself as me and to me as his being and nature."[21] Given that the Son or the Word is the revelation of the Father, the birth of God in the soul can be understood in terms of the uncovering of the image character at the heart of our being:

Giving birth is to be taken here as God's revealing self ... the more and the more clearly a person lays bare the image of God in himself, the more clearly God is born in him. And thus God's continual giving birth is to be taken to mean that the Father uncovers completely the image and is shining forth in him.[22]

The intellect is self-reflexive, which means that in our act of knowing we know that we know: the intellect "turns back upon itself" – cf. *ST* 1.14.2 *ad* 1.[23] This "turning back" or *reditio* (return) explains why in one of the previous quotations Eckhart writes that the intellect desires to "peel away"

---

[18] Ibid., trans., 314–15.
[19] Cf. *Sermon* 6, "Justi vivent in aeternum," trans. in *Essential Sermons*, 187.
[20] *Sermon* 30, *Teacher and Preacher*, 293, amongst many other places.
[21] *Sermon* 6, *Essential Sermons*, 187.   [22] *Sermon* 40, *Teacher and Preacher*, 301.
[23] The principle of *reditio completa* is derived from the Neoplatonic *Book of Causes*, proposition 15.

the distinctions of the Persons and go beyond into the nameless ground of the Godhead, "into the simple ground, into the quiet desert, into which distinction never gazed, not the Father, nor the Son, nor the Holy Spirit."[24] This teaching of the hidden ground of the Godhead beyond the Trinity is one of the most controversial aspects of Eckhart's doctrine.

Being Is God

In the *Prologue* to the *Work of Propositions* Eckhart states that Existence is God (*Esse est Deus*). The argument appears, at first sight, a startling reversal of the thesis defended earlier in the *Parisian Questions*: if existence were to be different from God, a created thing would receive its existence from something other than God, which is impossible. Again, if God and existence are different, he would exist by another, which is impossible. Therefore, God and existence are identical.[25]

In this argument, existence or being is attributed to God, and this appears at first to be radically different from what we learnt earlier about God as intellect. The two views are, however, not mutually exclusive. When Eckhart argues that existence and God are identical, he has in mind *esse simpliciter* – that is, simple or indistinct being. All beings are distinct and determinate ("this or that," as Eckhart usually puts it). God's being, however, is indistinct: it is not a thing; it is no-thing, absolute or indistinct being.

Esse est Deus can also be interpreted as a statement about creation rather than about God. In that case the statement "Being is God" should, of course, not be interpreted in a crude pantheistic sense, but rather in the sense that creatures have nothing of their own and their existence is utterly dependent upon God. Thus, what the creature possesses "it does not have from itself as something that inheres in it, but it has begged it and received it as something that is continually on loan . . . Thus, its act of existence is not its own, but it is from another and in another to whom is 'all honor and glory' because it is his."[26] Apart from God, creatures are nothing, and therefore, whatever perfections they have, they have from God: "All creatures are a pure nothing. I do not just say that they are insignificant or are only a little something: they are a nothing. Whatever has no being, *is* not. Creatures have no being because their being depends on God's

---

[24] *Sermon 48, Essential Sermons*, 198.
[25] *General Prologue*, trans. Maurer in *Master Eckhart: Parisian Questions and Prologues*, 85.
[26] The *Book of the Parables of Genesis* no. 25, translation from *Essential Sermons*, 103.

presence."[27] This statement about the radical nothingness of creation was considered "suspect of heresy" (cf. article 26 in the papal bull *In agro dominico*).

Given the notion that creatures are as nothing and whatever perfections they have are only "on loan," we should desist from treating them in a possessive manner. In other words, Eckhart's view on the nature of creation finds, again, a practical expression in his ideal of detachment. In his *Book of Divine Consolation* he writes about suffering in the following vein:

> Here is something that can console a man. . . . He ought to reflect that a man of his own nature has nothing of his own except sinfulness and weakness. Everything that is good and is goodness God has loaned him, not given him. . . . Since it is so, that everything which is good or comforting is only loaned to man, what cause has he to complain when he who has loaned it to him wishes to take it back? He ought to thank God, who has loaned it to him for so long.[28]

Before I consider this notion of detachment in more detail I want to examine the implications of the indistinct being of God in greater detail. We have seen that, insofar as creaturely perfections are from God and not our own, they can be called divine. It therefore comes as little surprise that Eckhart, in some of his more radical texts, does not allow for any distinction between divine and creaturely perfections. Moreover, the strong emphasis upon the otherness of God has, oddly enough, the same consequence – namely, that divine and creaturely perfections cannot be distinguished. God is so radically different from creation that he becomes indistinct and cannot be distinguished.

Denys Turner has eloquently described this dynamic of distinction and indistinction. He has demonstrated that in true apophaticism such as Eckhart's, God is conceived as being so different that language of distinction breaks down. While we can clearly distinguish things that have something in common (e.g., an oak tree and a spruce tree), it is much harder to say how two utterly different things (Bruckner's *Sixth Symphony* and time) are distinct. A fortiori, it is impossible to state how God differs from created things. Indeed, for Eckhart, God is distinguished by his indistinction (*esse indistinctum*) from distinct or created things.[29] Eckhart revels in the paradoxes yielded by this language of distinction and indistinction. In his *Commentary on Exodus*, nos. 113–14, for instance, he first states that nothing is as dissimilar as the Creator (who is indistinct) and creation (which is

---

[27] *Sermon* 4, "Omne datum optimum," translated in *Teacher and Preacher*, 246.
[28] The Book of "Benedictus": *The Book of Divine Consolation*, translation from *Essential Sermons*, 224.
[29] *Commentary on John* no. 562; *Teacher and Preacher*, 187.

distinct). He then argues that nothing is as similar as God and creature. The reason is well known by now: creatures owe their total existence and their perfections to God (*Esse est Deus*). In a third move he combines the two previous claims, writing that "nothing is both as dissimilar and similar to anything else as God and the creature": "What is as dissimilar and similar to something else as that whose 'dissimilitude' is its very 'similitude,' whose indistinction is its very distinction. God is distinguished from everything created, distinct, and finite by his indistinction and his infinity."[30] God's nature is not particularized or determinate – unlike created things which are all particular ("this or that": trees, flowers, women, books, chairs). God, on the other hand, is not a thing; he is no-thing, not "this or that," and therefore his very indistinctness is the only ground for his distinction.[31]

I have argued that Eckhart's two metaphysical views on God and his relation to the world are not mutually exclusive. In *Parisian Questions* he states that God is beyond being because God is intellect; in other texts he states that being is God, for the perfections of created being are utterly dependent upon God and receive their existence from him. Again, because God is radically distinct from creation he cannot be distinguished (or: his indistinction is his very distinction). And what makes God indistinct is just his intellectual nature (more specifically, its indeterminate character). Drawing on these philosophical insights I am now in a position to explore Eckhart's spiritual ideal of detachment in more detail.

Detachment

Eckhart writes that three things hinder us from hearing the eternal Word – namely, corporality, multiplicity and temporality.[32] The spark of the soul, being the apex of the intellect, which is beyond time, matter and multiplicity, is therefore the anthropological basis for attaining true union with God. This union is detachment.

---

[30] *Commentary on Exodus* no. 117, *Teacher and Preacher*, 82.

[31] Turner (*The Darkness of God*, 164) paraphrases: "In this alone is God distinct, that whereas one creature is distinct from another, God is not distinct from any of them. Thus, God's distinction from creatures consists in something no creature possesses, his indistinctness." As Eckhart himself writes in *Commentary on Exodus* no. 40: "Perhaps a more subtle reason can be given why there is no comparison between God and creature, and it is this. Every comparison implies that there are at least two things and that they are distinct, for nothing is compared to itself or is like itself. Every created being taken or conceived apart as distinct in itself from God is not a being, but is nothing. . . . Through this we can well grasp what Jerome [*Epistola* 15 (to Damasus) no. 4] says: "Our existence is not compared with God's"" (*Teacher and Preacher*, 55).

[32] *Sermon* 12, *Teacher and Preacher*, 267.

While Eckhart's philosophical analysis, discussed earlier, is important to understand his spiritual ideal, it would, however, be a mistake to ignore the important Christological aspect of this union. Exploiting the fact that the Word did not assume a particular person but a universal nature, without particularity, he encourages his readers to let go of their own particularity:

God assumed human nature and united it with his Person. At this point human nature became God because he took on a human nature and not a human being (*menschliche nature blôz und keinen menschen*). Therefore, if you want to be this same Christ and God, abandon all of that which the eternal Word did not assume. The eternal Word did not assume *a* man. Therefore, leave whatever is *a* man in you and whatever you are, and take yourself purely according to human nature.[33]

Eckhart argues for letting go of particularity by drawing on Christological (the universal human nature the Word assumed, as in the previous quotation), Trinitarian (breakthrough beyond the divine Persons into the divine ground[34]) or anthropological insights (intellect as universal and beyond multiplicity[35]). In all cases, however, his real concern appears to be to point his readers toward a new disposition with which to relate to God, self and the world. This disposition is detachment (*Abegescheidenheit, Gelâzenheit*).

Whoever really and truly has God, he has him everywhere, in the street and in company with everyone, just as much as in church or in solitary places or in his cell. But if a man really has God, and has only God, then no one can hinder him. Why? Because he has only God, and his intention is towards God alone (*meinet aleine got*), and all things become for him nothing but God. . . . No one can hinder this man, for he intends and seeks and takes delight in nothing but God, for God has become one with the man in all his intention (*meinunge*). And so, just as no multiplicity can disturb God, nothing can disturb or fragment this man, for he is one in that One where all multiplicity is one and is one unmulitplicity.[36]

The German words for "disturb" and "fragment" are *zerströuwen* (modern German: *zerstreuen*) and *vermanicvaltigen* (modern German: *vermannigfaltigen*) respectively. These words have strong connotations of being scattered, of losing oneself in distractions (in the sense in which Pascal

---

[33] *Sermon 24, Teacher and Preacher*, 286.
[34] See *Sermon 48, Essential Sermons*, 198: "[The spark of the soul] wants to know the source of this essence, it wants to go into the simple ground, into the quiet desert, into which distinction never gazed, not the Father, nor the Son, nor the Holy Spirit."
[35] See *Sermon 69*, quoted earlier; also see *The Book of the Parables of Genesis* no. 32; *Sermon 2* in *Essential Sermons*, 181: "I have sometimes said that there is a power in the spirit that alone is free. . . . It is free of all names, it is bare of all forms, wholly empty and free, as God himself is empty and free. It is so utterly one and simple, as God is one and simple, that man cannot in any way look into it."
[36] *Counsels on Discernment* no. 6, *Essential Sermons*, 251–52.

used the word) that divert us from what should be our real focus (*mei-nunge*) in life – God. This is not to say that creatures are somehow in competition with God. Nor is Eckhart asking us to become will-less or free from desire. On the contrary, as the beginning of the quotation suggests, Eckhart's spirituality is one that is very much embedded in our daily world. Indeed, he states that it is better to give a bowl of soup to a hungry person than to enjoy the delights of ecstasy.[37] The point he is trying to make is, therefore, that we should approach our world with a theocentric focus or intention. Rather than proposing we abandon desire he admonishes us that our will should become free from self-seeking and possessiveness (*âne alle eigenschaft*).[38] Indeed, Eckhart describes detachment by using the analogy of somebody consumed with a burning thirst. Everything this person does will be accompanied by his desire for water. Similarly, anyone who has detachment will have God present to him in all his activities.[39]

Denys Turner has captured the essence of detachment well when he argues that Eckhartian detachment is not an experience beside other experiences but rather a schema or category of experience – that is, detachment shapes all our experiences.[40] It is a disposition, a way of relating to the world, and not an experience in its own right: "Detachment and interiority are, for Eckhart, not so much the names of experiences as practices for the transformation of experience."[41] Because it involves a radical dispossession of self-centeredness it is actually the condition of possibility of genuine love.[42]

Eckhart thus asks us to reflect the gratuity of God himself: "God seeks nothing of his own. In all his works he is empty and free and works them out of genuine love. This is how the person acts who is united with God. He, too, is empty and free in all his works and he does them only for the glory of God, seeking nothing of his own."[43] Doing everything for the sake of God, seeking nothing of our own implies that we live and love "without a why" – just as God has no "why" outside or beyond himself.[44] The person who has attained detachment will be virgin and wife at the same time, fruitful in her works and yet detached and devoid of all self-centeredness in her dealings with God, world and self. Detachment is therefore radically

---

[37] *Counsels on Discernment* no. 10, *Essential Sermons*, 258.   [38] Ibid., 257.
[39] *Counsels on Discernment* no. 6, *Essential Sermons*, 253.   [40] Turner, *The Darkness of God*, 179.
[41] Ibid.
[42] See the text *On Detachment* (usually attributed to Eckhart) and Turner, *The Darkness of God*, 183.
[43] *Sermon 1*, *Teacher and Preacher*, 240.
[44] *Commentary on Exodus* no. 247 (*ut non habeat quare extra se aut praeter se*); *Commentary on John* no. 50; *Sermon 4*: "God and hence the divine man does not act for the sake of a why or wherefore" (*Teacher and Preacher*, 207).

different from escapism or Stoic indifference. On the contrary, detachment (and the radical theocentric focus it implies) results in a thorough engagement with the world in a non-possessive manner. The very selflessness of detachment allows us to treat the world in a non-instrumentalizing manner, without either idolizing it or abusing it. In this, Eckhart has given the most eloquent expression of the gratuity already implied in the Augustinian notion of fruition of God, or Thomas's understanding of Christian love in triangular terms.

BIBLIOGRAPHICAL NOTE

The critical edition is *Meister Eckhart: Die deutschen und lateinischen Werke herausgegeben im Auftrag der deutschen Forschungsgemeinschaft* (Stuttgart/ Berlin: Kohlhammer, 1936–). An inexpensive, bilingual edition of some works (with facing modern German translation and commentary) has been published in the Bibliothek Deutscher Klassiker by Niklaus Largier (ed.), *Meister Eckhart. Werke* I. *Predigten* (Frankfurt: Deutscher Klassiker, 1993) and *Meister Eckhart. Deutsche Werke* II *und Lateinische Werke* (Frankfurt: Deutscher Klassiker, 1993).

Two volumes in the Classics of Western Spirituality series are dedicated to Meister Eckhart: Bernard McGinn and Edmund Colledge (eds.), *Meister Eckhart: The Essential Sermons, Commentaries, Treatises, and Defense* (New York: Paulist Press, 1981) and Bernard McGinn (ed.), *Meister Eckhart: Teacher and Preacher* (New York: Paulist Press, 1986). M.O'C. Walshe has translated the German works in three volumes: *Meister Eckhart: Sermons and Treatises* (Dorset: Element, 1987). Fernand Brunner et al. had published some of the Latin works, with facing French translation in *L'Oeuvre Latine de Maitre Eckhart* (Paris: Cerf, 1984, 1989).

Bernard McGinn, *The Mystical Thought of Meister Eckhart: The Man from Whom God Hid Nothing* (New York: Herder & Herder, 2001) is an excellent introduction. For a brief but profound engagement with Meister Eckhart's thought (from which I have greatly benefited) see Denys Turner, *The Darkness of God: Negativity in Christian Mysticism* (Cambridge: Cambridge University Press, 1995), chapters 6–7. A rich collection is Jeremiah Hackett (ed.), *A Companion to Meister Eckhart* (Leiden: Brill, 2012).

CHAPTER 24

Jan van Ruusbroec and the Modern Devotion

Jan van Ruusbroec's original theology illustrates the ongoing vibrancy of Trinitarian thinking throughout the 14th century. Ruusbroec also develops a rich spirituality that is deeply shaped by this Trinitarian vision – and this constitutes one of the most attractive aspects of his thought.

Jan van Ruusbroec (1293–1381) first became a priest in Brussels, but later retired to a new monastery in the Zonien Forest, where the members of his community adopted the rule of St. Augustine (Augustinian canons). He wrote all his works in Middle Dutch (Flemish), although some of his letters survive only in Latin translation.[1] He wrote his most influential book, *Die Geestelike Brulocht* (*The Spiritual Espousals*) sometime in the early 1340s. As we saw in Chapter 14, vernacular religious literature flourished in countries with Germanic languages from the early 13th century onward. In countries in which Romance languages were spoken (closer to Latin) vernacular religious texts originated somewhat later.

Ruusbroec knew the writings of Hadewijch, but he draws on many other sources as well (Augustinian, Pseudo-Dionysian, 12th-century Cistercian, Bonaventurean, beguine and Rhineland influences) to develop a highly original mystical theology of the Trinity that shapes every aspect of his thought. The Bonaventurean influence shows itself in Ruusbroec's view that the Father generates his Son from the fruitfulness of his paternal

---

[1] Jan van Ruusbroec's own works (*Opera Omnia*, as edited by Guido De Baere) are available in a trilingual edition (Middle Dutch, Latin, English translation) in *CCCM* 100–10, published by Brepols in Turnhout (1988–2005). The following are some of his more important works: *The Spiritual Espousals* (*Die Geestelike Brulocht*), *A Mirror of Eternal Blessedness* (*Een Spieghelder Eeuwigher Salicheit*), *The Sparkling Stone* (*Vanden Blinkenden Steen*), *The Realm of Lovers* (*Dat Rike der Ghelieven*), *The Little Book of Clarification* (*Boecsken der Verclaringhe*), *The Four Temptations* (*Vanden Vier Becoringhen*), *The Seven Rungs* (*Van.vii.Trappen*) and *The Twelve Beguines* (*Vanden xii Beghinen*), amongst others. An easily accessible selection is found in The Classics of Western Spirituality series, *John Ruusbroec: The Spiritual Espousals and Other Writings*, trans. James Wiseman (New York: Paulist Press, 1985). An overview of Ruusbroec's theology and mysticism can be found in Rik Van Nieuwenhove, *Jan van Ruusbroec: Mystical Theologian of the Trinity* (Notre Dame, IN: University of Notre Dame Press, 2003).

nature. From the mutual contemplation of the Father and his Word, the Holy Spirit proceeds as their bond of Love. However, Ruusbroec then introduces an important innovation. He argues that the Holy Spirit, as the bond of Love between Father and Son, is the principle of the return of the divine Persons into their perichoretic unity, from which the whole dynamic process starts all over again. Ruusbroec therefore describes the Trinity as "an ebbing, flowing sea" in which (a) the Son and the Holy Spirit go out from the Father; (b) they flow back into the divine unity, where (c) they rest in enjoyment or fruition.

For this noble nature that is the principal cause of all creatures is fruitful. Therefore it cannot rest in the unity of the Fatherhood, because of the stirrings (*ghedueren*) of fruitfulness; but it must without cease give birth to the eternal Wisdom, that is, the Son of the Father. Always, without cease, the Son of God was born, and is born, and will remain unborn: nevertheless it is all one Son. Where the Father beholds his Son, the eternal Wisdom, and all things in the same Wisdom: there he has been born and is a Person other than the Father. . . . Neither out of the fruitful nature, that is, Fatherhood, nor out of the Father's giving birth to his Son does Love, that is, the Holy Spirit flow; but out of the fact that the Son is born a Person other than the Father, where the Father beholds him as born, and everything one with him as the life of everything, and the Son, in turn, beholds the Father giving birth and fruitful, and himself, and all things, in the Father – this is seeing and seeing-back in a fruitful nature – from this comes Love, that is, the Holy Spirit, a bond from the Father to the Son and from the Son to the Father. By this Love, the Persons are embraced and permeated and have flowed back (*wedervloeit*) into that unity out of which the Father without cease is giving birth. Now, even though they have flowed back into unity, there is no abiding, on account of nature's fruitfulness. This birth-giving and this flowing back into unity is the work of the Trinity. Thus, there is threeness of Persons and oneness of nature.[2]

The Bonaventurean influence is obvious in Ruusbroec's description of the processions of Word and Holy Spirit. The fruitfulness of the divine nature leads to the generation of the Son from the Father, and from their mutual contemplation the Holy Spirit proceeds as their bond of Love. The innovative element in Ruusbroec's view is the notion that the divine Persons flow back into the divine essence. This is *regiratio* in scholastic Latin or *wederboeghen* in Middle Dutch. The Holy Spirit is the principle of this return because the Holy Spirit, as the mutual bond of Love between Father and Son, is the unifying principle who initiates the loving return into the divine unity. After all, it belongs to the nature of Love to return

---

[2] *Opera Omnia*, vol. IV, *Dat Rijcke der Ghelieven*, lines 1597–1624 (translation partly modified). All references to the *Opera Omnia* include references to the lines in the Middle Dutch text.

what it receives (*Minnen natuere es altoes gheven ende nemen*), not because it feels indebted and wants to settle the balance, but rather out of sheer gratuity, in order to allow the other to give once more, in a never-ending dynamic of giving and receiving.[3]

Ruusbroec describes the Trinity as "an ebbing, flowing sea," with the Son and the Holy Spirit *going out* from the Father and then *flowing back* into the divine unity, where they *rest* in enjoyment. This never-ending dynamic of divine going out, flowing back in, and resting in enjoyment determines every aspect of Ruusbroec's thought. The notion of Love as bestowed and returned molds, for instance, his understanding of the economy of grace: God bestows his grace, but we need to "return" (or respond to) his gift through our charitable works. Similarly, the gift of the God-man can be seen in the same way: God bestows his Son, but in the humanity of the God-man we are allowed to participate in the return of this gift – a perspective that allows us to interpret the Cross and the Eucharist in terms of the Trinitarian dynamic of Love bestowed and returned.[4]

This dynamic vision of the Trinitarian life has important implications for the way Ruusbroec conceives of the Christian life. Indeed, in a beautiful passage from his short treatise *The Sparkling Stone* (*Vanden Blinkenden Steen*) Ruusbroec outlines how the Trinitarian life shapes our transformation. It is effectively a description of growing self-transcendence of the human person through participation in the Trinitarian life. Ruusbroec adopts the traditional distinction between hired servants, faithful servants, secret friends and hidden sons to describe this process.[5]

The *hired servants* only want to serve God for their own gain. They are profoundly self-centered. They have no idea what true love is about, and hence "they always remain alone with themselves."[6] Even if they fulfill religious obligations, they do so only out of fear, which illustrates their self-love and self-preoccupation (*minnen die si tot hem selven hebben*). They are effectively intent on themselves in all their activities (*want si soeken ende meinen hem selves in al hare werken*). However, when, with God's assistance, they overcome their self-centeredness (*sine eyghenheit*), God becomes

---

[3] *Opera Omnia*, vol. vii A, *Vanden xii Beghinen*, 2b 674; see Van Nieuwenhove, *Jan van Ruusbroec*, 136–38.

[4] Van Nieuwenhove, *Jan van Ruusbroec*, 138–56.

[5] *Vanden Blinkenden Steen* from *Jan van Ruusbroec. Opera Omnia*, vol. x, *CCCM* 110 editor in chief, G. de Baere (Turnhout: Brepols, 1991), lines 265–476 in Middle Dutch text. See Van Nieuwenhove, *Jan van Ruusbroec*, 67–70.

[6] *Vanden Blinkenden Steen*, 269–79.

their focus and they are intent upon God in everything they do. Thus they become *faithful servants.*[7]

Faithful servants lead a busy, active life of virtue. They are preoccupied with improving the world. God sent his servants out for his service "in all manner of outward (*uutwendighen*) good works." They remain, however, interiorly unenlightened and know little of a loving and fervent adherence to God. The latter is a feature of the *friends*: they are drawn inward (*inweert*), attracted to an interior, spiritual life.[8] The faithful servants are too preoccupied with or distracted (in the Pascalian sense of the word) by their works (*verbeelt met den werken*), and these become a source of self-satisfaction to them. As a matter of fact, the faithful servants are critical of the friends, claiming that the latter are wasting their time with their inwardness and inner devotion. Predictably, Ruusbroec refers in this context to the biblical story of Martha and Mary.[9] Mary chose the best part, an interior life desirous of God, unlike Martha, who lost herself in her busyness and preoccupations. But the interior life, symbolized by the secret friends, has its own temptations. The friends remain too preoccupied (*verbeelt*) with themselves and their interior practices. Religion and the spiritual consolations it offers may become a source of attachment in their own right. In that case devotion itself – or rather the self-centeredness still attached to it – may become a hindrance in our transformation. It is only the hidden *sons* who have attained the utter detachment or selflessness that allows them to rest in God with a love that is its own reason. Ruusbroec describes this as a passing away of the self and its possessiveness, in God (*in gode ghestorven haers selves ende alre eyghenscap*).[10] Whereas the faithful servants lead an active life (i.e., a life of charitable activity), and the friends an interior or God-yearning life, the hidden sons lead a contemplative life.[11]

There is nothing particularly original about these metaphors of servants, friends and sons. They are inspired by John Cassian (from a passage in the *Conferences* where he comments on the story of the prodigal son) and had been adopted by Bernard of Clairvaux.[12] There are, however, two aspects that make Ruusbroec's outline of particular interest to us. First, he points out that these dimensions of the spiritual life do not cancel one another

---

[7] Ibid., 307ff.   [8] Ibid., 325–29.   [9] Ibid., 329–84.   [10] Ibid., 429.

[11] Ibid., 477–78. Ruusbroec sometimes calls it a super-essential life; he adopts the Pseudo-Dionysian term "super-essential" because this life perfectly reflects and participates in our archetypal existence as idea in the Word.

[12] See John Cassian, *Conferences*, XI.vii.1–6 and St. Bernard of Clairvaux, *On Loving God*, chapters 13–14.

out. That is, even sons must still be servants (i.e., lead an active life) and friends (i.e., lead an inward or interior life). This implies that the contemplative life is not the highest life for Ruusbroec. The most perfect life is a life that combines all of these dimensions. This Ruusbroec calls the common life, which harmoniously integrates charitable activity and contemplation. I will come back to how Ruusbroec understands this combination.

Second, what is profoundly original is the Trinitarian interpretation Ruusbroec gives to these different dimensions of the spiritual life. The active life of the faithful servants, as a life of virtue and external activity, mirrors the "out-going" aspect of the Trinity (the generation of the Son and the procession of the Spirit). The inner or God-yearning life of the friends from *The Sparkling Stone* mirrors the "in-going" aspect of the divine Persons (*regiratio*) at the heart of the Trinity. The contemplative life of the hidden sons, in which we possess God in utter emptiness of self, detached and totally focused on God, mirrors the "fruition" or enjoyable "rest" of the divine Persons in their perichoretic unity.

The common life is then a combination of these aspects; that is to say, the mature Christian will engage in virtuous activity (thereby mirroring the "activity" of the divine Persons in the bosom of the Trinity) and also "rest" in God (just like the divine Persons "rest" in the shared essence). This is how Ruusbroec describes this integration of activity and rest in the common life (perhaps better translated as universal or catholic life):

God's Spirit breathes us out to love and perform virtuous works, and he draws us back into him to rest and enjoy: this is an eternal life, just like in our bodily life we breathe air in and out . . . to *go in*, in idle enjoyment, and to *go out* with works, and *always remaining united* with God's Spirit: that is what I mean. Just like we open and close our bodily eyes, so quick that we do not feel it, likewise we die in God and live from God, and constantly remain one with God. Thus we will *go out* into our ordinary life and *go in* with love and cleave to God, and always remain *united* with God in stillness.[13]

Ruusbroec's ideal of the common life echoes and radicalizes Gregory the Great's ideal of the *vita mixta* (the mixed life) in which charitable activity and contemplation are in perfect harmony with one another. But how exactly are we to understand this? How can we both enjoy and rest in God and yet be active? What does it mean to rest in God or to enjoy God?

Ruusbroec's language of "enjoying God" or "resting in God" (he treats the expressions as synonymous) recalls the Augustinian distinction

---

[13] *Van Seven Trappen, Opera Omnia* IX, CCCM 109, 1121–32 (my translation and italics).

between *frui* and *uti.*[14] As explained in Chapter 2, Augustine's notion of fruition of God refers to a radical theocentric focus we should adopt in all our dealings with the world. Only God should be our *ultimate* concern. Similarly, Ruusbroec explains the notion of "enjoying God" by developing the notion of the single intention (*die eenvuldighe meyninghe*), or theocentric focus – a term we encountered in Eckhart's writings as well (*meinunge*). "Resting in God" means that our love and knowledge have to be solely focused on God: "Whoever is not intent on God and does not love him above himself and all things (*die gode niet en meynt noch mint boven hem selven ende boven alle dinc*) will always be reckless and not heed the honour of God and all true virtue and God himself."[15] In a small treatise, entitled *The Four Temptations*, Ruusbroec stresses the importance of "dying to our own will," "breaking the bonds of disorderly affections for creatures,"[16] etc., so as to be raised above ourselves, "free in mind, unhindered, above all things into the eternal Good that is our inheritance and our bliss."[17] Again he emphasizes the importance of an intention (*meyninghe*) or disposition that focuses solely on God and that does not allow for disordered creaturely distractions or attachments. Once we realize that the contemplative aspect of enjoyment of God refers to a theocentric focus or intention we can begin to understand how this aspect can be combined with a life of virtue. Fruition of God refers to a radical theocentric focus in all our activities and practices (be they acts of virtue or more devotional acts). Ruusbroec puts it succinctly. "Therefore he has a common life, for contemplation and action come just as readily to him and he is perfect in both."[18]

In summary, Ruusbroec distinguishes between three "lives" or aspects of the mystical journey: an active life, which for him refers to a life of charitable activity, an interior or God-yearning life and a contemplative life in which we enjoy God. His spiritual ideal, then, is the common (or universal) life – that is, a life that combines virtuous "out-going" activity and interior and devout "in-going" practices with the fruitive aspect of contemplation – thus mirroring the threefold aspect of the intra-Trinitarian movement – that is, the going-out, the going-in and the moment of enjoyment of the divine Persons.

---

[14] Augustine too had associated enjoyment and rest, as in the following quotation from *De Trin.* x.13: "We enjoy things we know when the will reposes (*conquiescit*) in them because it is delighted by them for their own sakes; we use things when we refer them to something else we should enjoy. And what makes the life of men vicious and reprehensible is nothing but using things badly and enjoying them badly" (trans. E. Hill from St. Augustine, *The Trinity* [New York: New City Press, 1994], 296).

[15] *Vanden Vier Becoringhen*, 51–54.   [16] Ibid., 292–94, 329–30, 39–40, 302–05.   [17] Ibid., 340–45.

[18] Ibid., 948–49.

Ruusbroec's successors in the Low Countries did not retain his ideal of the common life conceived as a participation in the intra-Trinitarian dynamics. Henricus Herp (d. 1477), for instance, who incorporated huge chunks from Ruusbroec's works into his own *Theologia Mystica* (a work that exerted a profound influence upon the Spanish mystics of the 16th century) only focused on Ruusbroec's more phenomenological descriptions of the transformative effects of grace upon the soul. He does not, however, mention the common life. His spirituality therefore becomes more experiential and less Trinitarian.

Similarly, Geert Grote (d. 1384), the translator of some of Ruusbroec's works into Latin and founder of the Devotio Moderna (Modern Devotion) movement, develops a Christocentric spirituality that steers away from Trinitarian speculation.[19] The same can be said about the writings of Florens Radewijns, Gerard Zerbolt van Zutphen and Thomas a Kempis's *The Imitation of Christ*, the most celebrated exponent of the Modern Devotion. The Modern Devotion can therefore be best characterized as a practical, somewhat moralistic, ascetic, Christocentric, nonspeculative movement, with initially at least an important impetus from laypeople, aimed at reforming the Catholic Church in the Low Countries. It should be seen neither as a movement of Christian humanism (Albert Hyma) nor as a precursor to the Protestant Reformation or the Italian Renaissance. John Van Engen has argued, convincingly in my view, that the movement can be best understood as a Catholic Reform movement. It was not anticlerical and had no ambitions of making theological innovations. Its emphasis upon cultivation and discipline of the will must have struck Reformers as deeply alien to their way of thinking.[20]

If one wants to link the Modern Devotion with a Renaissance, one will first have to explore in more depth the nature of the Renaissance as it took place in Northern Europe (specifically the Low Countries) during the first half of the 15th century.[21] This Renaissance was very different from the Italian one, if only because it was deeply religious. It found its most magnificent expression in some of the paintings of the School of Flemish Primitives (Jan van Eyck, Rogier van der Weyden, Petrus Christus, Hans

---

[19] For texts from the Modern Devotion in English translation, see especially John Van Engen (ed.), *Devotio Moderna: Basic Writings* (New York: Paulist Press, 1988) and also Rik Van Nieuwenhove, Rob Faesen and Helen Rolfson (eds.), *Late Medieval Mysticism of the Low Countries* (New York: Paulist Press, 2008). The latter includes extracts from Herp.

[20] See John Van Engen, "Introduction," in *Devotio Moderna: Spiritual Writings*. Classics of Western Spirituality (New York: Paulist Press, 1988), 58–61.

[21] Susie Nash, *Northern Renaissance Art* (Oxford: Oxford University Press, 2008) offers a scholarly overview.

Memling, Hugo van der Goes). In their works, the religious aspect often grounds the portrayal of everyday life. For instance, in the famous painting by Jan van Eyck, *The Madonna with Chancellor Rolin* (ca. 1435), the gaze of the onlooker is drawn toward the center of the painting, which looks out to a town with people going about their daily business. This scene is sur-rounded or "framed," so to speak, by the Madonna and Child on the right and the praying chancellor on the left. (Rogier van der Weyden adopted this layout in his own painting of *St. Luke Drawing the Virgin.*) Similarly, Jan van Eyck's famous, homely portrayal of the *Arnolfini Marriage* (ca. 1434) is imbued with religious references and symbolism, such as the enclosed garden (cf. Sg 4:12), fruit on the windowsill (Gen. 3:2) and sandals (cf. Exod. 3:5). Thus the works of the Flemish Primitives portray our everyday world in perfect harmony with and permeated by the Christian faith, thereby expressing the Christian worldview of the medieval period in a superb artistic manner.

BIBLIOGRAPHICAL NOTE

Jan van Ruusbroec's own works (*Opera Omnia*, as edited by Guido De Baere) are available in a trilingual edition (Middle Dutch, Latin, English translation) in *CCCM* 100–10, published by Brepols in Turnhout (1988–2005). An easily accessible selection is found in the Classics of Western Spirituality series, *John Ruusbroec: The Spiritual Espousals and Other Writings*, trans. by James Wiseman (New York: Paulist Press, 1985).

An overview of Ruusbroec's theology and mysticism can be found in Rik Van Nieuwenhove, *Jan van Ruusbroec: Mystical Theologian of the Trinity* (Notre Dame, IN: University of Notre Dame Press, 2003).

CHAPTER 25

Epilogue

Undoubtedly in the 14th century we witness the gradual erosion of the medieval synthesis of faith and reason, theology and philosophy. William of Ockham is not the only thinker who represents this evolution, but he is perhaps its most celebrated (or reviled) exponent. Indeed, Ockham's universe, consisting of absolute substances that we access in an empirical manner, inaugurates some of the key intuitions of the modern world. I have suggested that his moderate voluntarism and fairly radical nominalism have to be interpreted in light of the changing nature of *ratio* and the growing division of faith and reason, theology and metaphysics at the end of the 13th century.

Instead of repeating some of this earlier analysis I would like to revisit the reasons why an engagement with medieval theology can both challenge and enrich our contemporary theological scene.

I find several aspects particularly appealing, such as the rich understanding of human intelligence (encompassing both reason and intellect), the sacramental understanding of creation, the profound Trinitarian vision of several of the key thinkers that passed our review and, above all, the thrust toward the transcendent that permeates the thought and desire of medieval theologians and spiritual writers.

Medieval theology offers an extraordinarily pluralist view on some of the most important theological issues. Thomas Aquinas's understanding of the Triune God is, for instance, rather different from that of Peter Abelard, William of St. Thierry, Bonaventure, Meister Eckhart or Ruusbroec. And yet this pluralism is supported by an overarching vision, which all major medieval theologians share – namely, that it is only in the fruition of God that our hearts can find ultimate fulfillment and peace.

Bibliography

While there are many excellent *Introduction to Medieval Philosophy* books (Etienne Gilson, Frederick Copleston, Gordon Leff, Armand Maurer, David Luscombe, John Marenbon), this book is the first *Introduction to Medieval Theology* in any language I know. A more exhaustive and broad-ranging survey by Giulio D'Onofrio, *History of Theology: The Middle Ages* (Collegeville, MN: Liturgical Press, 2008), covers many figures (including some minor ones I could not discuss in this book). Thankfully there are some outstanding introductions to individual medieval thinkers. Two series deserve special mention: The Great Medieval Thinkers (with Brian Davies as series editor), published by Oxford University Press, and Brill's Companions to the Christian Tradition with Christopher M. Bellitto as editor in chief, which contains many useful volumes on major figures from the medieval period.

The Internet offers an outstanding resource for lovers of medieval thought. Some key primary sources are now available on the Internet; I offer a sample:

Patrologia Latina (which contains the texts from all major Latin theologians until ca. 1200) is available in PDF on: www.documentacatholicaomnia.eu/25 _10_30_Volumina.html. The texts should be compared with more recent critical editions, such as those from Corpus Christianorum (Turnhout: Brepols) or Sources Chrétiennes (Paris: Éditions du Cerf). The text of the Latin works of Augustine (PL) is freely available on: www.augustinus.it/latino/index.htm.

A translation of Gregory the Great's *Moralia* is available at: www.lectionarycentral.com/GregoryMoraliaIndex.html.

Bernard of Clairvaux's works are available on: www.binetti.ru/bernardus.

The works of Albert the Great (Borgnet edition) are hosted by: http://albertusmagnus.uwaterloo.ca.

The complete works of Thomas Aquinas are available on: www.corpusthomisticum.org; for an online bilingual edition with English translation of the *Opera Omnia* by the Aquinas Institute, Wyoming, see https://aquinasinstitute.org.

I refer the reader to relevant chapters of this book for primary texts (and translations) of individual theologians. What follows is a basic bibliography of secondary literature.

SECONDARY LITERATURE

Aers, David. *Salvation and Sin: Augustine, Langland, and Fourteenth Century Theology* (Notre Dame, IN: University of Notre Dame Press, 2009).

Aertsen, Jan. *Medieval Philosophy and the Transcendentals: The Case of Thomas Aquinas* (Leiden: Brill, 1996).

Arblaster, John, and Rob Faesen (eds.). *A Companion to John of Ruusbroec* (Leiden: Brill, 2014).

Ayres, Lewis. *Augustine and the Trinity* (Cambridge: Cambridge University Press, 2010).

  Nicaea and Its Legacy: An Approach to Fourth Century Trinitarian Theology (Oxford: Oxford University Press, 2006).

Backman, Clifford. *The Worlds of Medieval Europe* (Oxford: Oxford University Press, 2003).

Bauerschmidt, Frederick. *Thomas Aquinas: Faith, Reason, and Following Christ* (Oxford: Oxford University Press, 2013).

Biard, Joël. *Guillaume D'Ockham et la Théologie* (Paris: Cerf, 1999).

Boulnois, Olivier. *Duns Scot. La Rigueur de la Charité* (Paris: Cerf, 1998).

Broadie, Alexander. *The Shadow of Scotus: Philosophy and Faith in Pre-Reformation Scotland* (Edinburgh: T&T Clark, 1995).

Brower, Jeffrey E. "Trinity," in Jeffrey E. Brower and Kevin Guilfoy (eds.), *The Cambridge Companion to Abelard* (Cambridge: Cambridge University Press, 2004), 223–57.

Brower, Jeffrey E., and Kevin Guilfoy (eds.). *The Cambridge Companion to Abelard* (Cambridge: Cambridge University Press, 2004).

Carabine, Deirdre. *John Eriugena Scottus* (Oxford: Oxford University Press, 2000).

Carpenter, Charles. *Theology as the Road to Holiness in St. Bonaventure* (New York: Paulist Press, 1997).

Chadwick, Henry. *Augustine of Hippo: A Life* (Oxford: Oxford University Press, 2010).

Clark, Mary T. *Augustine of Hippo* (New York: Continuum, 2000).

Colish, Marcia. "Christological Nihilianism in the Second Half of the Twelfth Century." *Recherches de théologie ancienne et médiévale* 63 (1996): 146–55.

  Medieval Foundations of the Western Intellectual Tradition 400–1400 (New Haven, CT: Yale University Press, 1998).

  Peter Lombard. 2 vols. (Leiden: Brill, 1994).

Coolman, Boyd Taylor. "The Comprehensive Trinitarianism of the *Summa Halensis*," in Lydia Schumacher (ed.), *The Summa Halensis: Doctrines and Debates* (Berlin: De Gruyter, 2020), 107–40.

  Knowledge, Love and Ecstasy in the Theology of Thomas Gallus (Oxford: Oxford University Press, 2017).

  The Theology of Hugh of St. Victor: An Interpretation (Cambridge: Cambridge University Press, 2010).

Copleston, Frederick. *A History of Philosophy: Augustine to Scotus* (Westminster, MD: Newman Press, 1950).

Courtenay, William. *Ockham and Ockhamism: Studies in the Dissemination and Impact of His Thought* (Leiden: Brill, 2008).

Cross, Richard. *Duns Scotus* (Oxford: Oxford University Press, 1999).

Duns Scotus on God (Aldershot: Ashgate, 2005).

Cullen, Christopher. *Bonaventure* (Oxford: Oxford University Press, 2006).

Davies, Brian. "Anselm and the Ontological Argument," in Brian Davies and Brian Leftow (eds.), *The Cambridge Companion to Anselm* (Cambridge: Cambridge University Press, 2004), 157–78.

The Thought of Thomas Aquinas (Oxford: Oxford University Press, 1993).

Davies, Brian, and Brian Leftow (eds.). *The Cambridge Companion to Anselm* (Cambridge: Cambridge University Press, 2004).

Davies, Brian, and Eleonore Stump (eds.). *The Oxford Handbook to Aquinas* (Oxford: Oxford University Press, 2011).

Decorte, Jos. *Raak me niet aan. Over middeleeuws en postmiddeleeuws transcendentiedenken* (Kapellen: Pelckmans, 2001).

Waarheid als Weg. Beknopte Geschiedenis van de Middeleeuwse Wijsbegeerte (Kapellen: Pelckmans, 1992).

De Libera, Alain. *Métaphysique et Noétique. Albert le Grand* (Paris: Vrin, 2005).

De Lubac, Henri. *Medieval Exegesis.* 4 vols. (Grand Rapids, MI: Eerdmans, 1998ff.).

Di Giovanni, Matteo. "Averroes and Philosophy in Islamic Spain," in John Marenbon (ed.), *The Oxford Handbook of Medieval Philosophy* (Oxford: Oxford University Press, 2012), 106–29.

D'Onofrio, Giulio. *History of Theology: The Middle Ages* (Collegeville, MN: Liturgical Press, 2008).

Dudden, F. H. *Gregory the Great: His Place in History and Thought, vol. II* (London: Longmans, Green and Company, 1905).

Dulles, Avery. *The Assurance of Things Hoped for: A Theology of Christian Faith* (Oxford: Oxford University Press, 1997).

El-Rouayheb, Khaled, and Sabine Schmidtke (eds.). *The Oxford Handbook of Islamic Philosophy* (Oxford: Oxford University Press, 2017).

Emery, Gilles. "Le Sacerdoce spirituel des fidéles chez Saint Thomas d'Aquin," *Revue Thomiste* 99 (1999): 211–43.

La Trinité Créatrice (Paris: Librairie J. Vrin, 1995).

Trinity in Aquinas (Ypsilanti, MI: Sapientia Press, 2003).

Evans, Gillian R. *Bernard of Clairvaux* (Oxford: Oxford University Press, 2000).

Evans, Gillian R. (ed.). *The Medieval Theologians* (Oxford: Blackwell, 2001).

Faesen, Rob. *Lichaam in Lichaan, Ziel in Ziel. Christusbeleving bij Hadewijch en haar tijdgenoten* (Baarn: Ten Have, 2003).

Feiss, Hugh, and Juliet Mousseau (eds.). *A Companion to the Abbey of Saint Victor in Paris* (Leiden: Brill, 2017).

Flanagan, Sabina. *Hildegard of Bingen 1098–1179: A Visionary Life* (London: Routledge, 1998).

Freddoso, Alfred. "Ockham on Faith and Reason," in Paul Vincent Spade (ed.), *The Cambridge Companion to Ockham* (Cambridge: Cambridge University Press, 1999), 326–49.

Friedman, Russell. *Intellectual Traditions at the Medieval University: The Use of Philosophical Psychology in Trinitarian Theology among the Franciscans and Dominicans 1250–1350*. 2 vols. (Leiden: Brill, 2013).

"Latin Philosophy, 1200–1350," in John Marenbon (ed.), *The Oxford Handbook of Medieval Philosophy* (Oxford: Oxford University Press, 2012), 192–219.

Medieval Trinitarian Thought from Aquinas to Ockham (Cambridge: Cambridge University Press, 2010).

Führer, Markus. "Albert the Great and Mystical Epistemology," in Irven Resnick (ed.), *A Companion to Albert the Great: Theology, Philosophy, and the Sciences* (Leiden: Brill, 2013), 137–60.

Gilson, Étienne. *History of Christian Philosophy in the Middle Ages* (London: Sheed and Ward, 1980).

John Duns Scotus: Introduction to His Fundamental Positions (London: T&T Clark, 2018).

Ginther, James. *The Westminster Handbook to Medieval Theology* (Louisville, KY: Westminster John Knox Press, 2009).

Gooch, Jason. "The Effects of the Condemnation of 1277," *Hilltop Review* 2 (2006): 34–44.

Guiu, Adrian (ed.). *A Companion to John Scottus Eriugena* (Leiden: Brill, 2019).

Hackett, Jeremiah (ed.). *A Companion to Meister Eckhart* (Leiden: Brill, 2012).

Hammond, Jay, Wayne Hellmann and Jared Goff (eds.). *A Companion to Bonaventure* (Leiden: Brill, 2013).

Harrison, Carol. *Augustine: Christian Truth and Fractured Humanity* (Oxford: Oxford University Press, 2000).

Harrison, Peter. "Voluntarism and Early Modern Science," *History of Science* 40 (2002): 63–89.

Hasse, Dag Nikolaus. "Influence of Arabic and Islamic Philosophy on the Latin West," in Edward N. Zalta (ed.), *Stanford Encyclopedia of Philosophy* (Spring 2020 Edition). https://plato.stanford.edu/archives/spr2020/entries/arabic-islamic-influence

Hayes, Zachary. *The Hidden Center: Spirituality and Speculative Christology in St. Bonaventure* (New York: Franciscan Institute, 2000).

Healy, Nicholas. *Thomas Aquinas: Theologian of the Christian Life* (Burlington, VT: Ashgate, 2003).

Hyman, Arthur, and James Walsh (eds.). *Philosophy in the Middle Ages: The Christian, Islamic and Jewish Traditions* (Indianapolis, IN: Hackett, 1973).

Illich, Ivan. *In the Vineyard of the Text: A Commentary on Hugh's "Didascalicon"* (Chicago: Chicago University Press, 1993).

Ingham, Mary. *Scotus for Dunces: An Introduction to the Subtle Doctor* (New York: Franciscan Institute, 2003).

Jolivet, Jean. *La Théologie d'Abélard* (Paris: Cerf, 1997).

Kerr, Fergus. *After Aquinas: Versions of Thomism* (Oxford: Blackwell, 2002).

Kilmartin, Edward. *The Eucharist in the West* (Collegeville, MN: Liturgical Press, 1998).

King, Peter. "Duns Scotus on Metaphysics," in Thomas Williams (ed.), *The Cambridge Companion to Duns Scotus* (Cambridge: Cambridge University Press, 2003), 15–68.

Krause, Katja. *Thomas Aquinas on Seeing God: The Beatific Vision in His Commentary on Peter Lombard's Sentences IV.49.2* (Milwaukee, WI: Marquette University Press, 2020).

Lahey, Stephen. *John Wyclif* (Oxford: Oxford University Press, 2009).

LaNave, Gregory. *Through Holiness to Wisdom: The Nature of Theology According to St. Bonaventure* (Rome: Istituto Storico dei Cappuccini, 2005).

Leclercq, Jean. *The Love of Learning and the Desire for God* (New York: Fordham University Press, 1982).

Leff, Gordon. *Medieval Thought from Saint Augustine to Ockham* (London: Pelican, 1958).

　William of Ockham: The Metamorphosis of Scholastic Discourse (Manchester: Manchester University Press, 1975).

Levering, Matthew. *Christ's Fulfillment of Torah and Temple: Salvation According to Thomas Aquinas* (Notre Dame, IN: University of Notre Dame Press, 2002).

　Scripture and Metaphysics: Aquinas and the Renewal of Trinitarian Theology (London: Blackwell, 2004).

　The Theology of Augustine: An Introductory Guide to His Most Important Works (Grand Rapids, MI: Baker, 2013).

Levy, Ian Christopher (ed.). *A Companion to John Wyclif: Late Medieval Theologian* (Leiden: Brill, 2011).

Louth, Andrew. *Denys the Areopagite* (London: Continuum, 2002).

Luscome, David. *Medieval Thought* (Oxford: Oxford University Press, 1997).

Marenbon, John. *Boethius* (Oxford: Oxford University Press, 2003).

　Early Medieval Philosophy (London: Routledge, 1988).

　Later Medieval Philosophy 1150–1350 (London: Routledge, 1991).

　The Philosophy of Peter Abelard (Cambridge: Cambridge University Press, 1997).

Marenbon, John (ed.). *The Oxford Handbook of Medieval Philosophy* (Oxford: Oxford University Press, 2012).

Markus, R. A. *Gregory the Great and His World* (Cambridge: Cambridge University Press, 1997).

Marmion, Declan, and Rik Van Nieuwenhove. *An Introduction to the Trinity* (Cambridge: Cambridge University Press, 2011).

Martos, Joseph. *Doors to the Sacred: Historical Introduction to Sacraments in the Catholic Church* (Liguori, MS: Liguori Publications, 2001).

Maurer, Armand. *Medieval Philosophy* (Toronto: Pontifical Institute of Medieval Studies, 1982).

　The Philosophy of William of Ockham in the Light of Its Principles (Toronto: Pontifical Institute of Medieval Studies, 1999).

McAvoy, Jane. *The Satisfied Life: Medieval Women Mystics on Atonement* (Eugene, OR: Wipf and Stock, 2009).

McCord Adams, Marilyn. *William Ockham* (Notre Dame, IN: University of Notre Dame Press, 1987).

McCosker, Philip, and Denys Turner (eds.). *The Cambridge Companion to the* Summa Theologiae (Cambridge: Cambridge University Press, 2016).

McGinn, Bernard. *The Mystical Thought of Meister Eckhart: The Man from Whom God Hid Nothing* (New York: Herder and Herder, 2001).

    The Presence of God: A History of Western Mysticism, vol. II: *The Growth of Mysticism: From Gregory the Great to the Twelfth Century* (London: SCM, 1995).

    The Presence of God: A History of Western Mysticism, vol. III: *The Flowering of Mysticism: Men and Women in the New Mysticism - 1200-1350* (New York: Herder and Herder, 1998).

    The Presence of God: A History of Western Mysticism, vol. IV: *The Harvest of Mysticism in Medieval Germany* (New York: Herder and Herder, 2005).

McGinnis, Jon. *Avicenna* (Oxford: Oxford University Press, 2010).

McGuire, Brian Patrick (ed.). *A Companion to Bernard of Clairvaux* (Leiden: Brill, 2011).

Merriell, D. Juvenal. "Trinitarian Anthropology," in Rik Van Nieuwenhove and Joseph Wawrykow (eds.), *The Theology of Thomas Aquinas* (Notre Dame, IN: University of Notre Dame Press, 2005), 123–42.

Mews, Constant. *Abelard and Heloise* (Oxford: Oxford University Press, 2005).

Möhle, Hannes. *Albertus Magnus* (Munster: Aschendorff, 2015).

Mommaers, Paul. *Hadewijch: Writer, Beguine, Love Mystic* (Leuven: Peeters, 2004).

Moran, Dermot. *The Philosophy of John Scottus Eriugena: A Study of Idealism in the Middle Ages* (Cambridge: Cambridge University Press, 1989).

Müller, Jörn. "*Duplex Beatitudo*: Aristotle's Legacy and Aquinas's Conception of Human Happiness," in Tobias Hoffmann, Jörn Müller and Matthias Perkams (eds.), *Aquinas and the* Nicomachean Ethics (Cambridge: Cambridge University Press, 2013).

Neil, Bronwen, and Mathew J. Dal Santo (eds.). *A Companion to Gregory the Great* (Leiden: Brill, 2013).

Newman, Barbara. *Sister of Wisdom: St Hildegard's Theology of the Feminine* (Berkeley: University of California Press, 1997).

Oberman, Heiko. *The Harvest of Medieval Theology* (Cambridge, MA: Harvard University Press, 1965).

Olszewski, Mikolaj. "The Nature of Theology According to Albert the Great," in Irven Resnick (ed.), *A Companion to Albert the Great: Theology, Philosophy, and the Sciences* (Leiden: Brill, 2013), 69–104.

O'Meara, John. *Eriugena* (Oxford: Clarendon, 1988).

Pelikan, Jaroslav. *The Christian Tradition: A History of the Development of Doctrine, vol.* III: *The Growth of Medieval Theology (600-1300)* (Chicago: Chicago University Press, 1978).

Pieper, Josef. *Happiness and Contemplation* (South Bend, IN: St. Augustine Press, 1998).

Pope, Stephen (ed.). *The Ethics of Aquinas* (Washington, DC: Georgetown University Press, 2002).

Power, Amanda. *Roger Bacon and the Defence of Christendom* (Cambridge: Cambridge University Press, 2012).

Resnick, Irven (ed.). *A Companion to Albert the Great: Theology, Philosophy, and the Sciences* (Leiden: Brill, 2013).

Reynaert, Joris. "Ruusbroec en Hadewijch," *Ons Geestelijk Erf* 55 (1981): 193–233.

Rorem, Paul. *Hugh of Saint Victor* (Oxford: Oxford University Press, 2009).

Rosemann, Philipp. *Peter Lombard* (Oxford: Oxford University Press, 2004).

Schockenhoff, Eberhard. "The Theological Virtue of charity," in Stephen Pope (ed.), *The Ethics of Aquinas* (Washington, DC: Georgetown University Press, 2002).

Schumacher, Lydia (ed.). *The* Summa Halensis: *Doctrines and Debates* (Berlin: De Gruyter, 2020).

The Summa Halensis: *Sources and Context* (Berlin: De Gruyter, 2020).

Early Franciscan Theology: Between Authority and Innovation (Cambridge: Cambridge University Press, 2019).

Sergent, F. Tyler (ed.). *A Companion to William of Saint Thierry* (Leiden: Brill, 2019).

Stoudt, Debra, George Ferzoco and Beverly Kienzle (eds.). *A Companion to Hildegard of Bingen* (Leiden: Brill, 2013).

Southern, Richard. *Saint Anselm: A Portrait in a Landscape* (Cambridge: Cambridge University Press, 1990).

Western Society and the Church in the Middle Ages (Harmondsworth: Penguin, 1990).

Spade, Paul Vincent (ed.). *The Cambridge Companion to Ockham* (Cambridge: Cambridge University Press, 1999).

Stewart, Columba. *Cassian the Monk* (Oxford: Oxford University Press, 1998).

Straw, Carole. *Gregory the Great: Perfection in Imperfection* (Berkeley: University of California Press, 1988).

Te Velde, Rudi. *Aquinas on God: The "Divine Science" of the* Summa Theologiae (Surrey: Ashgate, 2009).

Torrell, Jean-Pierre. *Saint Thomas Aquinas, vol. I: The Person and His Work* (Washington, DC: Catholic University of America Press, 1996).

Saint Thomas Aquinas, vol. II: Spiritual Master (Washington, DC: Catholic University of America Press, 2003).

Trottmann, Christian. *La Vision Béatifique. Des Disputes scolastiques à sa définition par Benoît XII* (Rome: École française de Rome, 1995).

Turner, Denys. *The Darkness of God: Negativity in Christian Mysticism* (Cambridge: Cambridge University Press, 1995).

Faith, Reason, and the Existence of God (Cambridge: Cambridge University Press, 2005).

Van Nieuwenhove, Rik. "'Bearing the Marks of Christ's Passion': Thomas' Soteriology," in Rik Van Nieuwenhove and Joseph Wawrykow (eds.), *The Theology of Thomas Aquinas* (Notre Dame, IN: University of Notre Dame Press, 2005), 277–302.

"In the Image of God: The Trinitarian Anthropology of St. Bonaventure, St. Thomas Aquinas and the Blessed Jan van Ruusbroec," *Irish Theological Quarterly* 66 (2001): 109–23 and 227–37.

Jan van Ruusbroec: Mystical Theologian of the Trinity (Notre Dame, IN: University of Notre Dame Press, 2003).

"Meister Eckhart and Jan van Ruusbroec: A Comparison," *Medieval Philosophy and Theology* 7 (1998): 157–93.

"The Religious Disposition as a Critical Resource to Resist Instrumentalisation," *Heythrop Journal* 50 (2009): 689–96.

"Ruusbroec, Jordaens and Herp on the Common Life: The Transformation of a Spiritual Ideal," in John Arblaster and Rob Faesen (eds.), *A Companion to John of Ruusbroec* (Leiden: Brill, 2014), 204–36.

"Saint Thomas Aquinas on Salvation, Making Satisfaction, and the Restoration of Friendship with God," *The Thomist* 83 (2019): 521–45.

"The Saving Work of Christ," in Brian Davies and Eleonore Stump (eds.), *The Oxford Handbook to Aquinas* (Oxford: Oxford University Press, 2012), 436–47.

"St. Anselm and St. Thomas Aquinas on 'Satisfaction': Or How Catholic and Protestant Understandings of the Cross Differ," *Angelicum* 80 (2003): 159–76.

Thomas Aquinas and Contemplation (Oxford: Oxford University Press, 2021).

Van Nieuwenhove, Rik, and Joseph Wawrykow (eds.). *The Theology of Thomas Aquinas* (Notre Dame, IN: University of Notre Dame Press, 2005).

Visser, Sandra, and Thomas Williams (eds.). *Anselm of Canterbury* (Oxford: Oxford University Press, 2008).

Von Balthasar, Hans Urs. *The Glory of the Lord, vol.* v (San Francisco: Ignatius Press, 1991).

"Theology and Sanctity," in *Explorations in Theology, vol. 1: The Word Made Flesh* (San Francisco: Ignatius Press, 1989), 181–209.

Vos, Antonie. *The Theology of John Duns Scotus* (Leiden: Brill, 2018).

Wawrykow, Joseph. *God's Grace and Human Action: "Merit" in the Theology of Thomas Aquinas* (Notre Dame, IN: University of Notre Dame Press, 1995).

The SCM Press A–Z of Thomas Aquinas (London: SCM, 2005).

Wilken, Robert. "Interpreting Job Allegorically: The *Moralia* of Gregory the Great," *Pro Ecclesia* 10 (2001): 213–26.

Williams, Thomas. "John Duns Scotus." Published in online version of *Stanford Encyclopedia of Philosophy*. See http://plato.stanford.edu/entries/duns-sco tus/.

"A Most Methodical Love? On Scotus's Arbitrary Creator," *Journal of the History of Philosophy* 38 (2001): 213–26.

"A Most Methodical Lover? On Scotus's Arbitrary Creator," *Journal of the History of Philosophy* 38 (2000): 169–202.

"Reason, Morality and Voluntarism in Duns Scotus: A Pseudo-Problem Dissolved," *Modern Schoolmen* 74 (1997): 73–94.

"Sin, Grace, and Redemption," in Jeffrey Brower and Kevin Guilfoy (eds.), *The Cambridge Companion to Abelard* (Cambridge: Cambridge University Press, 2004), 258–78.

Wippel, John. "The Condemnation of 1270 and 1277 at Paris," *Journal of Medieval and Renaissance Studies* 7 (1977): 169–201.

The Metaphysical Thought of Thomas Aquinas (Washington, DC: Catholic University of America Press, 2000).

Index

Abegescheidenheit. See detachment
Abelard, Peter, 84, 99–112, 121, 132, 299
abstraction theory, 234
Adam Marsh, 200
affectus, 206, 207, 255
affirmative way, 34, *See* apophaticism
Agnellus of Pisa, 201
Alain of Lille, 71
Albert the Great, 182, 183, 206, 247–62, 347
Albertus Magnus. *See* Albert the Great
Alexander IV, 221
Alexander of Hales, 158, 199, 200, 205, 206, *See Summa Halensis*
allegory. *See* Scriptures, four senses
Amaury of Bene, 71
Ambrose, 7
analogy, 276–79, 314, 316
angels, 67, 69, 93, 295, 339
Anselm of Canterbury, 16, 30, 71, 83–98, 237, 297, 299, 300, 317
   on freedom, 92–93
   soteriology, 94–98
Anselm of Laon, 72, 99
apophaticism, 8, 33, 89, 91, 258, 261, 276, 291, 316, 349
   in Eriugena, 68
appropriation, 22
Aquinas. *See* Thomas Aquinas
Aristotle, x, 9, 29, 78, 84, 182, 184, 185, 201, 202, 205, 206, 207, 217, 221, 233, 238, 248, 254, 257, 258, 259, 260, 262, 272, 274, 286, 289, 306, 307, 308, 310, 350, 373
Arius, 20, 21
aspectus, 206, 207
Augustine, 7–26, 30, 48, 53, 62, 109, 116, 135, 146, 159, 162, 193, 253, 302
Augustinian canons, 80, 359
Averroes, 182, 183, 185–86, 206, 248, 258, 259, 260, 306
Averroism, 186, 232, 245, 259, 262, 265, 306
Avicenna, 182, 185, 248, 273

Bacon, Roger, 183, 213–19
baptism, 170–71
Barth, Karl, 274, 277, 308
beatific vision, 257, 260, 261, 285
beatitude, 322
Beatrice of Nazareth, 186, 188
beauty, 122–24
beguines, 186, 187, 191
Benedict of Nursia, St., 28, 42
Benedict XII, 348
Berengar of Tours, 60, 83, 130, 171
Bernard of Clairvaux, 78, 79, 100, 104, 110–16, 158, 189, 206, 362
   criticism of Abelard, 110–12
Boccaccio, Giovanni, 333
Boethius, 29–33, 125, 167, 224, 290
Bonaventure, 147, 199, 204, 206, 232–46, 272, 308, 359
bonum diffusivum sui, 223, 238
Bruno of Cologne, 79

Carabine, Deirdre, 65
caritas. See love
Cassian, John, 27–29, 47
Cassidorius, 125
Catherine of Siena, 334
charity. *See* love
Charlemagne, 28, 56, 57
Charles the Bald, 56, 57, 58
Chaucer, Geoffrey, 333
Chenu, Marie-Dominique, 103
Chrétien de Troyes, 333
Christ. *See* soteriology
   and Incarnation (Bernard), 114–15
   and resurrection (Eriugena), 68
   and return, 69
   Body of, 18
   continues to suffer, 18
   encounter with (Hadewijch), 196
   hypostatic union, 167–68
   participation in, 16

Christ (cont.)
  priesthood, 302–3
  subject of theology, 204
Church
  Body of Christ, 299, 300–1
  in Augustine, 18
Cistercians, 41, 47, 55, 79, 80, 100, 112, 113, 116,
  117, 118, 119, 120, 134, 186, 187, 195, 266
Cîteaux, 79, 112
Clavis physicae, 71
Clement IV, 214
Clement VII, 332
Cluny, 79
common life, 363, 364, 365
communicatio, 288, 289
Conciliarism, 332
Condemnations of 1277, 236, 245, 257, 306–9, 313
condilectus, 143, 144, 225, 237
confirmation, 171
coniunctio. See conjunction
conjunction, 183, 186, 259, 260, 261
contemplation, 49, 62, 134, *See also* common life
  and action (Thomas Aquinas), 296–97
  and action in Gregory the Great, 51–54
  Richard of St. Victor, 138–41
  Thomas Aquinas, 294–97
contingency, 32, 33
contuition, 235
Council of Constance, 332
Council of Sens, 100
creation
  and Christ, 204
  and generation of the Word, 284
  and God (Eriugena), 64–71
  and sexual differentiation, 67
  as nothing (Eckhart), 353
  as sacramental, 67, 233, 244
  as sacramental (Hugh), 122–25
  as sacramental (Peter Lombard), 162
  eternal, 205, 207
  in Peter Lombard, 167
Cross, Richard, 324
crusades, 78
Cullen, Christopher, 234

Dante, 116, 333
David of Dinant, 258
Davies, Brian, 273, 277
deification, 35, 114, 204, 259
Descartes, 10, 11, 266
desire
  in Gregory the Great, 49–50
detachment, 2, 198, 355–58
devil, 16, 94, 104, 155
Devotio Moderna, 365

Dietrich of Freiberg, 262
divinity
  and existence (Eckhart), 353–55
  as intellect (Eckhart), 349–53
  eternity, 32
  foreknowledge, 32
  freedom (Duns Scotus), 340–41
  freedom and power (Ockham), 340–41
  honor (Anselm), 95
  indistinction (Eckhart), 354–55
  infinity, 315
  mercy and justice, 299
  proof of existence (Anselm), 87–91
  proof of existence (Duns Scotus), 317–19
  proof of existence (Ockham), 338–39
  proof of existence (Thomas Aquinas), 272–75
  simplicity, 163, 316, 318
  simplicity (Anselm), 91
  simplicity (Augustine), 20
  simplicity (Bonaventure), 238
  simplicity (Thomas Aquinas), 278
  transcendence, 34, 261
  transcendence (Hadewijch), 194–95
  transcendence and immanence, 66
  triple causal operation, 227
Dominic, St., 181
Dominican Order, 181, 188, 199, 247, 248,
  264, 297
Dominicus Gundissalinus, 184
double truth theory, 308
dualism, 228
Dulles, Avery, 287
Duns Scotus, 199, 310–27
Durandus of St. Pourçain, 343

ebullitio, 352
Eckhart, Meister, 191, 262, 347–58
El Cid, 78
emanation, 233, 238, 352
Emery, Gilles, 284
epektasis, 50
Eriugena, 56–73, 258
eschatology, 48, 101, 130, 204, 241, 249, 265
ethics
  divine command, 341
Eucharist, 195, 196, 204, 302
  controversy in 9th century, 58–60
  in Gregory the Great, 48
  in Peter Lombard, 171–73
  in Thomas Aquinas, 303–4
Eugene III, 112
evil
  absence of goodness, 9
exemplarism, 8–9, 233, 234, 242, 339
exitus, 198, 204

Faesen, Rob, 197
faith, 237, 275
  Abelard, 111
  and reason (Anselm), 86
  and reason (Eriugena), 62–63
  and reason (Roger Bacon), 216–19
  and reason (William of St. Thierry), 116–18
  and reason in Abelard, 105
  and reason in Augustine, 10–11
  and reason in Thomas Aquinas, 267–68
  and theology, 203, 267
  and theology (Ockham), 342
  definition (Thomas Aquinas), 285
  in Bonaventure, 245
  in Hugh of St. Victor, 132–34
  in Thomas Aquinas, 285–87
  models of, 286
Fall, 207
  in Hildegard, 154–55
Father, 284, *See also* Trinity, personal names
fides quaerens intellectum, 85, 268
Filioque, 58
  Augustine, 21
  Duns Scotus, 325–26
  in Eriugena, 60–61
five ways, 272–75
Flemish Primitives, 365–66
Florens Radewijns, 365
formal distinction
  (Duns Scotus), 318
forms, 9, 66, 183, 336, 350, *See* exemplarism
four senses. *See* Scriptures, four senses
Fourth Lateran Council, 201
Francis, St., 181
Franciscan Order, 181, 182, 199, 214, 220, 283, 308, 335, 371
free will, 322
  and divine foreknowledge, 31, 33
freedom
  (Anselm), 92–93
  in Augustine, 13
Friedman, Russell, 184, 225, 283, 324, 371
frui (enjoyment of God), 2, 159–61, 358, 364
  in Augustine, 25

Gabriel Biel, 345
Geert Grote, 334, 365
Gelâzenheit. See detachment
Gerard of Cremona, 184
Gerard of Wales, 200
Gerard Zerbolt van Zutphen, 365
gifts of Holy Spirit, 45
Giles of Rome, 331
Giotto di Bondone, 332
Glossa Ordinaria, 72

God. *See* divinity
Godfrey of Fontaines, 311
Gothic, 81, 181, 332,
Gottschalk, 14, 61
grace, 167
  in Augustine, 11–14
Great Schism, 61
Gregory of Nyssa, 56, 66, 69
Gregory of Rimini, 345
Gregory the Great, 40–55, 102
Gregory VII, 82
Gregory X, 266
Gregory XI, 331
Grosseteste, Robert, 200–13, 326

Hadewijch, 191–98
haecceitas, 318, 319, 337
happiness, 289
Harrison, Peter, 307
hell
  in Eriugena, 71
Heloise, 99, 100, 101
Henry of Ghent, 311, 314
Herp, Henrik, 365
Hildegard of Bingen, 148–56
Holy Spirit. *See also* Trinity, personal names
  and return (Ruusbroec), 360
  as Gift, 146, 243
  as Gift (Bonaventure), 242
  as love (Peter Lombard), 164–65
  procession, 224
  William of St. Thierry, 118
hope, 287
Hugh of St. Victor, 71, 121–37, 171, 244, 268
Hugh of Wells, 200
Hugh Ripelin of Strasburg, 262
Hugo van der Goes, 366
Hyma, Albert, 365

illumination, 234–35, 258, 259
imago Dei. See soul, image of the Trinity
Immaculate Conception, 326
In agro dominico, 348
Incarnation
  Duns Scotus, 326
  Robert Grosseteste, 209–10
  Summa Halensis, 229
Ingham, Mary, 320
intellect
  active, 183, 186, 258
  and reason (Eriugena), 63–64
  and will, 294–95
  distinct from reason, 11, 295–96, 344
  passive, 183

intellect (cont.)
    possible, 258
    universal and unmixed (Eckhart),
        350–51
intellectus. See intellect, distinct from
    reason
intellectus adeptus, 186, 257
intelligentia, 253
Islamic thought, 182–86

James of Venice, 184
James of Viterbo, 331
Jan Hus, 331
Jan van Eyck, 333, 365
Jerome, 57
John Buridan, 345
John Duns Scotus. *See* Duns Scotus
John of La Rochelle, 199, 219, 220
John of Paris, 331
John Wyclif, 331
John XXI, 306
John XXII, 266, 335, 348
Jordan of Saxony, 247
Julian of Norwich, 334

Kant, Immanuel, 266, 308, 322, 344
Kilwardby, Robert, 308
King, Peter, 318
Klapwell, Richard, 308
knowledge
    and love (Gregory), 50–51

LaNave, Gregory, 236
Leo IX, 81
Logica vetus, 29
Lollards, 331
love
    agapeic and erotic, 136–37, 189
    and knowledge (Gregory), 50–51
    and theology (Grosseteste), 206–8
    degrees of (Bernard), 113–14
    form of all virtues, 294
    gratuitousness, 192
    in Hadewijch, 192–94
    in Hugh of St. Victor, 134–37
    in Thomas Aquinas, 288–89, 291–94
    personal name of Holy Spirit, 242
    triangular, 135
    triangular (Thomas Aquinas), 293
Luther, Martin, 13, 159, 245, 344

macrocosm, 152–54
Manichaeism, 7, 15
Marguerite Porete, 186, 347
Mariology, 326–27

marriage, 177
Marsilius of Inghen, 345
Marsilius of Padua, 331
Maximus Confessor, 56, 67, 70
McCord Adams, Marilyn, 337, 342
McGinn, Bernard, 187, 190, 191, 349
Mechthild von Magdeburg, 186, 188–91
Memling, Hans, 366
memoria, 23, 252, 253
metaphysics of light, 208–9
Michael Scot, 184
microcosm, 152–54
Minne. See love (Hadewijch)
Modern Devotion. *See* Devotio Moderna
modus significandi, 277
monopsychism, 183, 259, 306
Müller, Jörn, 257
mystagogy, 87
mystical theology, 261

Natura (Eriugena), 64
Neoplatonism, 8–9, 68, 134, 257, 339, 344
Newman, Barbara, 149
Nicholas III, 335
Nicholas of Autrecourt, 345
Nicolas of Cusa, 71
nihilianism
    Christological, 167, 168
nominalism, 4, 84, 307, 334, 335, 343,
        345, 367
Norbertines, 81

Ockham's razor, 335
Odo Rigaldus, 219
Origen, 72
Oxford Calculators, 334

papacy, 331
paradise, 70
passion. *See* soteriology
Peckham, John, 308
pedagogy
    and sanctity (Bonaventure), 244–45
    and theology, 125–32
Pelagius, 12–13, 342
penance, 173–75, 298
per modum naturae, 224, 238, 239, *See* Trinity,
    processions
per modum voluntatis, 224, *See* Trinity,
    processions, Holy Spirit
perichoresis, 118, 238
persona media, 225, 241
personhood. *See* Trinity, personhood
Peter Aureoli, 182, 343
Peter Lombard, 121, 158–77, 205, 219, 267

Peter the Venerable, 100
Petrus Comestor, 121
philosophy. *See* theology, and philosophy
    reform of (Roger Bacon), 215
Photius, 61
Plato, 8, 29, 67, 84, 107, 125, 248
Plotinus, 8
Porphyry, 8, 29
positivism, 11
postmodern, 1–2
preambles of faith, 269, 270, 272, 274
predestination, 341
    and Eriugena, 61–62
    in Augustine, 14
priesthood, 176
Proclus, 8, 184
providence, 31, 300, 306
Pseudo-Dionysius, 33–35, 56, 121, 202, 223, 238,
    247, 258

quadrivium, 29, 125, 127, 128

Radbertus, 58–59
Rahner, Karl, 164
ratio. See reason
rationality
    fiduciary nature, 10
Ratramnus, 59–60
realism. *See* universals, voluntarism
reason. *See* faith and reason
    and faith, 237
    and intellect, 11, 32
    autonomous, 1
reditus, 64, 69, 198, 204, 233
Reginald of Piperno, 265
regiratio, 360, 363
res significata, 277
res tantum, 84
Richard Fishacre, 205
Richard of St. Victor, 138–47, 223, 237, 239,
    275, 323
Richard Rufus of Cornwall, 205, 209, 214
Richard Swinehead, 334
Robert of Molesme, 112
Rogier van der Weyden, 365
Roscelin, 82, 84, 86, 99
Roscelin of Champagne, 82
Rosemann, Philipp, 164, 165
Rupert of Deutz, 210
Ruusbroec, Jan van, 121, 359–65

sacra doctrina. See theology
sacraments, 342
    definition, 169
    in Peter Lombard, 168–77

sacramentum, 17, 18, 83, 124, 130, 131, 170,
    171, 174
sacramentum et res, 84, 174
sacramentum tantum, 84
sacrifice
    in Augustine, 17–18
    in Gregory the Great, 48
    in Thomas Aquinas, 302–4
sapientia. See theology as wisdom
satisfactio, 297
satisfaction (Anselm), 95–97
Schillebeeckx, Edward, 16, 94
Schleiermacher, Frederick, 2
Schockenhoff, Eberhard, 289
science
    and universality, 254
    in Aristotelian sense, 254
    Thomas Aquinas, 267
scientia experimentalis, 216, 217
Scriptures, 256
    four senses (Cassian), 47
    four senses (Gregory the Great), 43–44
    four senses (Thomas Aquinas), 270
    in Augustine, 14–16
    interpretation of in Gregory the Great,
    42–47
Siger of Brabant, 257, 306
sin, 69, 298
    (Abelard), 102
    in Augustine, 11–12
skepticism, 7, 10, 11, 112, 275, 307, 309,
    343, 344
Son. *See also* Trinity, personal names
    as middle Person, 225, 241
    birth of, in the soul, 352
soteriology
    Abelard, 103–5
    Anselm, 94–98
    Hildegard of Bingen, 155–56
    in Augustine, 16–19
    in Grosseteste, 210–11
    Thomas Aquinas, 297–304
soul
    image of God (Eriugena), 67
    image of the Trinity, 228
    image of the Trinity (Albert the Great),
    252–53
    image of the Trinity (Augustine), 22–24
    image of the Trinity (Grosseteste), 212
    image of the Trinity (Peter Lombard),
    162–63
    image of Trinity (Bonaventure), 244
    image of Trinity (Eckhart), 351
    participation in the Trinity (Ruusbroec),
    361–63

Southern, Richard, 80, 206
spark of the soul, 350, 351, 355, 356
subalternation, 202, 267, 312
subordination, 343
suffering, 19, *See* Christ, soteriology
Summa Halensis, 219–29, 238
super-eminent way, 34, *See* apophaticism
Suso, Henry, 333
Synod of Soissons, 105

Tauler, 333
Tempier, Etienne, 306, 308
theocentric focus, 2, 25, 52, 93, 137, 159, 244, 245,
    256, 267, 294, 296, 357, 358, 364,
theological anthropology. *See* soul, image of
    Trinity
theology. *See also* subalternation
  and philosophy (Abelard), 105–10
  and philosophy (Albert), 256
  and philosophy (Bacon), 216–19
  and philosophy (Bonaventure), 234
  and philosophy (Duns Scotus), 311–13
  and philosophy (Ockham). *See* William of
    Ockham, nominalism
  and philosophy (Thomas Aquinas), 235–36,
    266–72, 278–79
  and philosophy in Augustine, 10
  as practical, 235
  as science (Albert the Great), 253–56
  as science (Duns Scotus), 312–13
  as science (Grosseteste), 202–5
  as science (Ockham), 338–43
  as science (*Summa Halensis*), 202–5
  as wisdom, 203, 233–36
  reform of (Roger Bacon), 215
theophany, 66, 71, 151, 260, 261
theoria, 53
Thomas a Kempis, 334, 365
Thomas Aquinas, 135, 146, 182, 264–304
Thomas Bradwardine, 334
Thomas Gallus, 206
Thomas Malory, 333
Thomas of Cantimpré, 187
Thomas of York, 200
transcendentals, 226–27
transubstantiation, 131, 173, 342
Treaty of Verdun, 57, 77
Trinity
  Abelard, 105–10
  absolute property theory, 324
  appropriations, 106
  immanent, 20
  in Albert the Great, 249–52
  in Augustine, 19–24
  in Bonaventure, 236–44

  in Duns Scotus, 322–26
  in Grosseteste, 211–12
  in Hadewijch, 197–98
  in Peter Lombard, 161–67
  in Richard of St. Victor, 141–46
  in Ruusbroec, 359–61
  in *Summa Halensis*, 223–28
  in Thomas Aquinas, 279–85
  personal names, 22, 106, 166
  personal names (Bonaventure), 240–43
  personal names (Richard), 145–46
  personal names (Thomas Aquinas), 285
  personhood (Augustine), 20, 22
  personhood (Richard of St. Victor),
    143–44
  personhood (Thomas Aquinas), 282–83
  primacy of Father, 239
  processions, 224
  processions (Bonaventure), 238
  processions (Thomas Aquinas), 279–81
  relations (Augustine), 21
  relations (Duns Scotus), 323–25
  relations (Thomas Aquinas), 281–83
trivium, 107, 125, 128
truth, 227
  (Anselm), 93
  as affective, 256
Turner, Denys, 275, 295, 354, 357

Ulrich of Strasburg, 262
universals, 84, 318, 336, 340, *See also* William of
    Ockham, nominalism
  (Abelard), 100
univocity, 314, 315, 316, 327
Urban VI, 332
uti, 159–61, *See frui*

Van Engen, John, 365
Via Antiqua, 345
via experientiae, 216
Via Moderna, 345
Victorines, 80, *See also* Hugh of St. Victor,
    Richard of St. Victor
virtues
  cardinal, 265
  intellectual, 286
  theological. *See* faith, hope, love
vita mixta, 53
voluntarism, 307, 343
  (Duns Scotus), 319–22

William de Vere, 200
William of Auvergne, 205, 257
William of Champeaux, 80, 82, 84, 99, 121
William of Middleton, 219, 221

William of Moerbeke, 184
William of Ockham, 312, 334, 335–45
   nominalism, 336–37
William of St. Thierry, 110, 116–18, 192, 195, 206
Williams, Thomas, 316, 320

Wolfram von Eschenbach, 333
Wolter, Allan, 320
Word, 146, 242, *See* Christ, *See also* Trinity,
   personal names
   as archetype, 234